Sociology for Nurses

Sociology for Nurses

Shama Lohumi
MSc (N), PhD

Principal
Shivalik Institute of Nursing
Shimla, HP

Rakesh Lohumi
MSc, MPhil

Ex-Bureau Chief, *The Tribune*
Shimla, HP

ELSEVIER

ELSEVIER

RELX India Pvt. Ltd.
Registered Office: 818, Indraprakash Building, 21, Barakhamba Road, New Delhi-110 001
Corporate Office: 14th Floor, Building No. 10B, DLF Cyber City, Phase II, Gurgaon-122 002, Haryana, India

Sociology for Nurses, Shama Lohumi and Rakesh Lohumi

ISBN: 978-81-312-4010-6
e-Book ISBN: 978-81-312-4017-5

First Printed in Indian 2015
Reprinted 2017

Sr Project Manager— Education Solutions: Shabina Nasim
Content Development Specialist: Subodh Kumar
Project Manager: Nayagi Athmanathan
Sr Operations Manager: Sunil Kumar
Sr Production Executive: Ravinder Sharma
Sr Cover Designer: Milind Majgaonkar

Typeset by GW India
Printed in India by Rajkamal Electric Press, Kundli (Haryana)

Preface

It is now being widely accepted and acknowledged that a proper understanding of the social behaviour of individuals and groups and their value system is essential for effective delivery of health care. Scientific and biological knowledge alone are not enough for providing medical and nursing care.

Studies carried out by researchers have brought out that cultural, social and behavioural practices predispose certain communities to diseases and their health profile also changes with gender (male and female), area (urban and rural), literacy, religion and other such factors. As such the knowledge of sociology is essential for the development of professional nurses. It helps to appreciate the sociological aspects of health, which have a bearing on causes, incidence and spread of diseases, both communicable and noncommunicable, in the ever-changing social scenario.

Nurses have to deal with patients who come from diverse sociocultural backgrounds, and knowledge of sociology enables them to view and understand the behaviours of individuals and groups in the right perspective. They face many ethical questions in the profession, and a good grounding in sociology is immensely helpful in dealing with such situations and issues. This book aims to develop a sociological perspective among nurses so that the learning of this social science discipline increases their professional competence.

There are many books on sociology in the market but we have tried to make it more comprehensive. It not only covers the entire syllabus but also has additional content, which the students will find very useful while pursuing higher studies. Emerging problems of the modern society, particularly due to the changing family structure, drug abuse and growing population of the elderly persons, have been dealt with at length.

There are several topics like application of sociology in nursing, role of nurse as an agent of change and in social control, cultural competence and fallout of population explosion, which will be of interest to the student nurses.

Writing a book is always a tough job and involves hard work. It has been made possible with the cooperation of several persons who extended valuable assistance in sourcing and arranging all the relevant material. We are extremely grateful to all those who gave their unstinted support and valuable suggestions to help enhance the quality of the book.

One has to devote much time and energy to keep the deadlines, and in the process not only the writers but the family members also have to make sacrifice by way of restricted social life due to constraint of time. However, our son Tejaswi, daughter Garima and their uncle Nalin Lohumi have been very supportive throughout. But for their encouragement and constant goading it would not have been possible to complete the work in time.

—Authors

Contents

Unit - 4

SOCIAL GROUPS AND PROCESSES

Unit - 5

POPULATION

Unit - 6

FAMILY AND MARRIAGE

Unit - 7

SOCIAL STRATIFICATION

Unit - 8

TYPES OF COMMUNITIES IN INDIA

Unit - 9

SOCIAL CHANGE

Unit - 10

SOCIAL ORGANIZATION AND SOCIAL SYSTEM

Unit - 11

SOCIAL CONTROL

Unit - 12

SOCIAL PROBLEMS

UNIT - 1

INTRODUCTION

CHAPTER

1

Introduction to Sociology

LEARNING OBJECTIVES

After reading this chapter the learner should be able to

- Relate sociology with other subjects.
- Know why sociology is considered a science.

Sociology is a branch of social sciences concerned with the study of human social life, groups and societies. Relatively a new science, sociology is concerned with studies and analyses of how the society and the individual interact with each other deploying systematic methods of investigation. It observes and examines from a scientific point of view the structure and dynamics of society and its intricate connections, which shape the patterns of human behaviour and individual life.

Pursuit of truth and knowledge is an inherent trait of human beings. Man has been striving to explore and understand his physical and social environment and the associated issues that had a bearing on his life and survival. People have through the ages observed, analysed and reflected upon various aspects of human life. Religious thinkers and philosophers of various civilizations have studied the human behaviour and functioning of human societies and have also come out with their ideas for building a healthy society by drawing a distinction between moral and immoral conduct and actions.

The human endeavour to study various aspects of social life led to evolution of various social sciences like history, political science, economics, anthropology and psychology. However, none of these disciplines dealt with the human society as a whole and failed to provide a comprehensive picture. They did not fully explain the human behaviour and the underlying factors of social processes. The need to have a general science to study the society as an integrated unit gave birth to sociology. With its integrated approach it occupies the top place among social sciences as it tries to unify the conclusions drawn by other social sciences by taking a comprehensive view and also has its own specialized field of research.

Sociology takes a dialectical approach and explores and analyses the dynamic interconnectedness and the conflicts between the social groups. It views the human society as an interconnected whole and studies how the individual and society are dialectically linked.

SOCIAL IMAGINATION

We all have some knowledge about the functioning of our society and understanding of various aspects of the social processes. However, we lack the ability to study the social phenomena objectively. One requires social imagination to observe and analyse the functioning of the human society as an interconnected whole, particularly, how the society and an individual interact with each other.

The term *sociological imagination* was coined by American sociologist C. Wright Mills who observed and took notice of the inability of the individuals to see the intricate link between their own lives and the ongoing changes in the society.

According to him, 'Neither the life of an individual nor the history of a society can be understood without understanding both. Yet people are seldom aware of the intricate connection between the patterns of their own lives and the course of world history. They do not usually impute to the big ups and downs of the societies in which they live.'

Going into the reasons, he observes that ordinary people do not possess the 'quality of mind' essential to grasp the interplay of individuals and society, of biography and history, of self and world. He came out with the term *social imagination* to define the 'quality of mind' that will help them to use information and to develop reason to unravel what is going on in the world and of what may be happening within themselves.

In simple terms, sociological imagination is the ability to see the relationship between individual experiences and the larger society. It is the ability to have an objective view one's own society as an outsider, rather than having a limited perspective of personal experiences and cultural biases. It enables us to understand the link between our personal experiences and the social context in which they occur.

DEFINITION AND SCOPE OF SOCIOLOGY

The word 'sociology' has been derived from Latin word *socius* (meaning society) and Greek word *logos* (science) and it literally means 'science of society'. It was first used by French scholar Auguste Comte (1789–1857) who first used the term in 1839. He is considered to be the founder of the youngest of all social sciences. He rejected religion and royalty and shifted to the study of society to carry out reforms for the welfare of humanity.

He divided the subject into two categories: (1) social statics, the forces holding society together and (2) social dynamics, the forces driving social change. Comte's ideas and use of scientific methods lead to great advances in the field of sociology. He defined sociology as 'the science of social phenomena subject to natural and invariable laws, the discovery of which is the object of investigation'.

In the simplest words, sociology can be described as the study of human behaviour in groups, interaction among human beings, social relationships and the processes by which human activity takes place.

It has been developed to help study every social problem scientifically and objectively by eliminating subjectivity to the extent possible in examining human interactions. It is the systematic study of social behaviour and human groups and focuses primarily on the influence of social relationships upon people's attitudes and behaviour and on how societies are established evolve and undergo transformation.

Sociology has a very broad scope as a field of study and covers a wide range of area as it deals with a range of people and the whole range of human activities such as families, gangs, business firms, computer networks, political parties, schools, religions and labour unions. It is also concerned with issues like poverty, traditions, technology, discrimination, health, alienation, demography and community.

It looks at the social processes to understand how individuals and collective social entities construct, maintain and transform the society in different ways.

SOCIOLOGY AS SCIENCE

Sociology has evolved and understood as a science ab initio and it follows certain norms and procedures for making observations and draw conclusions. Unlike philosophers and religious thinkers whose observations and reflections are based on common sense, the findings of a sociologist must be arrived at through verifiable evidence that can be checked or replicated by others to make further studies. Thus, methods, rules and procedures followed while carrying out studies of human societies to generate sociological knowledge are of utmost importance. This is a crucial aspect that makes sociology a specialized discipline and differentiates sociological knowledge from common sense knowledge.

However, many consider only hard sciences like physics, chemistry and biology as the 'true' sciences and do not regard social or soft sciences such as sociology and psychology as sciences. There are, of course, some common basic principles of scientific inquiry that apply to both soft and hard sciences. Thus, the methods used to study any particular subject determine whether a discipline can be classified as science or not. Some scholars are not willing to accord the sociology the status of science and they maintain that sociology is not a perfect science, while others term it as a social science and not a natural science.

Sociology Is Both a Rational and an Empirical Science

Scientific investigations for gaining knowledge mainly entail two approaches: empirical and rational. The empirical methods are based purely on observation, measurement and experimentation, the results of which are analysed to explain various phenomena and put forward new theories. In the scientific terminology *empirical* refers to the use of working hypothesis that can be tested through observation and experiment.

The two major methods for obtaining data are measurement and observation, which refer to quantitative and qualitative measurements. Pure sciences like physics and chemistry mostly rely on quantitative measurements obtained through experimentation or observation. For example, the percentage of iron and other minerals in a water sample.

The qualitative measurements are based upon observation. They are arbitrary and require some kind of scaling to measure the intangible (abstract) responses. For instance, the level of stress, intelligence and other abstract qualities are measured by designing some numerical scale.

The rational approach is based on reason and logical argument and all knowledge is gained from logical reference. Sociology applies both empirical and rational methodologies to study and analyse the social phenomena and determine the general principles influencing it. It emphasizes that all evidence must be empirical which means it is based on evidence.

Sociology applies both the rational and the empirical approaches to gain knowledge. The empirical methodology involves objective observation and experience, direct or indirect, to collect facts and empirical evidence that can be analysed to formulate theories and draw conclusions. Theories and facts are both important as a theory has to be supported by facts. As German philosopher Immanuel Kant said, 'Experience without theory is blind, but theory without experience is mere intellectual play.' All modern sciences, including sociology, deploy both empirical and rational resources. It establishes that sociology is an independent social science.

Sociology Is Not a Special Science

Unlike other social sciences like political science, history and economics, which focus on certain aspects of human interaction and activities, sociology studies the human society and the social processes in general. Its field of investigation is not specialized or limited to any particular area and it studies all aspects of human society. Precisely for this reason, some sociologists call it the mother of all social sciences. It draws from other social sciences and in turn enriches them through its objective studies and analyses of the social phenomena.

It is concerned with human interaction and human life in general and more of a generalizing science. Other social sciences also study the human society and social life but they are only concerned with a particular aspect. Economics specializes itself in the study of economic activities. Political science specializes in political activities and so on. Sociology concentrates only on studying human activities in a general way and is not concerned with other subjects such as economics, political science, legal studies and moral science or any other special kinds of phenomena in relation to human life. It only studies human activities in a general way. This does not, however, mean that sociology is neither a basic social science nor does it simply is the general social science. Anthropology and social psychology often claim the mselves to be general social sciences.

The concepts and ideas of sociologists are different as their focus is not on the values and norms but how they work in actual societies. Their prime concern is the behaviour of humans as social beings. They study how the individual and society are interconnected and how they interact with each other. Sociology studies the human society as an interconnected whole and unravels how the individual is both constrained by it and can also contribute to effect a change in it.

The common sense observations and explanations are mostly unreflective as they are based on simplistic natural reasons for individualistic behaviour and generally do not take into consideration the interconnections or question the origins. In contrast, the sociological perspective has all through been constantly influenced by the developments in modern science and the systematic and questioning approach of sociology is rooted in the tradition of scientific investigation.

Historical Development of Sociology

Sociology is an offspring of philosophy and emerged as a reaction against speculative philosophy of eighteenth and nineteenth century to become a specialized discipline. The great advancements in the field of science and technology convinced scholars that methods of the natural sciences could be applied to study of human affairs.

It was the time when the European society was undergoing turbulent transformation following arrival of capitalism and ongoing industrialization. Most of the issues and concerns of sociology emerged from the contemporary society such as migration of people to the towns, urbanization, disintegration of rural communities and brisk population growth in the wake of the Industrial Revolution. French philosopher Auguste Comte coined the term *sociology* and it was used for the first time in 1839. Many of the issues that were raised then like urbanization, migration of workers and population explosion are relevant to all modern societies, particularly, in the developing world.

THE INDIAN SCENARIO

Indian sociology has been an offshoot of the Western sociology and continues to be dominated by it due to the countries colonial trappings. India is closely linked to the history of British capitalism and colonialism.

By the time sociology emerged as a formal discipline in India, scholars, philosophers and administrators of the pre-Independence era had already studied various aspects of Indian society and created a body of knowledge as contained in census reports, district gazetteers, books and other documents of the colonial era. The main objective of the studies was to have an understanding of the Indian society and learn about the social processes as they occurred.

However, the scenario changed in the second half of the twentieth century and sociological study was no longer limited to observing and explaining the social phenomena. The Indian sociology had reached a stage where descriptive and explanatory sociology was considered essential but not sufficient. The sociologists not only explained but also diagnosed the social phenomena, shifting focus to social dynamics and, in turn, to social change and social development, social exclusion, inclusive growth and nation building. The policymakers of independent India recognized the role of the social sciences in attaining the objectives of national reconstruction and development. They saw it as a tool for social engineering, paving the way for increased participation of social scientists along with economists and sociologists in research and development.

The state policies like making the practice of untouchability an offence and providing reservation for Scheduled Castes and Scheduled Tribes in the parliament and legislatures and jobs in the government and the public sector opened up new areas of study for sociologists.

SIGNIFICANCE AND PRACTICAL UTILITY OF SOCIOLOGY

Sociology has assumed great importance as it makes a scientific study of society and provides an objective view of the social phenomena. The study of society was carried out in an unscientific manner until the emergence of sociology.

- Sociology is essential for understanding a complex and diverse social structure like the Indian society. A society cannot be transformed without understanding the mechanism behind its construction. Sociological studies help in unravelling the intricate social processes and structures and framing suitable policies to solve the problems.
- Sociology studies role of the institutions through which the society the functions in the development of the individuals such as school and education, shrine and religion, industry and work and so on. Sociological studies help in taking measures to strengthen the institutions for the benefit of the individual.
- Sociology helps in identifying the social problems and assessing their magnitude. It is particularly helpful in planning strategies for stamping out deep-rooted social evils.
- Sociology plays a vital role in human resource planning as it enables objective assessing available human resources and also the human resources required for solving the social problems.
- It provides basic knowledge about human society, its strong and weak constituents and diverse structure, to facilitate conciliation and social reconstruction.
- It helps the state in promoting welfare of the disadvantaged sections through policy framework by generating authentic data about their socioeconomic status.
- By bringing out the high points of traditions and culture through objective studies, sociology actually helps in the preservation of the culture and values a society.

REVIEW QUESTIONS

1. Define sociology and write in detail about its scope.
2. Why sociology is considered to be a science?
3. What is the practical utility of sociology?

CHAPTER

2

Sociology and Other Social Sciences

LEARNING OBJECTIVES

After reading this chapter the learner should be able to

- Know how sociology is related with other social sciences.
- Differentiate between sociology and anthropology.

The social sciences study various aspects of the human world, and their domains are not demarcated clearly. As all these disciplines are concerned with human activity and interaction, there are overlapping areas. Various social sciences like history, political science, economics, anthropology and psychology evolved into specialized disciplines while studying the human behaviour.

The trend of researchers of one discipline conducting studies in areas falling in other disciplines is increasing, indicating openness to intellectual exchange with other disciplines. The *generalizing* nature of sociology affords it a vast scope not only for cross-discipline studies but also for various other areas related to social life such as health and education.

Sociology deploys the scientific methods like natural sciences but its field of study overlaps with other social sciences. They all have certain common issues interests, concepts and methods. At times when need for interdisciplinary approach is being emphasized due to focus on economic, social justice and gender-related issues, it is very important to understand this at the very outset and examine in some detail the overlapping subject matter.

ECONOMICS

Its domain of study is production and distribution of goods and services, and their consumption within the society. It deals with variables like price rise, inflation, demand and supply and money flows; the main objective has been to frame theories and laws to help understand the economic behaviour. The economists are able to predict trends with a fair degree of precision but things do go wrong when the social aspects are ignored. Studies pertaining to social basis of economic behaviour and the economic basis of social behaviour provide a vast scope for cross-discipline endeavours and lead to overlapping of subject matter.

Sociologists are aware that economic and material interests are a major influence in the functioning of the society but unlike economists they do not offer solutions to economic problems. They view the economic activities and behaviour in a broader social perspective keeping in view the norms, values and traditions and often question the very desirability of the goals and the basic assumptions.

Thus, sociology helps in providing a better understanding of the situation and this has led to growth of economic sociology in recent years.

POLITICAL SCIENCE

Political science has been mainly concerned with political theory, the government administration and the use of political power. The focus is on the operation of political processes and the ideas behind systems of government and its structure. It is not much concerned with the political behaviour and the actual operation of the government. The domain of political science has remained largely confined to the study of power as vested in the formal organizational structure.

The focus of sociological studies is on political behaviour, as reflected during the course of political movements, support or opposition to political issues and the connection between political and other social institutions.

Sociology and political science do share common areas related to study of political behaviour. Voting patterns have been studied to ascertain the behaviour on the basis of caste, gender and community. Studies have also been conducted in membership patterns of political organizations, reservation of seats for women in grassroot democratic institutions like panchayats and urban local bodies have opened up new areas for the emerging discipline of political sociology.

HISTORY

Historians record and study the past events in a chronological order. They ascertain and study facts to reconstruct the past events as they happened and know their causes by putting them in the proper perspective.

In recent years the approach has changed and the focus has shifted from merely delineating the accounts of events and the associated people and places to exploring the social processes and trends of the contemporary period.

While looking backwards in time historians are increasingly relying on sociological methods, concepts and tools to analyse the past events tracing the social history.

Sociologists have been traditionally drawing heavily from the history and using historical references to view the contemporary events in the right prospective. Historical references are often being used to help understand and shed new light on current social events.

PSYCHOLOGY

Often described as the science of mind, psychology is closely related to sociology, as psychologists use human behaviour to unravel the mystery of the mind, which cannot be observed directly. It is the most complex machine which distinguishes human beings from other living creatures.

Psychologists deal with individuals and they are primarily concerned with intelligence and learning, motivations, memory, nervous system, perception, hopes and fears. They believe that mostly human mind is greatly influenced by the social pressure and term psychology as the *science of behaviour*.

Psychological factors are important elements in social change, which are largely given shape by the psychology of man which undergoes change with every experience. Further, man is always eager to discover and invent new things. Human mind is behind the perpetually changing society, moral values, traditions, customs and other social aspects. The society adapts to the changes with time.

The intersection of psychology and sociology has given rise to social psychology, which serves as a bridge between the two disciplines. The focus of psychology is on individual experience, whereas sociology studies the human interaction, social processes and the society as a connected whole. Social psychology examines and explores the role social circumstances play in shaping the personality of an individual.

ANTHROPOLOGY

Anthropology is very close to sociology as it studies not only the biological evolution of human beings but also the cultural history across the world. The focus of physical anthropology is on human biological evolution, leading to differences in physical features of people living in various parts of the world at present. It is the aspect pertaining to culture and development of premodern societies which overlaps with sociology, which focuses on the modern societies and civilizations.

As very few premodern societies have left uninfluenced by the modern civilization, the area of anthropology has squeezed. The limited scope encouraged anthropologists to extend their area of study by including modern societies and communities into their ambit. On the other hand, sociologists, while drawing from the knowledge about the past have borrowed many concepts from anthropology and also adopted anthropological approaches to study and understand the human society. The overlapping of fields has given rise to new discipline of social anthropology.

Taking notice of the interdependence anthropology and sociology, anthropologist Kroeber termed the two sciences as *twin sisters*. Sociologists study man as a social animal and anthropologists observe and understand the behaviour of man in social situations. Many scholars consider social anthropology and sociology as the same and maintain that it is a branch of sociology.

SOCIOLOGY AND HEALTH

The scope of sociological study is vast and varied. One of the key areas relevant to nursing education is sociology of health. Sociologists have over the years established beyond doubt that the morbidity patterns and the spread of diseases is greatly influenced by the factors like socioeconomic status of individuals, ethnic traditions or beliefs, customs and other cultural traditions.

Health is a major social issue and as the physical and mental well-being of individuals is greatly influenced by the social factors. The health status of people varies from one society to the other and the yardstick for its assessment also differs. Sociological studies have established that the incidence of morbidity is influenced by the beliefs, traditions, customs and the socioeconomic status of individuals.

Sociologists have established that the spread of diseases is influenced by socioeconomic status of individuals, ethnic traditions, beliefs, customs and other cultural factors. Sociologists study and analyse the health statistics in a sociological perspective to identify the external factors responsible for outbreak and spread of diseases.

As per the definition of the World Health Organization (WHO), health is a state of complete physical, mental and social well-being and not merely the absence of disease or infirmity. It recognizes the fact that physical and mental well-being of an individual is influenced by societal factors and brings out health as a social issue. Health status of an individual is no longer considered merely a consequence of biological or natural conditions.

The standards of health vary from one community, society, country and culture to another. The health standards in poor developing countries are far from those of affluent developed countries.

RELEVANCE

While medical sociology is mainly concerned with the relationship between the medial professional and the patient, sociology of health investigates the sociological causes of diseases and illness and also studies how social life has an impact on morbidity and mortality rates. It is essential for nurses to be aware of the social circumstances of the patients and have basic knowledge about the social aspects of community and society. A sociological approach helps to identify the external factors responsible for spread of diseases. The academic importance of sociology of health is growing steadily and it has emerged as a significant field in Western countries. It is a playing a vital róle in social and preventive medicine.

The increasing focus on community health care, preventive measures, alternative therapies and dissemination of health information for promotion of over well-being makes it imperative for the nurses to have a modicum of sociological imagination for in-depth understanding to observe and evaluate the impact of culture, customs and other social factors on the health status in varied health care environments.

Sociology is extremely useful for health professionals in a country of sharp socioeconomic disparities and cultural and religious diversity like India as it enhances their understanding of the linkage and the impact socioeconomic conditions and cultural environment have on the levels of morbidly and wellness of the community.

It is essential for nurses, in particular, to have a good knowledge about the social factors as their role is no longer limited to clinical health care. In the changing health care environment they are required to play the role of a counsellor under the preventive initiative like total immunization and family welfare programmes.

The sociological approach has opened wide vast opportunities for nurses to carry out research in various health-related areas which will not only help in improving their understanding the impact of social environment on health but also provide useful information for the policymakers.

The health care to special groups in the society like the geriatric, physically and mentally challenged, children and people infected by incurable diseases like acquired immunodeficiency syndrome (AIDS), etc., cannot be provided without proper knowledge of the sociocultural backgrounds of the patients. The nurses have a major role in taking care of these special groups.

Even while providing clinical care knowledge of social circumstances helps the health professionals in understanding the behavioural pattern of the patients and their family members and they can deal with them accordingly.

REVIEW QUESTIONS

1. What is the relationship between sociology and health?
2. Why is anthropology considered to be very close to sociology?
3. Write a short note on the relationship between psychology and sociology.

CHAPTER

3

Application of Sociology in Nursing

LEARNING OBJECTIVES

After reading this chapter the learner should be able to

- Know the importance of sociology for nurses.
- Be efficient in applying the knowledge of sociology in various fields of nursing.

Knowledge of sociology is immensely useful for nurses as it helps to understand and appreciate the sociological aspects which have a direct bearing on causes, incidence and course of a range of both communicable and noncommunicable diseases in the changing scenario of the society. Apart from culture, religion, customs, values and beliefs and socioeconomic factors like poverty, malnutrition, poor sanitation, lack of education, inadequate housing and unemployment also play an important role in shaping the health of the society.

Research studies have revealed that cultural, social and behavioural practices predispose certain communities to diseases and health profile also varies with gender (male and female), area (urban and rural), literacy, religion and other such factors. It is being increasingly acknowledged that for effective delivery of medical care a proper understanding of the social behaviour of individuals and groups and their value system is essential, apart from scientific and biological knowledge. A patient is a human being with erratic habits, beliefs and other personal traits, which may influence his recovery. Nowadays, the concept of sociology is being increasingly used in studying the health profile and effective delivery of medical and nursing care. Medical specialists are seeking the help of social scientists to understand the social aspects health and diseases and the illness behaviour.

Nurses need to understand the complexities of the human relations and their impact on health. The impact of changing structure of family, with joint families giving way to nuclear families, on health of the population and other social transformations can be best understood by adopting a sociological approach.

Sociology helps nurses to know the social factors behind the causation of diseases and gather relevant information like the time of the year a particular disease occurs; the age group affected the most, any significant difference in prevalence rate among females and males or rural and urban population.

COMMUNITY HEALTH

Many health problems in the society are in fact social problems and these could be dealt effectively only by understanding the human behaviour. Nowadays, social scientists are often engaged to study the failures of various community health programmes and investigate the reasons for the reluctance of the people to accept the measures meant to improve their health status. It is now widely acknowledged that acceptance of a health programme depends on the human behaviour.

In India, many community programmes pertaining to family welfare, child and maternal health, immunization and total sanitation have been implemented which had only been partially successful. The low acceptability of such programmes among people has been the main reason for their indifferent outcome. People have been traditionally defecating in open and they consider it a healthy practice. They do not want toilets in or around their houses.

CULTURE

Cultural background plays an important role in delivery of health care and nurses and other medical professionals have to understand the human behaviour in relation to society to ensure cultural safety. Nurses have to provide care to patients coming from different race, caste, religion, tribes and socioeconomic background and sociology enables them to know about their customs, beliefs, food habits, attires, languages and values and enhances their tolerance for various cultures.

CLINICAL MEDICINE

Rapid advances in the field of medical science in recent years have provided treatment for most of the modern life-threatening diseases. However, still cardiovascular diseases, diabetes, arthritis, cancer, hypertension, ulceration, HIV positive and mental illness continue to be a major problem in Western countries and they are responsible for morbidity and mortality. Most of these ailments are associated with human behaviour and habits, and some of these have been categorized as *lifestyle* diseases.

Social scientists are undertaking studies to find the possible linkages between social conduct and the incidence of certain diseases. They are investigating why people from different sociocultural backgrounds respond differently to symptoms of a disease. It is now increasingly being realized that a health professional should not only have medical knowledge but also possess adequate social knowledge for effective delivery of health care.

EPIDEMIOLOGY

Cultural traditions and customs have a bearing on the health profile of communities. While certain traditional practices are really good for health, some others are based on misconception and have a negative impact in the long run. In India, there has been a long tradition of visiting temples located on hill tops which can be accessed only through trekking. It is a desirable practice as walking to distant temples is good for health. Similarly, the custom of fasting once in a week not only saves food grains but also prevents obesity. People consume a lot of fruits and nuts during fasting days which is good for health.

Certain customs during and after child birth are good for both the mother and the child. The practice of giving rich diet after child birth and providing a complete rest to the mother helps in overcoming the fatigue of delivery. It also ensures proper growth of the baby as the mother has all the time to take care and breastfeed.

On the negative side, intake of too many fats in the form of pure ghee and butter leads to obesity among women after delivery, nurses can advise about the right diet to be given after acquiring knowledge about the customary diet provided to pregnant and lactating women in a community.

Similarly, to understand the factors affecting the health like use of tobacco and beetle leaves and avoiding certain foods during pregnancy or lactation may have an adverse impact on health. Breastfeeding, adequate nutrition to pregnant women and lactating mothers are some social factors which should be encouraged.

There are certain practices in all the religions which promote healthy living. For instance, marriages within blood relations are prohibited in the Hindu religion, which prevents inbreeding, and in turn, genetic disorders.

If nurses are conversant with these traditional practices they can encourage the healthy ones and discourage those which mar the health.

Social Problems

Sociology provides knowledge about various social problems existing in society which have a bearing on the health status of the communities. In India, inferior status of women compared to men, dowry system and certain rituals are responsible for female feticide and infanticide and malnutrition among females. A consequence of this lack of gender equality is that maternal mortality rate is high because of repeated abortions after prenatal sex determination.

HEALTHY RELATIONSHIP

Sociology helps nurses to adjust and establish a healthy relationship with individuals and the community. They have to establish the relationship not only with patients but also with their family members to motivate them to change the lifestyle for a healthy living.

A deep understanding with the family also enables the nurses to know exact cause and real factors behind the diseases. Sociology is useful for nurses working in community in understanding the pattern of diseases in a particular population, relating the social causes like poor socio-economic status, gender discrimination, customs, dietary habits, occupation, educational status, and quality of health services.

REVIEW QUESTIONS

1. Why is the study of sociology important for nurses?
2. Write short notes on the following:
   a. Sociology and epidemiology.
   b. Sociology and community health.

UNIT - 2

INDIVIDUAL AND SOCIETY

CHAPTER

4

Individual and Society

LEARNING OBJECTIVES

After reading this chapter the learner should be able to

- Know the relationship between the individual and society.
- Get acquainted with various characteristics of a society.
- Have knowledge about the features of a community.

Human beings are biological creatures and an individual is a biological entity like animals and other living creatures. However, unlike animals, human beings are endowed with incredible mental traits and abilities through which he can learn, generate ideas, analyse, discriminate, interact and communicate in a manner no other species can. All these traits help a human being acquire extraordinary social abilities that differentiated him/her from animals and made thinkers like Aristotle to describe man as a social animal. Indeed, human beings have the most complex social structure. Some animals also have social abilities as evident from the tendency to live in groups but only human beings gather families, tribes, clans and nations.

Thus, the development of an individual depends only on its initial genetic endowment and exposure to social environment during the course of life. A human individual is a combination of biology and society in which he/she is brought up. The biological traits guide the responses to stimuli on the basis of the survival instincts developed through the responses of generations of ancestors.

An individual acquires certain traits through biological inheritance and it contributes to his/her personality in terms of physical features like height, colour, hair and psychological characteristics. Some of these traits are acquired by an individual from the parents and that is one of the hereditary factor that makes every individual different. According to Francis Galton, human beings are fundamentally unequal and differences are inborn. The inequality is mainly due to heredity and the environment.

The role of social environment in developing the personality is important as social structures regulate the behaviour of an individual by imposing restrictions and effecting alterations in carrying out biological responses. The relationship between the individual and society is important as Park says that 'Man is not born human but to be made human. No human being is known to have normally developed in isolation.' The skills of speech, language, interaction and communication and the concept of right and wrong are all learnt by an individual from the society.

Sociological studies have brought out that an individual's human nature is dependent upon the society. The attitudes, beliefs, moral values and ideals are shaped by the society an individual is born into. The process starts from the family and extends neighbourhood and friends as the individual grows up.

The relationship of an individual and society is continuously changing as the society also grows and evolves and with the changing attitudes and ideals of its members. A society is an aggregate of individuals and social life is an expression of the lives of the individuals.

The society affords opportunity for initiative, innovation and enterprise to an individual. The more sophisticated and organized a society is, the greater the degree of individuality its members are able to attain. The society not only provides all the resources to the members to develop their distinct personality but also to express their individuality. The society and the individual are interdependent and mutually support each other; there is no antipathy between the two.

According to Maclver, 'in the real world of man, society and individuality go hand in hand'.

However, it would wrong to infer that a perfect harmony exists between individuality and society. The relationship between individual and society is not one-sided. While an individual has his/her own mind, will and purpose, the same is not true for the society. However, it can be assigned any function keeping in view the aspirations, hopes, fears and larger interests of the dominant groups.

SOCIETY

The term *society* is derived from Latin word *societus*, which means companionship or friendship. The society is a group of individuals and companionship and friendship among them brings in the element of sociability in it. In common idiom, the word society is often used to denote specific groups like Arya Samaj, Dalit Samaj, Khasis or various other tribes. However, in sociology, the term *society* refers to norms and the intricate patterns of relationships among members and interaction among them and not merely to a group of people. A society is a process and not a tangible unit as a group of people. More important is the system of relationships, interaction by which a society sustains and the pattern of norms and values.

Some sociologists maintain that a society exists only when the members know each other and have common interests and goals. Not all relationships are social. There has to be a connect among the members in order to have a social relationship. A social relationship implies reciprocal awareness among individuals, direct or indirect. This reciprocal awareness is the characteristic of every social relationship. F.H. Giddings defined a society as 'a number of like-minded individuals who know and enjoy their like-mindedness and, thus, able to work together for common goals'.

A society is a web of social relationships among the people and it comes into existence when more than one individual live together. A mutual relationship develops among them and different social processes like cooperation, competition and conflict take place constantly and these intricate interactions give lead to establishment of society.

A society is a group of people who share a common culture, occupy a particular territory and have a feeling that they constitute a cohesive unit with a distinct entity. It is the mutual interactions and interrelations of individuals and groups.

Definitions of Society

Prominent sociologists and thinkers have given their own definitions of society. The father of sociology Auguste Comte described the society as a social organism possessing a harmony of structure and function.

Talcott Parsons defined society as 'a total complex of human relationships in so far as they grow out of the action in terms of means–end relationship inbuilt or symbolic'.

MacIver and Page defined society as a system of usages and procedures of authority and mutual aid of many groupings and divisions, of controls of human behaviour and liberties.

Morris Ginsberg viewed society as 'a collection of individuals united by certain relations or conduct and mode of behaviour which distinguish them from others who do not enter into these relations or who differ from them in behaviour'.

In the words of G.D.H. Cole, society is the complex of organized associations and institutions within a community.

As per Harkins, 'Society is any permanent or continuing group of men women and children which is able to carry on independently the process of racial perpetuation and maintenance on their own cultural level'.

F.H. Giddings terms 'society as the union itself, the organization, the sum of formal relations in which associating individuals are bound together'.

C.H. Cooley described society as a 'complex of forms or processes each of which is living and growing by interaction with others, the whole being so unified that what takes place in one part affects all the rest'.

Characteristics of Society

The meaning of the term *society* can be better understood if one undertakes a thorough analyses of its characteristics or elements. These distinct characteristics not only provide a wider understanding of the term but also make it clear how a society is different from a community. In a narrow term, society denotes to a group of people but in a broader sense it refers to the whole human society. However, society is characterized by some essential elements and the foremost is that it must have population as a society cannot be formed in the absence of a group of people. A society does not merely refer to a group of people but to a system of complex social relationships for which existence of a group of people is a prerequisite. Thus, population is the first and foremost requirement of society.

Some of the important characteristics of society are as follows:

Likeness

Likeness is the important feature as without a sense of likeness, there could be no mutual recognition of belonging together. Likeness of members in a social group is the primary basis of their mutuality.

The famous sociologist MacIver emphasizes that 'Comradeship, intimacy, association of any kind or degree would not be possible unless there is some understanding of each by the other, and that understanding depends on the likeness which each apprehends or anticipates in the other.' Likeness is the one element that can stir up a strong group feeling to bring men, women and children together. Likeness was found in early society on kinship and in modern societies this social likeness has broadened out into the principles of nationality.

Social likeness helps members to understand each other and develop close relationships. Society necessarily comprises like-bodied and likeminded individuals as friendship, camaraderie, intimacy and relationship of any kind would not be possible without likeness.

Differences

Likeness is an essential feature but not a sufficient condition for a social organization. Differences are also a prerequisite for a society as no two individuals are alike in their nature. Differences are complementary to social relationship because society involves differences and it depends on it as much as on likeness. The social structure of humanity is based on the family, the first society which is based on biological differences and differences in aptitude, interest and capacity. The biological differences between men and women are an example. The economic structure of society is based upon division of labour in which people are engaged in different or dissimilar economic activities.

If all the members will be alike in all respects, there would be little reciprocity and relationship and the society could not be formed. Further, it will severely limit interaction among members. In the opinion of Maclver, 'primary likeness and secondary differences create the greatest of all institutions-the division of labour'.

Though differences is necessary for society but differences by itself does not create society. Hence, differences are subordinate to likeness. Maclver says that 'primary likeness and secondary differences create the greatest of all social institutions- the division of labour'.

The culture of society prospers with the differences in thoughts, ideals and viewpoints. People differ from each other in respect of their interests, capacities, abilities, tendencies and other attributes but these differences do not necessarily mean mutual conflict. Instead, it further strengthens the organization of society.

A society based exclusively on likeness or uniformity is bound to lose in socialization as interaction will be limited, life would be monotonous and uninteresting. There would be little reciprocity, little give and take. They would contribute very little to one another. A society consisting of all adults, all old or all young people, is unimaginable.

Interdependence

Interdependence is an essential element to constitute society. It is not possible for human being to satisfy his/her desire in isolation. Interdependence is visible in every aspect of present day society. No individual is self-sufficient and the survival and well-being of every individual depends on this interdependence. It is dependence on others for food, shelter and security and other needs that makes the 'man a social animal' as stated by Greek philosopher Aristotle.

The interdependence starts from the family. The first society is based on the biological interdependence of the sexes, and continues to increase. None of the two sexes is complete by itself and depends on the other to start and maintain the family. With the advancement of society, the degree of interdependence increases manifold. Individuals apart, even the groups, communities, societies, countries and continents are interdependent.

Cooperation

Cooperation is an important characteristic without which the entire fabric of society may collapse. Cooperation forms the very basis of social life, without cooperation, a society cannot sustain and survive. If the members of the society are not united by a common purpose and they do not work together to achieve it, they cannot lead a happy and comfortable life. Cooperation avoids internecine tussles and results in inefficiency and economy.

In the words of P. Gisbert, 'Cooperation is the most elementary process of social life without which society is impossible.' C.H. Cooley points out that 'cooperation arises when men realize that they have common interests'. Family, the first society, cannot exist without cooperation.

Conflict

Like cooperation, conflict is an essential characteristic of society. Cooperation and conflict must coexist for constitution and sustenance of society. Conflict is an ever-present phenomenon present in every human society. In the words of the famous sociologist Maclver, 'society is cooperation crossed by conflict'.

Conflict is a process of struggle through which all things have come into existence. It is also necessary as it serves as a cementing force for strengthening social relations. In fact, cooperation and conflict go side by side in a healthy and well-developed society.

According to George Simmel, 'a conflict free harmonious society is practically impossibility'. Conflict, direct or indirect, makes cooperation more meaningful and these two universal processes lay the foundation of society. A society requires both 'harmony and disharmony' and 'cooperation and conflict' for its formation and growth.

Society Is a Network or a Web of Social Relationships

Social relationships are the foundation of society. These social relationships are based on mutual awareness and recognition. As social relationships are abstract in nature so also the society is abstract in nature. Without these social relationships, no society could be formed. Maclver described society as a network of social relationships.

Different kinds of social processes like cooperation and conflict constantly take place in society and relationships established around these give shape to society.

Permanent Nature

Society is a coherent, dynamic, stable and enduring organization. It is not a temporary organization of individuals and it continues to exist even after the death of individual members.

Society Is Abstract

Society is an abstract concept as it is a web of social relationships, which are intangible. One cannot see a relationship but one can feel it. Wright has rightly remarked that 'society in essence means a state or condition, a relationship and is, therefore, necessarily an abstraction'. Moreover, the essential elements of society like customs, traditions, folkways, mores and culture, which are all abstract in nature.

Society Is Dynamic

Society is a dynamic entity as it is a continuous and ever-changing process. No society is static and every society keeps changing incessantly and the process sees the old customs, traditions, folkways, mores, values and institutions modified or replaced by new traditions and values takes place. Society changes from its traditional nature to modern nature.

Comprehensive Culture

Society and culture are inseparable. Culture is an important characteristic as it distinguishes a society from others. Each and every society has its own culture which is the way of life of the members of a society. The value system, beliefs, art, morals are all part of culture and they are transmitted from one generation to the other through the cultural process. Culture is comprehensive as it fulfils the necessities of social life.

Interrelationship between Individual and Society

There is a close relationship between society and an individual. An individual is surrounded and encompassed by culture, a societal force, in the society and he/she has to conform to the norms, occupy statuses and become members of groups. Man depends on society and he has a meaningful relationship with it only because it supports and contributes to the ends, the purposes of individuals themselves. It is by helping the development of individuality of the individual that society achieves its purpose and significance.

The relationship between individual and society involves the question of values and that makes it the most intricate problem of social philosophy. The issue is more philosophical rather than sociological and closely connected with the question of the relationship of man and society. There are two major theories regarding the relationship of man and society.

1. The social contract theory
2. The organismic theory

CONTRACT THEORY

The social contract theory asserts that society came into existence because of the agreement entered into by the individuals. According to this theory, all men are born free and equal. The classical representatives of this school of thought are Thomas Hobbes, John Locke and Rousseau.

Thomas Hobbes

Thomas Hobbes was of the opinion that man in the state of nature was in perpetual conflict with his neighbours on account of his essentially selfish nature and found nothing but grief and misery in the company of his fellows. Since the conditions in the state of nature were intolerable, the yearning for peace made the people enter some kind of social contract to ensure security and certainty of life and property.

Thus, society came into being as a means for the protection of men against the consequences of their own nature. The agreement was of each with all and of all with each other. The contract became obligatory for the whole community as a perpetual social bond. Thus, man organized himself to protect against the evil consequences of his own nature to live in peace with all.

John Locke

British political philosopher John Locke maintained that man in the state of nature was enjoying total freedom and liberty from all sorts of rules and regulations. It was a state of peace, goodwill, mutual assistance and preservation but there was no recognized system of law and justice. As the population increased, equality was destroyed and a divide between rich started building up. The peaceful life was often upset by corruption, conflict and crime. The men were forced to live in full of fears and continual dangers.

In order to gain peace, stability and security people made a contract to enter into civil society. This contract called Locke social contract replaced the state of nature with civil society. The social contract was a surrender of rights and powers to help preserve the remaining rights. The contract was for specific purposes and the limited surrender of rights to the whole community and not to a man or to an assembly of men. According to Locke, the social contract subsequently contributed to the governmental control.

Jean Jacques Rousseau

Man enjoyed a pure, simple and innocent life of perfect freedom and equality in the state of nature. But the conditions changed as population increased, simplicity and idyllic happiness disappeared and the selfish nature of man started manifesting. Families were established, institution of property emerged and human equality was ended. Man began to think in terms of mine and yours.

French writer of the eighteenth century Jean Jacques Rousseau in his famous book *The Social Contract* described man in the state of nature as a noble savage who led a life of primitive simplicity and blissful joy. He was independent, contented, self-reliant, healthy, fearless and good. It was only primitive instinct and sympathy, which united him with others. He was free from all prejudices, knew neither right or wrong and had no idea about the notions of virtue and vice.

When equality of early state was lost, war, murder, conflicts became the order of the day. The way out was found in the formation of a civil society in which natural liberty gave way to civil freedom through a social contract. Rousseau said that by virtue of this contract everyone while uniting himself to all remains as free as before. The unique feature was that it represented collective good as distinguished from the private interests of its members.

However, the theory of social contract attracted widespread criticism as there was no historical evidence to show that the society has ever been deliberately created through a contract. Further, it is beyond imagination to believe that man could ever think of entering into a contract with others at a time when he lived under conditions of extreme simplicity, ignorance and even brutality.

The advocates of the theory hold that the early individuals entered into the contract for their individual safety and security of property. However, the early laws were more communal than individual and the unit of society was not the individual but the family. The most primitive people even lived in some form of society however rudimentary or unorganized. Another relevant point that arises is that there are always two parties to the contract and there can be no one-sided contract as was conceived by Hobbes.

According to Sir Henry Maine, contract is not the beginning of society but the end of it.

They Are the Social Contract: The Organismic Theory of Society

The organismic theory views the society as akin to a living organism and describes its relationship between an individual as similar to that of a limb to the body and that of a leaf to the plant. Plato, Aristotle, Herbert Spencer, Spengler and Novico were the main exponents of this theory. According to them, society is nothing but a kind of living organism, possessing organs, which perform functions analogous to those of a plant or animal.

Spencer developed the organismic theory by making an elaborate comparison between the society and the organism. He compared individual to a cell as the basic building blocks and thought of society as a biological system a greater organism. The society is also subject of the same process of gradual development from a simple to complex like an organism. It also exhibits differentiation in functions and integration in structure and as per this theory society is an organism whose structure and function resemble those of the human beings and which also develops according to the same laws.

Besides these similarities, Spencer also draws a number of structural analogies between the society and organism. An individual cell of an organism may die with little effect on its life; similarly, the death of an individual has no bearing on the society.

The organismic theory is not free from criticism as there are some dissimilarities too due to which sociologists found faults and consider the theory unsatisfactory. Organs of a human body cease to exist when a man dies. But the society does not cease to exist and continues its functions. Also society and individual cannot be like a structured human body as it cannot explain the relationship of an individual and society like an organism.

One can metaphorically explain of the relationship in terms of the organic form, but in reality the picture is different. Individuals of society are not fixed like parts of the body. A society does not come into existence from the union of two organisms and it grows of its own conscious efforts. Thus, it cannot be like an organism.

However, the significance of the theory cannot be undermined as it establishes an inseparable relation of individual and society and asserts that individual and the society cannot live without each other.

COMMUNITY

Community is an important fundamental concept in sociology. MacIver defined community as 'an area of social living characterized by some degree of coherence'.

The origin and growth of community goes back to the origin of human civilization and man has been living in community ever since his arrival. Community is the original and first abode in the lap of which human civilization itself reared up of human civilization. During prehistoric era man was leading a nomadic or barbarian life and was wandering here and there for food and could not settle up anywhere.

It is natural that people residing in a definite area develop likeness, cooperation and fellow-feeling among themselves. As a result they share common traditions, culture and develop common social ideas among themselves. This common social living within a geographical area gives rise to community life. Thus, the minimum basic elements for a community to exist include a collection of people in a geographical area.

The term *community* has been derived from two Latin words *com* (together) and *munis* (servicing). It comprises a group of people with common and shared interests. However, in common parlance the term *community* is often wrongly used to indicate a racial community or a religious community. Gradually community life expands as socioeconomic, cultural and political relations develop among the people living in a particular area. It leads to emergence of a full-fledged community with the creation of different social, political, economic and cultural institutions. Sociologists differ over approach to the meaning of community and they have given various definitions of the term. A perusal of these definitions will provide a better understanding of the term. Some sociologists lay emphasis on area or ecological aspects, while focus more on psychological aspects.

Maclver stated that 'Community is an area of social living marked by some degree of social coherence.'

According to Kingsley Davis, 'Community is the smallest territorial group that can embrace all aspects of social life'.

In the words of Ogburn and Nimkoff, 'Community is the total organization of social life within a limited area.'

Arnold Green described a community as a cluster of people, living within a contiguous small area, who share a common way of life.

According to E.S. Bogardus, 'Community is a social group with some degree of' we-feeling' and living in a given area.'

G.A. Lundberg defined a 'community as a human population living within a limited geographic area and carrying on a common inter-dependent life.'

From all these definitions, it can be concluded that community refers to a group, small or large, whose members live together sharing a common life and have developed a strong sense of community sentiment or consciousness among them, which distinguishes them from others.

Analysing the characteristics of a community will make the meaning of the term further clear as we discuss further.

A Group of People

A group of people, small or large, is the most fundamental or essential characteristic of community. There can be no community life without a group of people as community. Living starts only when a group of people live together and share a common life. When they develop a strong sense of community consciousness, a community comes into existence. Thus, a group of people is an essential element of a community.

A Definite Locality

Community is a territorial group and, thus, it is the next important characteristic of a community after a group. A group of people alone is not sufficient to form a community. They have to reside in a specific territory to form a community. The territory need not be fixed forever as is the case of nomadic people who may change their habitations. But a majority of the communities are settled and closely bound and their solidarity is derived from their living in a definite locality.

Community Sentiment

It is another important characteristic as without community sentiment a group of people living in a definite territory will not form a community. A strong sense of 'we' feeling among the members or a feeling of belonging together is created because of common living within an area for a long time. The sentiment of common living that exists among the members of a locality results in the members emotionally identifying themselves and this new identity distinguishes them from the members of other community.

Naturality

Communities are naturally organized and grow spontaneously. They are neither a product of human will nor they come into existence by an act of government. Individuals became its member by birth.

Permanence

Community is always a permanent group and it refers to a lasting and stable living of individuals within a definite area.

Similarity

The members of a community are similar in many ways. They live within a definite locality, lead a common life and share some common ends. Among members, it is characterized by similarity in language, culture, customs and traditions and in many other things. Similarities in these respects play an important role in the development of community sentiment.

Wider Ends

A community has wider ends as its members associate not for the fulfilment of a particular goal but for a variety of ends.

Total Organized Social Life

A community is marked by total organized social life. It is a society in miniature as it includes all aspects of social life.

A Particular Name

Every community has a particular name by which it is known to the world and its members are identified by that name. For example, people living in Punjab are known as Punjabis.

No Legal Status

A community is not created by the law of the land, and it has no legal status. It has no rights and duties in the eyes of law.

Size of Community

A community is classified on the basis of its size. For instance, village is an example of a small community, whereas a nation is an example of a big community.

Exists within Society

A community exists within society and possesses distinguishable structure which distinguishes it from others.

DIFFERENCES BETWEEN SOCIETY AND COMMUNITY

1. A society is all pervasive and has a universal character. It is not bound to a definite geographical territory. However, a definite geographical area is an essential element of a community.
2. Society is a web of social relationships and includes every relationship established among the people. This social relationship may be direct or organized or unorganized, conscious or unconscious. A community consists of a group of individuals and exists within a society.
3. Community sentiment or a sense of 'we feeling' is not essential in a society. But there can be no community without a community sentiment. It is indispensable for a community.
4. Society is an intangible network of social relationships, which cannot be seen or felt by a touch. On the other hand, community is a group of people living in a particular area, the existence of which can be located. A community is, thus, tangible and concrete.
5. Society is a wider entity and there can be more than one community in a society. Community is smaller than society and there cannot be more than one society in a community.
6. Common interests and common objectives are not necessary in society. But common interests and common objectives are necessary for a community. People in a community live together for the achievement of common interests and common objectives.
7. Society involves likeness as well as difference and both common and diverse interests are present in a society. However, in a community, likeness is more important than difference.

REVIEW QUESTIONS

1. Write in detail about the relationship between an individual and the society.
2. What are the various characteristics of a society?

CHAPTER

5

Socialization

LEARNING OBJECTIVES

After reading this chapter the learner should be able to

- Know about the process of socialization.
- Have knowledge about the various agencies of socialization.

We are all familiar with Greek philosopher Aristotle's famous quote 'Man is by nature a social animal'; however, socialization is a long-drawn learning process. The human being enters this world as a biological entity like animals, but he acquires the social traits from the society to grow up into a social being. A baby learns the language, habits and ways, norms, traditions of the group or society in which he or she is brought up and his thinking, emotions, feelings and attitudes develop accordingly. Interacting with other members of the society play the most important role in this process of moulding which ensures continuation of society. The learning process continues throughout life. Values, customs, traditions, norms and ways of the society are inherited and passed on from one generation to the other in this manner.

MEANING AND DEFINITION

The process of interaction by which growing individuals imbibe the values, attitudes, habits, beliefs and various other cultural traits from the group or society into which they have been born is called socialization. It is a wide-ranging process by which the personality of an individual takes shape.

Famous sociologists Horton and Hunt described socialization as the process that helps individuals to internalize the values and norms of the groups and develop a distinct personality. The interactive learning shapes an individual into a social person.

MacIver explains socialization as 'the process by which human beings establish wider and profounder relationships with one another in which they become more bound and develop other associations'. As socialization transforms an individual from a human being to a social being, MacIver maintains that socialization and individualization are two sides of the same coin.

According to Lundberg, socialization involves complex processes of interaction through which the individual learns the habits, skills, beliefs and values and behaviours essential for effective participation in social groups.

Green defined socialization as 'the process by which children acquire the cultural traits, a distinct self- and a unique personality', while Peter Worsley views socialization as the process of 'transmission of culture, whereby men learn the rules and practices of social groups'.

In the words of H.M. Johnson socialization is 'learning that enables the learner to perform social roles. It is the process by which individuals acquire the traits of an already existing culture of groups they come into'. Kingsley Davis views it as the emergence and gradual development of the self or ego, leading to development of distinctive personality and mind.

Socialization is also important for the continuation of society as it facilitates transmission of its culture from generation to generation and that is how it maintains itself. It is a process of cultural learning by which a new person acquires necessary skills and knowledge to effectively participate in a social system.

PROCESS OF SOCIALIZATION

The process of socialization starts even before birth as a baby begins to learn from his mother's womb. While growing up the child keeps learning and acquires behavioural skills and knowledge to live in society and, thus, becomes a social being. Socialization is a life-long phenomenon and it takes place at different stages such as primary, secondary and adult. In the primary stage, the child grows up in the family and the socialization happens within family and interaction with close relatives. The secondary stage involves schooling when the child goes out and mixes with fellow children and neighbours and gets greater exposure to people outside the family. The third stage is adult socialization when an individual adopts an adult roe and learns the practices and expectations associated with a social role and social circumstances.

Primary Socialization

It is the socialization that takes place early in life, as a child and adolescent. A child is socialized by education, surroundings, cultural environment and social lifestyle in his family. The process starts at birth and during childhood, when the basic behaviour pattern is formed, the child learns from the family members.

This is the most important developmental stage of a human being, because it sets the groundwork for all future socialization. The child learns the attitudes, values and actions appropriate to individuals as members of a particular culture during this stage.

As a child one is not aware of 'one-self' and the process of primary socialization makes one 'self-aware' through interaction with people with whom one has the primary relationship like mother, father and grandparents.

There are four stages in this socialization:

The Oral Stage. It starts very early as baby learns sucking and satisfies hunger. Before birth the child is cosy in the mother's womb but after birth the infant has to breathe himself and has to cope with discomforts like cold, wet and heat. The only way he can express himself is by 'crying'. The infant establishes its oral dependency by means of crying. It develops some definite expectations about the feeding time and is involved in himself and his mother. It also learns to give signals for his felt needs. This stage continues till the completion of infancy.

The Anal Stage. This stage starts after the completion of first year and continues up to three years. The child learns to an extent to take care of himself and does not remain totally dependent on the mother. As the child grows up and learns to control urination and defecation. Toilet training is a part of this stage of socialization. This stage continues till the child is three years old. The child is taught to distinguish between correct and incorrect actions through the system of reward and punishment.

The Oedipal Stage. It starts from the fourth year and continues till the beginning of adolescence stage (around 13 years). According to famous psychoanalyst, Sigmund Freud, the boy develops the 'Oedipus complex', feeling of jealousy towards father and love towards mother during this stage. Similarly, the girl develops the 'Electra complex', feeling of jealousy towards the mother and love towards the father. Usually, girls love their father more than their mother, whereas boys are more attached to their mothers.

The child becomes the member of the family as a whole and identifies himself with the social role assigned to him on gender basis. Social pressures compel the child to identify with the right sex. The boy tries to identify himself with the father and the girl with the mother. In school, the children prefer to mix with those of their own sex. The child internalizes his own role and that of father, mother and siblings (brother and sister).

The Stage of Adolescence. This stage is important as the children undergo physiological and the psychological change during adolescence. Boys and girls try to break free from parental control and become assertive and often find themselves in conflict. They want to indulge in various activities, while parents continue to exercise control over them, especially, sexual activity.

The parents want the adolescent children to become responsible and learn the new roles as adults and the associated norms. The transition from the adolescent stage to the adult stage is more difficult in the traditional societies where parents have the final say.

Secondary Socialization

The secondary socialization takes place outside the home. They learn from their friends, teachers and people around them. The interaction with people outside family and home enables the adolescents to learn how to behave and act in a particular situation.

Peer groups play an important role in the learning process. The peer groups influence the behaviour irrespective of the fact they are friendly or unfriendly or even bully at times.

Like primary socialization, secondary socialization also involves agents and agencies. However, unlike primary socialization, the learning is from people who are not emotionally close. Secondary agents could be those one has not met at all. For instance, a celebrity can influence a whole generation.

Tertiary Socialization

It starts with adulthood and continues all through. A person learns the practices and expectations associated with a social role of an adult. He becomes independent, responsible and independent.

AGENCIES OF SOCIALIZATION

Socialization includes the following agencies:

Family: The process of socialization immediately after birth of a baby is initiated by the family. Mother is the first teacher of the child. Mother tongue is the language the child learns from his family. Child picks up the habits from family, and eats what the family members cook.

Neighbourhood and community: Child learns a lot from the neighbourhood and community as he has maximum interaction with the neighbours after the family members.

School: School plays an important role in socialization of a human being as every school-going child spends around eight hours a day in the school. He spends more time in school than his home.

Peer groups: Each child learns a lot from his friends as competition, sharing, cooperation, morality and fashion from his age group persons.

Mass media: Television, newspapers, radio and magazines are very crucial in socialization in modern times.

Religion: A person follows the religion of the family he is born into. A person's religion is determined at birth only. Religion is a major influence in the process of socialization as religious practices are important part of life.

FACTORS INVOLVED IN SOCIALIZATION

The following factors are involved in socialization:

Imitation: Imitation is a major factor involved in socialization of children. Usually, they learn by imitating others. A child learns language and pronunciation by imitating his family members only. Fashion is mainly imitation as every individual tends to be trendy.

Suggestion: Suggestions mould the behaviour of human beings. Parents give lot of suggestions to children and they do get influenced by suggestions.

Language: Language has impact on a man right from childhood. Language is the medium of social interaction.

Identification: Everybody identifies herself or himself with someone and tries to behave in a similar manner. Children may identify themselves with the toys they play with or the picture books or the characters in the cartoon movies.

REVIEW QUESTIONS

1. What is socialization? Explain in detail.
2. What are the various stages of process of socialization?
3. Write down about various agencies of socialization.

CHAPTER

6

Brief Review of Human Growth and Development

LEARNING OBJECTIVES

After reading this chapter the learner should be able to

- Learn about the factors affecting the growth and development of a child.
- Know the role of environment in the social development of a person.

A human baby is also like the baby of any animal at birth. It is through the process of socialization that an infant undergoes which makes him or her different from animal passage of time and acquires a distinct identity. An infant does not have awareness of self and environment. He only cries to get his basic needs fulfilled as and when he is hungry or wet and cold. He responds only to sudden loud sound or very bright light. The cultural learning process in childhood is much more intense as compared to adulthood, though the process of learning continues till a person is alive.

Primary socialization occurs during infancy and childhood. Language and basic behavioural patterns are learnt during the period that forms the foundation for the learning. The main agency for the primary socialization is family. Secondary socialization begins sometimes in childhood and the agencies responsible for the process include neighbourhood, peer group, school and the media, besides the family. In modern society, early socialization occurs in a small family unit having mother, father and a sister or brother. Unlike the traditional joint families, grandparents, uncles, aunts and cousin brothers and sisters are missing, and thus, not a part of the early socialization process. Instead, children are looked after by servants in the families where both the parents are working. In many cases, the children are looked after by a single parent if husband and wife are stationed at different stations or separated by divorce.

EARLY SOCIALIZATION

Family remains the major agency for socialization from birth to adulthood and throughout the life and plays an important role in connecting the generations. A child's ability to learn depends upon the opportunities available from various social groups surrounding him. Children do not just acquire the information available passively but choose and interpret what they perceive from the world around them through seeing, hearing and feeling. The first stage of learning is up to 2 years of age when he starts speaking. Vocabulary building is a bit difficult for the child as he has to attach the meaning to the sounds and many words have multiple meanings. Initially, young children usually do not attach meaning to a word as they learn to call 'mamma'. They may call everybody 'mamma'. Gradually, they start associating the words with objects.

During the first 4 months of age, child cannot differentiate between the objects and human beings and is not aware of anything that exists beyond his vision. But gradually after that age, they start differentiating between objects and human beings and also start recognizing people constantly staying around him as mother, father, brother, sister, grandparents or baby sitter. They become aware of their environment and feel comfortable with familiar persons and become uncomfortable with strangers and unfamiliar places. During this stage, children start relating words with objects and persons and also learn to speak. A child makes many meaningless sounds in the first 6 months, he may respond when somebody talks to him but he cannot imitate the words. This is an echo reaction. Attempts to imitate keeps on increasing with age and number of words imitation also increases. The language he learns and pronunciation of words is like people surrounding him. Children feel happy when their demands are fulfilled as they have been fed, left clean and dry. They feel discomfort with extremes of temperatures, very cold or very hot. During this stage, child starts eating normal food, what an adult consumes. Usually, breastfeeding is over by the end of infancy. A newborn sleeps for most of the time but his sleeping pattern keeps changing as he grows and by the time he is 2 years old, he sleeps only for 10–12 h. Most of the toilet training also happens during this period as child starts exercising control over urination and bowel movement and starts giving indications when he has urge for these. He now has a set of temporary teeth, starts sitting, turning around, crawling and ultimately walking. Much of the learning is by touching, manipulating and exploring the objects.

From 2 to 7 years of age, a lot of growth and development occurs and this is also very important phase of socialization. Children acquire mastery over their mother tongue and are able to express their demands. They use a lot of expressions and signs along with words to express and explain things. They make certain sounds to show that they are happy, excited or unhappy. But they are self-involved during this stage and they feel the world around them as they understand the different roles of family members. They go to school, play with toys and get involved in playful activities with friends. They imitate what other members do like trying to wear big shoes, driving toy cars, cooking, washing clothes, polishing shoes or dressing up like adults. Their language is fully developed but continuity in expression of thoughts may not be there. Concept of number, weight and amount is not very clear to them. Children enjoy repetition and love hearing the same story again and again, while adolescents and adult find repetition very boring. Learning in this age is by trial and error, imitation and training. No significant differences in motor development are seen in early childhood as far as sex of the child is concerned. It is only the cultural practices that have impact on the development with girls wearing pink colour, frocks, bangles and playing with dolls and boys wearing certain colours, shirts trousers and playing with motor toys and guns.

By the time children are 5 years old, they are capable of dressing up, pulling up the socks and wearing shoes. They become skilled in tying laces, manipulating buttons, zippers and buckles by the age of 6 or 7. Children also become proficient in throwing ball and catching it. They start running between the age of 5–6 and they run as they get enjoyment out of it and not to reach a destination fast. Climbing stairs starts at the age of 2 with assistance. Children place one foot on the step and then draw the other and use the same foot each time to step upstairs. The ability to climb steps like adults is attained by the age of 4.

Children are able to brush their teeth by the age of 3. They develop muscles coordination of fingers, hands and wrist gets fully developed and ready to write by the age of 6. Between the age of 3 and 5, most of the children can copy geometric figures. Swimming depends on the opportunities and many children, if given a chance, learn it before the age of 4.

The third period in child development is from 7 to 11 years of age when they are capable of handling ideas like causality, sickness without difficulty. They get to understand the concepts of amount, numbers and weight and start carrying out mathematical operations like addition, multiplication, division and subtraction. This is also the prepubertal age when growth rate increases suddenly.

The period between 11 and 15 years is the stage of puberty when a lot of physical changes occur in the body along with hormonal changes. The changes are very rapid and pronounced. This is the time when physical differences start emerging between girls and boys. The changes start early in girls and the puberty period for them is between 11 and 13 years and for boys it is from 12 to 15 years. This period is also called preadolescence period during which the entire body goes through a metamorphosis, externally as well as internally. Changes are not only physical but also behavioural. Secondary sex characteristics develop during this period, which distinguishes male child from female child. Children in this age group are anxious for independence and get frustrated by restrictions imposed by parents. Children develop a positive attitude towards certain kind of work and negative attitude towards others. Choosing right kind of vocation as per the interest, capability and attitude of the child is very important in this age.

After the age of 17, the concept of self starts establishing and the children start understanding themselves. A realistic concept about oneself and one's abilities is formed and realistic vocational goals are set. Children learn socially acceptable behaviour and also how to like others and show affection so as to be liked by others. Achievements are important for a person as he grows up.

SOCIAL DEVELOPMENT

There are three processes involved in the social development of a person, learning socially acceptable behaviour, performing the approved social roles and development of attitude so that an individual interacts with people and participates in social activities. Most of the persons grow up covering their real feelings and thoughts that are not socially acceptable. But socially approved behaviour is not expected from very young children.

EFFECT OF ENVIRONMENT ON CHILDHOOD AND ADOLESCENCE

The childhood is important as primary socialization takes place during this period. Environment plays an important role in childhood development. During early infancy, the amount of crying among babies varies as it depends on how promptly and adequately the needs of a child are met. They may express their needs by noncrying methods like smacking the lips or ejecting the tongue when hungry and squirming when wet. If these signals are understood then the babies hardly cry but if these signals are ignored then the babies cry. Some babies cry when other methods of conveying their needs fail. Excessive crying is physically and psychologically damaging for the child at any age.

Physical environment: Type of housing, surroundings, recreational facilities and environmental cleanliness effect the development of the child. Safe house is essential to protect the child from injuries. Sufficient space for playing and recreational facilities is required to promote the overall development of a child.

The environmental factors are closely related to the speech development during childhood as number of family members and friends play a role. Family relationship is equally important as a healthy relationship between child and family members, especially mother, facilitates speech development, whereas unhealthy relationship may lead to speech retardation in a child apart from certain speech disorders as lisping, stuttering and slurring.

Emotional deprivation: This does not mean child is totally deprived of emotions but he is deprived of adequate pleasant emotional experiences such as curiosity, joy, happiness and affection. Children who grow up in an environment with abundant unpleasant emotions, such as anger, fear, jealousy and envy, are emotionally starved. They suffer a delay in development, physical, motor, speech and even intellectual. These children tend to be hostile and uncooperative. They express their resentment by aggressiveness and disobedience. These children are mostly selfish and demanding.

Inadequate nutrition: A child may not grow to his height potential if not given adequate nutrition and sunlight. Breastfeeding is also very important for the growth and development of a child. Apart from it, a child suffers from stunted growth if forced to work too heavy for his underdeveloped body.

Environmental pollution: Air, water and soil contamination is the cause of many childhood diseases like diarrhea, gastroenteritis, tuberculosis, pneumonia and many other killer diseases effecting the normal growth and development of children.

Childhood illnesses: Any illness, physical or psychological, affects the physical, behavioural and personality development of a child. Obesity, drug and alcohol use, sexual activity and emotional disorders are some of the major health issues faced by adolescents. Schools seek to affect student's health in a number of ways, including teaching exercise via physical education, Yogic exercises, extracurricular activities, nutrition through mid-day meals and the provision of health education services. The students are under constant pressure to do well in studies and it can have negative effects on their mental health due to high level of stress. School is a primary cultural milieu for students as they spend so much time there each day, which may lead to drug, alcohol and cigarette use among students and risky sexual activities also.

Social environment: Both the parents and their relationship are considered to be important for the overall development of children. If the parents are having strong and supportive relationship, the children tend to develop positive social relationship while children from broken families encounter developmental problems. Good social relationships inculcate self-esteem among children, and these children are less prone to experience mental health problems like depression and anxiety as compared to children lacking such social relationship. It also improves their cognitive development and educational attainment.

Environment of the educational institute: A safe environment is a prerequisite for effective learning. In many countries, schools are required to have programmes in place to reduce levels of violence as part of larger plans to improve academic performance.

Economic deprivation: Financial constraints in the family lead to depression and anger among its members and inconsistent parenting. The increased conflict among family members because of economic deprivation and hardships increase the risk behaviours in adolescents, including smoking, fighting and drinking. It affects the emotional security of young children and reinforces the use of aggression and interpersonal hostility.

Effect of peers: Adolescents have a lot of peer pressure. They try to follow what the youths around them are doing. They dress up like actors in the Bollywood. They try to be trendy and fashionable. Bad habits like smoking, alcohol consumption and drug abuse are picked up by adolescents from their friends. Even if they have awareness about right and wrong, it becomes difficult for them to escape from peer pressure.

Physical defects: It becomes difficult for a disabled person to establish his identity as he may be dependent on others to perform certain tasks. Specifically during the period of transition, when his peers are getting jobs, getting married and having children, disabled feel isolated and depressed. Persons with disabilities may not have normal growth pattern as a child with cerebral palsy may have short stature or involuntary movements of neck and limbs, some may have to use wheel chair or crutches. So, certain deformities make them look different. Lack of resources also makes it difficult for them to cope up with disabilities. India has large number of disabled people and social support to disabled is not adequate.

IMPACT OF ENVIRONMENT ON ADULTHOOD

Socioeconomic status: Research has established that exposure to socioeconomic disadvantage during childhood and adolescence increases the chances of poor health in adulthood. It is related with their living environment, which includes housing, safety, food, health care, transportation and neighbourhood and friends.

Lack of education: Proper education and skills are essential for getting jobs and lack of education and adequate skills become a great disadvantage that could lead to socioeconomic exclusion. An illiterate person with no skills had limited opportunities for jobs and has to live with this disadvantage throughout the life.

Physical environment: Apart from family and neighbourhood, the environment at workplace, particularly colleagues, has maximum influence on a person during adulthood. Stressful condition in the workplace, air and noise pollution, traffic congestion and problems in commuting in big cities adversely affect physical and mental health. A person often picks up bad habits like drinking, smoking and consumption of drugs in the company of colleagues, which has implication not only for the individual but also the entire family with undesirable habits.

Social environment and social support: The social environment extends beyond family and neighbourhoods during adulthood as a person comes in contact with new people and colleagues from diverse socioeconomic and cultural backgrounds. It improves his social interaction skills and widens the mental horizon.

Culture and traditions: Beliefs, customs, values and other cultural traditions influence a person throughout the life. However, the influence is more in rural areas and in big cities and towns where people come from diverse cultural backgrounds and have their own cosmopolitan culture. Those who have to migrate to urban areas miss the sociocultural life and it makes an impact on them.

EFFECT OF ENVIRONMENT ON OLD AGE

Financial independence: After a certain age, a person either gets retired from or stops working due to old age and may not have any source of income. In a country like India, where there is no social security, elderly members are dependent financially on their family members. Social security schemes for old persons can make the both ends meet for them.

Social support: Social support is must for the well-being of any person, especially for elderly people. Usually, the source of social support are the family members. Social support from various sources can be useful for overall health and for combating psychological problems like depression and anxiety. At times, it becomes difficult for the family members to provide support to their elderly members due to various reasons such as financial problems, death of spouse, job relocation or having a disabled child. Unavailability of other sources of social support affects the life of elderly people. Lack of religious affiliations, adult day care centres and assisted living facilities may lead to loneliness and isolation among elderly people. Most of the places in India do not have social activities for old people like mobile libraries, singing groups, group exercises or yoga and meditation, which are helpful in enhancing their self-awareness. The lack of self-awareness causes negative impact on the quality of life of old people.

Type of family: Joint family system has advantage for the elderly persons, who are looked after well by their family members. They feel that they are wanted by the family. Old persons are occupied with their grand children. Nuclear families hardly have space for elderly people of the family.

Health care facilities: People require health care in old age because most of them have one or the other chronic disease.

Lifestyle: Economically weak old persons cannot afford to have a good lifestyle. They have to cook for themselves and do all the household chores without any help. After certain age, life becomes miserable for them as they develop senile changes. To arrange for the grocery, vegetables and fruits, paying electricity and phone bills does not seem possible. Financially sound old persons can pay to get various works done. They can hire a maid for household chores and a driver to take them around to maintain social circle.

Type of house: Usually, people like to have a house that is comfortable, especially in old age, everything should be there within reach. House should be such which is safe for them; no slippery floors, proper stairs with support. Many cities have a list of elderly people with police, who regularly visit them to ensure their safety as crime against them is very high. Social support should be available for old people who feel insecure.

Environmental threats: Effects of extremes of temperature as cold wave or heat wave are very intense in elderly people. There is decline in biological strength, in old age they feel the severe impact of the pollutants in the air, water and food. The knock-on effects of natural calamities like flood, storms, cyclones and earthquakes are felt the most by elderly people.

Loss of life in the family: Loss of loved one can be very painful experience in old age, specially the loss of spouse. Death of loved one usually has severe physical, psychological and social effect on an elderly person. Physical symptoms can be sleeplessness, loss of appetite, whereas emotional instability, emotional numbness, introversion, a disorganized lifestyle, anxiety, anger, depression, mood disorders and maladaptive strategies are some of the psychological symptoms. Social symptoms are social isolation and negative coping behaviour. These symptoms are more pronounced in widowed people as most of them lack social support.

REVIEW QUESTIONS

1. What are the various factors affecting the growth and development of a child?
2. Describe the impact of environment on adulthood.

CHAPTER

7

Rights and Responsibilities of an Individual in a Democratic Society

LEARNING OBJECTIVES

After reading this chapter the learner should be able to

- Be aware of the rights of a citizen in a democratic society.
- Know about the responsibilities of a citizen.

India is a 'sovereign socialist secular democratic republic' with a parliamentary system of government. With a population of 1.25 billion, second only to China, India is the biggest democracy in the world. The republic is governed in accordance with the provisions of the Constitution of India, which lays down the framework defining fundamental political principles, powers and duties of government institutions and sets out fundamental rights and the duties of citizens. The protection of basic human rights is accepted as the responsibility of the state worldwide. It is embodied in written constitutions of counties across the world and it also figures in the Charter of the United Nations. Governments make efforts to protect inalienable rights. These rights are not destroyed when civil society is created, and neither society nor government can remove or 'alienate' them.

FUNDAMENTAL RIGHTS

Democracy cannot work if the people do not have these rights. Without the fundamental rights, no one can live in a democratic manner. The basic rights serve as safeguard against governments becoming despotic. Fundamental rights are essential for moral and material development and human progress. These are fundamental in the sense that without these no one can live in a democratic manner. In the absence of these rights, citizens cannot develop their personality and their own self and democracy cannot work. Fundamental rights are not like the ordinary rights of citizen, and these rights are enshrined in the Constitution. While ordinary rights are protected by the ordinary law of the country, the fundamental rights are protected and guaranteed to the citizens by the Constitution. Fundamental rights are inviolable in ordinary situation. The state can suspend these rights temporarily during proclamation of emergency to maintain public order, security and other such exigencies. If someone's fundamental rights are violated, he or she can go to the court seeking legal assistance. Without these rights, democracy becomes meaningless. Fundamental rights are contained in Part III of the Constitution of India and the citizens can enjoy these rights with some limitations.

Every democratic state incorporates the fundamental rights in the Constitution to ensure a good life to the citizen.

The fundamental rights listed in the Constitution are as follows:

- Right to freedom of speech and expression
- Right to freedom of religion
- Cultural and educational rights
- Rights against exploitation
- Right to constitutional remedies
- Right to equality
- Right to elementary education
- Right to information.

RIGHT TO FREEDOM OF SPEECH AND EXPRESSION

It is one of the inalienable rights and it is the backbone of any democracy. It covers everything from right to debate and vote, to assemble and protest, to worship and to ensure justice for all. They are all dependent on the unrestricted flow of speech and information. Freedom of speech means right to express one's own convictions and opinions freely and publicly by words of mouth, writing, printing, pictures or any other mode of communication without any hindrance from the government but without deliberately causing harm to reputation or character of others by levelling false allegations. In modern times, the right to freedom of speech is the essence of free society and it must be safeguarded at all costs.

In a democracy the citizens live with the conviction that through the open exchange of ideas and opinions, truth will eventually triumph over falsehood, the views of others will be better understood and appreciated, areas of compromise will be clearly defined and the path of progress will open. Democratic governments do not control, dictate or judge the content of written and verbal speech.

At times a democracy has to defend the rights even those individuals and groups who themselves advocate such non-democratic policies such as curtailing the freedom of speech. Citizens defend this right out of the conviction that open debate will lead to greater truth and wiser public actions.

Freedom of peaceful assembly is another important right along with freedom of speech. It is the right of the people to assemble peacefully and demand that the government hear and take notice of their grievances. Without the right to gather and be heard, freedom of speech would be severely undermined and devalued. The right to gather, protest and demand change ensures a vibrant democracy. Democratic governments cannot use state authority to suppress protest or to prevent dissident groups from making their voices heard. They can only legitimately regulate the time and place of political rallies and marches to maintain the peace and order.

FREEDOM OF RELIGION AND FAITH

Freedom of religion, or more broadly freedom of conscience, means that every person is at liberty to choose any religion and that no person should be forced to follow any religion against his or her desire. No one can be punished or penalized in any way for choosing one religion over another or opts for not following any religion at all. A democratic nation feels that a person's religious faith is a profoundly personal matter.

In essence freedom of religion means that government cannot compel anyone to profess a particular religious faith or recognize an official church or faith. Children cannot be forced to go to a particular religious school, and it is not obligatory to attend religious services, to pray or to participate in religious activities against one's own will. Many democratic nations had earlier established churches or temples that receive state support. The government has the responsibility of protecting the freedom of individuals whose religious beliefs differ from that of the officially sanctioned religion.

RIGHT TO EQUAL PROTECTION BEFORE THE LAW

As per Article 14 of the Constitution, 'the State shall not deny to any person equality before the law or equal protection of law within the territory of India'. There are two aspects of this article: one is *equality before law*, which implies there should be no special privilege to anyone on the basis of birth, sex, religion, etc., and the equal subjection of all the classes to the ordinary law. The second aspect is equal protection of law, which aims at equality of treatment to all citizens in equal circumstances. It means whether someone is Prime Minister or President, he should be treated with same law as normal citizen is dealt with. Democratic societies also assert such civil rights as the right to a free and fair trial. Every democratic regime has the responsibility to put in place constitutional, legal and social structures to protect the human rights of the people. However, the procedures for formulation of laws to protect these basic human rights will necessarily vary from society to society.

CULTURAL AND EDUCATIONAL RIGHTS

The Constitution states that all minorities, religious or linguistic, can set up their own educational institutions to and promote their culture. The Constitution of India guarantees cultural and educational rights for all section of people irrespective of their religious, racial and cultural diversities. Articles 29 and 30 take care of the cultural and educational rights. Article 29 bestows to the minorities the right to preserve their language, script and culture, notwithstanding the provisions of Article 343, which makes Hindi in Devanagari script as the official language of the state.

The Constitution also guarantees that the state shall not impose upon any minority group any culture preserve other than the community's own culture. It also provides that no one can be denied admission to state and state-aided educational institutions on the grounds only of religion, race, caste or language. Article 30 confers the right to establish and administer educational institutions to all communities and the state shall not discriminate against them in providing grants on grounds of religion, race or language. It allows various communities the right to impart instruction to the children of their own community in their own institutions in their own language.

The right has also some limitations as the state is empowered to regulate its affairs in the interest of efficiency of instruction, discipline, morality and public order.

RIGHTS AGAINST EXPLOITATION

This is meant to prevent exploitation any citizen, particularly the weaker and deprived sections. Articles 23 and 24 provide protection against trafficking in human beings, beggary and any other form of forced labour are prohibited and any contravention of this provision shall be an offence punishable in accordance with law. They also safeguard women and children and others against various forms of exploitation. Article 24 of the Indian Constitution prohibits abolition of employment of children below the age of 14 years in dangerous jobs like factories and mines and the Child Labour Act (1986), provides penalties for violators of law and relief and rehabilitation measures for those affected.

RIGHT TO CONSTITUTIONAL REMEDIES

The fundamental rights are of highest importance for the citizens of a nation. These are basic things for the development of personality. The right to constitutional remedy is itself a fundamental right. Dr Ambedkar referred to this right as the very soul of the Constitution. Article 32 empowers the Supreme Court to issue directions in the nature of habeas corpus, mandamus, prohibition, quo warranto and criterion for the enforcement of any of the rights conferred by fundamental rights. The Supreme Court is thus a protector and guarantor of fundamental rights.

RIGHT TO EQUALITY

No discrimination should be made on the basis of race, colour, caste, sex, region, age, disability, ethnicity, gender, gender identity, height, nationality or religion.

Equality before Law

No person or groups of people can demand for any special privileges.

Social Equality and Equal Access to Public Areas

Every person shall have equal right to enter public places like public wells, bathing ghats, museums, temples and so on. However, the special privilege for women and children or for the backward classes or scheduled castes or scheduled tribes.

Equality in Matters of Public Employment

Article 16 of the Constitution of India mentions that every citizen will be treated equally in the matters of employment. There will be no discrimination against anyone in respect of any employment on the basis of race, caste, religion, creed, descent or place of birth. However, there are some exceptions to this right where the position requires the knowledge of the locality and language spoken there.

Abolition of Untouchability

Practice of untouchability is declared as a crime as per the Constitution of India and anyone doing so is punishable by law. Prohibiting a person from entering a place of worship, or source of water is a punishable offense as per Untouchability Offences Act of 1955.

Abolition of Titles

Titles like Rai Bahadur and Khan Bahadur given by the British government have been abolished. Citizens of India are not allowed to accept such titles from foreign nations.

Right to Elementary Education

The Right of Children to Free and Compulsory Education (RTE) Act, 2009, confers the means that every child in the age group of 6 to 14 years has a right to free, compulsory and full time education.

Right to Information

Right to information (RTI) is a powerful tool to the citizens to get information from the government as a matter of right. RTI Act is a big step towards making the citizens informed about the activities of the government. It is a fundamental right of citizens to request information from a 'public authority' (a body of government or "instrumentality of state') and reply is required to be given within 30 days.

RESPONSIBILITIES OF A CITIZEN

Fundamental duties were enshrined in the Constitution of India when it came into force in 1950. They were incorporated into Article 51 A in a new chapter by the 42nd Amendment in 1976. In all, 10 fundamental duties have been added in Part IV of the Constitution. These duties are important and necessary for the vital interest of our country. The fundamental duties are some obligations on the citizens to perform for peace and prosperity of the country.

Democracies rest upon the principle that government exists to serve the people who are the real masters. The people do not exist to serve the government and they are not its subjects. While the state protects the rights of its citizens, the citizens reciprocate by extending their loyalty to the state. Whereas, in an authoritarian system, the state expects loyalty and service from its people without any reciprocal obligation.

In democratic nations when citizens vote, they are exercising their right and responsibility to decide who shall rule on their behalf. But in an authoritarian state the voting serves to legitimize the already selected persons. The selection is made by the regime, so voting in such a society is a show of public support for the government. Elections in such an authoritarian state involve neither rights nor responsibilities exercised by citizens.

Citizens in a democracy enjoy the right to join non-governmental organizations of their choice and to participate freely in the recreational activities and public life. Citizens must accept the responsibility of educating themselves about the various issues pertaining to the welfare of state, demonstrating tolerance towards those holding opposing views, and also compromising if necessary to reach an agreement. A successful democracy requires cooperation, compromise and tolerance among all citizens. Freedom does not mean freedom from responsibilities.

Authoritarian states either do not have voluntary groups or have very few. Individuals in such states have no means to debate issues or run their own affairs, but they are the subjects in positions of obedience only.

As far as the rights and responsibilities of the citizens are concerned they are the opposite sides of the same coin. As a citizen exercises his rights, it is also his or her responsibility to protect the rights of others. In fact, even citizens of well-established democracies often take full advantage of rights but ignore their responsibilities.

The basic rights such as freedom of speech, assembly and religion impose limits on any democratic government to shield the citizens against misuse of power by the government or political majority.

Rights of individuals do not function in isolation as these rights are not the private possession of individuals. But their existence is there as far as they are recognized by other citizens of the society. The electorate is the ultimate custodian of its own freedom.

The responsibilities of a citizen entail participating in the democratic process to ensure its functioning. Citizens should educate themselves to vote intelligently for candidates running for power. Otherwise democracy will begin to wither and become the preserve of a small number of persons or organizations with vested interests.

Active involvement in public life is not the struggle for political position. Citizen participation in a democratic society is much more than voting or just contesting elections. At the panchayat or municipal level, citizens may serve on school committees or become members of community groups as Mahila Mandals and Yuva Mandals or contest elections to the local body. At the state or national level, citizens can raise their voices and use pens for debate over public issues. They can join political parties and contest polls, labour unions or voluntary organizations. Democracy is a process, a way of living and working together; so, a healthy democracy depends upon such contributions and informed participation of its citizens. Fundamental duties were not prescribed in the Constitution originally but these duties were included in the Constitution under Article 51A on the basis of the recommendations of Swaran Singh Committee.

A citizen of India is expected to perform following fundamental duties faithfully.

1. To abide by the Constitution and respect its ideals and institutions, the National Flag and the National Anthem
2. To cherish and follow the noble ideals which inspired the struggle for the country's freedom
3. To uphold and safeguard the sovereignty, unity and integrity of India
4. To defend the country and respond to the call for national service whenever required
5. To promote harmony and the spirit of common brotherhood among the people rising above religious, linguistic and regional or sectional diversities
6. To preserve the rich heritage of our composite culture
7. To protect and improve the natural environment, including forests, lakes, rivers and wild life
8. To develop the scientific temper and spirit of inquiry
9. To safeguard public property and shun violence
10. To strive towards excellence in all spheres of individual and collective activity

To Respect the Constitution, National Flag and National Anthem

To abide by the Constitution and respect its ideals and institutions, maintain the dignity of the Constitution by not indulging in any activities in violation of the letter or spirit of the Constitution is the duty of every citizen. Every citizen has a duty to give proper respect to the National Flag. The National Flag is a symbol of the nation's pride. There is unfurling of National Flag on the Independence Day and Republic day in every organization. Every participant of the ceremony must stand straight during this ceremony. Flags made of paper and plastic are sold on the roadsides and people enthusiastically buy them, but we find these flags being discarded on roads or in dustbins, which is wrong and miscreants must be prevented from showing disrespect to our national symbols. Similarly, National Anthem is a symbol of our history, sovereignty, unity and pride. Showing any disrespect to our Anthem would tantamount to an anti-social and antinational activity. India is proud of its citizens because of their dedication, sincerity and patriotism. We, the citizens of India, have to be proud of our nation and show respect to the Constitution, our National Flag and our National Anthem.

To Protect the Sovereignty and Integrity of the Nation

It is the fundamental duty of every citizen of India to not do anything that undermines the sovereignty, unity and integrity of India. Each citizen must not only refrain from any such activity but also do his best to prevent any miscreant trying to weaken the unity of the nation or show disrespect to our national symbols.

To Protect the Motherland to Promote the Spirit of Common Brotherhood among the People of India

Every citizen is bound to be ready to defend the country against war or external aggression. This is obviously addressed to all citizens other than those who belong to the army, the navy and the air force and, thus, it concerns the common man as indicated by the expression 'when called upon to do so'.

To Preserve the Rich Heritage of Our Nation

We feel our cultural heritage is one of the noblest and the richest in the world. What we have inherited from the past. It is our duty as a citizen of India as to preserve and pass it on to the future generations as they always draw inspiration from the nation's history, as it stimulates them to achieve greater heights of achievement and excellence. We all should ensure that our monuments and pieces of art are preserved and not damaged or disfigured.

To Protect and Improve the Natural Environment

It becomes the duty of every citizen to protect and improve natural environment in the rising pollution and environmental degradation. Our forests, lakes, rivers and wild life are part of environment. We must have compassion for living creatures as pollution and large-scale deforestation is causing immense harm to all creatures on earth. The mindless and wanton deforestation in the name of needs of development is taking a heavy toll on the fragile environment and causing havoc in the form of natural calamities and imbalances. We all should make efforts to protect the environment and save it for future generations. Some of these efforts are afforesting wasteland, conserving the forest, cleaning rivers, conserving water resources and controlling pollution by industrial units and traffic.

To Protect Public Property

The Constitution prescribes that it is the fundamental duty of every citizen to shun violence and to protect public property, as it is an increasing trend of individuals to adopt violent means instead of peaceful protest for their demands. Destruction of public property during protests is a common scene. As citizens of India we all need to protect our society from such antisocial activities.

To Develop Scientific Temper, Humanism and Spirit of Enquiry and Reform

To eradicate the prevailing evil practices, customs and traditions, the Constitution prescribes that people should develop a scientific temper a rational attitude, quest for knowledge and thirst for learning. Talents of individuals and resources should be used for reforming and developing the society.

To Strive towards Excellence in all Spheres of Individual and Collective Activity

The Constitution of India makes it a fundamental duty of the individuals to make all efforts to attain all-round excellence. Progress of a nation is not possible without the willing and sincere efforts of the people. All the citizens must be motivated to develop their facilities and achieve excellence in all spheres of human activity.

It is the duty of the parents to provide education to children. Right to education is a fundamental right of every child from 6 to 14 years of age. The Indian Constitution prescribes it as a fundamental duty of parents to send their children to school.

To Promote the Spirit of Common Brotherhood Amongst all the People of India

Our nation has different castes, languages, religions and varied cultural streams but we are all governed by one Constitution and have one National flag and one citizenship. Spirit of brotherhood should exist among the citizens considering the entire nation as one family. Citizens should rise above narrow cultural differences and need to strive towards excellence in all spheres of collective activity.

To Protect the Dignity of Women

This is also our fundamental duty to ensure that all practices derogatory to the dignity of women are given up. It is a belief that gods reside where women are worshipped and our country is land of gods. Disrespect to women is tarnishing the image of our society. So, discrimination against women in any form should not be there. Many laws have been passed by the Union Government and the State Governments to prevent practices that are derogatory to the dignity of women as dowry prohibition law, commission of sati prevention.

To Cherish and Follow the Noble Ideals that Inspired Our National Struggle for Freedom

As per the Indian Constitution, it is the fundamental duty of its citizens to follow the ideals of freedom fighters, who sacrificed their lives for the nation.

To Defend the Country and Render National Service When Called Upon to Do So

Though we have a strong army to defend our nation from enemy, the Constitution has a provision that every citizen should be ready to defend the country in the hour of need.

REVIEW QUESTIONS

1. Write in detail about various rights of a citizen.
2. What are the different responsibilities of a citizen in a democratic country?

UNIT - 3

CULTURE

CHAPTER

8

Culture

LEARNING OBJECTIVES

After reading this chapter the learner should be able to

- Have knowledge about culture.
- Know about the process of culture development.

Culture is broadly defined as the way of life of a group of people giving rise to distinctive social behaviours, beliefs, values, language, attitudes, religious practices, notions, concepts and knowledge over a period of time. In short, it is the acquired collective behaviour of a group of people. It is the lens through which one views the world and is passed from one generation to the next.

The word 'culture' is derived from the Latin word *colere* that means 'to cultivate'. The way we live is culture. It is reflected in what we wear, what we eat, how we behave and how do we perform our daily activities. All the activities we perform intentionally or unintentionally are a part of culture. It includes our thinking, moral values, beliefs, ideas, relationships, ways of celebrating events as birth marriage and festivals.

IMPORTANCE OF CULTURE

Culture is an inseparable part of human life and its in-depth understanding is essential for study of any society. Its importance can be understood from the fact that there is no culture at sub-human level and all the animals live in natural environment. Only the human beings live and grow up in a social environment. It is the distinguishing feature of the human society. Culture is not an individual heritage but a social product shared by members of a group.

The basic concept of culture is fundamental to sociology and provides the main basis for disciplines like anthropology. It is widely used in several other disciplines like psychology, political science and economics.

MEANING OF CULTURE

Given its wide application in various streams of study 'culture' has acquired a range of meanings and interpretations. It is a very broad term that embraces entire gamut of life, philosophies, ethics, morals, customs and traditions, manners and modes of behaviour, political, economic and other activities. It is represented through the art, literature, costumes, customs and traditions of a community. Culture includes all that man has acquired in his individual and social life. In the words of MacIver and Page, culture is the 'realm of styles, of values, of emotional attachment, of intellectual adventures'. It is the entire *socially transmitted heritage*, which the individual receives from the group.

In common parlance, the term *cultured* is used to refer to an educated person or group and *uncultured* to one lacking on or devoid of education. However, in sociology, the meaning of culture is quite different. But common men often speak of culture as synonymous with education.

Unlike historians who mostly use the term *culture* to refer to *higher* achievements of group life, sociologists use culture to mean *all* the achievements of group life. Culture is a treasure-trove of knowledge and covers all aspects of social heritage including political, mythological and philosophical concepts, arts, science and literature. It plays a vital role in shaping attitudes, personality and behaviour and defines values and goals. However, no individual is completely shaped by culture. Every individual is unique in any culture as differences in ability, aptitude and learning results in distinctive personality traits. Moreover, culture does not always influence individuals in a uniform and identical manner and various biological and social factors also contribute to their uniqueness in any cultural environment.

Culture is a unique possession of human beings as its influence leads to distinctive way of life and unique character to every individual. A clean culture may seem strange to a person from a different cultural background. One does feel the difference in customs, eating habits, behaviour and other aspects of life in an unfamiliar cultural environment but landing in a totally alien environment one may get a cultural shock. The differences are so vast and deep at times that people often find it difficult to get adjusted in a new cultural environment. Culture evolves over a period of time and it is a continuous process with no definite beginning in time.

DEFINITIONS OF CULTURE

Sociologists and anthropologists have given their own concepts of culture and defined it in different ways. It has rightly received prime attention in sociological research owing to its centrality in understanding the nature and performance of the social arrangement called *society*. Culture is one of the most important concepts in sociology being central to the study of individual in society. With literacy scholars and social psychologists also showing immense interest in the concept to understand human social behaviour, the study of culture has gained increasing importance over the last few decades and as a result the definitions of the term are also numerous.

American anthropologist Edward Sapir tersely defined culture as 'any socially inherited element of the life of man, material and spiritual'.

Widely regarded as the founder of cultural anthropology, Edward Burnett Taylor described culture as 'a complex whole, including knowledge, belief, art, morals, customs and any other capabilities and habits acquired by man as a member of society'.

Eminent sociologist E.S. Bogardus put it rather simply by stating that 'Culture is all the ways of doing and thinking of a group'.

Culture is created by human beings and it is not innate or ascribed. It is achieved through the continuous process of socialization, interaction and learning. Culture is transmitted from one generation to the next and having grown up in the cultural environment most individuals do not question or view the prevailing cultural practices critically.

COMPONENTS OF CULTURE

All cultures essentially comprise of five basic elements:

Beliefs: Ideas about how the world operates
Values: Ideas about the meaning of life
Norms and Sanctions: Guidelines for behaviour
Expressive Symbols: Material representations of ideas and values
Language: Mode of learning and transmission of culture.

Every society has its own distinctive culture and people in different societies across the world have cultures, which are not only diverse but also unique.

Material Culture and Nonmaterial Culture

Along with cultural diversities and disparities, societies throughout the world also have certain cultural similarities. For instance, modes of worship may differ but societies have some religion. Similarly, occupations, rituals, ceremonies and customs also have similarities. Every culture consists of such nonmaterial things along with material things of different kinds.

1. **Material culture:** It comprises architecture, sculptures, tools, machines, art pieces and other physical objects.
2. **Nonmaterial culture:** The ideas, values, language, beliefs, taboos, customs and other associated traditions.

The concept of *material culture* is relatively more precise, while the concept of nonmaterial culture is more ambiguous and less clear. The physical world created by man such as roads, railways, aeroplanes, buildings, implements, furniture, automobiles and other tangible objects represent the material culture. It also includes the banking system, currency system, and computer networks, Internet, schools, churches, synagogues, temples, mosques, offices, factories and plants, tools, means of production, goods and products, stores, and all such things that symbolize the physical aspects of culture.

Nonmaterial Culture

In the normal discourse, the term culture represents nonmaterial culture comprising ideas, knowledge, values, morals, ethics, beliefs, habits, attitudes, language and institutions. It reflects the inner nature of the man and the intrinsic value system, knowledge and refinement achieved by the society.

VALUE SYSTEM

The moral values and norms which serve as the broad guidelines for socially acceptable behaviour.

Language

Culture evolves through social interaction and communication is the key to meaningful interaction. Language and dialects is the most important mode of communication and often lends identity to a culture. People with the same native tongue often share the same culture. Many societies have a large number of people who speak different dialects or languages but are part of a common culture.

BELIEFS, SUPERSTITIONS AND TABOOS

Beliefs are integral to every culture and superstitions and taboos are a part of it.

Religion

It is the most important component of the culture as it relates the man's communion with the invisible cosmic force called god.

RITUALS, RITES, CEREMONIES, FESTIVALS AND CELEBRATIONS

Rituals and rites are performed on particular occasions like marriage rituals, death and birth of a child. Festivals are usually events to celebrate life and they are also observed on specific occasions.

Festivals, ceremonies and rituals play an important role in sustaining the culture.

Social Norms

Norms govern the behaviour of the members of a society. These are the set of rules created for ensuring minimum standards for behaviour.

CHARACTERISTICS OF CULTURE

Culture is the collective social heritage of a group of people. Every culture is unique and has its own characteristics.

Culture Is Not Static

It is dynamic and keeps evolving all the time. As it gets influenced and modified by other cultures, new cultural traits are acquired and old ones are lost as they become irrelevant and no longer useful. All cultures change over time, however, the rate of change and the aspects of culture that change vary from society to society.

It Is Passed on from One Generation to the Next

Culture is transferred from generation to generation in terms of customs, traditions, language, festivals, rites and rituals.

Culture Is Symbolic and Lends a Distinct Identity to the People

It is a collective social heritage and not an individual legacy of man. An individual acquires the cultural traits of the society in which he is living. Language is not only the means of communication but also the carrier of culture. Without the integration of language into the fabric of the culture, there will be confusion and the culture traits will be lost with passage of time.

The Process of Acquiring Culture Is Socialization

Culture cannot exist in isolation. A person learns culture through his senses and the experiences he undergoes in the society he grows up. All the societies in the world have a distinct culture. For, instance, the Indian culture is radically different from African culture and the Western culture.

All Cultures Are Concerned with Survival

Like individuals cultures go through the cycle of birth life, and death. Culture plays an important role in the development of human beings.

Culture Shapes the Personality of People

According to Kimball Young, 'Personality consists of habits, attitudes and ideas which are built up around both people and things'. Personality development of a child takes place as per the culture of the society he is brought up. Culture has a deep impact on the personality of a person.

Cultural Lag

Eminent sociologist Ogburn introduced an interesting concept of *cultural lag* while exploring the relationship between material and nonmaterial culture. In the process of social change, the material and nonmaterial parts of culture are changing constantly. While the material culture of a society such as technology may undergo change rather rapidly, the process of transformation in nonmaterial culture is very gradual. The *gap* that arises due to difference in the pace of transformation of the material and nonmaterial components is termed as *cultural lag*. Advances in technology, particularly inventions, discoveries and new weapons, instruments and equipment bring quick transformation in material culture. This change in the material part of culture sets in process leading to subsequent changes in the nonmaterial aspects of life like norms, values and customs but it lags behind as the process of change is much slower compared to material part.

Development of Culture

The development of culture is an incessant process during which elements from other cultures are also infused through contact, diffusion and accommodation. New elements are added to the aggregate of accumulated cultures handed from one generation to the other and. culture progresses as a result of their unification. The distinctive cultures evolve and it is a long drawn process. The existing culture of any region or country is an outcome of these processes carried over a period of thousands of years. The development and growth of culture takes place at varied pace depending on the conditions. The progress in cultural growth is rapid if there are people with the required initiative, otherwise there will be cultural stagnation in the society. Other factor like discontent with some of the existing things among the people and their willingness to give up these and find a solution also influence the pace of change.

THEORIES OF CULTURAL GROWTH

Anthropologists have given significant attention to the subject and come out with three theories to explain the growth of culture.

1. Evolutionism
2. Diffusionism
3. Acculturation

Evolutionism

Believing that human societies have evolved from lower into higher types anthropologists came out with the concept of *psychic unity of humankind* as per which psychic make-up man was the same everywhere. It essentially meant that given the same problems man would think out similar solutions anywhere. Thus, culture will grow from simpler to complex forms through the process of evolution. The similarity in traits or cultural parallels was a consequence of the psychic unity of mankind. Similarities in the elements of cultures or institutions were termed as cases of convergent evolution.

Most of the researchers maintain that the evolutionary theory of culture has been influenced by the Darwin's theory of evolution definitely influenced. As per the evolutionary theory, cultural growth follows a unilinear sequence with definite stages through which all the societies passed. Some remnants of the primitive stage are retained in the higher stage of a culture, which provide insight into earlier stages. The developed and higher traditions stay longer in society.

Diffusionism

In the simplest terms diffusion means spread of a cultural traits from their place of origin to other places. This theory is based on the premise that evolution tempered with diffusion through which discrete culture traits are transferred from one society to another by way of migration, trade, war, or other contact.

Theory was based on belief that various culture complexes develop at various times in different regions and subsequently spread across through the continuous process of diffusion. Layers of culture traits diffused in may be identified in a culture.

Acculturation

As culture traits spread from one culture to the other another, life starts changing. If the influence of an alien culture is so overwhelming that the whole system of life the native culture begins to change, the process of under, it is the process of acculturation sets in.

The exchange of culture traits between two cultures, it is transculturation. However, when the influence of other culture is so strong that one system of life in any culture starts giving way to establishment of another system, it is acculturation. It happens in stages and the afflicted culture first disintegrates and thereafter process of improvement and enrichment begin. However, the individuality of the affected culture is lost and it takes a new form. Scholars maintain that that no culture of the world today exists in its unadulterated form and every culture has taken a lot from other cultures.

REVIEW QUESTIONS

1. What do you mean by culture and how do you distinguish between material and nonmaterial culture?
2. Write in detail about various theories of cultural growth.

CHAPTER

9

Culture and Nursing

LEARNING OBJECTIVES

After reading this chapter the learner should be able to

- Have knowledge about the characteristics of culture.
- Identify the relationship between culture and health.

Cultural beliefs and practices of the patient play an important role in delivery of health care, particularly in a diverse country like India where the people are deeply rooted in traditions. The perception of illness and disease and their causes vary with culture and they have to be taken into consideration while deciding approaches to health care. Culture also influences the manner in which health care is delivered and how the patient responds to it. For effective delivery of nursing care to a patient of another culture, it is imperative to recognize the impact that a nurse's own personal culture on his or her professional practice. Any action that undermines or demeans the cultural identity of a patient tantamounts to unsafe cultural practice.

Thus, nurses have to acquire a degree of cultural competence by obtaining adequate information about the culture of the receiver of health care to avoid misapplication of medical knowledge. Awareness about culture enables a nurse to take a holistic view, which helps in improving the quality of care and health outcomes. They have to be tolerant and willing to adapt to different cultural beliefs and practices and flexible enough to understand and respect the view point of others.

A nurse will have to be receptive and make a conscious effort to find out and learn about the patient's beliefs regarding health and illness. They must possess requisite knowledge along with the ability to communicate and understand how health behaviours are influenced by culture. It will go a long way in eliminating barriers to the delivery of health care. These issues show the need for health care organizations to develop policies, practices and procedures to deliver culturally competent care.

CULTURAL COMPETENCY

In a diverse society like ours, nurses encounter all sorts of cultural differences, such as ethnic customs, rituals, beliefs and traditions, which have a bearing on the health, illness and related issues. Thus, a nurse has to be culturally competent for effective and culturally safe delivery of health care. Restrictive cultures where the patients are reluctant to talk about personal matters pose a greater challenge to the nurses.

For acquiring cultural competency a nurse must have the capacity to recognize and value cultural diversity along with ability for cultural self-assessment. They must have tolerance, patience and requisite communication skills to interact meaningfully with patients from different cultures. It is essential to know the culturally influenced behaviours to provide culturally appropriate care. Cultural awareness is sine qua non as it allows one to see a *holistic picture* and immensely helpful in delivery of quality of quality health care.

INFLUENCE OF CULTURE ON HEALTH AND DISEASES

Studies have over the years established that health is not solely determined by factors like genetic inheritance, access to quality health care and the environment, social and cultural factors also have an important role in health and well-being of people. Cultural backgrounds of people have tremendous impact as cultural factors inevitably interact with biology to impact health. Defined as a system of shared thoughts, beliefs and behaviours of a group of people, culture virtually serves as a template for the organization of social and psychological processes. It influences the health of individuals to a great extent.

Its importance is well recognized by the World Health Organization (WHO), which has defined health as 'a complete state of physical, mental, social and spiritual well-being and not merely absence of diseases'. It brings out two important aspects, social health and spiritual health. Both of these aspects are related to culture. The perception of health, illness and death is largely influenced by culture as it depends on beliefs, ethics and customs. Unhealthy cultural norms, habits and lifestyle are very difficult to change as human behaviour is motivated towards group conformity. Cultural practices are deep-rooted and require a very long time to change or modify. Cultural issues play a major role in patient compliance.

CULTURE AND PERCEPTION OF ILLNESS

Culture and health are interdependent and health is influenced by culture to a great extent. A society comprises many cultures and every culture has systems of health beliefs to explain causes of illness and remedy for its cure. The perception of illness and disease depends on cultural beliefs. For instance, Western industrialized societies like the United States view disease as a natural scientific phenomena and advocate medical treatments to combat microorganisms or use sophisticated technology to diagnose and treat disease. In some underdeveloped countries, illness is perceived as some supernatural phenomenon and they go for spiritual interventions and rituals to cure it. Problems arise when health care professionals and patients are from different cultural backgrounds as beliefs, values, perception and lack of patient compliance act as barriers to effective treatment.

BENEFICIAL AND HARMFUL CULTURAL PRACTICES

It is also true that all cultural practices are not a bane for health. Some of these practices promoting adequate nutrition, good sleep and regular physical exercise are based on centuries of trial and error and have positive values. One has to identify the cultural beliefs and practices that are deleterious and beneficial. For instance, the practise of making the woman to stay away from other members of the family after delivery of a child for 40 days ensures adequate rest and also helps in preventing infections. The practise of breastfeeding is good for the heath of infant. The habit of brushing teeth and having bath in the morning ensures good hygiene. In contrast, the practice of *purdah system* (keeping the woman behind a veil) is not good for health as it denies them fresh air and sun. The food habits, good or bad, are dictated by culture and they cannot be changed easily as they are ingrained in the behaviour of individuals. Early marriage, gender bias and cultural importance attached to male offspring and other such traditions have implications for health as they give rise to the heinous practices like female foeticide.

In countries like India and Pakistan the people are reluctant to accept a diagnosis of severe emotional illness or mental retardation because it is a seen as stigma and affects marriage prospects of other members of the family. In Vietnamese culture, mystical beliefs explain physical and mental illness instead of medical diagnosis. Good health is attributed to harmonious balance between the poles of hot and cold that govern bodily functions. Vietnamese are averse to readily accepting the Western mental health counselling and interventions, particularly when self-disclosure is expected.

Cultural differences have a bearing on the attitude of patients to medical care and their ability to understand, manage and cope with illness. Cultural influence cannot be overlooked as patients and their families bring in culture specific ideas and values related to health and illness, reporting of symptoms expectations regarding delivery of health care. The common practice of chewing tobacco in rural India has rendered a large section of population vulnerable to cancer and other diseases. Similarly, the social culture of smoking and consumption of liquor is responsible for a host of health problems.

Medical scientists and sociologists are increasingly focusing on cultural factors while looking into health problems. A society may have many cultures and every culture has its own customs, which may have a bearing on health. Some of the key factors influencing health are the following.

ROLE OF FAMILY

Family is the primary unit of a society and each family has culture of its own. All the members have blood relations and live under the same roof and share the same food, customs, beliefs and value system. The culture of the family also reflects the culture of the society and, in turn, determines the attitude and behaviour of individual members.

The joint family system prevalent in India and some other Asian and African countries is significant from the point of view of health as the presence of parents, grandparents, uncles and aunts help in proper development and shaping the attitude and behaviour of the child. However, the nuclear family system in the urban areas is not conducive to proper growth of child and puts more burden on the parents and the child lacks adequate parental care if both husband and wife are working.

Beliefs in the Family

In a developing country like India there are misconceptions and taboos among the rural people have many misconceptions related to the family size and structure. The common belief that children are a gift of god and that more children means more hands to work and earn lead to large families. The lack of adequate spacing in birth of children can cause maternal malnutrition and anaemia, low birth weight and increased maternal and infant mortality rates. The belief that a family is not complete without the birth of a male child is at the root of gender bias. These wrong cultural beliefs have a significant impact on the economic status and, in turn, on the health of people.

Sex and Marriage

Sexual customs and behaviour vary widely among different religious and ethnic groups. In some religious communities orogenital sex and intercourse is prohibited during menstruation. Similarly, orthodox Jews are barred from intercourse for seven days after menstruation ceases. The practices of polygamy (one man marrying several women) and polyandry (one woman marrying several men) prevalent in many tribal communities of the country increases the risk of sexually transmitted diseases. In developed countries like the United States of America excessive racial mixing may lead to increase in incidence of jaw and tooth size discrepancies, and, in turn to malocclusion. This may be the reason for high rate of malocclusion in the United States as compared to other populations lacking in racial mixing.

Maternal and Child Health

Mother and child health (MCH) has been an area of concern in the developing countries and it is greatly influenced by various customs and beliefs all over the world. The cultural practices have been classified as good, bad, uncertain and insignificant depending on how they influence health. Prolonged breastfeeding, oil bath, massage and exposure to sun and thus these are among the good customs. However, avoidance of healthy foods like papaya, milk, fish, meat, egg and leafy vegetables due to wrong notion that they may induce heat in the body of a pregnant woman are bad for the health of the foetus. The application of *kajal* (black soot mixed with oil) to the eyelids partly for beautification and partly for warding off of the evil eye falls in the category of uncertain habits.

There are some adverse practices in childrearing like home deliveries conducted by untrained *dais*, who have very minimal knowledge on asepsis and sterilization. The villagers have greater faith in them than the trained health care workers in many rural areas and it is a cause of high infant mortality. The new born baby is not given breastfeeding up to three days after birth in some parts of the country like Gwalior region due to wrong belief that colostrum is harmful. This may prevent the transfer of maternal antibodies and make the child vulnerable to infections. Wrong practices like adulteration of milk and delay in the start of weaning foods may cause protein energy malnutrition and affect the child's health. A general misconception is that diarrhoea is common among children during teething and needs no care. The belief that diarrhoea will take off the heat from the body and child should not be fed milk and other liquids adds to the problem as it results in dehydration.

FOOD HABITS

Food habits are ingrained in any culture and deeply rooted in psyche. They are influenced and nurtured by religious beliefs and the local environment and climatic conditions. Food habits are passed from generation to generation in the families, which have a major role in shaping eating habits along with external environment. It has been observed that the people whose staple food is rice suffer from ariboflavinosis due to deficiency of riboflavin. In India rice-eating regions are mostly in the east and south. Similarly, people of Telangana region in Andhra Pradesh, where staple diet is maize or jowar, have deficiency of niacin and they suffer from pellagra. The problem is caused by excess leucine created due to amino acid imbalance among jowar and maize eaters. Similarly, the high concentration of molybdenum, a health hazard, in jowar facilitates retention of fluoride in the body, and consequently it may increase the severity of fluorosis among the population whose staple diet is jowar.

The diet of tribal people consists of coarse food grains and fibrous edibles free from refined carbohydrates. It reduces the risk for dental caries and also facilitates adequate stimulation of the jaws, jaw muscles and teeth eruption, curtailing the risk for malocclusion. In contrast, the Western diet is dominated by refined foods, which increases the risk for caries as well as malocclusion, which is caused due to inadequate stimulation of jaw. The food habits of Scandinavians comprise a variety of fishes and cheese, which provide some protection against caries. Similarly, the Caribbean diet in the form of local fruits, vegetables, cassava and a great variety of fish also protects against dental caries. The Africans use trona salt extensively as a preservative, tenderizer, flavouring agent in food and a medicine in the treatment of dyspepsia. The salt contains high concentration of fluoride, as high as 7,900 parts per million, which increases risk of dental fluorosis.

Religious Restrictions in Food Habits

Religion plays a role in determining food habits and in Hindu religion vegetarianism is a virtue. Orthodox Hindus are mostly pure vegetarians and they strictly shun animal foods. Vegetarian diet may cause deficiency of vitamin B12, leading to Moeller's glossitis. Adulteration of milk is done with the motive of economic gain but there are also some wrong notions that boiling pure milk may dry secretion in the donor animal. The overdilution of the milk due to adulteration degrades its nutritive value and it may lead to protein energy malnutrition among the consumers.

Hindus consider cow as a sacred animal and they do not eat beef and Muslims avoid pork as pig feeds on human excreta and garbage. These are good habits from the health point of view as they help prevent the occurrence of taeniasis caused by an adult form of *Taenia saginata* and cystecercosis, which manifest as oedematous oral ulcers, gingival bleeding and lesions mimicking mucocles. Fasting is a frequent practice among orthodox Hindus, and Muslims also observe fast during the month of Ramzan. However, excessive fasting is not good for health as it causes gastritis, peptic ulcer, malnutrition, nutritional anaemia and loss of weight and other ill-effects on health. In many orthodox Indian families, the practice of men eating first and women last is still prevalent. It is not a healthy practice as it may cause maternal malnutrition, leading to high maternal and infant mortality rates. Excessive consumption of spicy food, particularly chillies, commonly prevalent in some parts of Andhra Pradesh and northern Karnataka is also not good, as it makes people prone to peptic ulcer, oral submucous fibrosis and oral malignancies as well.

Personal Hygiene

The open defecation culture in rural areas of India is a big health hazard but villagers are averse to constructing latrines as they have a wrong notion that latrines are needed only by city dwellers where open fields are not available. They are not much concerned about the health risks associated with human excreta, which contaminates water, food and soil and provides breeding ground for mosquitoes and flies. Villagers heap solid wastes for decomposing in the vicinity of their houses inviting all the health risks. The wells are the major source of drinking water in rural areas along with tanks and ponds and they are all subject to contamination due to human activities like open defecation, bathing, washing of clothes and utensils. Often animals are also given bath and made to drink water from these sources.

On the positive side, some rivers, springs and other natural sources of water are considered holy only to help preserve water quality. However, people carry samples of holy water in bottles, preserve them for long duration and carry them over long distances for distribution among relatives and friends, which can lead to epidemics like cholera and gastroenteritis. The rural houses are usually damp, bereft of requisite natural light and ventilation and lack of separate kitchen, latrine and proper drainage. Animal rearing is common practice in the villages and animal waste is also a health hazard. All these increase the risk for most of the communicable diseases among them.

Oral Hygiene Practice

Hindus, particularly Brahmins and priests, in many parts of the country, clean their teeth using cherry wood early in the morning hour, facing the rising sun. This may promote oral health if it is done appropriately. However, orthodox Jains clean their teeth using fingers and without using the brush, which is not good for oral health. Muslims offer prayer in the form of *namaz*, five times in a day and each time they use miswack stick, tooth picks and do gum massaging as part of the ritual, which is good for oral health.

The rural people in Udupi region of Karnataka use the twigs from mango or cashew tree, while *datun* is used in North India. Neem and banyan twigs are commonly used in the rural areas of Tamil Nadu and coconut twigs in the rural areas of Kerala. Such practices are not confined to India. They are prevalent in many other countries. In African countries, twigs from *Salvaodora persicca* are used for cleaning the teeth. Besides mechanical cleaning action, some twigs may be endowed with antimicrobial properties. The *Salvadora persicca* twig has high concentration of fluoride, which may offer anticaries benefit. Improper use may lead to gingival and periodontal trauma over a period of time. There are other dental hygiene practices among rural people such as use of brick, charcoal, rangoli powder, mud, salt and ash, which can cause gingival recession, abrasion and dentin sensitivity.

PERSONAL HABITS

Purdah System

Practiced among Muslims and high-caste Hindus, *purdah* has both positive and negative effects. It protects against harmful sunrays and thus prevents the occurrence of basal cell carcinoma. However, inadequate exposure to sunlight may affect synthesis of vitamin D, leading to hypoplasia of the teeth. Studies have revealed that the frequency of droplet infections like tuberculosis and diphtheria are relatively high among people who practice the *purdah* system.

Smoking and Alcoholism

The consumption of alcohol is prohibited among Muslims and high-caste Hindus and it is good for oral health. But in the Western countries, it is part of social culture and considered something glamorous, which is harmful for overall health and well-being of people. Smoking and alcoholism are culturally acceptable among some tribes and females are equally involved in these habits. The habit of reverse smoking, which increases the risk of palatal malignancies, is widely prevalent among the fishing communities in the districts of Srikakulam and Vishakhapatnam in Andhra Pradesh.

Pan Chewing as a Custom

Guests in North Indian states like Rajasthan, Uttar Pradesh, Maharashtra and West Bengal are welcomed by offering pan, betel leaf, slaked slime, areca nut and catechu. It encourages the habit of chewing pan and tobacco is a proven risk factor for periodontal diseases, oral submucous fibrosis and oral malignancies.

Drug Addiction

In India, Hindu sadhus of some sects have been using charas, bhang and ganja in various forms and the habit is spreading in the younger generation in India. This unhealthy practice, which results in physical and psychological dependence, is common in the Western culture.

CULTURALLY RESPONSIVE TREATMENT

In the increasingly globalized world, the societies are becoming multicultural. Large-scale migration of population is bringing in immigrants into developed countries like the United States, Australia, Canada and other parts of the world. Health care professionals are realizing the need for adequate cultural assessment of the patient to draw up a culturally responsive treatment plan. Cultural assessment will enable the health authorities to provide culturally competent care to patients.

REVIEW QUESTIONS

1. How does culture influence health?
2. What are the various characteristics of culture?
3. What is the impact of family on culture?

CHAPTER

10

Cultural Diversity

LEARNING OBJECTIVES

After reading this chapter the learner should be able to

- Know about cultural diversity.
- Know about uniformity in culture diversity.

The importance of cultural diversity cannot be over emphasized at a time when societies are becoming increasingly multicultural. Cultural diversity means understanding and becoming aware of different cultural norms and recognizing that each individual is unique. Individuals may differ on account of race, ethnicity socio-economic status, gender, physical abilities, beliefs, rituals, ideologies or other such factors and these differences are nurtured by being sensitive to the needs and concerns. Awareness of different cultural norms and intercultural cooperation is the ideals sought through an emphasis on diversity.

Cultural diversity also makes our country stronger in the modern globalized world as people from diverse cultures bring different language skills and the new ways of thinking to help provide creative solutions to difficult problems. Thus, cultural pluralism makes a society more competitive in the new global economy. The importance of cultural diversity has been recognized by the the United Nations Educational, Scientific and Cultural Organization (UNESCO) which adopted a universal declaration in November 2001 emphasizing that 'As a source of exchange, innovation and creativity, cultural diversity is as necessary for humankind as biodiversity is for nature. In this sense, it is the common heritage of humanity'.

The General Assembly of the United Nations has declared May 21 as the World Day for Cultural Diversity to preserve and promote cultural pluralism and deepen the understanding of its values.

Definition

Cultural diversity is recognition and appreciation of the fact that differences in race, ethnicity, language, nationality, religion, socio-economic status, rituals and sexual orientation make every individual in a society unique. Cultural diversity or multiculturalism is based on the idea that cultural identities should not be discarded or ignored but rather maintained and valued. A culturally diverse community has members of different groups. Multiculturalism provides scope for cultural variations and does not allow dominant culture to assimilate various cultures. It recognizes that apart from shared cultural tenets some cultural differences are also important. Cultural diversity has both visible and invisible features. Age, gender or colour of the skin is visible but the more significant features of diversity like socio-economic background, cultural origin, religion/philosophy, family situation are invisible.

The cultural diversity of India is reflected everywhere from cuisine and food habits to art and craft which differs in various parts of the country. Not only the staple food and delicacies differ but the methods of cooking also vary in different regions. Each Indian cuisine has its own specialty and it is relished revered all over the world. Indian cuisines are famous for both vegetarian and non-vegetarian delicacies and judicious use of herbs, condiments and spices.

The varied art forms are an integral part of Indian culture and they are known for their finesse. There is a wide variety of art including painting, idol making, stone carvings, wood sculptures, metal statues, ornaments, jewellery and terracotta. As every region of the country has its own art there is huge diversity in the forms and it also lends uniqueness to Indian culture.

The clothing people generally wear varies across the country and the style of dressing also varies. For example, saree is the most popular attire of the women throughout the country but it is worn in different styles. The Bengali women do an *ulta pallu* (draping the *aanchal* of the saree over your shoulder to the back of the body), while in rest of the country the women mostly have a *sidha pallu* (draping the aanchal of the saree over the shoulder to the front of the body). The south Indian women wear sarees in a little different style. The type and texture of cloth used for making sarees also differs. In various places, silk sarees are the most popular and hence cost much more than the other variants.

The north Indian women mostly wear salwar-kameez, while in Rajasthan and Gujarat lehenga-choli is the traditional attire. Similarly, kurta-pajama is the preferred traditional costume in large part of the country but in some southern part lungi is preferred over pajama. Pagri is worn by all the Sikh men who also maintain long hair and men carry a *safa* or a cloth which has multiple use from shielding from dust and wind to serve as a handkerchief if required.

Uniformity in Cultural Diversity

Yet cultural unity is also vital for nation as disunity would lead to conflicts and threaten its very existence. It is important for the people of a culturally diverse country to have a national culture that somehow unifies them. For instance, India is a country known for its diversities in religion, languages, cultures, beliefs, food preferences and many more such things, but more astounding the unity or uniformity in such diversity. While retaining a strong identity of various cultures the country has also seen an assimilation and synthesis of different cultures to give rise to a unique culture.

No other country in the world has such a diversity with people belonging to different religions, castes and races and speaking different tongues, having different norms and values, food habits, beliefs and worshipping different Gods and yet living in harmony. They are all the proud citizens of the country, governed by a central authority.

The most important feature of the Indian society that stands out is the coexistence of different ethnic groups which have retained their separate identity by formulating their own inter group behaviour to ensure that there is no mutual interference. The social customs and traditions which the Indians observe across the country irrespective of caste, race and creed contain within them a sense of unity. There are several bases for diversity of culture in India.

Religion. Considered as a land of spirituality and faith, India has the highest diversity in terms of religion with Hinduism, Islam, Christianity, Sikhism, Buddhism and Jainism, and many other religions flourishing together. India also has a significant and flourishing population of 'Parsees' community, which follows Zoroastrianism. Religion has a great impact on the Indian society and it is an integral part of the life of the people. Some religions like Sikhism, Buddhism and Jainism have originated in the country. The Indian philosophy has developed on Indian soil and not been borrowed from anywhere. It blended the various cultures together and bound the people together despite differences in overall concept of gods, and modes of worship.

The religious differences also have seeds of disunity and conflict but the basic philosophy based on theory of Dharma and Karma, rebirth, purification of soul, salvation, heaven and hell has been the same for all. The emphasis is on spirituality and not on material wealth. Religious tolerance is the unique feature of India, and this is the main factor behind the coexistence of followers of different religions.

Language. With 1652 languages and dialects as per 1961 census, India also has the highest diversity in terms of languages. Over the last five decades many of these languages and dialects have been lost but still the country has vast linguistic diversity. Almost every state has its own language like Punjabi, Malayalam, Kannada, Telugu, Tamil, Bengali, Oriya, Hindi and English. Most of these languages have their roots in Sanskrit, the mother of all languages. The national song Vande Mataram, with which the people are emotionally attached, is in Sanskrit language. The great motto Satyameva Jayate (truth alone triumphs) is part of the State Emblem of India. Thus, Sanskrit plays an important role in cultural unity in spite of the fact that it is no longer the language of communication by the people.

Fairs and Festivals. The important fairs and festivals like Holi, Diwali, Christmas, Id, Buddha Jayanti, Dussehra, Vaishakhi, Pongal and Mahavir Jaynti are celebrated collectively by the people and it provides the best example of unity in diversity. There are many other regional festivals that are celebrated across different parts of India and most of the people celebrate and participate in these festivals irrespective of their religion. Besides, the Republic Day, Independence Day, Gandhi Jayanti and some national days are also celebrated unitedly. Thus, the diversity of fairs and festivals is underscored by unity in celebrations.

Family and Marriage. Different communities have different norms, rules and forms of marriage depending on caste, religion and region. For instance, in Hindus, marriage is monogamous and dowry is given, while in the case of Muslim marriage is polygamous and *mehar* is given. However, the institution of marriage has the common objectives of entering a family life through socially sanctioned ways.

Similarly, families are either monogamous or polygamous, patriarchal or matriarchal or of any other form, yet they are all bound to have *we feeling* among the family members providing an underpinning of uniformity in diversity.

Political Organization. India is the largest and most vibrant democracy in the world with a number of political parties, both at the national level and in various states, which profess different ideologies indicative of political diversity. However, despite radically different ideologies and rivalry, the political parties unite whenever an issue involving national interest or larger public interest comes to fore. Thus, all the national and regional political parties have uniformity in objectives which are driven by public or national interest.

Transcultural Society

The increasing churning and mergers of cultures are due also to large-scale migrations of populations; this leads to emergence of multicultural societies and further to transcultural societies. With the passage of time the need for intercultural relations in multicultural societies grows and there is increased and intensive exchange of values, behaviours and mutual respect and acceptance of different culture also grows. It leads to the evolution of transcultural, which is much more than multicultural societies.

Transcultural societies require a strong acceptance by different cultures and exchange of different values but without dominance or prevalence of anyone over the other. The process takes centuries but with increased mobility and the world already becoming a global village many cultures flourishing together in a transcultural manner will take less time than in the past. It is a deep process as it impinges on the values which are at the basis of each and all cultures.

Cuban anthropologist Fernando Ortiz coined the term *transculturation* in 1947 to describe the phenomenon of merging and converging cultures. Transculture encompasses more than transition from one culture to another. It is not a case of uprooting of one entrenched culture by another culture but merger of cultures that leads to creation of a new culture. Transculturation can often be the result of colonial conquest and subjugation, especially in a postcolonial era as native peoples struggle to regain their own sense of identity.

The word transcultural indicates movement across time, space and other cultural boundaries. The process of transculturation reflects the natural tendency of people to resolve conflicts over time, rather than exacerbating them. In the era of global mobility, both conflicts and resolutions are amplified by communication as the tendency of ancient cultures of remaining apart has been replaced by stronger forces that bring societies together. In short, transculturation is one aspect of global phenomena.

The emergence of profession societies has implications for health care and already transcultural nursing has become an essential aspect of health care today. The ever-increasing transcultural population in countries like the United States poses a significant challenge to nurses providing individualized and holistic care to their patients. Transculturally competent care requires nurses to recognize and appreciate cultural differences in health care values, beliefs and customs. They must acquire the necessary knowledge and skills in cultural competency which goes a long way in ensuring patient satisfaction and, in turn, positive outcomes.

REVIEW QUESTIONS

1. What are bases of uniformity in culture?
2. Explain in detail about the transcultural society.

grows and there is increased and intensive exchange of values, behaviours and mutual respect and acceptance of different culture also grows, it leads to the evolution of transcultural, which is much more than multicultural societies.

Transcultural societies require a strong acceptance of different cultures and exchange of different values but without dominance or imposition of any one over the other. The process takes centuries but with increased mobility and the world already becoming a global village many cultures coming together in a transcultural manner will take less time than in the past. It is a deep process of imposing on the values which are at the basis of each and all cultures.

Cuban anthropologist Fernando Ortiz coined the term transculturation in 1947 to describe the phenomenon of merging and converging cultures. Transculture encompasses more than transition from one culture to another; it is not a case of imbibing of one culture ('culture' by 'inculcation') but the genesis of culture that leads to emergence of a new culture. Transculturation may often be the result of colonial conquests and subjugation, especially in a postcolonial era as native peoples struggle to regain their own sense of identity.

Its overt transcultural nature, its movement across time, space and cultural boundaries, the process of transculturation reflects the natural tendency of people to resolve conflicts over time, rather than exacerbating them. In the era of global mobility both conflicts and resolutions are multiplied by communications; the influence of new traditions or remaining apart has been replaced by stronger forces that bring societies together. In short, transculturation is one aspect of global phenomena.

The emergence of transculturalism has implications for health care, and thereby transcultural nursing has become an essential aspect of health care today. The ever-increasing transcultural population in countries like the United States gives a signal to the need for nurses providing individualised and holistic care to their patients. Transculturally competent care requires nurses to recognise and appreciate cultural differences in health care values, beliefs and customs. They must acquire the necessary knowledge and skills in cultural competence which goes a long way in ensuring patient satisfaction and achieving positive outcomes.

REVIEW QUESTIONS

1. What are bases of uniformity in culture?
2. Explain in detail about the transcultural phenomenon.

UNIT - 4

SOCIAL GROUPS AND PROCESSES

CHAPTER

11

Group

LEARNING OBJECTIVES

After reading this chapter the learner should be able to

- Have knowledge about the process of group formation.
- Get acquainted with various types of groups and their characteristics.

Most of the animals live in groups and a human being is no different by nature. In fact, a human being is much more gregarious and cannot survive in isolation. It is rightly said that 'man is a social animal'. The habit of living in groups is intrinsic to human beings and every individual is part of more than one group, starting from family at home. A man belongs to more than one group. The routine life of an individual consists of his participation in groups. He is a member of a primary group called family. He is also a member of the community and has a group of friends.

MEANING OF GROUPS

As per the simple dictionary meaning a group is set of two or more things located together. However, a group refers to a collection of individuals who are bound by social relationships and recognize themselves as a distinct social unit. They have regular interaction that causes them to identify with one another and share values and beliefs. Identification and participation in a group leads to frequent and close interaction strengthening its solidarity. Social groups are the most stable and strong units and they are not only important for members but have a key role in the society. Their members have a common feeling of camaraderie, mutual influence, common interests and they work together to achieve a common set of goals.

Groups are the basic building blocks of the society. There are varied types like a family, village, town, city, political party and trade union. It must be noted that social groups are different from social classes, status groups and other entities which lack structure and whose members are not much aware of the existence of the group. These are essentially quasi-groups which could give rise to social groups. For instance, many political parties have emerged from social classes and, thus, the line dividing social groups and social classes is thin. Organization of a group may be done formally or it can gradually evolve and come into existence unintentionally.

Similarly, disorganization of a group can happen suddenly or a group may cease to occur without the awareness of its members.

While all groups are important to their members and society, some groups are more important than others.

CHARACTERISTICS OF GROUP

Defining boundaries: Groups have boundaries as evident from the family can be a joint family or a nuclear family but member of another family cannot be its member. Similarly, a football team cannot have a cricketer as a member. The number of members in certain groups keeps changing but each group, big or small, has its boundaries. The members work for the welfare of their group and compete with other groups.

Leadership: Each group has a leader to coordinate its activities. Leader is meant to guide the group.

Decision making: A group is not static but a dynamic entity and decisions are required to be made for the progress of the group.

Setting goals: A group sets various goals, both short term and long term, and performs multiple functions to achieve them. It may not necessarily stick to one function and pick up a different function after accomplishing one.

Controlling members' behaviours: Members of the groups have control over each-other's behaviour. A person belongs to many groups and plays different roles in different groups. For example, a youngest member of the family obeys the decisions of the elders of the family, but he may be the head of an organization where he issues orders.

TYPES OF GROUPS

Groups can be of the following types:

- In-groups and out-groups
- Primary and secondary groups
- Reference groups
- Spatial groups

In-Groups

It is a group that a person is a loyal member of and strongly identifies with. These groups are closely related to each other and share the same house, food, economy. For example, Savita and Rakhi are both women (in-group) and volleyball players (in-group). Once people identify themselves as belonging to an in-group, they start to perceive differences between the in-group members and the members of other groups and out-groups. Family is an in-group and its members may belong to many out-groups such as neighbourhood, community, club and professional group. Everyone who is not a part of their in-group belongs to an out-group.

Out-Group

It is a group that a person has no loyalty to and is not a member of. Since Savita and Rakhi are both women, men form an out-group for them. A man, Mike, would be a part of the out-group from the perspective of Savita and Rakhi.

At times, artificial boundaries are created within members of groups. The members form in-groups and out-groups. Members of in-groups have loyalty for each other, whereas they are antagonistic towards the out-groups. Every social group creates boundaries within itself, but a cohesive in-group typically has three main characteristics.

Members of the group use titles, external symbols, and dress up differently to distinguish themselves from the out-group.

Members of the in-group tend to view members of the out-group as rivals and compete or even clash with them. This competition with the other group can also strengthen the unity within each group.

Members of the in-group try to establish their superiority applying positive stereotypes to their own and negative stereotypes to the out-group.

An individual usually has more contact with people who are a part of his or her in-group than with members of any out-group. Consequently, opportunities to learn about the individual characteristics of out-group members are limited. Information related to in-groups is organized in more personal terms, whereas only abstract characteristics of out-groups are recalled. There is more incentive to make distinctions among in-group members than out-group members as one knows that there will be more contact with them in future. It also leads to in-group favouritism.

In-group favouritism: It refers to preference and affinity for one's in-group over the out-group. One of the key determinants of group biases is the need to improve self-esteem. The members of the in-group constantly strive to enhance their self-esteem and even as individuals they will find a reason, no matter how insignificant, to prove to themselves why their group is superior.

Inter-group aggression: It is any behaviour intended to harm another person, because he or she is a member of an out-group. Such behaviour is viewed by its targets as undesirable. Loyalty to the in-group may lead to antagonism and aggression towards the out-group, including fierce competitions for the same resources.

Out-group homogeneity effect: It is one's perception of out-group members as more similar to one another than are the members in the in-group. In short, the overwhelming feeling is that 'they are alike; we are diverse'.

Prejudice: It is a hostile or negative attitude towards the people in a distinct group, based solely on their membership within that group. It significantly influences our behaviours in evaluating others and this leads to forming incorrect conclusions.

Stereotype: It is a result of the natural tendency of human beings to form groups based on a common identity. In this generalization all the members of a group are assigned identical characteristics, regardless of actual variation among the members. The stereotype can be used to convince and make the people to view a certain group as inferior and undeserving.

Primary Groups and Secondary Groups

Primary Group

It is a small group having close association, cooperation, and face-to-face interaction among members who work together for the welfare of each other. A family, sports team, class mates, group of friends and a tribe are examples of a primary group. The term *primary* is used with these groups because they are the principal source of relationships and socialization. The relationships in our primary groups provide love, security and companionship to members. Social values and norms are imbibed from family and friends who remain a part of an individual's life all through.

Primary groups are close-knit, include intimate relationships, stable and are usually long lasting. The members of primary groups feel a strong personal identity with the group. Primary groups are closely knit with members having deep concern for one another, sharing activities and culture and spending long periods of time together. They are psychologically comforting and play an important role in developing personal identity.

The family, the child's play group and the neighbourhoods or community are almost universal in all societies. They are instrumental in development of the social life and facilitate integration of their members in the larger society.

Characteristics of Primary Group

Primary groups are universal groups. They are the chief basis of what is universal in human nature and human ideals. The self is developed and moulded by the primary group relations. Primary groups socialize the individuals. Before the growth of cities, the majority of associations occurred in primary groups.

Small size: The main characteristic of primary group is its small size. The character and nature of the group tends to change with its size. Increase in the size of the group weakens bonds of relationship having a negative effect on intimacy of the members.

Physical proximity: Physical proximity provides an opportunity for the very development of primary groups. Eating, playing and studying together are the symbols of closeness.

Direct cooperation: Primary group is characterized by direct cooperation between its members. The members do not act independently; all of them participate in the same process. Work is essentially a mode of sharing a common experience. Thus, its members work directly and in cooperation with each other to achieve their common interests.

Identity of ends: The identification of end is connected with the fusion of personalities within the group. They work together for the attainment of their common ends without disagreement. They look at the world through the same eyes.

Personal relationship: The primary relationship is a matter of persons; it exists because of the person, not despite of him. This means the relationship in primary group is personal and disappears if a particular person disappears from it.

Stability of the group: Primary group is relatively a permanent group. It is one of the main features of primary group. The longer the group remains together, the deeper are the contacts between its members.

Limited self-interest: Members of the group subordinate their personal interests to the interests of the group. The common interest of the group is strong enough to override and control individual interests.

Similar background: The members of a primary group must have more or less the same background. Each must have something to contribute, to give as well as to take. The person, who is too far above or below it, disturbs the process of group participation.

Unspecialized character: A primary group is neither deliberately created nor it is specialized in character. It has not come into being for the pursuit of any particular interest of the people. On the other hand, the interest of primary groups is always comprehensive. Hence, the group is unspecialized in character.

Communication: In case of primary group, communication is very quick and effective. Direct or face-to-face contact helps easy communication among the members.

Informal relationship: Members come together spontaneously. They are directly in contact with each other.

Motivation: Members of the group motivate each other.

Unity: Members of the group have we feeling. They all work together to perform a certain task or achieve a goal.

Importance of Primary Groups

- Social control
- Authority
- Compromise
- Decision on the basis of majority
- Integration

Secondary Group

Such groups can be small or large. They are mostly marked by impersonal and infrequent interaction, usually short term. These groups are typically found at work and school. An example of a secondary group is a committee organized to plan a holiday party at work. It holds meetings occasionally and for a short period of time. The group members may have similar interests; the purpose of the group is to accomplish the assigned task instead of the relationships. Usually in a secondary group, members indirectly influence each other. There is not much face-to-face contact among the members.

Characteristics of Secondary Groups

Large in size: Secondary groups are usually huge in size with a large number of members spread across the world. For example, the Red Cross Society, its members are scattered across the world. The large size results in indirect relations among the members.

Definite aims: Secondary groups are formed to fulfil some definite aims and objectives. The success of a secondary group is indicated and judged by the extent to which it became able to fulfil those aims like setting up a school, college or university to provide education.

Voluntary membership: The membership of a secondary group is not mandatory in nature, whether one will be a member of a secondary group or not it depends on his own volition. There is no compulsion for anyone to be a member of any secondary group. For instance, it is not necessary that one should be a member of a particular political party.

Formal, indirect and impersonal relation: The relationship among the members of a secondary group is indirect, formal and impersonal in nature. People do not develop personal relations in a secondary group as they interact among themselves in accordance with formal rules and regulations. It is not possible to establish direct relation among themselves due to large size of secondary groups. Moreover, the members are least concerned with the other aspects of each other's life and such relations among members are mainly indirect.

Active and inactive members: The secondary group comprises both active and inactive members. In the absence of intimate relationship and lack of personal interaction some members become more active, while others remain inactive. Political parties provide the best example of such groups where some members take active interest in the affairs of the organization, others are dormant.

Formal rules: A secondary group is characterized by formal or written rules and the members function accordingly. Anyone who does not obey these formal rules and regulations loses his membership. A secondary group is organized and regulated by formal rules and regulations. There is decentralization of power and clear-cut division of labour.

Status of an individual depends on his role: It is another important characteristic of a secondary group because the status and position of each and every member depends on his role that he plays in the group. Birth or personal qualities do not decide one's status in a secondary group.

Individuality in person: Secondary group is popularly known as *special interest groups* as people become member of secondary group to fulfil their own self-interest. Hence, they always give stress on the fulfilment of their self-interests and once the end is achieved they are no longer interested in the group. As a result, in secondary group individuality in person is found.

Self-dependence among members: Another feature of secondary group is that members are self-reliant and also selfish. Every member tries to safeguard his own interests by himself.

Dissimilar ends: Secondary group is characterized by dissimilar ends. The members of a secondary group have different and diverse ends and people join the secondary groups to achieve these ends.

Relationship is a means to an end: Secondary relations are not an end in itself rather it is a means to an end and an individual establishes relationship to fulfil his self-interest. Even friendship is struck for specific purposes.

Formal social control: Secondary group exercises control over its members in formal ways such as police and law courts.

Division of labour: A secondary group is characterized by division of labour. The duties, functions and responsibilities of members are clearly defined. Each member has to carry out duties and functions assigned to him or her.

Importance of Secondary Group

The rising population and urbanization is the basic reason for formation of secondary groups. Primary groups serve the purpose of small and simple society but not appropriate for large and modern society. The large size of secondary group affords ample opportunities to the members. It provides better and wider opportunities for the members to develop their faculties and talents. There are numerous and varied career openings available and an individual can rise to unbelievable heights in business, industry, education and other fields due to talent and hard work.

A secondary group increases efficiency of its members as they work diligently for their self-interest and specific goals. A clear-cut division of labour and formal set-up along with rules ensures effective management of the secondary group.

Secondary group helps in broadening the outlook of its members as it accommodates a large number and variety of individuals and it is more universal in its judgement than the primary group.

Secondary groups are functional in character as relations are instrumental in accomplishing certain specific tasks, unlike primary group, bereft of no sentiments.

Reference Group

A reference group is a group to which we compare ourselves. An individual can look to a group of which he has been a part in the past or a group he may become a member in the future as a reference group. For instance, a married man may still look to his single friends as a reference group, even though he no longer belongs to the group. Similarly, for women who get pregnant for the first time women with children serve as a reference group, even though they do not yet belong to this group.

Informal Versus Formal Reference Groups

Most reference groups are informal and based on the shared interests and goals of group members. Informal groups are not structured with a specific goal in mind. They work and interact on a very personal level. Informal reference groups include the following:

- Families
- A group of elderly people

- Peer groups
- Mahila Mandals
- Group of adolescent girls

Formal reference groups have a specific goal or mission. They also have a specific structure and positions of authority. Examples of formal reference groups include the following:

- Labour unions
- Alcohol anonymous group
- Women against domestic violence

Positive Reference Groups and Negative Reference Groups

Positive reference groups: These are the ones an individual wants to be accepted by. Thus, if one wants to be a film actor, he might carefully observe and imitate the behaviour of film actors. These are the groups that provide the person with a guide to action by explicitly setting norms and espousing values.

Negative reference groups: These are the groups one does not want to be identified with but they also serve as sources of self-evaluation. A person might, for example, try to avoid resembling members of a particular religious group or a circus group. A group rejected by or in opposition to ego's own group is 'the enemy' or the negative group.

FORMATION OF GROUPS

If we bring together some strangers in a restricted space and environment and provide a common goal and maybe a few rules, then a highly probable course of events will follow. It would not be long-lasting group like passengers travelling together to reach a destination, though these passengers have same destination, same environment and are in a restricted space. Interaction among individuals is the basic requirement for the formation of a group. Initially, the members interact differentially in the groups of two or three. Usually, interactions occur among the individuals having some common interests or skills or share common economic and cultural background. Individuals may move from one group to the other temporarily but will return to the same groups rather consistently bringing some stability in relationships. These small groups ultimately integrate to form larger groups, depending on the common goals and objectives. The process is marked with further differentiation of roles, revision of territory and dominance ranking.

Conflict or disagreement is integral part of the process of group formation. There are tussles over distribution of resources, the choices of means and different subgoals, the development of appropriate norms, rewards and punishments. All this rarely takes place without conflict. Jealousy over roles, or locations, or favoured relationships and territorial conflicts are a common feature but most serious struggles pertain to status, ranging from mild to violent protests. Sociologists draw analogies to animal behaviour, to classify such behaviours as territorial behaviours and dominance behaviours. Once the relationships take concrete shape, differentiations of leadership, dominance, or authority will develop depending on the pressure of the common goal and various skills of individuals, to bring productive groups into existence.

Some of the individuals may be excluded and others may withdraw during the process of group formation because of conflicts of interests or unsettled dominance order. A reproductive group requires that both dominance order and territorial arrangements be settled with respect to the common goal and within the group. Eventually, competition for territory and dominance gets manifested leading to emergence of one or more competing groups depending on the number of individuals in the original collection of strangers, and the number of *hangers-on* that are tolerated.

REVIEW QUESTIONS

1. Differentiate between formal and informal groups.
2. Explain the difference between primary group and secondary group.
3. How does formation of groups occur?

CHAPTER

12

Social Groups and Social Processes

LEARNING OBJECTIVES

After reading this chapter the learner should be able to

- Gain knowledge about economic, political, religious groups.
- Be aware about crowd, public, audience and social processes.

All social interaction is essentially a form of collective behaviour. It is through the lens of collective behaviour that one sees individuals affecting the group and being affected by it and gets an idea about forces that contribute to the intended and unintended social change. Simply put, if two persons behave in a similar way, it may be termed as collective behaviour. In a broad sense the term *collective behaviour* will include all behaviours involving more than one person. As such all group activity can be thought of as collective behaviour.

However, sociologists use this term in a limited sense and consider it as an occasional episode rather than a regular feature. They define it as the behaviour of individuals under the impulse that is common and collective. Collective behaviour is crucial to understanding human beings as social animals.

In the words of sociologist N.J. Smelser who specializes in this field of study, collective behaviour is 'relatively spontaneous and unstructured behaviour of a group of people who are reacting to a common influence in an ambiguous situation'. Mob, crowd and panics are prime examples of collective behaviour. Public crazes, fashions, social unrest, social movements and revolutions are other manifestations of collective behaviour.

Kurt Lang and Gladys Lang describe collective behaviour as 'the sequences and patterns of interactions that emerge in a problematic situation'. They defined crowd behaviour to include the disorderly street mob and social upheaval to the peaceful and comparatively trivial shifts in the orientations of individuals and small groups that can produce major changes in taste, fashion or public opinion. All societies constitute a social order, but there is an inherent disorder within. Collective behaviour is frequently the form in which it manifests itself.

ECONOMIC GROUPS

There is a tendency for class formation with urbanization in India despite a well-entrenched caste system. It is happening in rural areas also where agriculture workers are from low caste and landholders are from upper castes and household workers are from middle castes. Class system seems to be emerging in rural areas also because of distribution of resources and access to political control.

Three levels of classes exist in villages as per some anthropologists. Forward class (higher castes), backward class (middle and lower castes) and harijans (very low castes). Members of these groups are like they are large-scale farmers, small-scale farmers and landless labourers.

In cities, economy, education, business and certain professions crosscut caste boundaries, suggesting the possibility of forming classes in the future. There are groups of prosperous industrialists and entrepreneurs who contribute to the development of the nation to a great extent, bureaucrats and political officeholders, who have money and power, and working class people who enjoy good salaries.

Members of the upper class, who are just around 1 per cent of the population, own large properties and have all the luxuries of life. They become members of exclusive clubs and enjoy vacations in foreign lands. They include industrialists, former maharajas and top executive.

Economically the lowest group comprises individuals engaged in menial jobs and they constitute the growing underclass, which is taking shape in both villages and urban areas. These low-ranking menial workers remain economically insecure and they join hands cutting across lines of class and religion to muster political support to achieve their common interests.

India's rapidly expanding economy has provided the basis for the emergence of a new group, the middle class, which is increasingly dictating India's political and economic direction. This class is mobile, consumer-oriented and, to some extent, forward-looking. This class exists in cities, towns and countryside, making its voice heard everywhere. It is constituted by farmers, white-collar workers, businessmen, military personnel, professionals and various others, all of whom have reasonable earnings with substantial savings to lead a prosperous life. Middle class people own cars, televisions and other consumer goods, and educate their children in public schools.

The new middle class is booming and appears to be expanding rapidly. There is no single set of criteria defining the middle class and also it is not possible to estimate its numbers with accuracy.

RELIGIOUS GROUPS

India's complex society also has groups of religious persons, organized under numerous sects and headed by sadhus (holy men). The members of these groups have voluntarily stepped outside the usual bonds of kinship and caste to join the religious groups.

There are several thousand Hindu and Jain *sadhus* and *sadhvis* (women ascetics), Buddhist monks and nuns in India who have given up affiliation with their caste and kin. In many sects the new entrants undergo rituals of funeral ceremony rebirth, to start the life afresh as an ascetic. They come from all walks of life, and range from illiterate villagers to well-educated professionals and are devoted to spiritual concerns. They choose to wear white or saffron robes, or perhaps no clothing at all, as is the case with Jain saints. Some of them daub their skin with holy ash, pray and meditate, and wander from place to place, depending on their needs solely on the generosity of others. Some of them live in ashrams and temples to learn and also to preach the public.

They live in renunciation but each of them is affiliated with an ascetic order governed by strict religious regime comprising dress code, itinerancy, diet, worship and ritual ceremonies. The temples, ashrams and monasteries depend on the donations from public. Although these sadhus are out of many of the trappings of ordinary life, they do follow the hierarchy and interdependence so pervasive in Indian society.

But there are extremes of renunciation also turning normal rules of conduct completely upside down. These extremes are sadhus called Aghoris who do not live in groups. An aghori lives alone at cremation grounds, eating and drinking in a human skull bowl, in quest of great spiritual attainment. He consumes his own urine, excreta and pieces of human flesh from burning corpse, violating the basic norms of the civilized society.

POLITICAL GROUPS

In democratic countries, individuals contest elections on behalf of some political party. Some democratic countries have predominantly a two-party system, as in the United States, whereas others like India have multiple party systems. Individuals can contest election as independent candidates. Labour unions also play an important role as they pursue their own agenda and fight for the rights of workers. They support political parties and help some parties in winning elections. These are typical secondary groups having following characteristics.

Relationship

There is formal relationship among the members of the political party. Some of the members of a political party hardly meet each other, whereas indirect communication exists among the members.

Size

The size of the political party is large as most of the political parties exist throughout the country.

Membership

It is not mandatory for everyone to be the member of any political party. There are some active members of the political party who work for the party but there are members who are not actively involved and just support a particular party as an inactive member.

Formal Rules and Regulations

Political parties get stability by implementing rules and regulations. There is division of labour among the members of the party that makes it successful. A political party has a team to manage it affairs usually consisting of a president, vice president and secretary, and convener, spokesperson at district, state and national levels. They also have executive bodies at all levels for taking decisions.

Limited Influence on the Personality of a Member

Members of a political party work for the welfare of the party but there is hardly any impact of the party on the personality of the individuals.

Formal Social Control

Each political party has various office holders at various levels so that all the party members are under the control.

CROWD

Crowd is a gathering of large number of people in a place in an unruly way. Crowd is thought to be an undesired social phenomenon, but still fulfils an important function in the society. Crowd helps in releasing pent-up feelings. In general, crowd is a gathering of individuals of varied nationalities, religions, age groups, professions or sex and even the circumstances that have brought them together. It can be a group of friends or gathering of people for a common cause or a group of people with similar interest. Interpersonal relationship among people in a crowd is minimal. For instance, there is an accident and all the passers-by stop to see the extent of damage and injury to the persons involved in the accident. Looking at the gathering of the people, more and more people start joining to see what has happened out of sheer curiosity. Crowd is a temporary gathering which dissolves with the removal of cause of gathering.

Characteristics of Crowd

Collective Behaviour

It is not the behaviour of an individual in the crowd, but everyone in the crowd behaves in a similar manner. That is why it is called collective behaviour. It is not possible to regulate the behaviour of crowd by any set of rules. The behaviour is unpredictable most of the time and guided by beliefs, hopes and emotions.

Gathering of People

Persons gathered at a particular place and their attention is focussed on a particular object or person.

Transient Group

Crowd is a temporary gathering of people and it gets disseminated once the focus of attention gets disappeared.

Loosely Structured

Crowd is a gathering of people in an unorganized manner, having no definite aim. There is no leader and individuals in a crowd do not follow any social norms.

Anonymity

Individuals in the crowd do not know each other and they are not even keen to know about each other as it is a casual collection of people. Anonymity is there in the crowd because of being temporary gathering and large. Moral responsibility is shifted from an individual to the group.

Limited Attention

There is some centre of attention and each individual's attention is directed towards it.

Irrational

Rational analysis in the crowd is impossible. Crowd has no culture or tradition of its own and crowd can turn even a sane person into a beast.

Suggestibility

People in a crowd do not want to face any opposition to their views. They accept the suggestion which is favourable to their temper. It is difficult to lead the crowd in a different direction. Crowd requires careful handling to avoid violence or destruction.

Emotionality

It channels the feelings and thoughts of individuals in a definite direction. Usually people, who are unable to express their feelings, break free in a crowd and indulge in such activities which as an individual they lacked courage to do.

Lack of Sense of Responsibility

No one in the crowd has a sense of responsibility. They can do anything at the spur of the moment and have a feeling of repentance afterwards. The collective behaviour of the crowd can be devastating and uncontrollable. It is radically different and deviated from normal behaviour.

TYPES OF CROWD

Crowd can be classified in various categories like homogeneous and heterogeneous, casual, expressive, conventional, active and inactive.

Homogeneous

These crowds belong to a religion, class or sect and marked by some kind of commonality.

Heterogeneous

This type of crowd may be anonymous like gatherings seen in markets and streets crowd or may not be anonymous assemblies.

Casual Crowd

A crowd at the place of accident, gathering of people in a fair or people in theatre watching a movie are the forms of casual assemblies. In such a gathering individuals are less likely to remember people who were part of the crowd.

Expressive Crowd

Individuals get together to express their demands or sentiments. The aim is to voice their grievances. Any effort to disperse the expressive assembly without any assurance may turn it into an aggressive crowd.

Conventional Crowd

Individuals coming together for regularly organized events fall in the category of conventional crowd. Theatre audience, radio listening audience and spectators at a cricket match are its examples.

Active Crowd

It is accidental and momentary gathering of individuals. It can be an aggressive crowd capable of doing anything. Expressive crowd has no significant or long-term purpose. There can be free expression of emotions as yelling, crying, jumping or laughing. Aggressive crowd is usually seen during agitations. It has characteristics of intense emotionality, suggestibility and influence of rumours, similar behaviour and tendency of imitation. All the individuals in the crowd are emotionally charged. Such crowd follows suggestions without assigning any reason. Individual in such a crowd just follow the rumours and do not even check the truth. The role of a leading individual in such a crowd is very crucial as he can arouse emotions and excite the members of the crowd.

Inactive Crowd

Individuals gather for some peaceful purpose like an audience at a religious discourse.

MOB

Mob is a disorderly gathering of people with an intention of causing trouble or violence or a riotous group of people. The word *mob* is also used for a gang involved in extortion and drug trafficking. Mob has its own immediate objectives and focus on fulfilment of these objectives.

The mob can be classified into purposive, active, confused and random gathering.

Purposive and Active Mob

These are preplanned by some parties to achieve certain purposes.

Confused and Random Mob

These are not preplanned and leaders hardly give any directions to the members. A gathering may get panicky because of confusion.

PUBLIC

Public is a gathering of individuals having common interest in an issue, though these individuals may not know each other. An individual may be the member of various public. A public has core members who influence the decisions and fringe members who hardly influence decision.

Characteristics of Public

A Dispersed Group

Public is a dispersed group, which may never meet again.

A Deliberate Group

There is no emotional intensity, though there may be exchange of ideas among the members of public. There is quest for knowing new things. Debate can be there on an issue to reach the consensus.

A Definite Issue

If there is a definite issue, the important thing is that public should have an interest in the issue. Public gather when an issue arises.

Loosely Organized

Members do not have fixed status roles. They do not have we feeling. It is like a group having no shape and size also varies with kind of issue.

Self-Awareness

Members of the public do not get carried away by each other's opinions. Each member is aware of his own interest.

AUDIENCE

Audience is a kind of institutionalized crowd. Because gathering is for a specified period and there is an accepted sequence of events with a formal beginning and formal end.

Characteristics of Audience

Specific Purpose

The audience are there to listen to a musician or to see a drama, so specific purpose is there for each of the audience.

Specific Time and Place

Audience gather at a specific place like a theatre, ground or auditorium at a specified time when performers are going to perform.

Two-Way Communication

Though audience stand apart from the performers but they participate in communication in the form of clapping, cheering or whistling

TYPES OF AUDIENCE

Audience have been classified in various ways but most common are:

Information-seeking audience: People gather in a ground to listen to a party leader to get information about that particular political party. Individuals assemble in an auditorium to listen to an academician as an information-seeking audience.

Entertainment-seeking audience: Individuals have come to a place for enjoyment and recreation. Audience in a movie theatre or people in a playground to watch a match are the entertainment-seeking assembly.

Conversational audience: Individuals go to attend meetings to clarify their stand or dispel doubts about their beliefs.

Pedestrian audience: It is a gathering of onlookers who get attracted by something and stop there. It can be an audience enjoying the show of a snake charmer or a magician by the roadside.

TRIBE

A tribe is a social group having various clans, nomadic bands and other subgroups having definite geographical area. Numerous tribes, notified as scheduled tribes, are also integrated into the caste system and are further divided into groups similar to subcastes. Some tribes are more like ethnic groups than castes. Basically a tribe is a group of families speaking a common dialect, living in a common territory, professing a common religion and a common culture. Some tribes live separately from others in the forested centres of the country and some live in villages with non-tribal people. Usually they are considered members of separate castes ranking low on hierarchical scale.

Characteristics of a Tribe

Common territory: A tribe live in a particular geographical area.
Common dialect: Members of a tribe speak a common dialect.
Blood relationship: Members of a tribe are related to one another by blood though they are not endogamous groups.
Political organization: Each tribe has a chief and has authority over all the members. So, tribes have their own political systems.
Common religion: Religion being very important to tribal people, all the members believe in common religion and follow the religious ceremonies strictly.
Common name: Each tribe has a name.
Unity: There is strong unity among the members of a tribe.
Common culture: A common culture exists in a tribe.

CLAN

This is a group with a belief having common origin and descent. Clan is constituted by all the relatives of either mother's or father's lineage. They believe that they all are the offspring of one ancestor. Members of a clan have 'we feeling'

Characteristics of a Clan

It is exogamous. Marriages within a clan are not allowed.
They believe to be having an ancestor (mythical or real).
It is unilateral consisting of families from mother's side or father's side.
Clans are known often named after some ancestor like seers Saraswat, Attri and so on.
They have great control over their members and do not allow its member to do unsocial acts.
The head of a clan is usually a priest.

Band

Band is an original form of a local group. It is an informal small group. It might not have a leader but have a strong community feeling. Usually the group is nomadic and does not have a definite place to live. They keep on moving from one place to another with their pets and tents.

CASTE

In a caste system social position of a person is determined at birth and exists for life time. It is an organized group. Members of a caste marry within caste, so it is called *endogamous*. There are four major castes in India associated with occupation. The lowest of four castes *Dalits* are oppressed people. India's constitution forbids discrimination on the basis of caste but caste ranking and caste-based discrimination have occurred for centuries and still exists more in the rural areas than in urban settings and more in the realms of kinship and marriage than in personal interactions.

Some correlation between ranking on the basis of caste hierarchy and economic prosperity still exists. Members of high castes tend to be more prosperous than members of lower castes. Many lower-caste people live in conditions of poverty and lack basic facilities and are socially disadvantaged group.

There are thousands of castes and subcastes in India. Each caste is part of a locally based system of interdependence with other groups, involving occupational specialization, and is linked in complex ways with networks that stretch across regions and throughout the nation.

Characteristics of a Caste

Unchangeable: Individual belongs to a caste by birth and it can never be changed.

Endogamy: Marriages are acceptable within the caste.

Discrimination against lower castes: Discrimination against lower castes is quite prevalent especially in villages.

CLASS

It is a grouping of people on the basis of economic status. Economic resources influence the life style and individuals of a common class have similar standard of living by and large.

Characteristics of a Class

Class systems are fluidic in nature: There are no clear-cut boundaries among the classes. With improvement in economic status people may shift to higher class and vice versa.

Class is economically based: Economic resources decide the class of individuals.

Class positions are achieved: Class is not determined at birth and is not forever.

Class system exists in urban areas: Class system exists in urban areas. Individuals in rural areas are known by their caste not by the class.

REVIEW QUESTIONS

1. What do you mean by a crowd? What are the various characteristics of a crowd?
2. Explain in detail about economic group and political group.
3. What are the characteristics of a tribe and a clan?
4. Explain the difference between caste and class.

CHAPTER

13

Competition, Conflict, Coopeartion and Accommodation

LEARNING OBJECTIVES

After reading this chapter the learner should be able to

- Know about the importance of cooperation and competition.
- Have an understanding of the causes of conflicts.

Interaction between individuals and groups is the essence of social life and that makes a society is an ever-changing entity. Social interaction is the basic process that gives shape to human nature and social structure.

Sociologists have defined and classified social processes in different ways and the fundamental social processes on which they focused are cooperation, conflict and competition, accommodation and assimilation.

COOPERATION

Man is a social animal and cooperation is a social and psychological necessity for him. It is difficult for an individual to survive without cooperation and it is a universal phenomenon among human beings.

The word cooperation is derived from the Latin words *co* and *operart*. *Co* means together and *operart* means to work. So, cooperation means working together. It means working together in the pursuit of common interests or common goals.

In the words of A.W. Green cooperation is 'the continuous and common endeavour of two or more persons to perform a task or to realize a goal that is commonly cherished'.

Characteristics of Cooperation

- It can be conscious or unconscious.
- It gives satisfaction to people.
- It needs readiness to help people.
- People should be sympathetic, kind hearted and concerned for others to cooperate.
- The outcome of cooperation is positive.
- People or groups work together to achieve common goals.
- Progress of individuals, community and country is based upon cooperation.

Types of Cooperation

Primary Cooperation

Primary cooperation is found among the primary groups like family, friends and neighbourhood and play groups. Each individual works for the welfare of the other members of the group. Rewards of cooperation are shared by all the members of the group.

Secondary Cooperation

It is very formal and specialized cooperation found in secondary groups like political, religious, educational and commercial groups. An individual works in the group for his welfare in terms of salary, promotion or profits. People work for the group as they have some loyalty towards the group but welfare of the group is not their only consideration.

Tertiary Cooperation

This type of cooperation is found between bigger groups like two political parties to defeat the third political party. Management and workers may cooperate for different ends.

DIRECT COOPERATION

Members of the group work together performing similar functions like playing a game, cooking together, pushing a car having starting problem or constructing a building. It is performance of a task by group of persons to achieve a common goal.

INDIRECT COOPERATION

This is based on division of labour. Each member of the group performs the task assigned to him. Activities are different but goal is same.

Importance of Cooperation

Personality development of an individual occurs because of cooperation of others as parents, family members, friends and teachers.

Cooperation is essential for the progress of an individual, community and nation.

Cooperation is necessary for the organizations as division of labour helps in completion of any task. For instance, professionals with different specializations work together in a hospital to achieve a common aim.

Culture and traditions are transferred from generation to generation through cooperation.

Inventions are not possible without cooperation, as number of persons work together for some innovation.

Nothing in a society is possible without cooperation.

We feeling in groups, welfare of the society and unity exist because of cooperation.

COMPETITION

Competition exists when things are scarce. Human desires are unlimited and resources to satisfy these desires are limited, giving rise to competition. Struggle to satisfy the desire with limited resources is competition.

Competition is continuous, which never comes to an end, driven by desire for status, wealth and fame.

Competition brings about social changes. Individuals in society struggle and modify their behaviour to achieve something. Modification in behaviour to attain desired ends leads to innovations or inventions.

Competition is not against an individual but it is directed towards an aim. But it can lead to conflict between two persons as two leaders contesting elections have rivalry against each other.

Competitions are governed by certain norms to avoid unfair means.

Competition is universal as it is present in all the societies to a certain extent. It is found in all types of classes evenly.

Competition is unconscious as competitors themselves are not aware of other competitors.

Competition exists for things in scarcity. Things in abundance do not have competition as people do not have to struggle to acquire them.

Types of Competition

Personal or Conscious

When competitors know each other, they work to attain same position contesting an election.

Impersonal or unconscious: When competitors are not aware of each other as is the case while appearing in a competitive examination.

Constructive or healthy: This type of competition is helpful and stimulating for others. It is called healthy competition as students in a class work hard to get more marks than others, which adds to their performance.

Destructive or unhealthy: When an individual wants to win at the cost of others, as a big shopkeeper may work in way that petty shopkeepers lose business.

Social competition: This type of competition is encouraged in democratic societies. Abilities and potentials of individuals are recognized. Social competition can be there between the groups of males and females.

Economic competition: Competition in production, distribution and consumption of goods. It can be at individual level or at group level for higher salary, promotion or increment.

Political competition: Political competition among various political parties to rule the nation is always there. Even competition exists among various nations to become world power.

Cultural competition: This is basically to preserve a culture. There is competition between the natives and the invaders to preserve the culture of each like the British and the Indians.

Importance of Competition

There is a strong association between social status and competition as competition assigns a respective position to an individual.

Competition makes an individual, society and nation progressive.

Competition plays an important role in the development of personality of individuals.

Competition gives rise to innovations and inventions.

Opportunities are provided to the persons with abilities through competitions.

Competition makes people to work hard to acquire better status.

Competition provides motivation to achieve. It helps us to dig deep and find resources and explore ways to succeed.

Competition is related to growth and poverty reduction, Effective competition leads to productivity.

CONFLICT

It is incompatibility between two or more forces or characters. It is an essential part of human growth. Conflict occurs when an individual or a group strives to gain certain reward at the cost of others.

It is a universal process found in every society at one time or the other. It is an important and inevitable aspect of the human life.

Types of Conflict

Interpersonal conflict: Conflict between two individuals may occur simply because they are different from one another. They have different personalities, choices and views. We have varied personalities, which usually lead to incompatible choices and opinions.

Intrapersonal conflict: Conflict within an individual is called intrapersonal conflict. It takes place within the person's mind involving the individual's thoughts, values, principles and emotions. Interpersonal conflict maybe trivial like whether or not to go for a walk and maybe a major one like deciding a career path. The major conflicts can be quite difficult to handle and may lead to restlessness and anxiety, or even cause depression. In such occasions, it would be best to seek a way to let go of the anxiety through communicating with other people.

Intragroup conflict: It is a type of conflict among individuals within a group. The incompatibilities or misunderstandings among these individuals and disagreements and personal differences in views and ideas are the causes of intragroup conflict.

Intergroup conflict: Misunderstanding among different teams within an organization leads to intergroup conflicts. For example, marketing department of an organization is in conflict with the customer care department due to the varied sets of goals and interests of both the groups. Conflict among political parties, social groups or economic classes is quite common.

International conflict: Conflict between two nations can be there because of religion, economy or ideology.

Class conflict: Social classes may have conflicts because of having opposing interests.

Racial conflict: Because of differences in physical features conflicts arise. Some races may have a sense of superiority over others and may try to suppress those causing conflicts.

Caste conflict: Some caste groups have a sense of superiority and inferiority of high and low or holy and unholy, leading to conflicts.

Positive Impact of Conflicts

Conflicts help in personal growth or developing healthy relationships with others. In addition, coming up with adjustments is necessary for managing this type of conflict.

When conflicts within self get resolved, a person finds himself out of the situation, and becomes more empowered as a person. Thus the experience evoked a positive change, which helps in personal growth.

Conflict can be helpful in decision-making, which will eventually allow individuals attaining their objectives.

Conflict may ultimately lead to peace through victory of one contestant over the other.

Conflicts may lead to development of non-violent ways for resolving crisis.

Conflict may lead to renewal of relationships and creativity when brought into open for resolution.

Negative Impact of Conflicts

The degree of conflict may disrupt harmony among the members and may require mediation or guidance from a third party to settle the issue.

Conflicts may lead to stress interfering in communication and coordination, diverting attention from the goal.

Conflict may lead to damaging of social relations creating winners and losers, which maybe the source of conflicts in future.

Conflicts between management and workers may lead to material losses.

Conflicts can be the source of confusion and social disorder, if not resolved.

ACCOMMODATION

Accommodation is a balance between individuals and groups. It is natural and an unconscious process, which results from conflicts. Accommodation is not required if there are no conflicts. It is a continuous, social process that resolves conflicts and helps in adjustment to the physical and social environment. Conflicts need to be resolved to have a peaceful life as these can be exhausting. Accommodation is universal, continuous and combination of both the emotions of love and hatred.

Every individual makes efforts to accommodate himself in the society. There are different ways of accommodation.

Pressure: The conflict may force a weak person to surrender or continue conflict till defeated by the powerful person. Admittance of defeat by weaker person who gets overpowered by other person as the conflict is between two persons with unequal strength.

Compromise: If conflict is there between persons who are equally strong, both of them may patch up by making some adjustment.

Mediation: Conciliation or meditation between two parties is done by a third party. Many international disputes are settled through mediation. At times contestants do not find any way out to resolve the conflicts, and the mediator plays an important role to resolve those conflicts by suggesting basis for settlement and even common meeting ground. The decision is not forced upon the individuals by the mediator.

Consensus: The conflicting parties reach a consensus and promise not to behave in a manner to offend the other party and expect the same from the other party. Thus, conflicts are resolved through consensus.

Tolerance: There is no possible way of settling the conflicts, so avoidance is considered to be the best way. Groups must bear with each other. No compromise is made by either of the parties. Best example of consensus is existence of capitalist and communist parties in a state.

Sublimation: This is conviction on the part of one of the conflicting parties by adopting new point of view. It occurs not only in religious parties but also commonly seen among political, social and economic parties.

Rationalization: It is justifying one's action or behaviour by rationalization, involving plausible excuses or explanations for one's failure, instead of accepting his limitations or inability that the real defect is in one's own self. It happens even with groups who justify their actions with excuses.

Superordination and subordination: It involves superordination and subordination. Perfection is achieved by making the position of an individual fixed in an organization to avoid conflicts. In all the political parties, there are leaders and followers. Leaders give orders and followers obey them. This happens in slavery and caste system also. Slaves accept that they are meant to serve their owners by accepting their inferiority. Similarly, in caste system, certain castes are considered to be higher to other castes and there are no conflicts and their positions are accepted by them that the existing order of things is regarded as the only proper one.

ASSIMILATION

It is process by which an individual acquires social and psychological characteristics of group. So, assimilation is also social adjustment. Assimilation requires more fundamental changes than accommodation. Assimilation is basically identifying with another group by bringing about the changes and becoming similar to that group. Thus, one group acquires the culture of other group.

Characteristics of Assimilation

It is an unconscious process: Usually people discard their cultural habits unconsciously and adopt the cultural habits of others. It may take decades to adopt the culture of other groups.

It is a two-way process: Assimilation involves giving and taking. It is also called *acculturation*, which means taking cultural elements from the group in contact and incorporating them into their own culture. Contact between two groups leads to the exchange of cultural traits and essentially it has impact on both, though the culturally 'weaker' group adopts most of the traits from the culturally 'stronger' group. The culturally stronger group is much more stronger than the culturally weaker group. For instance, the Indians adopted a lot of cultural elements of the Britons during the British rule.

It is a very slow process: Assimilation does not occur all of a sudden. It takes very long to bring about the changes in culture and personalities of individuals. It requires continuous and direct contacts between the groups.

Assimilation is not confined to single field only. It embraces various components of the life style. The term *assimilation* is generally applied to explain the fusion of two distinct cultural groups but this process is not limited to a particular field. There is gradual assimilation of children into adult society and husband and wife, with no similarities, start their marital life and develop likeness and unity.

It is a complex phenomenon: Assimilation is not a simple process as it is not related to a particular aspect of life, rather it happens in various aspects of life such as religious, educational, political and cultural.

Factors Affecting Assimilation

Tolerance: It is the basic requirement for assimilation. Tolerance helps people to come together and accept the cultural differences.

Equality: Equal economic opportunities and equality in wealth distribution is mandatory to create favourable conditions for assimilation.

Cultural similarities: Homogeneity in culture of groups brings them together.

Intimate social relations: Frequent close contacts and communication between two groups are required for initiation of process of assimilation.

Education: Education is an important factor for bringing about awareness among people, so very helpful for assimilative process.

Isolation: Communication gap leads to isolation hindering the process of assimilation.

Racial differences: Physical traits like skin colour, features make people look different and these differences are obstacles for assimilation.

Cultural differences: Difference in language, religion and traditions constituting culture may hinder assimilation.

Prejudice: It may create social distance between two groups creating barriers in assimilation.

Basically assimilation is important, which can be initiated by eliminating barriers between the groups.

ISOLATION

Lack of interaction or social contact is isolation. Isolation can be of individuals or groups.

Types of Isolation

Spatial: Distances are maintained between the groups or individuals and lack of contact leads to isolation. As criminals are excommunicated or are socially isolated they get deprived of social interaction, which may lead to aggression and antisocial behaviour.

Organic: Certain factors like deafness or blindness are also responsible for social isolation of individuals. Though these are not created by human beings but these factors deprive these individuals of common leading to isolation.

REVIEW QUESTIONS

1. What are the various causes of conflicts?
2. Write short notes on the following:
   a. Assimilation
   b. Accommodation
   c. Isolation

UNIT - 5

POPULATION

CHAPTER

14

Society and Population

LEARNING OBJECTIVES

After reading this chapter the learner should be able to

- Comprehend of the causes of growing population in India.
- Know about the effects of population explosion.

As the human population continues to grow, the pressure on the earth's resources also increases. However, the rate of population growth varies across the world as it depends on the stage of the demographic transition a region is passing through.

The population in some countries has already completed the demographic transition from high fertility rates to high death rates and their population has already started declining. Most of these developed countries are in Europe and North America. On the other hand, most of the developing countries are still in the intermediate phase of low mortality and high fertility rates and they are witnessing rapid population growth. These countries are already stressed and more people will affect the ability of the governments to provide the basic necessities like food, shelter and clothing. As the natural resources are already under a severe strain in these countries and the environment is degrading fast, they are not in a position to cope with the increasing burden of people.

POPULATION GROWTH

It is defined as the average annual percent change in the population size due to a surplus or deficit of births over deaths and the balance of migrants entering and leaving a country. The rate may be positive or negative. It depends on fertility rate, mortality rate, immigration and emigration.

The human population has been growing for centuries and scholars, particularly philosophers, have been trying to understand trends to know how it will change over time. They have also been observing and analysing its impact on the natural resources to help establish a linkage since long. The common view till 1700 was that the size of the population will be maintained as human knowledge and moral constraint will enable society to generate the necessary supplies required for survival by exploiting the abundant natural resources. In case the population started growing rapidly, the people would start exercising sexual restrain to contain the growth.

EFFECTS OF POPULATION EXPLOSION

Population explosion is intricately linked to socioeconomic development and it affects the quality of life and environment. It increases pressure on land, water and natural resources and impedes development as a large part of the gross domestic product has to be utilized for expanding the basic amenities, housing, energy, transport, water supply, health and education infrastructure to meet the ever-growing requirement. Some major consequences of rapid population growth are food shortage, loss of biodiversity, air and water pollution, unemployment and overcrowding.

Environmental Degradation

The accelerated exploitation of the fast-depleting natural resources and, in turn, the increased production of wastes degrades the environment. It leads to loss of forest cover and biodiversity and causes air, water and noise pollution. The increasing human activity results in build-up of greenhouse gases and thus, hastens the process of climate change.

POLLUTION

Air pollution: The increase in vehicular traffic and industrial activity causes air pollution and noise pollution. The use of fossil fuel for producing energy and burning of biomass also adds to air pollution.

Water pollution: Release of effluents from industries causes water pollution. Unscientific disposal of urban waste is also a major source of water contamination along with accelerated soil erosion due to loss of green cover. The rivers are getting polluted as they do not have the carrying capacity to carry such heavy load of pollutants.

Noise pollution: Ever-increasing volume of vehicular traffic and industrial activity not only pollute air and water but also cause noise pollution.

Poverty: The communities dependent on natural resources suffer as their livelihoods are threatened due to environmental degradation. It also affects agriculture production due to over exploitation of land and water resources.

Urbanization: As livelihood becomes unsustainable and pressure on land increases more and more people are forced to move to towns and cities to eke out a living. It leads to unbridled and unplanned urbanization and mushrooming of slum colonies, lacking basic facilities like drinking water, proper housing and sanitation. The concrete jungle is expanding as cities and towns spill over into the green belts.

Deforestation: Large-scale mining, unbridled urbanization, diversion of land for commercial and industrial activity are taking a heavy toll of the green cover. As per the 2011 report of the Forest Survey of India the total forest cover of the country is 692,027 km^2, which is only 21.05% of the geographical area of the country, and far below the norm of 33% laid down under the national forest policy.

Overcrowding: Large concentration of population over relatively a small area has led to overcrowding in India. The trains, buses, streets, markets are overflowing with people. We find long queues everywhere, be it a railway or bus ticket counter, a bank or any other public service outlet. The religious shrines are also overcrowded. Some of the cities have become very congested due to very high density of population.

Unemployment and underemployment: Population growth is aggravating the problem of unemployment as jobs are not being generated at the same pace. The well-educated youths are being forced to take of lower levels of jobs which are leading to large-scale underemployment. It is making youth vulnerable to exploitation and causing frustration among them.

Industrialization: More and more in industries are coming up though industrialization is the part of development of a country.

Social evils: Many social evils as prostitution, crime, female foeticide and drug addiction arise because of population explosion. The large-scale migration of people to cities and increasing frustration among youth due to unemployment are the main factors behind it.

REVIEW QUESTIONS

1. What is meant by population explosion? Write in detail about causes of population explosion.
2. How does growing population affect various aspects of life?

CHAPTER

15

Population of India

LEARNING OBJECTIVES

After reading this chapter the learner should be able to

- Have knowledge about the demography of India.

The population of India increased by a whopping 181 million over the 2001–2011 decade. As per the latest headcount, the total population was 121,01,93,422 as on 1 March, 2011 up from 102,87,37,436 in 2001.

It is the second most populous country after China (134.10 crore). Comparative data reveals that the population gap between India and China was fast decreasing and it has come down from 238 million in 2001 to 131 million in 2011. Further, the gap with the USA, the third most populous country, increased from 741 million to 902 million. Projections made by the United Nations (UN) indicate that India will overtake China by 2028 when its population will cross 145 crore. India's population will continue to grow until the middle of the century, while China's will start slowly declining from 2030.

Table 15.1 shows that the average annual growth rate increased steadily from 0.56 during the 1901–1911 decade to 2.22 in 1971–1981. Thereafter, it started declining and came down to 2.16 per cent during the 1981–1991 period and further to 1.97 per cent in 1991–2001 period. The annual growth rate for India during 2001–2011 is still lower at 1.64 per cent but much higher than the overall growth rate of 1.23 per cent of the world population. On the other hand, China registered the third lowest annual growth rate of 0.53 per cent. In fact, as per UN projections China's population will start declining from 2030.

In absolute terms the number of net additions to the population declined for the first time during 2001–2011. While the population increased by 18,23,16,397 during 1991–2001, the figure for 2001–2011 was 18,14,55,986, a decline of 8,60,411. Thus, 2001–2011 is the first decade (with the exception of 1911–1921) when less population has been added compared to the previous decade and percentage decadal growth witnessed the sharpest reduction of 3.90 percentage points (from 21.54 to 17.64 per cent) since Independence.

Table 15.2 shows that Uttar Pradesh remains the most populous state as per the 2011 Census with a headcount of 19,95,81,477, and it now accounts for 16.49 per cent of the country's population as against 16.16 per cent in 2001. It is followed by Maharashtra with a population of

TABLE 15.1 Population Growth Since 1901

Census Year	Population	Decadal Growth (%)	Average Annual Growth Rate (%)	Growth Over 1901
1901	23,83,96,237			
1911	25,20,93,390	5.75	0.56	5.75
1921	25,13,21,213	–0.31	–0.03	5.42
1931	27,89,77238	11.00	1.04	17.02
1941	31,86,60,580	14.22	1.33	33.67
1952	36,10,88,090	13.31	1.25	51.47
1961	41,92,34,771	21.64	1.96	84.25
1971	54,81,59,652	24.80	2.20	129.94
1981	68,33,29,097	24.66	2.22	186.64
1991	84,64,21,039	23.87	2.16	255.05
2001	1,02,87,37,463	21.54	1.97	331.52
2011	1,21,01,93,422	17.64	1.64	407.64

Source: Registrar General and Census Commissioner, India, Census of India 2001: Series-I: India, General Population Tables (2006): Table A-2 and 2011 Census Data.

11,23,72,972 but its share has dwindled from 9.42 to 9.29 per cent. Bihar is not far behind with 10,38,04,637, 8.58 per cent of the total population, up from 8.07 per cent in 2001.

The percentage decadal growth declined during 2001–2011 compared to previous decade for all states, except Tamil Nadu, Chhattisgarh and Puducherry (Table 15.3). The fall was highest in case of Delhi (26 percentage points), followed by Haryana (8.53) percentage points), Rajasthan (6.97 (percentage points) and Maharashtra (6.74 percentage points), and lowest for Andhra Pradesh (3.5 percentage points). There was an increase in case of Tamil Nadu (3.9 percentage points), Puducherry (7.1 percentage points) and Chhattisgarh (4.3 percentage points).

Nagaland is the only state which recorded a negative growth rate over the decade, while Goa, Lakshadweep, Kerala and Andaman and Nicobar registered a single-digit decadal growth.

Density of population up from 325 in 2001 to 382 person per sq. km in 2011, an increase of 57 (17.5%). Delhi with 11,320 person per sq. km is the most densely inhabited city, followed by Chandigarh (9,258). The state of Arunachal Pradesh has the minimum density with 17 persons per sq. km.

The government has under national population policy (NPP) adopted in 2000 set a goal of stabilizing the country's population by 2045. However, the projected population of 110.7 crore by 2010 has been exceeded by 11 crore in 2011 itself. As such there is little possibility of the country achieving the target set under NPP.

Sex Ratio

The overall sex ratio (number of female per 1000 males) increased by 7 points from 933 in 2001 to 940 in 2011. This is the highest sex ratio recorded since Census 1971 and a shade lower than 1961. Increase in the sex ratio has been observed in 29 states/UTs but three major states (J&K, Bihar and Gujarat) have shown a decline as compared to Census 2001.

TABLE 15.2 Population of States and Union Territories (Census 2011)

Rank 2011	State/Union Territory	Population as per 2011 Census	% to the total 2011	% to the total 2001	Rank 2001
1	Uttar Pradesh	19,95,81,477	16.49	16.16	1
2	Maharashtra	11,23,72,972	9.29	9.42	2
3	Bihar	10,38,04,637	8.58	8.07	3
4	West Bengal	9,13,47,736	7.55	7.79	4
5	Andhra Pradesh	8,46,65,533	7.00	7.41	5
6	Madhya Pradesh	7,25,97,565	6.00	5.87	6
7	Tamil Nadu	721,38,958	5.86	6.07	7
8	Rajasthan	6,86,21,012	5.67	5.49	8
9	Karnataka	6,11,30,704	5.05	5.14	9
10	Gujarat	6,03,83,628	4.99	4.93	10
11	Orissa	4,19,47,358	3.47	3.58	11
12	Kerala	3,33,87,677	2.76	3.10	12
13	Jharkhand	3,29,66,238	2.72	2.62	13
14	Assam	3,11,69,272	2.58	2.59	14
15	Punjab	2,77,04,236	2.29	2.37	15
16	Chhattisgarh	2,55,40,196	2.11	2.03	17
17	Haryana	2,53,53,081	2.09	2.06	16
18	Delhi	1,67,53,235	1.38	1.35	18
19	Jammu & Kashmir	1,25,48,926	1.04	0.99	19
20	Uttarakhand	1,01,16,752	0.84	0.83	20
21	Himachal Pradesh	68,56,509	0.57	0.59	21
22	Tripura	36,71,032	0.30	0.31	22
23	Meghalaya	29,64,007	0.24	0.23	23
24	Manipur	27,21,756	0.22	0.22	24
25	Nagaland	19,80,602	0.16	0.19	25
26	Goa	14,57,723	0.12	0.13	26
27	Arunachal Pradesh	13,82,611	0.11	0.11	27
28	Puducherry	12,44,464	0.10	0.09	28
29	Mizoram	10,91,014	0.09	0.09	30
30	Chandigarh	10.54,686	0.09	0.09	29
31	Sikkim	6,07,688	0.05	0.05	31
32	Andaman and Nicobar	3,79,944	O0.03	0.03	32
33	Dada and Nagar Haveli	3,42,853	0.03	0.02	33
34	Daman and Diu	2,42,911	9.92	0.02	34
35	Lakshadweep	64,429	0.01	0.01	35
36	**India**	**1,21,01,93,422**			

Source: Registrar General and Census Commissioner, India, Census of India 2011 Census Data.

TABLE 15.3 Comparison of Percentage Decadal Growth (2001–2011 and 1991–2001)

S. No.	State/Union Territory	Growth rate 2001–2011 (%)	Growth rate 1900–2001 (%)
1	Uttar Pradesh	20.1	25.9
2	Maharashtra	16.0	22.7
3	Bihar	25.1	28.6
4	West Bengal	13.9	17.8
5	Andhra Pradesh	11.1	14.6
6	Madhya Pradesh	20.3	24.3
7	Tamil Nadu	15.6	11.7
8	Rajasthan	21.4	28.4
9	Karnataka	15.7	17.5
10	Gujarat	19.2	22.7
11	Orissa	14.0	16.3
12	Kerala	4.9	9.4
13	Jharkhand	22.3	23.4
14	Assam	16.9	18.9
15	Punjab	13.7	20.1
16	Chhattisgarh	22.6	18.3
17	Haryana	19.9	28.4
18	Delhi	21.0	47.0
19	Jammu and Kashmir	23.7	29.4
20	Uttarakhand	19.2	20.4
21	Himachal Pradesh	12.8	17.5
22	Tripura	14.7	16.0
23	Meghalaya	27.8	30.7
24	Manipur	18.7	24.9
25	Nagaland	–0.5	04.5
26	Goa	9.2	15.2
27	Arunachal Pradesh	11.1	27.0
28	Puducherry	27.7	20.6
29	Mizoram	22.8	28.8
30	Chandigarh	17.1	40.3
31	Sikkim	12.4	33.1
32	Andaman and Nicobar	6.7	26.9
33	Dada and Nagar Haveli	55.5	55.7
34	Daman and Diu	53.5	59.2
35	Lakshadweep	6.5	17.3
36	India	17.6	21.5

Source: Compiled by authors using official data from India's 2001 and 2011 Census.

Kerala with a sex ratio of 1,084 and Puducherry (1,038) are the top two states with highest sex ration, while Daman and Diu (618), and Dadra and Nagar Haveli (775) are at the bottom.

Population (0–6 years) 2001–2011

The number of children in the 0–6 years age group declined by 3.08 per cent, indicating a fall in the fertility levels. However, the decline is higher in case of female (–3.80%) compared to male (–2.42%), which is a matter of concern.

	2001	2011	Difference	Growth (%)
Persons	16,38,37,395	15,87,89,287	–50,48,108	–3.08
Males	8,50,08,267	8,29,52,135	–20,56,132	–2.42
Females	7,88,29,128	7,58,37,152	–29,91,976	–3.80

The total number of children in the age group of 0–6 is 158.8 million. The maximum number of children was in Uttar Pradesh (29.7 million), followed by Bihar (18.6 million), Maharashtra (12.8 million), Madhya Pradesh (10.5 million) and Rajasthan (10.5 million) constitute 52% children in the age group of 0–6 years. The proportion of child population (0–6 years) to total population has come down to 13.1 per cent from 15.9 per cent in 2001. The decline has been to the extent of 2.8 points.

The child sex ratio (CSR) has declined from 927 in 2001 to 914 in 2011. The CSR of 914 at the all India level is the lowest since independence (Table 15.4).

Increasing trend in the CSR (0–6 years) was recorded in Punjab, Haryana, Himachal Pradesh, Gujarat, Tamil Nadu, Mizoram and Andaman and Nicobar Islands. However, the situation was quite bad in rest of the country and all the remaining 27 states and union territories saw a decline in the CSR over Census 2001.

Mizoram with a CSR of 971 and Meghalaya (970) are the top two states with the highest CSR, and Haryana (830) and Punjab (846) are at the bottom with lowest CSR. Lahaul and Spiti (Himachal Pradesh) with a CSR of 1013 and Tawang (Arunachal Pradesh) with 1,005 are the top two districts and Jhajjar (774) and Mahendragarh (778), both in Haryana, are at the bottom.

Literacy

The literacy rate has gone up from 64.83 per cent in 2001 to 74.04 per cent in 2011 showing an increase of 9.21 percentage points.

The literacy rate for males is 82.14 per cent and females 65.46 per cent. The increase in literacy rate of 11.79 in females is higher than 6.88 per cent in males. It is encouraging to note that out of total of 217,700,941 literates added during the decade, females (110,069,001) outnumbered male (107,631,940).

TABLE 15.4 Child Sex Ratio (0–6 years)

	2001		2011	
	Population (0–6 years) in million	**Proportion (0–6 years) in%**	**Population (0–6 years) in million**	**Proportion (0–6 years) in%**
Males	85.0	51.89	82.9	52.24
Females	78.8	48.11	75.8	47.76

The gap of 21.59 percentage points recorded between male and female literacy rates in 2001 has reduced to 16.68 percentage points in 2011 but it was higher than the target of 10 percentage points set by the Planning Commission by the year 2011–2012. Another remarkable feature was that there was a decline of 31,196,847 among illiterates and the female (17,122,197) contributed more to the decline compared to males (14,074,650).

The literacy rate improved significantly and it increased to over 85 per cent in Kerala, Lakshadweep, Mizoram, Tripura, Goa, Daman and Diu, Puducherry, Chandigarh, NCT of Delhi and Andaman and Nicobar Islands, meeting the target set by the Planning Commission for 2011–2012.

Further, Chandigarh, Nagaland, Mizoram, Tripura, Meghalaya, Lakshadweep, Kerala and Andaman and Nicobar Islands have achieved the target of reducing the gap in the literacy rate in male female to 10 percentage points.

Kerala (93.91%) and Lakshadweep (92.28%) are the two top states with the highest literacy rate, and Bihar (63.82%) Arunachal Pradesh (66.95%) are at the bottom. Serchhip (Mizoram), 98.76 per cent, and Aizawl (Mizoram), 98.50 per cent, are the two top districts and Alirajpur (Madhya Pradesh), 37.22 per cent, and Bijapur (Chhattisgarh), 41.58 per cent, are at the bottom.

Census 2011 Highlights

POPULATION		
Persons 1210.2 million	Males 623.7 million	Females 586.5 million

The percentage decadal growth rate has come down in the six most populous states of the country, as compared to 1991–2001.

Uttar Pradesh (25.85% to 20.09%)	Maharashtra (22.73% to 15.99%)
Bihar (28.62% to 25.07%)	West Bengal (17.77% to 13.93%)
Andhra Pradesh (14.59% to 11.10%)	Madhya Pradesh (24.26% to 20.30%)

The number of states and union territories registering a growth of less than 1.5 per cent per annum has gone up to 15 from just only 4 during the previous decade.

REVIEW QUESTIONS

1. Write down about the thickly populated states in India.
2. What do you mean by the density of population?

CHAPTER

16

Population Growth and Malthusian Theory

LEARNING OBJECTIVES

After reading this chapter the learner should be able to

- Gain knowledge about Malthusians and neo-Malthusians theory of population.

As the human population continues to grow, the pressure on the earth's resources also increases. However, the rate of population growth varies across the world as it depends on the stage of the demographic transition a region is passing through.

The population in some countries has already completed the demographic transition from high fertility rates to high death rates and their population has already started declining. Most of these developed countries are in Europe and North America. On the other hand, most of the developing countries are still in the intermediate phase of low mortality and high fertility rates, and they are witnessing rapid population growth. These countries are already stressed and more people will affect the ability of the governments to provide the basic necessities like food, shelter and clothing. As the natural resources are already under a severe strain in these countries and the environment is degrading fast, they are not in a position to cope with the increasing burden of people.

POPULATION GROWTH

It is defined as the average annual percent change in the population size due to a surplus or deficit of births over deaths and the balance of migrants entering and leaving a country. The rate may be positive or negative. It depends on fertility rate, mortality rate, immigration and emigration.

The human population has been growing for centuries and scholars, particularly philosophers, have been trying to understand trends to know how it will change over time. They have also been observing and analysing its impact on the natural resources to help establish a linkage since long. The common view till 1700 was that the size of the population will be maintained as human knowledge and moral constraint will enable society to generate the necessary supplies required for survival by exploiting the abundant natural resources. In case the population started growing rapidly, the people would start exercising sexual restrain to contain the growth.

MALTHUSIAN THEORY

All this changed after British philosopher and economist Thomas Robert Malthus (1766–1834) came out with a theory based on radically different idea that the human population will always tend to outgrow the food production and that no uplift of the people is possible without controlling reproduction.

In an article titled 'An Essay on the Principle of Population', published in 1798, he observed that food output did not grow at an exponential rate like population and, instead, it would increase rather slowly. With an exponential growth rate the population will increase more rapidly in proportion to the increasing total size. For instance, a population of 2 will increase to 4, 8, 16, 32, 64, and so on, at an exponential growth rate. On the other hand, the food production is likely to grow in arithmetic progression 1, 2, 3, 4, 5, 6, 7, 8 and so on. Consequently, he predicted that the gap in population size and food availability will widen progressively and it would lead to a situation where humans would have no resources to survive on. He maintained that controls on population growth would be imperative to avoid such a catastrophe. It was the first systematic analysis of population and resources, which changed the views of several contemporary thinkers.

Malthus predicted that uncontrolled population growth would result in depletion of resources and lead to problems like increased pollution, overcrowding and unemployment. With availability of limited food there would be starvation, diseases, crime, poverty and eventually war. The populations would continue to grow until reversed by disease, famine, war or calamity. The consequent increase in death rates and decline in birth rates would help control the human population and bring it to a manageable size for which available resources would suffice. A section of the population has always been poor and miserable and that this was unlikely to change and this eventually helped in containing population growth.

Malthus was of the view that size of the population should be kept down to manageable levels through preventive and positive checks. His emphasis was on exercise of moral restraint, and delaying marriage was one such proposition put forward by him. Men should marry later in life than usual and only when they are capable of supporting a family. He was not in favour of birth control within marriage.

Assumptions

Malthus based his theory on the assumption 'passion between the sexes is an inevitable phenomenon' and thus the population will multiply at a rapid rate, and this tendency cannot be checked by progress in science and society. The basic urge to procreate will prevail.

Further, the population will grow much faster, if not controlled, than the power of the earth to provide subsistence for man and it would outstrip food supply. He believed that with land being a limited resource, the agriculture production cannot be increased at the desired rate and eventually the nature will take over and population will be controlled through high mortality caused by disease, food shortage, starvation, natural calamities and war.

According to Malthus, man was by nature a lazy animal and he would procreate as long as the requisite supply of food was available. A shortage in food supply due to increasing population might lead to an increase in agriculture production but the man will return to his complacent ways after the needs are met. A cycle of overpopulation and food shortage will be triggered and suffering due to limited food supply would persist.

WAS THOMAS MALTHUS CORRECT?

Thomas Malthus's theory was controversial and generated considerable debate at that time and it led to a new intellectual discourse among demographers and social thinkers. It is still debated and population theorists like Paul Ehrlich, Julian Simon, Garrett Hardin and Barry Commoner have carried on with the discussion in the second half of the twentieth century.

Malthus attracted criticism for the bleak future he predicted for the humankind and some later thinkers found fault with his theory. They maintained that he failed to foresee the role technology could play in influencing the growth of population and improving the quality of life. The food supply has indeed kept pace with the growth of population as advances in technology have made it possible to produce more food. Even a developing country like India with second highest population in the world has generated a food surplus using technology.

There are others who believe that fundamentally the Malthusian theory is correct because the prosperity of people depends on the resources available in this world. His prediction has come true at least in parts of the world as evident from outbreaks of famines, epidemics, natural disasters and wars, and they have been reeling under extreme poverty and hunger due to excessive population.

However, it is most effectively countered by the theory of democratic transition as per which the affluence and education bring down the birth rate. In fact, the world population is actually stabilizing because of the demographic transition.

KARL MARX VERSUS THOMAS MALTHUS

The strongest opposition to the Malthusian theory came from Karl Marx (1818–1883) who maintained that poverty was the result of unjust practices resorted by a capitalist who exploited the manpower. Marx who founded Communism believed that in a capitalist economy where the worker is paid less than the value of his productivity and deployment of machinery also leads to unemployment. The surplus earned by the capitalist is the gap between the productivity of workforce and the wage level. The injustice is perpetrated on the poor and their exploitation under the capitalist system.

NEO-MALTHUSIANS

According to neo-Malthusians, population problem as it presently exists in underdeveloped countries is an inevitable result of the reproductive behaviours of man. An American biologist Paul Ehrlich published book titled *Population Bomb* in 1968 in which he observed that the population growth was overtaking the growth of agricultural production and the capacity for renewal of earth's resources. He saw a 'certain' demographic disaster in the making due to food shortages and disease. He predicted that food shortages in the developing world would lead to geopolitical crises that could even trigger a thermonuclear war.

Critics termed Ehrlich's work as a mere repetition of Malthus's nineteenth-century argument. Economist Julian Simon maintained that the impact of population pressure on natural resources was overstated and that the relationship between population growth and economic growth was not as simple as Ehrlich believed. The people were the ultimate resource and they had the capacity to develop high-yielding crops, build inexpensive housing and provide other necessities to the growing populations.

REVIEW QUESTIONS

1. Write about Malthusian theory and population growth.
2. Write short notes on the following:
   a. Neo-Malthusians
   b. Views about Malthusian theory

CHAPTER

17

Population Explosion and Its Implications

LEARNING OBJECTIVES

After reading this chapter the learner should be able to

- Have knowledge about population explosion.
- Get acquainted with causes and effects of population explosion.

The rapid growth of human population has been a matter for concern as every new addition puts more pressure on the fast depleting natural resources. The population growth peaked in 1970 and it has started declining slowly in recent years. However, the annual growth rate of 1.18 per cent is still too high for comfort. In fact, as per the latest projections (2013) of the United Nations (UN), the global population will increase by about 40 per cent to reach 9.6 billion by 2050. Thus, almost 2.5 billion people will be added over the next three and half decades. The world population may reach 11 billion by the end of the century (2100).

The maximum numbers are coming from countries with high-fertility rates, mainly in Africa and Asia. The UN has identified high-fertility countries, which include 39 countries in Africa, 9 in Asia, 6 in Oceania and 4 in Latin America, where most of the growth will take place. The population bomb is really exploding in Nigeria, which is expected to add 730 million people, to acquire a size of 914 million by 2100 if the current trend continues.

According to the UN Population Division in the best-case scenario it will take 13 years to add the 8th billion, 18 years to add the 9th billion and 40 years to reach the 10th billion.

Rapid population growth leads to a range of socio-economic problems like unemployment, poverty, tardy economic development, poor health care and education facilities. In short, it affects the quality of life.

POPULATION EXPLOSION

A sudden spurt in growth of population is called population explosion. It is a curse for a developing country like India, which supports 17 per cent (121 crore) of the world's population with only 2.3 per cent of the world's area. It is the second most populous country after China and it is expected to become the most populous country by 2028, with a population of 145 crore.

The growing number of people will put further pressure on the already scarce land and other natural resources and strain the basic amenities. The population density of India has more than doubled over the past four decades, an indication of the increasing pressure on land and other resources.

Table 17.1 will give the idea about the increasing population density of India.

The trend shows that the population density will be almost 500 persons per sq. km over the next two decades. The individual population of some of its states is equal to the total population of many countries. For example, the population of Uttar Pradesh (a state in India) almost equals the population of Brazil.

TABLE 17.1 Density of Population

Year	Number of Persons per sq. km
1901	77
1911	82
1921	81
1931	90
1941	103
1951	117
1961	142
1971	177
1981	216
1991	267
2001	325
2011	382

REASONS FOR POPULATION EXPLOSION

A high birth rate, declining death rate an immigration from the neighbouring countries like Bangladesh, Nepal and Sri Lanka are the main reasons for rapid population growth in India.

High Birth Rate

Poverty: India still has a large number of poor people living under poverty line who consider having a large number of children an advantage as the family will have more earning hands.

Low status of women: Many families are obsessed with male child and they go on producing children till they have a son as women are still not treated at par with men. Even most of the women want to have a son instead of a daughter because it adds to their status in the society.

Illiteracy: Literacy and education, especially of females, affect fertility through greater access and practice of contraception. They are well aware of the benefits and need to have a smaller family size. Research studies have shown that women who get married after matriculation tend to have smaller families than illiterate women. Though Right to Education Act has been implemented by the government, but still many children, especially girls, do not go to school. The literacy rate has gone up from 64.83 per cent in 2001 to 74.04 per cent in 2011 but the literacy rate for females is still 65.46 per cent.

Religious beliefs and traditions: Some religions are opposed to family planning as children are considered to be the gift of god. In some societies traditionally, last rites are performed by sons only so it becomes mandatory to have a son.

Early marriage: As per the law the minimum age for marriage of girls is 18 years and boys 21 years. Child marriage has been prohibited by law but still many parents, particularly in the rural areas, marry their children at a tender age because of poverty, illiteracy and traditions. Early marriage increases reproductive span of women.

Death Rate

Improvement in health care: Advances in medical science and improvement in health infrastructure, better sanitation, awareness, education and increasing number of working women is leading to a decline in death rate.

MCH (Maternal and Child Health) services: Availability of maternal and health services including immunization and family planning services is helping to control maternal mortality rate and infant mortality rate, which are important indicators of a country's health.

National Health Programmes: The implementation of various national health programmes to contain and stamp out communicable and non-communicable diseases have helped in controlling many diseases such as smallpox, polio, plague, malaria and leprosy.

Migration: Migration of people also adds to the population. A large number of people from Bangladesh, Sri Lanka, Nepal and Tibet have migrated and settled in India. The entry of crores of illegal migrants from the neighbouring countries has significantly increased the population size.

EFFECTS OF POPULATION EXPLOSION

Population explosion is intricately linked to socioeconomic development and it affects the quality of life and environment. It increases pressure on land ,water and natural resources and impedes development as a large part of the gross domestic product has to be utilized for expanding the basic amenities, housing, energy, transport, water supply, health and education infrastructure to meet the ever-growing requirement. Some major consequences of rapid population growth are food shortage, loss of biodiversity, air and water pollution, unemployment and overcrowding.

Environmental Degradation

The accelerated exploitation of the fast depleting natural resources and, in turn, the increased production of wastes degrades the environment. It leads to loss of forest cover and biodiversity and causes air, water and noise pollution. The increasing human activity results in build-up of greenhouse gases and thus hastens the process of climate change.

Pollution

Air pollution: The increase in vehicular traffic and industrial activity causes air pollution and noise pollution. The use of fossil fuel for producing energy and burning of biomass also adds to air pollution.

Water pollution: Release of effluents from industries causes water pollution. Unscientific disposal of urban waste is also a major source of water contamination along with accelerated soil erosion due to loss of green cover. The rivers are getting polluted as they do not have the carrying capacity to carry such heavy load of pollutants.

Noise Pollution: Ever-increasing volume of vehicular traffic and industrial activity not only pollute air and water but also cause noise pollution.

Poverty: The communities dependent on natural resources suffer as their livelihoods are threatened due to environmental degradation. It also affects agriculture production due to over exploitation of land and water resources.

Urbanization: As livelihood becomes unsustainable and pressure on land increases more and more people are forced to move to towns and cities to eke out a living. It leads to unbridled and unplanned urbanization and mushrooming of slum colonies, lacking basic facilities like drinking water, proper housing and sanitation. The concrete jungle is expanding as cities and towns spill over into the green belts.

Deforestation: Large-scale mining, unbridled urbanization, diversion of land for commercial and industrial activity are taking a heavy toll of the green cover. As per the 2011 report of the Forest Survey of India, the total forest cover of the country is 692,027 sq. km, which is only 21.05 per cent of the geographical area of the country, and far below the norm of 33 per cent laid down under the national forest policy.

Overcrowding: Large concentration of population over relatively a small area has led to overcrowding in India. The trains, buses, streets and markets are overflowing with people. We find long queues everywhere, be it a railway or bus ticket counter, a bank or any other public service outlet. The religious shrines are also overcrowded. Some of the cities have become very congested due to very high density of population.

Unemployment and underemployment: Population growth is aggravating the problem of unemployment as jobs are not being generated at the same pace. The well-educated youths are being forced to take up lower-level jobs, which is leading to large-scale underemployment. It is making youth vulnerable to exploitation and causing frustration among them.

Industrialization: More and more industries are coming up. Industrialization is part of a country's development.

Social evils: Many social evils such as prostitution, crime, female foeticide and drug addiction arise because of population explosion. The large-scale migration of people to cities and increasing frustration among youth due to unemployment are the main factors behind it.

REVIEW QUESTIONS

1. What are the various causes of population explosion in India?
2. How does population explosion affect the various aspects of life?

UNIT - 6

FAMILY AND MARRIAGE

CHAPTER

18

Family Welfare Programme

LEARNING OBJECTIVES

After reading this chapter the learner should be able to

- Know about the objectives of the National Family Welfare Programme.

Family planning programme was launched as early as 1952 to control the rapid growth of population in India. The United Nations recognized family planning as a human right much later in 1968. Family planning means planning the number of children a couple will have along with the space between the birth of two offsprings.

Family planning clinics were already working in India since 1931 and the clinic approach was adopted during the First and Second Five Year Plans. However, it was replaced by 'Extension and Education Approach' in 1961. The Family Planning Programme was widened to cover nutrition, maternity and child care to make it more acceptable and effective. In 1976, the Government of India announced the National Population Policy with the objective of reducing the fertility period of reproductive couples. The policy discouraged child marriages and increased the minimum age of marriage to 18 years for girls and 21 years for boys. The family planning programme was implemented on a war-footing during the emergency period (1975–77). Compulsory sterilization was introduced and nearly 10 million men and women were sterilized. Financial initiatives were given to the people for undergoing sterilization.

However, the programme was virtually rejected by the people in view of the target-oriented approach of field functionaries and use of coercive methods in the implementation of the programme during the period 1976–77 in some areas. The government took notice of the resentment among the people and made it clear that there will be no compulsion or pressure in the implementation of the programme. It was made a part of the part of 'Family Welfare' relying solely on mass education and motivation. The government renamed the programme as Family Welfare Programme in 1977 and put emphasis on the health and welfare of the family as a whole.

The aim of the Family Welfare Programme was to bring down the birth rate, infant mortality rate in addition to reducing the average size of the family.

OBJECTIVES OF THE FAMILY WELFARE PROGRAMME

- Proper spacing between pregnancies
- Limiting the number of children
- Avoiding unwanted births and bring about wanted births
- Premarital counselling
- Marriage counselling
- Sex education
- Genetic counselling
- Preparing for parenthood
- Facilitating adoption
- Services to unwed mothers
- Teaching home economics and nutrition
- Prevention of sexually transmitted diseases.

IMPLEMENTATION OF THE FAMILY WELFARE PROGRAMME

Family welfare programme was launched in 1977 purely on a voluntary basis, with emphasis on promoting spacing methods, securing maximum community participation and promoting maternal and child health care. The objective was to arrest population growth by bringing down the birth rate, besides promoting child and maternal health to help reduce the infant mortality rate (IMR). The Universal Immunization Programme (UIP) was launched in 1985 to protect the infants and children from preventable diseases by providing universal coverage of infants and pregnant women with immunization against identified diseases through vaccination. Mahila Swasthya Sanghs (MSS) were constituted for effective community participation in the programme) at the village level in 1990–91. MSS consisted of 15 persons, out of which 10 represented various social segments in the community. The remaining were village-level functionaries like the adult education instructor, primary school teacher, anganwadi worker, traditional birth attendant and others associated with women's welfare activities. In 1992–93, the UIP was strengthened and upgraded to Child Survival and Safe Motherhood (CSSM) Project. The focus was on sustaining the high immunization coverage level under UIP, and augmenting activities under oral rehydration therapy (ORT) to prevent child mortality due to diarrhoea. It also included administration of vitamin A drops as a prophylactic measure for the prevention of blindness in children and control of respiratory diseases. Safe motherhood was an important component, under which traditional birth attendants were imparted training and provided aseptic kits for conducting deliveries. Further, to deal with obstetric emergencies, the first referral units were strengthened.

STRATEGIES OF THE FAMILY WELFARE PROGRAMME

The basic objective of the programme was to improve the quality of life by restricting the size of the family and stabilize the growing population by bringing down the fertility rate.

Various strategies were adopted to make it a people-centred programme by merging various social welfare programmes into it.

Accessibility to information and services for contraception with a wide range of choices.

Bringing down the infant mortality and maternal mortality rates through improved maternal and child health services.

Various activities under the National Family Welfare Programme include the following:

Immunization: Vaccination of children to protect them from 12 diseases such as tuberculosis, tetanus, polio, diphtheria, whooping cough, hepatitis, measles mumps rubella, typhoid, pneumonia and meningitis. To improve the immunization services Accredited Social Health Activists (ASHA) workers have also been involved.

Contraceptives: All the health centres provide contraceptives free of cost to reduce the unmet need of the eligible couple. Contraceptives are also commercially sold by different manufacturing companies without getting any subsidy from the government.

Condoms: Apart from health centres, condoms are also distributed through various shops and condom-vending machines under free distribution scheme and at subsidized rate under social marketing scheme.

Oral contraceptive pill (OCPs) and emergency contraceptive pills (ECPs): OCPs are also distributed through free distribution scheme and at subsidized rate through social marketing scheme. The ECPs are used to prevent unwanted pregnancy after an unprotected sexual intercourse. These can also be used in case of sexual assault, rape or contraceptive failure. But ECPs should be taken on prescription of medical practitioners.

Intrauterine devices (IUD): IUDs with at least 5 and 10 years of duration are provided under free distribution scheme only.

Permanent or Terminal Methods

Eligible couples are also offered permanent or terminal methods of family planning like tubectomy and vasectomy free of cost under the National Family Welfare Programme. Rather to encourage people to adopt permanent methods of family planning, there are many schemes by the government to benefit those who undergo these procedures like special leave, increment in salary or promotion in the job.

Tubectomy: Various procedures like mini lap tubectomy and laproscopic tubectomy are conducted for women as a permanent method of family planning. Laproscopic tubectomy is considered to be safer and quicker method than others.

Vasectomy: This is a permanent family planning method for males and there are two types of procedures done for vasectomy: conventional vasectomy and no-scalpel vasectomy. The new method, no-scalpel vasectomy, has no complications at all, so this method is being promoted for the participation of males in the family welfare programme.

Indian Government has been investing more and more money in the family welfare programme through five-year plans and the programme seems to be having greater acceptance from 1990s onwards. Still, this programme could not achieve expected results.

REVIEW QUESTIONS

1. Write short notes on the following:
   a. Objectives of the National Family Welfare Programme
   b. Spacing methods of family planning
   c. Permanent methods of family planning

CHAPTER

19

The Institution of Family

LEARNING OBJECTIVES

After reading this chapter the learner should be able to

- Have knowledge about family.
- Get acquainted with the general characteristics of family.

Marriage is an institution developed over a period of time but families existed in some form or the other from the primitive times. The institution of family is as old as humankind and it is the basic unit of the human society. The institution of marriage emerged gradually probably from some kind of pairing of men and women. There is not much evidence regarding the origin of marriage as it evolved over the years at different times in different cultural milieus. It emerged and existed in varied forms. As marriage is cultural-specific, the rules and regulations differ from one culture to another.

FAMILY

Family is the basic unit of the society and typically consists of parents and their children, the prime function of which is to provide for its members. Family structures of some kind are found in every society.

The word family has been derived from the Latin word *familia,* meaning *household; household servants,* which came from another Latin term *famulus*, which refers to a group having parents, children and servants. Initially, the word family referred to the servants of a household and subsequently to both the servants and the descendants of a common ancestor. It was only in the later half of the 17th century (around 1667) that the term was used specifically for the group of persons consisting of parents and their children.

Relationships in a Family

The associations among members give rise to different relationships like husband and wife, parents and children and brothers and sisters.

Family remains the pivot of contemporary life despite the changing pattern of life and increasing personal mobility. Families offer companionship, security and a measure of protection against an often uncaring world. However, the family structure has undergone significant changes in recent years. The types of families that have evolved as a result of the change in structure and inherent dynamics of family system have been discussed hereunder.

General Characteristics of a Family

A family has the following common features:

Mating Relationship

A mating relationship is a sine qua non (essential) precondition for the establishment of a family. The mating relationship maybe permanent or temporary but there can be no family without it. The social institution of marriage, which mostly forms the basis of mating relationship, also lends a distinct character to the family, depending on the fact whether the marriage is monogamous or polygamous or polyandrous.

System of Nomenclature

Each family is identified by its distinctive system of nomenclature which is essentially an arrangement for reckoning descent of the members. In matriarchal society it is traced from the mother and in patriarchal society from the father. In some societies, it is traced from both father and mother.

Economic Provision

Every family has a provision to cater to the economic needs of its members. It is mostly the head of the family who strives to make the economic provisions but all the members share the provisions available to the family.

Common Habitation

All the family members live together and share a common home. The residential set-up provides the space and environment for producing offsprings and raising them.

Distinctive Features

Besides general characteristics, a family also has some distinctive features.

Universality

Family is the basic unit existing universally in all types of groups, associations and institutions in the human society from the ancient times to the present modern across the world. Every human being is or has been a member of some family.

Formative Influence

A family has its own distinctive customs, traditions, culture, value system and norms which have a great influence on its members. All the members of the family religiously observe family norms which inculcate social qualities like obedience, tolerance, sympathy, love, affection and sacrifice and also help in developing the personality of the children who learn the first lessons in socialization in the family. Thus, the family exerts a deep influence on the members and plays a vital role in shaping their personality and character.

Emotional Bonding

A family is held together by emotional ties and serves as emotional anchor for the members. The overwhelming affection, love, sympathy and compassion find expression in mating, procreation and parental care.

Limited Size

As a primary group the size of the family is quite limited as it generally comprises persons who are born in it and are closely related by blood relationship or brought in through adoption. A family consisting of father, mother and their children is small and it facilitates strong relationships among the members.

NUCLEAR POSITION

Family occupies a nuclear position in the social structure. Every part of social organization emanates from the family, the hub of all human activities, and the social structure is built around it.

Responsibilities of the Members

The members are responsible towards the family and they have a deep sense of obligation to the family as a whole. They share the pleasure and pain and face the problems and hardships together and discharge their duties and responsibilities unitedly. In a way the members have unlimited responsibilities as they make sacrifices and toil for their families throughout their lives.

Social Regulations

The customs, traditions, culture, value system and regulations are important as they shape the personality and character of the members. The family set-up ensures that they never violate the rules and regulations and that is why families are hard to break up.

Permanent and Temporary in Nature

As an institution, family is a very stable and permanent structure. After marriage some members, a son or a daughter, may leave but the family is never completely dissolved and it continues to exist in some form or other. As an association, it is temporary and transitional and undergoes variations in its structures and functions from time to time.

REVIEW QUESTIONS

1. What do you mean by family and what are the characteristics of a family?
2. What are the distinctive features of family and responsibilities of its members?

CHAPTER

20

Functions of Family

LEARNING OBJECTIVES

After reading this chapter the learner should be able to

- Get acquainted with the functions of family.
- Know about the changing trends of families.

As a core of all social groups, the institution of family performs diverse functions in human society. Sociologists have classified these functions into different categories.

The functions of family have been broadly divided into two categories: *essential* and *nonessential*.

ESSENTIAL FUNCTIONS OF FAMILY

Essential functions, also termed *primary functions,* are those which are fundamental in nature and no other institutions can perform these functions as successfully as a family. They are essential for the continued existence of the family. The essential functions include stable satisfaction of sex needs, production and rearing of children, provision of home and socialization.

Stable Satisfaction of Sexual Needs

This is the most important essential function which the family has been performing since the dawn of human civilization. Gratification of sexual desire of the members in a stable and legitimate way is the primary function of family. It regulates the sexual behaviour of its members through the institution of marriage which is designed to provide a long-term partnership between spouses. Satisfaction of sex needs in a desirable way helps to avoid sex rivalry and ensures normal development of personality.

Procreation and Rearing of Children

Perpetuation of family is vital and this makes procreation the most important function and the family provides the legitimate basis for production of children. Further, it also provides institutional framework for the upbringing of children who are incapable of surviving on their own. It provides food, shelter, affection, protection and security to all its members and plays a vital role in the socialization of a child. Family takes care of the needs of the children and affords them an atmosphere congenial for proper development of their personality.

Provision of Home

The members of a family need a home to live happily in a peaceful and secure environment. Thus, providing a home for common living becomes another important function of the family. It is only in a home that children are born and brought up. Besides, a home also provides emotional and psychological support to the members and also the space for recreation.

Socialization

The family is the primary agent of socialization and plays a vital role in instilling values, morals, norms and ideals of the society among children. An individual imbibes the culture and traditions of the society and develops his personality and character while living in family.

NON-ESSENTIAL OR SECONDARY FUNCTIONS OF FAMILY

Along with the essential functions family also performs some nonessential functions. These functions are considered secondary as they are also performed simultaneously by other social institutions in family. Functions pertaining to economic, religious, educational, health and recreational activities fall in the nonessential category.

Economic Functions

Being both a production and a consumption unit, the family has been performing several economic functions since ancient times. Basic economic needs of members like food, clothing and housing used to be met by the family which was a self-sufficient unit. In recent times, the economic functions of family is considerably modified and taken over by other agencies. It has been reduced mainly to a consumption unit and it does not produce anything. The members of family go out for working. It still performs some economic functions of purchasing, protecting and maintaining property and distributing it among the members.

Educational Functions

As a primary educational institution, family provides a platform for the formal learning of children and helps members acquire knowledge and skills and learn the tricks of trade. The mother is the first teacher of a child who imbibes virtues of moral values, discipline, obedience and manners through informal education in the family. Most of the educational functions of family have been taken over by school, college and universities these days but the family still continues to play a vital role in imparting the first lessons in primary education to its members.

Religious Functions

Family is the centre for imparting training customs, rituals and other religious activities. The members who follow a particular religion offer prayers together, celebrate religious ceremonies and observe various rites and rituals collectively. The religious beliefs, traditions and values are passed down from the parents to the children, from one generation to another. In the modern era secularism is becoming the order of the day, diluting the religious activities in the family but they still play an important role in shaping the religious attitude of the members.

Health-Related Functions

Family is the basic unit for providing nutritive diet and health care to the members. It also looks after the sick and aged persons of the family. Thus, for building a healthy society, proper health education of the husband and wife who manage the household is essential. The mothers, in particular, have a major role in improving the health of the infants through breastfeeding and adopting other recommended practices.

These days, major health functions are performed by hospitals and unlike past, the delivery of a baby is also conducted in hospitals by trained medical staff.

Recreational Function

The family is the hub of recreational activities as all the festivals, feasts, ceremonies and other such occasions are celebrated by the members together. It serves as a recreation club for the members who engage themselves in various activities for entertainment.

CHANGING TRENDS AND ASSOCIATED ISSUES

Working Parents and Single Parent

Economic compulsions make it incumbent on both the parents to work. While it helps achieve financial stability, the children suffer as the parents are not able to give time. It is leading to problems, particularly, in the nuclear families as the children are neglected.

The number of single parent is increasing due to increasing number of divorces and live-in relationships. Raising a child is not easy for a single parent.

The age of marriage is increasing and many parents have offsprings late in the life. They face problems in raising children as they lack the vigour and also face financial problems at times.

REVIEW QUESTIONS

1. What are the important functions of a family?
2. Explain the health-related functions of a family in detail.

CHAPTER

21

Types of Families

LEARNING OBJECTIVES

After reading this chapter the learner should be able to

- Get familiar with various types of families.
- Know about advantages and disadvantages of nuclear and joint families.

ON THE BASIS OF SIZE

Families are of two types on the basis of their size: nuclear family and joint family.

Nuclear Family

A family comprises husband, wife and children. These are small families mostly in urban areas with working women.

Advantages of Nuclear Families

- Families are small and require less space.
- Family members enjoy privacy.

Disadvantages of Nuclear Families

- Children mostly get neglected as there are no elderly people to take care of them when both husband and wife go out to work.
- Elderly people are deprived of care and attention as youngsters move out to work in other cities.

Joint Family

It is an extended family consisting of at least three generations, such as children, parents and also grandparents. These are large families as sons continue to live with their parents even after marriage. At times even uncles, aunts and their offsprings are also part of the joint family.

These are large units as the members live under one roof and have common kitchen and hold common property.

Advantages of Joint Families

The joint family system, which has been prevalent in India since ancient times and has been in vogue to the present day, has many advantages.

Stable economic unit: A joint family is more stable than a nuclear family and ensures economy in expenditure because of their large size as purchases are made jointly and no individual has the rights over assets. The head of the family controls everything and the members have no option but to be spendthrift.

Division of labour: Joint family benefits from proper optimum of labour as work is distributed among the members on the basis of age, sex and ability. Every phase of each member is taken care of by the family which is practically managed as a cooperative unit.

Social and economic security: Joint family structure provides social and economic security to the members and widows, orphans, physically challenged and other weak members are well looked after. The basic needs such as food, shelter and clothing are provided irrespective of the fact that a member is contributing to the earnings of the family or not.

Socialization and social control: The joint families are the training schools for socialization and promote social virtues like discipline, cooperation, selfless service, sacrifice and obedience among members under the care and control of elders.

The control exercised by elders prevents the younger members from indulging in undesirable and antisocial activities. The members learn subordinate their individual interests to the group interests. The elders keep a close watch on every individual and as such the chances of deviant behaviour are minimal.

Perpetuation of cultural traditions: They also provide a good platform for recreation as all the festivals and ceremonies are celebrated jointly. In the process, they ensure continuance of cultural traditions. They help promote community living and discourage individualistic tendencies.

Disadvantages of Joint Families

The joint family system has over the years lost many of its advantages due to socioeconomic changes. In fact, in recent times many of its disadvantages have come to fore which was leading to the disintegration of the age-old system.

Affects personality development: The younger members do not get adequate exposure as the elders take all the responsibilities; consequently, they do not get enough opportunities to develop their personality and talent. Thus, the joint family system does not provide an environment conducive to the growth of individuals who lack initiative.

Lack of privacy: Couples, particularly the newlyweds, lack privacy due to presence of other members and there is little scope for free interaction between husband and wife. The parents are not able to give adequate personal attention to their children who are invariably more attached to their grandparents.

Undermine productivity: As the basic needs of all the individuals are met they do not feel any need for engaging in productive activity and make savings for the future. They lack initiative for hard work and do not take interest to earn their livelihood. The joint families are not good for promoting productivity and accumulation of capital as there is no commensurate reward for hard work.

Squabbles and litigation: Disputes over property and internal dissensions lead to frequent squabbles and often to litigation. At times the members, particularly women, fail to make adjustment which mars peace and happiness in the family.

Thwart social change: The joint families are orthodox and perpetuate traditions. Their conservative environment is a great hindrance to social change. Even desirable changes required to keep pace with the changing times are resisted by members.

Low status of women: The joint family system is disadvantageous to women who have to live under the control of father as a child, husband during youth and son during old age. They do not enjoy equal status and have no right over family property.

TYPES OF FAMILIES BASED ON MARRIAGE

Families have been classified on the basis of the type of marriage as under:

Monogamous Family

In this family, the married couple and their children stay. It is formed on the basis of a single marriage.

Polygamous Family

When one male or a female marries more than one female or male, a polygamous family is formed. This type of family is neither common in modern societies, nor it bears the approval of the society.

ON THE BASIS OF DESCENT AND AUTHORITY

On the basis of authority that a person holds in a family, families are of two types: matriarchal families and patriarchal families.

Matriarchal Families

The mother heads the family and holds major authority. Sociologists maintain that matriarchal family is the earliest form of family structure, though it is now quite rare and found only among some tribes in India. The mother and her family stay together and the family name of the mother's side is given to her children. The husband comes to stay with the wife's relatives. The women play a major role in decision-making in the mother-dominated families.

Matrilineal

The descent is matrilineal and the lineage is traced through the mother. The daughters inherit the property from their mother and they succeed them and the sons.

Matrilocal

Some societies are matrilocal, as per marriage and family customs the newly married couple stays with the woman's parents.

Patriarchal Families

The father or the eldest male is the head of the family and holds authority. The wife goes to stay with her husband and his relatives after their marriage. Children carry father's name. The father holds the authority to take major decisions.

Patrilineal

The patriarchal families are patrilineal and the lineage is traced through father. The sons inherit the property of their father and in some societies the eldest son enjoys special rights and status. The men exercise all the authority and take decisions in the male-dominated family structure.

Patrilocal

Patriarchal societies are patrilocal as the newly married couple stays with the husband's parents on the following basis:

ON THE BASIS OF COMMUNITY

On this basis, the families can be either rural type or urban type.

Rural Family

A rural family may be defined as a group of persons constituting a family which lives in an agricultural or open country environment. It is generally characterized by a relatively early age of marriage, high birth rate and low divorce rate. These families are orthodox in outlook and religiously follow the traditions.

Urban Family

Such families generally dwell in big cities and townships. They are characterized by their small size, higher age of marriage, progressive outlook, freedom of women and are less rooted in traditions.

ON THE BASIS OF ORIENTATION AND PROCREATION

On this basis, families are of two types:

Family of Orientation

It is the family in which an individual takes birth and lives along with his parents and siblings.

Family of Procreation

It is the family which an individual establishes or adopts after marriage. It comprises the individual, his wife and the children produced after marriage. An individual can be a member of either or both types of families.

ON THE BASIS OF RELATIONSHIPS

A family can be either consanguineous or conjugal by classification based on relationships.

Consanguineous Family

It refers to families in which blood relatives stay together. Besides husband and wife, other blood relatives are also part of the family.

Conjugal Family

A conjugal family consists of husband, wife and their children. It is smaller in size and less stable. Marriage-based relations have more importance in such families and they are strongly bound emotionally.

ON THE BASIS OF RELIGION

On this basis families can be classified into three main groups in India: Hindu, Muslim and Christian families.

Hindu Family

In a Hindu family marriage is considered to be compulsory and an important ritual. Generally, it is a monogamous family with a joint family system, although the trend is now shifting from the joint family system towards the nuclear family. Culture and traditions have important roles to play in day-to-day life.

Muslim Family

Marriage is considered compulsory in Muslim families also. These are mostly polygamous families. They are quite orthodox and women are strictly kept in veil and granted very little freedom.

Christian Family

Monogamous families are a tradition in the Christian community also. Generally, nuclear families are found and boys and girls are given equal importance and freedom.

REVIEW QUESTIONS

1. How can you classify the families on various basis?
2. Differentiate between nuclear family and joint family.

CHAPTER

22

Laws Governing Marriage in India

LEARNING OBJECTIVES

After reading this chapter the learner should be able to

- Get familiar with various laws related to marriage.
- Know the various grounds for the dissolution of marriage.

The cultural and religious diversity makes it imperative for a country like India to have different marriage laws for various communities. The various laws governing marriages are Hindu Marriage Act, 1955, Muslim Marriage Act, Sikh Marriage Act (Anand Marriage Act), Christian Marriage Act and Parsi Marriage and Divorce Act, 1936.

There is also a complete freedom for an individual to get married with any other individual of opposite gender irrespective of factors like religion and culture so long as the legal condition of minimum prescribed age for marriage is met. Apart from community-specific laws, a Special Marriage Act, 1954, and a Foreign Marriage Act, 1969, are also in force under which marriage can be solemnized and registered, irrespective of the religion of the partners involved. The Special Marriage Act is meant for those getting married within the country and the Indian citizens who may marry abroad can get it registered under Foreign Marriage Act.

The Indian citizens have a choice between their respective religion-based and community-specific marriage laws and the common law of civil marriages. The specific laws are generally described as *personal laws* which take care of all the related issues right from rules to be followed for marriage, eligibility for marriage, procedure to be followed, documentation and also the guidelines to settle disputes in case of a marital discord.

THE SPECIAL MARRIAGE ACT

The Special Marriage Act is an optional law, an alternative to each of the various personal laws, available to all citizens. Religion of the parties intending to enter wedlock is immaterial under the Act and one can marry under its provisions both within and outside one's community.

Any person, whichever religion he or she professes, can marry under provisions of the Special Marriage Act either within his or her community or in a community other than his or her own, provided the conditions for marriage laid down in it are met. The Act also provides the facility of turning an existing religious marriage into a civil marriage by registering it.

The Special Marriage Act does not by itself or automatically applies to any marriage; it can be voluntarily opted for by the parties in preference to their personal laws. It contains its own elaborate provisions on divorce, nullity and other matrimonial causes.

The Special Marriage Act provides an alternative to the Hindus, Buddhists, Jains and Sikhs for marriages solemnized within these four communities to the Hindu Marriage Act 1955. Similarly, Muslims also have a choice between their personal law and the Special Marriage Act.

However, the Indian Christian Marriage Act, 1872, lays down that all Christian marriages shall be solemnized under its own provisions and as such the availability of the Special Marriage Act for a marriage where both the parties are Christians remains unresolved.

In Muslim law marriage with all first cousins both on the paternal and maternal sides is permitted, and the personal law of the Jewish and Bahai communities also allows marriage with a cousin. Under Christian law, marriage with a cousin may be permitted by a special dispensation by the Church.

However, the Special Marriage Act, 1954, does not allow marriage with any first cousin and it is in accord with the Hindu Marriage Act, 1955, in this regard. Relaxation of the net of prohibited degrees on the ground of custom is also permissible under that Act. The Hindu Marriage Act also disallows marriage with second cousins (father's first cousin's children) due to the restriction known as *sapinda* relationship [Section 5(v)], but the Special Marriage Act does not place any second cousin in its two lists of prohibited degrees in marriage.

The Law Commission has in its 212th report considered the conflicts and their legal consequences and suggested certain amendments to the Special Marriage Act law to resolve the conflicts of its provisions with various personal laws. A Hindu, Sikh, Buddhist or Jain can marry a second cousin under the Special Marriage Act, though it is not allowed under the Hindu Marriage Act. Whereas the Muslim personal law permits such a marriage unconditionally, on the contrary, a Muslim cannot marry a first cousin under the Special Marriage Act. Members of all those other communities whose personal law allows marriage with a first cousin are also in the same position as the Muslims.

However, not many opt for the Special Marriage Act as the linkage between civil marriages and the applicable law of succession deprives them of their laws of succession although personal laws of succession are given lot of importance by Muslims and Parsis.

There are other issues which inhibit marriages under the Special Act as it contains its own elaborate provisions for divorce, making the marriage null and void and other matrimonial remedies. As such the Indian Divorce Act 1869 would not be applicable to the marriages governed by it. There is a further conflict with the Indian Divorce Act which lays down that it will apply even if only one party is a Christian.

Interreligious Marriages

Certain interreligious marriages are allowed as per the Muslim law but to be governed by its own provisions. A man can marry a chaste woman of the communities believed to be Ahl-e-Kitab (Arabic word which refers to people of the book or people who were given previous scriptures by Almighty God). It includes Christians and Jews and followers of any other monotheistic faith and as such Muslim law permits interreligious marriages.

However, there is no conflict with the Special Marriage Act as the Muslim Law does not require that such a marriage must take place under its own provisions.

The Indian Christian Marriage Act (1872) has areas of conflict with the Special Marriage Act, as it lays down that the marriage of a Christian with a non-Christian must also be solemnized under this Act. The Special Marriage Act says that any two persons, irrespective of their religions, can marry in accordance with its provisions. Thus, there is a conflict in respect of marriage of a Christian with a non-Christian.

Foreign Marriage Act

Under the Foreign Marriage Act, 1969, a marriage can be solemnized between an Indian and a foreigner and also between two Indians, in any foreign country irrespective of their religions and personal laws. Such marriages are held in the presence of consular and diplomatic staff appointed by the Government of India for the purpose.

The Act prohibits marriage within prohibited degrees of marital relationship but does not specify any such list. It only says that the expression 'degrees of prohibited relationship' will have the same meaning as under the Special Marriage Act, 1954. Thus, all first cousins are deemed to be within the prohibited degrees of marriage under the Act.

However, it specifically mentions both custom and personal laws of the parties as grounds for relaxation of the rule of prohibited degrees in marriage as per the Hindu Marriage Act, 1955.

The Hindu Marriage Act is applicable to all Hindus, Buddhists, Jains and Sikhs.

The prescribed minimum age of bride and bridegroom at the time of marriage is 18 years and 21 years, respectively.

Void and Voidable Marriages

A marriage is held void under any of the following conditions:

- Either party has a spouse living at the time of marriage, meaning that the marital status of the parties has to be single.
- Parties are within prohibited relationship.
- Parties are sapindas of each other.

A marriage may be annulled by a decree of nullity on any of the following grounds:

- Impotency of spouse.
- Spouse is incapable of giving a valid consent to marriage because of unsound mind or suffering from mental illness. Person is as unfit for marriage to such an extent that there is inability for the procreation of children or he or she suffers from recurrent attacks of any form of insanity.
- The consent for marriage was taken by force or by fraud.
- The woman was pregnant from some other person at the time of marriage.

Provisions regarding restitution of conjugal rights and grounds for divorce: Court may pass a decree for restitution of conjugal rights when either spouse has withdrawn from the society of the other without any reasonable excuse.

Divorce can be obtained under the Act on the following grounds:

- In case of voluntary sexual intercourse with any person other than the spouse after the marriage.
- Cruelty.
- Either spouse deserting the other for a continuous period of not less than two years.
- A spouse ceased to be a Hindu.

- Incurably of unsound mind or suffering from virulent and incurable form of leprosy or venereal disease in a communicable form.
- If either spouse renounces the world by entering any religious order.
- If a spouse is not heard of as being alive for a period of seven years or more.
- The couple has not stayed together for a period of one year or more after decree of judicial separation or no restitution of conjugal rights for a period of one year or more after decree for restitution of conjugal rights.

Wife can also seek divorce on the following grounds:

- The husband has been guilty of rape, sodomy or bestiality after marriage.
- There has been no resumption of cohabitation for one year or more since passing of decree for maintenance against husband.
- Marriage of girl was solemnized before 15 years of age and she has repudiated the marriage, after attaining the age of 15 years but before 18 years.

A petition for divorce may be filed after one year of the marriage and in exceptional circumstances a petition may be allowed to be presented before one year.

Remarriage After Divorce

A person can remarry after a marriage has been dissolved by a decree of divorce and there is no right of appeal against the decree or the time for such a right of appeal has expired without an appeal having been presented or an appeal has been presented but has been dismissed.

Muslim Marriage Law

Husband is entitled to have as many as four wives as marriage is considered to be only a civil contract and not a sacrament under the Muslim Marriage Act.

There are some essential requirements for a valid marriage under Muslim Law:

- Proposal and acceptance. As the Muslim marriage is in the nature of contract, it requires free and unfettered consent of the parties. The consent should not be vitiated by the fraud or force.
- Capacity to contract marriage. If a party is a minor, he or she should be represented by the guardian.

Marriage among the persons related by affinity (is not considered to be legal as marrying a foster mother and others related through such foster mother).

Marrying a fifth wife, a woman undergoing iddat, woman contracting a second marriage during the subsistence of the first marriage and absence of proper witness also makes a marriage illegal. Marriage with a pregnant women and own divorced wife are also prohibited

An obligation of *mahr* is imposed upon the husband at the time of the marriage as a mark of respect to the wife. Mahr can be in cash or in kind and till it is paid the widow has the right to retain possession of her husband's property.

A Muslim woman has to undergo Iddat, the period of chastity, on the death of her husband or divorce and during this period she is not permitted to marry another man. The period is 3 months if the marriage is dissolved by divorce, and 4 months and 10 days in case of the death of husband.

The right of custody of child, called Hizanat, of the mother is not lost by divorce. The mother is entitled to the custody of her male child until he has completed the age of seven years and in case of the daughter, until she is married.

Christian Marriage Law

Marriage under the Christian Law is in the nature of a contract and hence there should be a free and voluntary consent between the parties. The Indian Christian Marriage Act, 1872, is applicable to marriage of persons professing Christian religion.

Under the Act, marriage between parties falling within the prohibited degrees of relationship under Section 19 is not allowed.

When there is a minor involved the consent of father or guardian is necessary. There is no legal impediment for marriage between a Catholic and a Protestant. The law regarding divorce, judicial separation and allied matters is contained in the Indian Divorce Act, 1869. Either spouse can seek divorce on the following grounds:

- Impotency at the time of marriage and institution of the suit.
- Parties falling within the prohibited degree of consanguinity or affinity.
- Either party suffering from a mental disorder or a lunatic or idiot at the time or marriage.
- If the spouse of either party was alive at the time of marriage and the said marriage had taken place by fraud or by force.

Under Section 10, the wife can seek dissolution of marriage on the following grounds:

- Having sexual relation with a relative.
- Having another wife.
- Husband has been held guilty of rape, sodomy or bestiality and cruelty;
- Adultery associated with desertion without any substantial cause for two years or more.

Sikh Marriage Act

The Anand Marriage Act governing the Sikh marriages was enacted in 1909 to recognize marriages solemnized as per Sikh rites (anand karaj).

The Act was amended in 2012 as Sikhs faced problems abroad as their marriages were registered under the Hindu Marriage Act, even as they identified themselves as Sikhs. The amended law will enable the Sikhs to register their marriages under the Anand Marriage Act instead of the Hindu Marriage Act.

Anand Karaj (Punjabi) is the Sikh marriage ceremony, meaning 'Blissful Union' or 'Joyful Union', which was introduced by Guru Amar Das.

Parsi Marriage and Divorce Act, 1936

The Parsi Marriage and Divorce Act, 1936, governs the matrimonial relations of Parsis. The word *Parsi* is defined in the Act as a person who professes the Zoroastrian religion. Every marriage as well as divorce under this Act is required to be registered in accordance with the prescribed but failure to fulfil requirements does not make a marriage invalid. The Act provides only for monogamy. The scope of certain provisions of the Act has been enlarged through the Parsi Marriage and Divorce (Amendment) Act, 1988, to bring them in line with the Hindu Marriage Act.

However, there is no codified matrimonial law in India for the Jews till now as they are very few in number. They are governed by their religious laws. Marriage by Jews is regarded as a sacred relation between two persons, and not a civil contract. Divorce can be sought through the courts on grounds of adultery or cruelty.

REVIEW QUESTIONS

1. Write short notes on the following:
   a. Special Marriage Act
   b. Muslim marriage law

CHAPTER

23

The Institution of Marriage

LEARNING OBJECTIVES

After reading this chapter the learner should be able to

- Have knowledge about the various types of marriages prevalent in India.
- Appreciate the advantages and disadvantages of polygamy and monogamy.

Marriage has almost universally been defined as a formal union of a man and a woman, recognized socially and by the law by which they are bestowed the status of husband and wife. Sociologist Max Weber defined marriage as a 'stable sexual relationship' allowed and legitimized by the larger kin group and used to determine rules about property rights for children. Marriage regulates sex life of human beings and provides stability to relationship between men and women.

Legally speaking, marriage is a contract between a man and a woman. Entering into a marriage contract creates new rights and obligations and changes the legal status of both parties, the husband and the wife. The institution of marriage is vital to preserve the family unit and morals and civilization.

The children born through the wedlock of husband and wife along with other close relatives constitute a family. It is united by moral, legal, economic, religious, and social rights and obligations.

FORMS OF MARRIAGE

There are two basic forms of marriage, monogamy and polygamy, the latter is further classified into polygyny and polyandry.

Monogamy

This is the usual form of marriage in the modern world which is recognized and acceptable in most of the societies. In this form of marriage, one man has marital relations with one woman at a given period of time. The one-to-one relationship between a man and a woman is the most modern civilized way of living. Only in the case of death of the spouse or one of the partners seeking divorce, they can establish such relationship with other persons. However, one cannot have two or more wives or two or more husbands.

Of late some countries have legalized marriages between persons of same sex adding a new dimension to the institution. Women can marry women and men can marry men in such countries.

Often a marriage between persons of same sex is not long lasting as it does not achieve stability, and after certain period the tendency is to end their relationship and remarry. If second marriage is also monogamous as then, it is referred to as sequential monogamy, serial monogamy or remarriage.

In monogamy, the marriage partners give undivided attention to maintain and strengthen the marital bond. It is the most straightforward and uncomplicated way of marital life.

Advantages of Monogamy

There are several advantages of monogamy:

Better adjustment: In this form of marriage men and women have to live with one partner only and this leads to better adjustment between them.

Greater intimacy: A small family with limited number of persons ensures more love and affection, leading to friendly and deep relations.

Better parenting and socialization of children: In a monogamous marriage, there is a greater possibility of the partners getting more involved in bringing up the children. The parents are fully devoted to and focus undivided attention on the children and they are well looked after. There is no jealousy between the parents in looking after their children.

Happy family: Family happiness is maintained under monogamy which is usually not the case in other forms of marriage as conjugal bliss destroyed because of jealousy and other reasons. Thus, in this form of marriage, the family is defined as a happy family.

Equal status to woman: In this form of marriage, the status of a woman in family is equal. If the husband works, the wife looks after the household duties or both of them work for strengthening the economic condition of the family.

Equalitarian way of living: It is only under the monogamous way of living that husband and wife can have an equalitarian way of life in which the husband and wife not only share the familial role and obligations but also make joint decisions. They become equal partners in the process of decision-making.

Population control: Some sociologists have the view that monogamy helps in controlling the population as single wife can have a limited number of children.

Better standard of living: It is possible to maintain the standard of living with limited resources as a small family entails less expenditure.

Respect to parents: The parents receive love, affection, respect and care from their children under monogamy.

Law is in favour: Monogamy is legally sanctioned form of marriage, while some other types of marriage are prohibited.

More cooperation: In such a family, there is close bond between the couple and the chances of conflict are reduced and there is much more cooperation between husband and wife.

Stability: It is a more stable form of marriage. There is a smooth and better division of property and other assets after the death of parents.

Disadvantages of Monogamy

It also has some disadvantages such as the following:

Maladjustment: Monogamy is a marriage between one husband and one wife. If the partner is not of choice, there is a mismatch and the life loses its charm. They have to adjust between themselves throughout life but nowadays they are resorting to divorce which has its own implications.

Monopoly: According to Sumner and Keller, monogamy is monopoly. Wherever there is monopoly, there is bound to be both 'ins and outs'.

Childlessness: If one of the partners has some problem, the couples cannot have children. They have to suffer from childlessness.

Adultery: When they do not get partner of their own choice they have sexual relations with other people. This also promotes the social evils like prostitution.

Polygamy: Unlike monogamy, a man is married to more than one woman or a woman has more than one husband in this form of marriage. These two forms of marriages are further classified as polygyny and polyandry.

Polygyny: A man marries more than one woman in this form of marriage and it is being practised in India by some tribal communities, such as Nagas and Gonds.

Often two sisters are married to one man and it is than termed as a *Sororal Polygyny*. The word *sororal* is derived from Latin word *soror* which means sisters.

In case the wives are not related as sisters the marriage is termed as non-sororal polygyny.

Polygamy

Polygamy is illegal for the Hindus in India and some other religious groups under the Hindu Marriage Act. However, it is legal for the Muslims to have more than one wife at a time as per the Muslim Personal Law (1937), which is called *Shariat*. However, polyandry is not that very common among Muslims as evident from 1961 census, which shows that polygamy was much less prevalent among Indian Muslims (5.7%) than among several other religious groups. The incidence was highest among the tribals and the Buddhists. The Hindus, in comparison, had an incidence of 5.8%. Although there have been movements to end polygamy by the progressive sections, the orthodox members of the Muslim community seek to preserve the practice.

Polygamy is criticized vehemently and abhorred in modern progressive societies. However, many countries, which do not permit polygamous civil marriages, recognize them under the customary law.

Advantages of Polygamy

Though not recognized under law in most of the developed countries, the polygamous marriages do have some advantages.

Prevention of adultery: When there is a mismatch or disliking for one partner the husband can still have marital bliss by having sexual relations with other spouses. He does not have to find leads to the problem of prostitution.

Offers hope for widows and divorcees: In an orthodox country like India where widowhood and divorce are still viewed as social stigmas, polygamy offers scope for a dignified life. The women still not enjoy equality with men in matters like remarriage. Unmarried men are not inclined to marry a woman who had been married before. More so, if she has offsprings from the first wedlock. In such situations, polygamy provides a solution as already-married men who are financially well-off can marry them and enable them to lead a dignified life by providing shelter and protection.

Stable support system: If the wives are financially independent and supplement the income of the family polygamous marriages can provide larger and more stable support systems.

Better socialization of children: Polygamous families provide greater exposure to children as they have to deal with diverse personalities in large joint families under one roof.

Disadvantages of Polygamy

There are some inherent disadvantages of polygamy which denies equal rights to spouses.

Inequitable deal: The husband may not be able to give a fair deal to all the spouses and it could lead to injustice and give rise to jealousy which could rob the family of peace and happiness and marital bliss.

Financial challenge: In a polygamous marriage, the man has to support a large family and it entails a large financial burden which may weigh down any advantages that polygamy may offer.

Problems in raising children: A polygamous marriage can have adverse effects on the upbringing of children due to multiple wives.

Polyandry

Polyandry is the practice of one woman being married to two or more men. The custom evolved in the human society mainly due to the need to preserve the scarce land and food. However, in some parts the scarcity of females, largely on account of female infanticide and poor survival rate of neglected female children, also encouraged this practice.

Polyandry prevented division of land and allowed families to pool resources and live comfortable lives. Polyandry was practised from the ancient times across the world, including the Indian subcontinent.

The polyandry practised in India is mostly fraternal, where brothers share a wife. The close bonding among brothers ensures stability of polyandrous families. Non-fraternal polyandry, where a group of unrelated men share a wife, is virtually non-existent because of its inherent instability as parenting a child collectively is not easy for an unrelated men.

Polyandry is common in certain parts of India, Bhutan, Nepal and Tibet. The Chinese government has imposed a ban on polyandry in Tibet. The practice is heading for a natural death due to increasing female literacy in tribal communities. The educated girls are aware of their rights and are resisting such marriages. They are also agitating to secure rights in the family property.

In India, it was mainly prevalent in the Kinnaur region, a part of Himachal Pradesh which is located close to Tibet. Polyandry was also practised in some parts of South India specially among the Toda tribes of Nilgiris, Nairs of Travancore and Ezhavas of Malabar. Polyandry has virtually vanished from the traditions of most many groups and tribes in recent years. It is now prevalent only in some isolated pockets of hill regions like Kinnaur in Himachal Pradesh.

REVIEW QUESTIONS

1. What do you mean by polygamy and what are its various advantages and disadvantages?
2. Write short notes on the following:
   a. Polyandry in India
   b. Monogamy

CHAPTER

24

Problems of Modern Family and Marriage in India

LEARNING OBJECTIVES

After reading this chapter the learner should be able to

- Get acquainted with problems of modern families.
- Know about different issues regarding marriage in our country.

The problems of the modern family and marriage are interwoven and emanate mainly from the virtual collapse of the traditional joint family system and the emergence of the modern nuclear family. The transformation in the family structure has also given rise to many new problems, while some of the old ones, such as dowry, divorce, lack of intergenerational solidarity, discord between siblings and domestic violence have got further intensified.

Increasing longevity of women, up from 23 years in 1910, to 67 years (3 years more compared to men) in 2011 and rise in number of female-headed households, rise in the incidence of separation and divorce, growing conflicts between wife and husband, parents and sons and between brothers, increased freedom of marital choice, shrinking of kinship ties, continuous consultations between sons and parents on familial matters, rising level of female education and decline in total fertility rate are having long-term implication for the family system.

The small size of the modern family, mostly comprising parents and offsprings, itself is the root cause of many social problems. The process of family formation and dissolution has become faster compared to past. There has been large-scale migration from rural to urban and nuclear families are becoming order of the day. The divorce rate is increasing and the proportion of single member household is on the rise.

PROBLEMS OF NUCLEAR FAMILY

There are distinct advantages and disadvantages in both the joint family and nuclear family systems. However, advantages outweigh the disadvantages in a joint family set-up. The major advantage that a nuclear family affords is the opportunity to create an individual identity, something all human beings crave for and denied in a joint family set-up.

Child Rearing

There are no grandparents or other relatives and in most cases both husband and wife are working. The absence of elders in the home affected the upbringing of children and also led to erosion of values.

When both parents are working, the children are neglected, as there are no grandparents to take care of them. The children are left in the care of servants at home or in a day care centre. They are not only denied love and affection but also did not get exposed to the virtues and traditional values of the joint family system. In absence of experienced elders, dealing with the problems of growing children is a problem. Many parents resort to disciplinary techniques similar to what they gone through their childhood.

Marital Discord and Divorce

There is no support system in the nuclear family and minor issues between spouses turn into major problems. Often such situations lead to domestic violence and even divorce as marriage is no longer considered to be a 'divine match' or a 'sacred union'. Men and women are walking out of wedlock on flimsy and superficial reasons and this is not a good trend though divorce rates in India are among the lowest in the world. In urban areas divorce rates have started mounting.

The women are more concerned about their marriage than men and they also suffer more in case of marital discord. They are expected to take the lead to resolve marital conflicts and if they give up the marriage is over.

Children whose parents get divorced face social problems and at times encounter difficulties at school also. Children feel emotionally drained and often face psychological problems for want of adequate parental care.

Insecurity and Problems of Elderly

There is no one to take care in case a family member falls sick or have some other problem. The modern family is haunted by insecurity as they are more vulnerable like theft, robberies and murders, as it is easier to commit such a crime when someone is alone at home or only children are there.

The nuclear family system is also resulting in neglect of the elderly who left to fend for themselves in the twilight years of their life. The aged parents have to lead a lonely life without any emotional support. The increase in life expectancy has posed a big challenge of looking after the elderly people.

The new generations are slowly realizing that the advantages of the joint family system outweighed the comfort, independence and conveniences the nuclear families offered.

In the joint family working couples could comfortably go for jobs when parents are there at home. The children get better physical care from their grandparents and they also imbibe traditional family values under them. The problem of looking after the elderly people is also taken care of as they live in the family with their children and grand children.

Marriage a Must for Women

In Indian society, a woman has to get married to lead a dignified life as marriage not only confers her status in society but also provides security. Marriage and family dominates the life of women. The primary duty of the woman is to be loyal to the husband and his relatives. After marriage, husband and relatives control her all outside relationships. Woman worships her husband as her God and prays for his long life. The primary role for an Indian woman is still 'marriage' and 'motherhood'. If daughter remains unmarried or gets divorced, it brings the entire family under stress.

The nurturing roles as daughter, mother, and wife and as daughter-in-law make a woman's life completely dominated by male. The feeling of helplessness and dependence leads to stress and affects woman's mental health. Problems like infertility takes a heavy emotional toll as not being able to conceive is often considered as a social stigma.

Money Matters

Financial problems can also break a marriage, particularly when both the spouses are working. Enjoying financial independence before marriage the couples take time to make adjustments and at times matters get complicated. In certain families husband and wife maintain their separate accounts, while some husbands expect their partners to give their salary to have financial control over the family income. In some families, financial control maybe with women but problem arise when a spouse is not comfortable being under the financial control of the other.

Domestic Violence

Domestic violence is another problem many families are facing. Women and children are the victim of domestic violence, which may be physical brutality or psychological abuse. It may be in the form of intimate-partner violence or child abuse. Majority of family violence takes place within the four walls of home and a very small percentage of cases is reported. At times violence may take an ugly turn inflicting a serious injury or even causing death. Many violent acts among family members are still not considered crimes. Violence between spouses increases risk of mental health problems such as depression, anxiety and posttraumatic stress disorder. Violence in the family has serious effect on members, particularly young children, leading to addictions, suicide attempts, truancy and other behavioural problems. It is common to see aggression and criminal behaviour among adolescents who have been exposed to parental violence.

When all forms of violence are considered, women and men are found to be equally responsible for physically abusing children. They are known to sexually abuse them, though it is perpetrated by males in a majority of cases. Preschool children who become the victims of abuse resulting from parents' attempts to control behaviour of children and discipline them.

Nonresident Indian (NRI) Marriages

The NRI marriages, generally involving a woman from India and an Indian man residing in another country, have peculiar problems. The families usually ignore the common precautions that are to be observed in traditional matchmaking due to fear of losing a lucrative marriage offer. They do not even ponder over that in case things go wrong in an NRI marriage, the woman's recourse to justice is greatly constrained and complex. The woman is at great risk in NRI marriages being far away from home in an alien land, facing language problem, lack of family support and having no knowledge about the local laws and judicial system. They are subjected to all sorts of atrocities, battered, assaulted, abused both mentally and physically, ill-treated and forced to flee or are forcibly sent back to India. In certain cases, women end up entering wedlock with an NRI who is already married and abandoned even before being taken to the foreign country of his residence. In other cases ceremonies of engagement, followed by a massive wedding, a huge dowry and a honeymoon and then the NRI husband flies out of India, leaving the wife behind, never to return. The woman continues to wait endlessly.

A lot of the women are abandoned in the strange country with absolutely no support and without even the legal permission to stay on in that country. In most of these cases women are denied maintenance in India on the pretext that the marriage had already been dissolved by the court in another country.

Dowry and Hindu Marriage

Dowry is a custom in Hindu marriage since times immemorial. According to tradition the marriage of a girl is *kanyadan* which is not complete until the bridegroom is given a *varadakshina* in the form of dowry. The daughter was given costly garments and ornaments and other gifts in marriage by her parents and relations, out of love and affection. However, gradually this tradition acquired the form of social evil called 'dowry', making most of the marriages a bargain with the family of the bridegroom making all sorts of demands. The evil spread to the communities in the tradition of dowry had not been prevalent. Demand for dowry has even resulted in cruelty, domestic violence and murder of the bride by the in-laws or forcing her to commit suicide. The evil of dowry has forced parents to raise loans or /dispose of their property to marry their daughters.

Modern Families

A traditional family mostly comprises a husband, his wife and their biological children. However, a modern family may consist of a single parent, a gay couple or unrelated adults who live and rear children together. The divorce rate has increased considerably as more women are able to pursue their own careers. Young adults are aware of the realities of divorce and are quite supportive. Many urban women opt to remain single as the economic concerns of single women faced in the past do not exist anymore. The number of single member family is also increasing.

REVIEW QUESTIONS

1. Write short notes on the following:
   a. Modern families and problems of the elderly
   b. Domestic violence in modern families
   c. Dowry problem

CHAPTER

25

Family, Marriage and Their Influence on Health and Health Practices

LEARNING OBJECTIVES

After reading this chapter the learner should be able to

- Have knowledge about the influence of family on health.

Family and marriage have a bearing on the health of the members to a great extent. Similarly, health also has impact on family and marriage. Family is the primary unit of society, a group of biologically related individuals living under the same roof and eating from the common kitchen. Family-oriented care helps the members to maintain health and prevent diseases. Marriage is associated with physical health, psychological well-being, and improved longevity. Married people have better overall well-being and they live longer as compared to those divorced, separated, single or widowed.

The relationship between marriage and health is difficult to understand. Healthy people have a better chance of marrying and staying married as they maybe seen as desirable marriage partners based on their physical attractiveness, earnings potential, mental well-being and self-sufficiency. This pattern is viewed as *selection* of healthy people into marriage. Married people live a healthier life than unmarried people. A stable marriage provides a secure, coherent, regulated and healthy environment.

This overall positive effect is strong and consistent. It has been observed that the unmarried have higher levels of depression, anxiety and other forms of psychological distress compared to married people.

Effects of marriage on health: Marriage has impact on the health of both men and women to a great extent and the effect maybe positive or negative. Changes in behaviours, influencing not only physical but also mental health, are quite common. For instance, reduction in consumption of alcohol, drugs and smoking by men is some of the positive changes in behaviours after marriage. Recent research has shown that marriage has significant effects on the health behaviours of both men and women but the pattern is mixed. Marriage is mostly associated with healthier behaviours, though in some cases it leads to unhealthy behaviours. A happy marriage reduces heavy drinking and overall alcohol consumption. Compared to married people, the divorced and widowed persons have higher mortality due to cardiac disorders, paralytic stroke, pneumonia, cirrhosis of the liver, road accidents and suicide, all of which are leading causes of death.

Effects of marriage on mental health: A happy and stable marriage is associated with improved psychological well-being. It reduces depressive symptoms for both men and women but divorce increases them. Depressive symptoms after divorce are long lasting and the prevalence of these symptoms remains elevated years after the marital breakup. The effects of divorce on depression appeared to be more significant for women than for men. Mental health of couple locked in a stable marriage is much better than those who remain unmarried as living with someone provides emotional support and economic well-being. Married people almost always live together and often with children, their privileges and obligations revolve around the home and family. On the other hand, a person who lives alone may be isolated from an important network of social and economic ties.

Effects of marriage on physical health and longevity: People who marry live longer and enjoy better physical and mental health than those who do not marry. Marriage is associated with lower mortality risk.

Support from one's spouse may improve physical health in several ways: by improving emotional health, by reducing risky behaviour as alcohol consumption as for men and women, marriage appears to reduce alcohol abuse. Wives, in particular, often discourage smoking, drug use, or heavy drinking in the house, cook low-cholesterol meals and keep fattening food out of the house and schedule check-ups. The fact that women generally have a healthier lifestyle than men may explain why marriage improves men's health.

Married people are less likely to drink heavily, to get into fights, to drive too fast, and to take risks that increase the likelihood of accidents and injuries decreases the risk of lung cancer, emphysema, stroke, coronary heart disease and respiratory infections, including pneumonia. A balanced diet low in calories and cholesterol and high in fruits and vegetables decreases the risk of coronary heart disease, adult-onset diabetes, atherosclerosis, high blood pressure and colon cancer. Driving safely and not drinking and driving decreases the risk of accidents. On the other hand, when a spouse expects more than he or she is willing to give back, acts like the only important person in the family, and cannot be counted on for esteem and advice, men and women feel demoralized, tense, worried, neglected, unhappy and frustrated.

Marriage may improve physical health by aiding early detection and treatment, and by helping recovery which is called secondary prevention. Married people are more likely to see the doctor for check-ups, screening and other early detection than the unmarried with the same symptoms, functioning and general level of health.

Weight change: A stable marital status is unassociated with any weight change, though marriage is associated with weight gain. However, divorce and widowhood seems to be somewhat associated with weight loss, particularly among men. Entry into wedlock appeared to be associated with weight gain for women, but not for men, who experience weight loss instead. Similarly, divorce or separation or death of a spouse appeared to be associated with weight loss for men but not for women.

Lack of exercise: Married individuals tend to spend less time exercising than unmarried, divorced, or separated individuals. It is evident from some research studies that, unmarried individuals devoted 2.5 h more and divorced or separated individuals spent 1.9 h more time on exercise as compared to married individuals over a period of 2 weeks. Among those who were never married, men devoted 2 h more on exercises than women. The effects of marriage on a healthy lifestyle are generally positive but not completely consistent. A few healthy behaviours are not increased by marriage. Married people are more likely to be overweight, and they are less likely to engage in physical activity and exercise than the unmarried.

These ties may help create a stabilizing sense of security, belonging and direction. Without them a person may feel lonely, adrift and unprotected. Emotional support is the sense of being cared about, loved, esteemed, and valued as a person and having someone who cares about you and your problems. Married people are more likely to report that they have someone they can turn to for support and understanding when things get rough, and that they have a confidant they can really talk to. Emotional support decreases depression, anxiety, sickness, various psychological problems and mortality.

Economic effect of marriage: Marriage is advantageous for both the partners, though the economic benefits of marriage are greater for women than for men. Household income drops precipitously after divorce and remains low throughout the life especially for women. Economic well-being, in turn, has a large effect on health and mental health. The health benefits of marriage—social support and economic well-being—may weigh differently for men and women, the ways in which divorce increases the psychological distress of men and women. When divorced, women suffered more of a loss of household income than did men, whereas men suffered more of a loss of social support than did women. Both men and women gain economic well-being and emotional support from marriage, but marriage maybe more of an economic benefit to women and an emotional support benefit to men.

Employment of women: Employment may improve a mother's well-being under some conditions but degrade it under others. Effect of children on a married woman's depression depends on her employment, child care arrangements and husband's participation in child care. The most stressful situation occurs if a woman is employed, has young children, has difficulty arranging child care, and gets no help from her husband with child care and household chores. Thus, children seem to have very different effects on employed mothers, depending on the availability and affordability of child care and the husband's participation in child care. Support from people in the household other than the husband also can reduce the burden of children. However, in the best circumstances children may improve well-being of parents. Some of these circumstances are adequate family income to prevent economic hardship, a working wife, availability of affordable child care services, and shared participation in child care along with emotional support from husbands or other relatives.

Sickness in the family: If one member of the family in India gets sick all the members get involved in the care. Right from taking care of the diet to trying home remedies. Family members constantly stay with the sick person and even do not sleep in the night if required. If there is any chronic disease in the family as cancer, cardiovascular disease or disability, that affects the whole family. Apart from emotional distress, the whole family also goes through the financial stress and gets disturbed. Family has to spend money on hospitalization, medication, diet and rehabilitation. If the sick member is the earning member of the family then the financial loss is even more, otherwise some family members have to stay with the person in hospital or home during sickness.

Child Health: Antenatal care, intranatal care and breastfeeding are the key care practices that could have an impact on child health. Factors like feeding young children, care of children during illness, psychosocial care of children, food preparation and storage and hygiene are also very important for keeping the children healthy. However, these practices can be modified by availability of resources to the caregiver for its implementation. These resources include knowledge and beliefs about child rearing, the health and nutritional status, and employment of the care provider. Besides, factors like autonomy for child care, workload and time constraints for providing child care; social infrastructure; father's role; and community support also have a bearing on quality of child care. The growth and nutritional outcomes of children depend upon competence of the parents in providing child care. Conducive child care settings foster positive development of eating behaviours of children.

Type of family: In joint families, the presence of parents, grandparents, uncles, aunts and other near relatives plays a vital role in child rearing as well as in shaping the attitude and behaviour of the child. On the other hand in nuclear family system, there is so much burden on the parents of bringing up the children due to lack of any other help and the problem gets magnified if both the parents are working. The lack of parental attention in the nuclear families and peer pressure may provoke the child into deleterious habits like smoking, alcoholism and drug addiction These habits in turn increase the incidence of oral cancers, venereal diseases and mental illnesses.

Incomplete or broken family: Children are supposed to grow up in a healthy family where they could receive love, care and concern from their parents. However, in the broken families, children are invariably denied attention, affection and care and consequently they grow up with behavioural problems. It is not surprising that the children indulging in bad behaviour, rivalry and displaying discontentment in the school or other gathering places are usually from a broken family. A majority of children in the remand homes and juvenile centres are from broken families. Mistakes in bringing up children are the main reason for delinquent behaviour among children from broken families.

Loss of children causes grief and anxiety in parents. As a consequence, their mental health gets affected adversely. The breaking of a family is great loss for each and every member of the family.

Marriage has long-term effect on the health of children. Childhood family environment is linked to adult mortality risk, and it has been observed that males who grew up in stable families if compared with those who lived with their biological fathers, but not their biological mothers, were less susceptible to adult mortality. There was no difference in risk of adult mortality between those who lived with both parents and those who lived with their biological mothers but not their biological fathers.

Violence in the family: Violence in family takes a great toll on a victim's health. Victims of family violence are mostly women who suffer from chronic pain, psychosomatic symptoms, gastrointestinal disorders and other health problems, besides immediate injuries from the assault. Psychological abuse is often considered less severe than physical violence but its harmful consequences for mental health are increasingly being recognized. Apart from anxiety, post-traumatic stress and depression, women who are abused suffer an increased risk of unplanned or early pregnancies. Substance abuse is also very common among the victims of family violence. Family violence also makes women more vulnerable to attacks during pregnancy and, thus, these women are more likely to experience medical difficulties in their pregnancies.

REVIEW QUESTIONS

1. Write in detail about the impact of broken or incomplete family on child health.
2. What are the long-term effects of marriage on health?

UNIT - 7

SOCIAL STRATIFICATION

CHAPTER

26

Social Stratification

LEARNING OBJECTIVES

After reading this chapter the learner should be able to

- Know the meaning and process of social stratification.
- Get familiar with caste and class system in India.

Human societies are inherently heterogamous entities and as they evolve, social inequalities also start emerging. Apart from the natural differences, human beings are also socially differentiated on the basis of their status, power and income giving rise to social inequalities. The differences not only result in a more diverse society but also lead to disparities in the way they are treated and the opportunities available to them, their earnings and respect they command in the society. Thus, power, prestige and assets are three important premises on which social stratification is based.

The term *social inequality* simply refers to the existence of socially created inequalities. However, social stratification not only involves social inequalities but also beliefs. These differences create layers or strata in society. How stratification occurs and the effects it has on people are major concerns of sociologists. In all societies, people differ from each other on the basis of their age, sex and personal characteristics. Human society is not homogeneous but heterogeneous and members are differentiated not only on the basis of natural features but also distinguished in accordance with socially approved criteria.

MEANING OF SOCIAL STRATIFICATION

Social stratification is basically a form of social inequality. Almost all the societies arrange their members in a form of a social hierarchy based on economy, race, superiority, inferiority and equality. Stratification is essentially a process of differentiation whereby some groups and individuals come to be ranked higher than others.

Social inequality is a universal phenomenon that exists in every society in some form, which differs across societies. Social stratification occurs when individuals and groups are ranked in a hierarchy of status as per some commonly accepted norms based upon the inequality of social positions. Social stratification in simple terms means division of society into different strata or layers. Members of a particular stratum have a common identity and a similarity in the lifestyle.

The society in which divisions of social classes exist is known as a stratified society. The Indian caste system provides an example of social stratification. However, stratification in modern societies fundamentally differs from stratification of primitive societies. Social stratification involves two phenomena based on characteristics of groups and individuals and social evaluation. The social processes define certain types of goods as valuable and desirable and these goods are distributed across various positions as per allocation rules in the division of labour. The social positions in society are matched to *reward packages* of unequal and disproportionate value. For instance, power, status and income that go with the social positions like advocate, engineer, doctor, farmer and housewife vary vastly.

Accordingly, some individuals or groups come to be ranked higher than others on the basis of possession of certain characteristics. Further, the ranking of individuals is in accordance with some basis of evaluation.

The sociologists are concerned with the facts of social differences and also with their social evaluation.

DEFINITION

Social stratification is defined as a system by which categories of groups and individuals are ranked in a hierarchy in a society. Sociologists have described the process of social stratification in different ways.

According to Ogburn and Nimkoff 'it is a process by which individuals and groups are ranked in more or less enduring hierarchy of statuses', while in the words of Lundberg 'a stratified society is marked by inequality, by differences among people that are evaluated by them as being *lower* and *higher*'.

Raymond W. Murray terms it as 'a horizontal division of society into *higher* and *lower* social units'. Gisbert describes it somewhat differently as 'division of society into permanent groups of categories linked with each other by the relationship of superiority and subordinations'. In the words of Williams, 'it is the system for ranking of individuals on a scale of superiority–inferiority–equality as per some commonly accepted basis of valuation'.

ORIGIN OF STRATIFICATION

There are two main theories of origin of stratification as listed hereunder:

1. Conflict theory that attributes the emergence of difference in social strata to economic factors.
2. Functional theory as per which inherited individual and differences in environmental conditions are the cause of social stratification.

According to the proponents of conflict theory like Karl Marx, economic factors are responsible for the emergence of difference in social strata or social classes. He linked social stratification to the means of production by their ownership or nonownership. On its basis, there are two mutually conflicting classes, the capitalists and the workers, in every society. Marx defined *Capitalists* as the people who own factories and other productive business and *Proletariat* as those who sell their productive labour to the capitalists. One is rich and the other is poor, with mutually opposite interests, making conflicts inevitable.

However, Gumplocer, Oppenheimer and some others maintained the conquest of one group by the other led to social stratification. The conquering group normally dominates the conquered group, which is forced to accept the lower or inferior state and class.

On the other hand, Kingsley Davis, Mac Iver and other votaries of functional theory social stratification originated due to the functional necessity of the social system. They rejected the conflict theory asserting that conflict may facilitate stratification but never originated it. Social stratification is an unconsciously evolved system to ensure that the most important positions are occupied by the most qualified persons. Prof. P.A. Sorokin attributed social stratification mainly to inherited difference in environmental conditions.

While the conflict theory lays stress on conflict between large and stable groups driven by strong community sentiments, the functional theory underscores the integrating function of social stratification based upon individual merit and reward. The theory of Marx attracted criticism for nonrecognition of the system of unequal rewards that may be necessary to motivate people to perform their social roles effectively.

TYPES OF SOCIAL STRATIFICATION

Social stratification is based upon a variety of principles and it takes different forms based on different criteria in different societies. These forms are slavery, caste, class and estate, as discussed in the following sections.

Slavery

It is the earliest form of social stratification and a legally recognized division of society. It had an economic basis and every slave had a master to whom he was subjected. It mostly existed in Europe and some other ancient countries around 500–600 BC.

Caste

It is a system of classification as per which a man's status and its accompanying rights and obligations are ascribed on the basis of his birth into a particular group. As per the declassification of Indian caste system, there are four groups: Brahmins, Kshatriyas, Vaisya and Sudra. An individual born in a particular caste remains its member forever and no action on his or her part can change it. Castes are ranked in a social hierarchy and each caste has a fixed specified occupation.

Social Class

It is a consequence of economic factors and stratification on the basis of class that is dominant in modern society. Those who have the means of production like land and capital forms one class, whereas those who do not, forms the other class. Thus, the two classes represent the haves and have not.

Estate

It is alternatively the later form of social stratification that existed in medieval Europe under which emphasis was laid on birth as well as wealth and possessions. Estates include serfs, the commoners, clergy and the feudal lords.

CHARACTERISTICS OF SOCIAL STRATIFICATION

Eminent scholars have attributed the following characteristics to social stratification.

Social Stratification Is Universal

Social stratification has been in existence in one form or the other ever since society came into being. Difference between the rich and the poor, weak and the powerful existed in all the ancient civilizations. No society in the world is free from stratification, though it differs vastly from primitive societies to the modern societies. According to Sorokin 'all permanently organized groups are stratified'.

Stratification Is Social

Age, sex, intelligence and other biological factors may form the basis for differentiating statues but one's education, property, power, experience, character and personality are much more important than biological qualities. Thus, stratification is largely a social phenomenon by nature.

It Is in Diverse Forms

The forms of stratification are not uniform and it varies across societies depending on the criteria. The ancient Greeks were divided into freemen and slaves and the ancient Romans into the patricians and the plebeians. In the modern world class, caste and estate are the general forms of stratification. In India, a peculiar type of stratification in the shape of caste system has been prevalent. In the ancient era, the Aryans were divided into four varnas: the Brahmins, Kshatriyas, Vaisyas and Sudras. Thus, diversity in stratification has been there in every society, past or present, big or small.

Social Stratification Is Consequential

Social stratification has two important consequences, *life chances* and *lifestyle*. The members of a class have equal social opportunities but these vary in across societies. Besides opportunities for education and good health, it also includes chances of obtaining justice, marital conflict, separation and divorce.

Lifestyle is indicative of a particular social status and it includes matters like housing, means of recreation, the kinds of dress, the kinds of books, television shows and overall social environment one is exposed to. It can be viewed as a subculture in which one layer of the strata differs from the other within the structure of a commonly shared overall culture.

REVIEW QUESTIONS

1. How the social stratification occurs on the basis of caste and class?
2. What are the various characteristics of social stratification?

CHAPTER

27

Caste System and Class System in India

LEARNING OBJECTIVES

After reading this chapter the learner should be able to

- Get acquainted with the caste system prevalent in India.
- Have knowledge about the merits and demerits of the caste system.

The Indian caste system is considered as a form of social stratification. Social status is determined by the caste a person is born into and it is unchangeable. It is thus considered a closed system of stratification. There are limits on interaction and behaviour with people from another social status. It is rooted in the country's prominent religion, Hinduism, though the Buddhist revolution and British rule saw significant changes in it.

Under the Indian caste system, people have been classified into four hierarchically ranked castes, called *varnas*, on the basis of occupation. Differentiation on one or the other forms exists in all human societies; it becomes a social issue when such a system results in unequal access to resources, power and status as has been the case with Indian caste system.

MEANING OF CASTE

The word *caste* is derived from Spanish word *casta*, meaning lineage, breed, strain or race. The Portuguese used it to describe the classes of people described as *jati* in India.

Sociologists have given different definitions of the word *caste*.

1. According to Lundberg, a caste is merely a rigid social class into which members are born and from which there is virtually no escape. It is the type of stratification system which is most rigid in matters of mobility and distinctness of status.
2. In the words of E.A.H Blunt, a *caste* is 'a collection of endogamous groups, bearing a common name and the membership of which is hereditary. Generally regarded as forming a single homogeneous community, it imposes on the members certain restrictions in respect of social intercourse and follows a common traditional occupation or claims a common origin'.

3. Terming it as special case of class H. Cooley states that 'when a class is somewhat strictly hereditary, we may call it a caste'.
4. MacIver observes, 'When status is wholly predetermined, so that men are born to their lot without any hope of changing it, then class takes the extreme form of caste'.
5. Ketkar defines caste on the basis of two important group characteristics:
   a. Membership is confined to those who are born of members and include all persons so born.
   b. Membership is forbidden by an inexorable social law to men outside the group.
6. Martindale and Monochesi define caste as 'an aggregate of persons whose share of obligations and privileges are fixed by birth, sanctioned and supported by religion and usage'.
7. According to Anderson and Parker, 'Caste is that extreme form of social class organization in which the position of individuals in the status hierarchy is determined by descent and birth'.
8. According to Williams, 'Caste is a system in which an individual's rank and its accompanying rights and obligations are ascribed on the basis of birth into a particular group'.

Thus, thinkers have variously defined the term *caste*. But as Ghurye states, 'With all the labour of these students, however, we do not possess a real general dilation of caste. The best way to understand the term *caste* is to examine the various factors underlying the caste system'.

Greek traveller Megasthenes, who came to India in the 3rd century BC, made two important observations about the caste system:

1. It does not permit to contract marriage with a person of another caste.
2. Forbids members to undertake an occupation other than ancestral.

ORIGIN OF CASTE SYSTEM

The caste system is supposed to have originated in India but its exact origin cannot be traced. There are different theories, some religious, some biological and others sociohistorical, about how the caste system started. The religious theories explain how the 'varnas' were founded, the biological theory is based on the *sattva, rajas* and *tamas,* the inherent qualities, and the sociohistorical claims that the caste system originated with the arrival of Aryans around 1500 BC.

Religious or Traditional Theory

As per this theory, the caste system has a divine origin. The theory cites the Vedic literature wherein it is stated that supreme creator, brahma, created the castes for harmonious and smooth functioning of the society. According to the ancient Hindu book, *Rig Veda,* the primal man—Purush—destroyed himself to create a human society and different varnas were created from different parts of his body. The brahmins were created from his head; the kshatriyas from his hands; the vaishyas from his thighs and the shudras from his feet. Accordingly, the varna hierarchy is determined in descending order of the different organs from head downwards from which the varnas were created.

Biological Theory

Claims that all existing things inherit one of three qualities (*gunas*), *sattva, rajas* and *tamas*, and the varnas are based on the predominance of the qualities. The combination of these qualities in various proportions constitutes the group or class of people all over the world with temperamental differences. Sattva qualities are associated with wisdom, intelligence, honesty, goodness and other positive qualities. Rajas qualities are related to passion, pride, and valour, while tamas qualities are associated with negative traits like dullness, stupidity and lack of creativity. People having these inherent qualities in different proportions end up adopting the appropriate occupation.

Accordingly, brahmins inherit the sattva qualities and they are serene, self-controlled and lead an austere life. They are known for uprightness and forbearance and have passion for knowledge and wisdom. The kshatriyas and vaishyas inherit the rajas qualities, and the shudras inherit the tamas qualities.

Racial Theory

According to this theory the caste system emerged due to coming in contact of different races and the consequent of clash of cultures. According to Dr Mazumdar, the caste system took its birth after the arrival of Aryans in India. The Aryans considered themselves to be superior to the non-Aryans because of their better complexion, robust physique and appearance. They considered the native people as inferior and placed themselves above them in the social hierarchy. The Indo-Aryans used certain words like *varna* (colour) to assert their separate existence. They spoke of the *dasa* varna. Rig Vedic literature stresses the differences between the *arya* and *dasa*, not only in their colour but also in their speeches, religious practices and physical features. The three classes, brahmin, kshatriya and vaishya, are frequently mentioned in the Rig Veda, while the fourth class, the shudra, occurs only once in the Rig Veda.

The brahmin and kshatriya represented the professions of the poet–priest and the warrior-chief, while vaishya comprised all the common people. The shudra class represented domestic servants who were no different than slaves.

Political Theory

According to this theory, the caste system did not originated on the basis of race but a result of manipulations by those who wanted to exercise authority. It was an invention of brahmins to occupy the highest position in the social hierarchy. In the words of Dr Ghurye, 'Caste is a brahmanic child of Indo-Aryan culture cradled in the land of the Ganges and thence transferred to other parts of India'.

The next three classes in the social ladder were ordered to live according to the teaching of the brahmin, who declared their duties, while the king also is exhorted to regulate his conduct accordingly. The pre-eminence of the brahmins brought them many social privileges. As their influence grew in India, complicated rules of ritual and conduct were built up and incorporated into the religious books. To maintain their superiority over other classes brahmins closed their ranks and other castes also followed suit.

Occupational Theory

The caste system is considered a natural outcome of the division caused in the Hindu society on the basis of occupation. Its origin can be found in the nature and quality of social work performed by the various groups of people. According to Nesfield, 'Function and function alone is responsible for the origin of caste structure in India'.

Functional differentiation led to occupational division and as a result host of subcastes such as lohar, sonar, chamar, bhangi, barhai, pawa, teli, nai, tamboli, kahar, gadaria and mali came into existence. The persons engaged in professions regarded as better and respectable became superior to those who were performing lower or dirty work.

Evolutionary Theory

This theory says that the caste system evolved gradually through a long-drawn process and did not come to into existence suddenly. Its development was influenced by a number of factors such as hereditary occupations, the desire of the brahmins to maintain their purity, the unwillingness of rulers to enforce a uniform law, beliefs in reincarnation and the doctrine of Karma, ancestor worship, clash of cultures, foreign invasions, colour and racial prejudices and the static nature of the Hindu society.

The caste system is not specifically an institution of the Hindus but is a typical Indian institution. It was not peculiar to India, it existed and still prevalent in various parts of the world in some form. For instance, ethnic groups such as Jews and Negroes are still treated as low castes in many countries, including the United States. The feudal system of medieval Europe was also a type of caste system.

Characteristics of Caste System

The caste system is highly complex in nature and not a well-defined entity but a grouping of people with different origins over time. According to Dr G.S. Ghurye caste is not possible because of the complexity of the phenomenon. Instead he described the main characteristics of caste which have been featuring traditionally in the caste system.

Hierarchical Social Structure

The castes system is a gradational structure in which groups are arranged in a hierarchical order from superior to inferior. The brahmin caste is at the top and the shudra caste is at the bottom. In between there are two intermediate castes, the kshatriyas and the vaishyas. The supremacy of the brahmins and the low status of shudra (harijans or dalits) is an accepted fact in the Indian society, though there are disputes regarding the exact position of the intermediary castes.

Segmental Division of Society

It is not a homogeneous society. It is divided into various small social groups called *castes*, each of which is a well-developed social group. The membership of the group is determined by the consideration of birth. An individual belongs to the caste of their parents and it is an indisputable and unalterable fact by which ones social status position solely determined. Even if an individual changes in his status, occupation, education, economic condition take place, the membership of an individual does not change. There is practically no social mobility.

Endogamy

The most fundamental characteristic of the caste system is endogamy. The members of a caste or subcaste have to marry within their own caste or subcaste and anyone who violates this rule is ostracized from the caste. Endogamy is a common rule for a caste and it is still being followed rigidly, making intercaste marriages difficult.

Hereditary Occupation

Members of a particular caste are expected to follow the hereditary occupations meant for the caste. Change in occupation was not allowed in the traditional caste system. A member was prohibited from taking up any degraded occupation not only due to moral restraint imposed by own caste but also because of the restriction put by other castes whose members did not permit others to enter their traditional occupation. For instance, traditionally a brahmin was allowed to function as a priest. Anyone not born as a brahmin was not allowed function as a priest.

Restriction on Food and Drink

The caste system imposed certain restrictions on the food habits of the members and usually cooked food from a caste placed lower in the social hierarchy was not accepted. The food habits of various castes differ and who should accept what kind of food and from whom was often decided by caste. A person belonging to a higher caste believes that he gets polluted by accepting food or drink from a person belonging to the low caste.

In north India and some other parts, a brahmin would only accept 'pakka' food (cooked in ghee) only from some castes lower than his own but have 'kachcha' food (prepared with the use of water) from his own caste. However, any kind of food prepared by the brahmins is acceptable to all the caste people. Brahmins dominated the hotel industry for a long time only because of this factor. Restrictions are also imposed on the use of certain vegetables for certain castes. Some traditional brahmins do not consume onions, garlic, cabbage, carrot, beetroot and other vegetables, while eating beef is not allowed in any caste, except for the harijans.

Cultural Difference

Various castes have their own set of rules and regulations with regard to endogamy, pollution, purity, occupational specialization, food habits and other aspects as such each caste develops its own subculture. The behaviour of an individual is governed by the requirements of his caste, and it has a bearing on the life style and behaviour pattern. According to Dr Gharya, castes are a 'small and complete social worlds in themselves', marked off definitely from one another, though subsisting within the larger society.

Each caste in a way has its own way of life, customs, traditions, practices, rituals, informal rules, regulations and procedures. The conduct of members was regulated through caste councils or 'caste panchayats'.

Social and Religious Disabilities

A common feature in traditional caste societies is that the groups placed low in the social hierarchy suffered from social and religious disadvantages. For instance, the shudras were not allowed to draw water from public wells used by higher castes and they were barred from entering religious shrines and many other public places. These discriminatory practices are still prevalent in some backwards areas of the country.

Varna and Caste

Caste and varnas are two different concepts, though some people wrongly consider as the same. The peculiarity of the Hindu theory of social organization is its *Varnashrama* organization. The varna organization and ashram organization are two separate organizations yet the two go together as they refer to the problems of nurture and nature of man.

The Ashram organization refers to the conduct of an individual in the world (nurture) in different stages of his life and the Varnashrama organization refers to the work that individuals undertake in the society according to the nature and memberships of their respective varnas.

Varna originates from the word *Vri*, which means the choice of occupation as per inherent traits, and literally, refers to colour. Thus, *varna* can be interpreted in two ways: As the colour of the skin it refers to classification on the basis of racial differences, and as choice of occupation based on inherent traits it means social division on the basis of occupational differences.

The division of society in four varnas, brahmin, kshatriya, vaishya and shudra, was based on the division of labour. There was nothing like lower or higher varna in the Vedic period. There was no restriction on occupation and persons belonging to a particular varna could take up any profession they liked. There was no restriction regarding food, drinking or diet and inter-marriage between the different classes of the Aryan race were allowed, indicating that varnas were open classes, based on individual traits and not on birth.

Varnas were relatively flexible as compared with the castes. With the acquisition of skills, talents and virtues, an individual could improve his status by moving to higher class and vice versa was also true.

Varna is considered an abstract classification of people of a mythical origin. The system is believed to be derived from the Purushashukta and the Rig Vedic hymn which describes the creation of priests (brahmins), warriors (kshatriyas), traders (vaishyas) and menials (shudras) from the mouth, arms, thighs and feet of the creator, respectively.

Caste is different in many ways. The term caste originates from the root word *jana,* which implies 'taking birth'. Thus, caste is concerned with birth.

Unlike varna castes are very large in number and there are also many regional variations, mostly based on linguistic differences. Determined by birth caste is a concrete grouping based on ritualistic and occupational criteria. The caste system imposes many restrictions on the members.

Merits and Demerits of the Indian Caste System

The caste system has been an integral part of the Hindu society, one of the oldest in the civilization, which has not only survived all these years but also remained active and vigorous. The caste system did serve as a stabilizing force for a long time but it had its own merits and demerits. It was even seen as a bane as caste system promoted discriminatory and undemocratic practices which created division among the people. This is the main reason leading to its disintegration.

Merits

Harmonious division ensures definite social environment: Every society undergoes social stratification and the caste system provided a perfect system in ancient India based on division of work. The whole society was divided into four classes, namely, brahmins, kshatriyas, vaishyas and shudras, which is not rigid but open. It provides definite social environment as culture of each caste is different. Everyone was free to improve status and attain the highest social dignity. The scientific classification based on principles of heredity and economy of labour, which helped to preserve the social integration.

Caste systems as a constitution of Hindu society: Some European writers considered the caste system as a blessing and observed that 'It is this foundation of Hindu social constitution that has sustained the nation without being shattered to pieces, despite of the numerous political and religious upheavals that occurred during the last thousand years'. Similar views have been expressed by Sir Henry Cotton, who stated that 'The caste system has rendered most important service in the past and still continues to sustain order and solidarity'.

Promotes cooperation and economic pursuit: The caste system instils *we* feeling among the members which automatically promotes cooperation. As the occupation is determined by caste, the young generations are given the required training by family or other senior members in the caste.

Racial purity and evolution of higher race: The caste system helps in preserving social purity by prohibiting intercaste marriages. Each caste is able to preserve its culture in this manner.

According to Havell, such laws 'were laws of spiritual engines designed to promote the evolution of a higher race'.

Segregation of social life and political life: The caste system separated the social life from political life and this was the main factor that the Muslim invaders and those from Europe failed to convert the Hindus to their religion.

Demerits

The caste system promoted orthodoxy and became a hurdle in the social progress. It also brought in many social evils and thinkers from time to time wanted the society to do away with it.

Social disorganization: A uniting force for centuries the caste system has become a dividing element in the Hindu society. The caste hierarchy brought created sharp divisions in the society and brought in inhuman practice like *untouchability*. The shudras were prohibited from using common facilities and deprived of all social privileges which were available to members of high castes. They were discriminated against and forbidden from all the public places such as temples, ghats, wells and even schools. In the process a large chunk of people was thrown out from the main stream of Indian social life.

It also divided the Hindus into numerous subcaste groups and sects which promoted disorganization. The process of stratification of society into high and low even led to division even among brahmins, the highest caste and the also got into a hierarchy from high to low and no sections of the Hindu society was left untouched.

Political disunity: The caste divisions divided the whole society into innumerable subdivisions and political unity became impossible. The national disunity enabled foreigners to conquer and rule over the country without much difficulty. The casteist forces have been very active in our society even after independence and still creating divisions and coming in the way of socioeconomic of the underprivileged.

Domination of upper caste: The caste system was exploited by the upper castes to suppress the lower castes and to perpetuate their hegemony over them. The widening chasm between the higher and lower castes weakened the unity of the whole community.

Religious conversions: The dominance of upper castes forced lower castes to convert their religion by embracing Islam or Christianity. The rigidity of caste system which denied equal rights to lower castes only facilitated religious conversions.

Lower status of women: Besides suppression of lower castes the system also worked against the women who did not enjoy equal status with men. They were deprived of education and all other opportunities for progress and even married off at a tender age. They were not permitted to remarry even if they became widows soon after marriage and in certain communities forced to commit *sati* by jumping into burning pyre of the husbands.

Impedes social progress: The rigid caste system made the society resistant to change, and in the process social progress was hampered. The caste system made the people very conservative and their strong desire to preserve the customs and traditions did not allow to effect changes necessary for social progress.

Disintegration of Caste System

With all these negative features the caste system became the bane of the Hindu society and it also set in the process of its decay. A number of factors came into play and the once rigid system has starting disintegrating.

Modern education: As the religious education which promoted caste system gave way to modern education, the process of social change started. The modern education promoted secular and democratic principles like equality, liberty, brotherhood and harmony. It also developed scientific outlook and exploded traditional myths and taboos. The coeducational institutions also promoted women education and intercaste marriages which weakened the caste system as a whole.

Industrialization and urbanization: The advances made in the field science and technology and the process of industrialization also undermined the caste structure as members from all castes got employment in factories. The occupational barriers set-up by the caste system were brought down. Members of different castes worked together in industries and it strengthened the intercaste social discourse. The members of lower castes came to occupy higher positions in industries and government offices turning the caste hierarchy upside down.

Industrialization also led to urbanization as people from rural areas migrated to towns for employment in the industries. The people coming from different areas do not know the caste background of each other and the caste factor gets diluted.

Rapid development of transportation and communication: Rapid modes of transportation and communication like buses, trains and motorcars made the caste restrictions redundant. The caste rules, regarding food, drink and social intercourse could not be observed while travelling in these means. The modern means of transportation have increased special mobility of the people and ended geographical isolation of villages and promoted social intercourse.

Social reform movement: The discriminatory caste system made many social thinkers to launch movements to reform the society. These included Raja Ram Mohan Roy, Swami Dayananda Saraswati, Acharya Harihar, Swami Vivekananda, Ramakrishna Paramahansa and Swami Vinoba Bhave. The emergence of sects like Brahma Samaj, Arya Samaj, Prathana Samaj and Ramakrishna Mission was the outcome of the efforts made to reform the society.

Political movement: Father of the Nation, Mahatma Gandhi, spearheaded the political movement for the abolition of caste system. He launched a drive for the emancipation of harijans and the democratic set-up after independence allowed equal opportunity to all to assert their political identity. Different political parties have been wooing the lower castes and in the process the caste lines are fading from the society.

Intercaste marriage: The Hindu Marriage Act allowed freedom to individuals to get married to anyone and it has gradually weakened the tradition of endogamous marriages promoted and preserved by the caste system.

Government efforts: The laws enacted by the government and other initiatives taken to eradicate social evils and unjust practices have also helped in disintegration of the caste structure. Apart prohibiting *untouchability* by law, the government also provided reservation to lower castes in jobs and educational institutions. A number of schemes have been implemented for the socio-economic uplift of the lowers castes to improve their lot.

Emergence of Class

In the words of Max Weber, caste and class are both status groups. While castes are perceived as hereditary groups and a kind of closed stratification, social classes represent the groups of people who have a similar socio-economic status in relation to other classes in the society. Unlike caste system, ritual norms have no importance at all in the class system; instead, power and wealth alone determine one's status.

According to MacIver, Davis and Bottomore caste and class are polar opposites and antithetical to each other. The *class* represents a *democratic society* having equality of opportunity; *caste* is obverse of it.

The class system started emerging during the British period when the agriculture economy underwent a change with the new revenue system and it was given a push by the agrarian reforms carried out after the independence which led to increasing commercialization of agriculture. The new economy based on trade, commerce and industrial enterprise and along with modern education provided impetus to social transformation leading to creation of new classes in India.

Change in Agriculture

During the British rule private property in the form of Zamindari and Ryotwari systems was recognized and it led to two new classes of the zamindars and the peasant proprietors. A new form of local power structure emerged with these zamindars as the British empowered them with the specific authority to get commission on the land revenue collected for the imperial government. The zamindar ruled over the raiyats (proprietary cultivators) and the landless labourers. Traditionally, land owners constituted the highest caste, followed by poor peasantry, the cultivators and the landless labourers, mostly untouchable castes.

After independence changes in class structure and landownership have taken place. There are instances of structural change particularly during the early years of our independence. Land reforms benefited the tenants who got ownership of land and the Jagirdari and Zamindari system was also disbanded. The landless were given land in many states.

Industrialization

The development of modern transport system, particularly, railways and road transport, industrialization and state administration led to emergence of new working class not connected with agriculture and the employment in government and other sectors gave rise to middle class.

The rise of new social classes was also uneven as certain communities already engaged in definite economic, social or educational vocations in the pre-British period took the lead in taking advantage of the new opportunities. For instance, baniyas, the trading community, were the first to take up modern commerce banking and industrial enterprises, and brahmins went for modern education ahead of others.

Differences between Class and Caste

1. Caste is hereditary and determined by birth and it is a closed group with no possibility of change, fixed, while class is an open group based on economic differences and inequalities in possessions and control of material resources,
2. The caste is an endogamous group and members have to marry within the group, whereas class is an open group with no restriction on marriage and an individual was free to marry anyone.
3. The status of an individual is determined by birth in caste system, whereas in class the status is achieved by an individual through education, skills and economic prosperity.
4. In caste system noneconomic factors such as influence of religion, rituals, customs, beliefs like rebirth are important, while class system is secular and it has nothing to do with religion.
5. There is no social mobility in caste system, whereas social mobility is possible by improving the social status.
6. The caste system is based on the concept of inferiority or superiority of human beings and undemocratic, while the class system based on social status of an individual and they promote democracy.

7. There is no occupational mobility in the caste system and members have to adopt the traditional occupation, whereas members of social class can adopt any occupation and change it at will.
8. Social gap between members of different castes is too wide, which is not the case with class system where the gap is narrow in comparison.
9. Caste system imposes restriction on food and social intercourse, while in the class system there are no restrictions on interdining and social interaction.
10. Caste system is an organic system but class system encourages competition among various segments.

REVIEW QUESTIONS

1. How caste system came into existence in India?
2. What are the various reasons of emergence of class system?

CHAPTER

28

Social Stratification and Social Mobility

LEARNING OBJECTIVES

After reading this chapter the learner should be able to

- Know the relationship between social stratification and social mobility.
- Get familiar with different types of social mobility.

The dictionary meaning of the word *mobility* is ability to move freely and easily. However, in sociology, it refers to the movement within the social structure, from one social position to another. It means a change in social status. In the social ladder, the movement could be from lower to higher level or from higher to lower level. All societies afford some opportunity for social mobility, though extent to which individuals can move from one class or status level to another varies from one society to the other.

According to eminent sociologist P.A. Sorokin, no society is completely closed or completely open and no two societies are exactly same in allowing or discouraging movement. The pace of movement also varies from one period of time to another. The greater the amount of social mobility, the more open the class structure. The concept of social mobility is vital for ascertaining the relative *openness* of a social structure. Social mobility largely depends on the nature and types of social stratification, which also determines its forms, direction and magnitude. An open society with a class system encourages mobility as social positions in this stratification system depend more on achieved status, like education, than on ascribed status, like gender and caste. The general notion that social mobility is always positive and that an open society is better than a closed one is not true. A closed society with little social mobility shelters individuals from cut-throat competition and the consequent stress and frustration of failure. Besides, it does not raise expectations that cannot be fulfilled.

Social mobility constantly exposes individuals to socially unfamiliar situations and they have to adapt to new class, new norms and values. In contrast, members of a closed society spend their entire lifetime in a familiar environment.

However, a closed society that does not give opportunities to talented people from the lower strata to move to higher social positions of leadership will not fare well in the long run.

TYPES OF SOCIAL MOBILITY

Social mobility takes different forms at different periods of time. Individuals achieve new position by way of a change in occupation with a consequent change in status, through promotions in the same occupational group or change in occupation from one generation to the other. For instance, son of a farmer becomes an engineer or doctor and an industrial worker becomes a businessman.

There are many different patterns of social mobility depending on the social stratification. The movement takes place from lower to higher, higher to lower and between two positions at the same level.

The main types of social mobility are as follows:

1. Vertical mobility
2. Horizontal mobility
3. Intergenerational mobility
4. Intragenerational mobility
5. Structural mobility

Vertical Mobility

It refers to the movement of people from one stratum to another or from one status to another. It occurs when a person or group of people moves up or down in social status. It brings changes in class, occupation and power within the lifetime of an individual. It involves movement from lower to higher or higher to lower. There are two types of vertical mobility: upward mobility and downward mobility.

The movement of an individual from lower status to higher status is called upward mobility. For example, if the son of a worker sets up an industry or any other enterprise, it is an upward social mobility. Similarly, the case when the son of a peon becomes an IAS officer, there is a change from lower to higher status.

However, if a farmer loses his land for some reason and he is forced to do petty jobs to make a living, it is a case of downward mobility. When circumstances compel a person to quit a lucrative job and settle for a lower position, he is downwardly mobile.

Horizontal Mobility

It involves movement of individuals from one social group to another social group situated on the same level. If a person moves between jobs or careers of the same social status, it is horizontal mobility. It indicates change in position without any change in status. For example, if a doctor shifts from one hospital to another performing the same job, there is no change in the status. It is horizontal mobility.

Intergenerational Mobility

When changes in status take place over generations, it is called intergenerational mobility. For example, son of a farmer becoming an officer involves change in status through change in occupation. There is intergenerational mobility when people are able to achieve new statuses through their own efforts, irrespective of the circumstances they were born in.

Intragenerational Mobility

Time factor is an important element in determining the type of social mobility. When changes in status take place within one generation, it is an intragenerational mobility. It is the mobility occurring within a person's lifetime. For example, the rise of a person from a low supervisory level to the managerial level during the career is an example of intra-generational mobility.

Structural Mobility and Individual Mobility

It is a vertical movement of a specific group, class or occupation relative to others in the stratification system brought about by changes in stratification hierarchy itself. It occurs because of the structural changes and not because of individual efforts. For example, globalization has brought about changes in the labour market that have led to rise of some occupational groups and decline of others. Changes in society, which afford opportunities to large numbers of people to move up the social ladder at the same time, are a form of structural mobility. Thus, in structural mobility, changes occur because of structural changes in society.

Individual mobility is determined by characteristics like race, ethnicity, gender, religion, level of education, occupation, place of residence, health and other such factors.

STRATIFICATION AND CASTE

Under the caste system the status is hereditary and ascribed by birth. The rigid and closed caste system does not encourage vertical mobility and once such positions are assigned, the individuals cannot improve their social status in any way.

Social Stratification and Class

Unlike the caste system, class is an *open* system that facilitates vertical mobility. The status is based on achievement and movement from one status to another has no barrier. An individual is free to move up the social ladder by hard work, talent, money, intelligence, power and education.

Gender

Differentiation on the basis of gender is the oldest type of social stratification like caste. It is a socially constructed category rather than biologically determined and means much more than sex. The gender of a man is masculine and a woman is feminine. In recent years, gender has emerged as a conceptual tool for analysis to provide a deeper insight into various structural relationships of inequalities existing between men and women. Relationships between men and women vary widely across societies and cultures and change over periods of time.

Gender is the most potent significant and immensely useful analytical concept used by the feminists who prefer the term *gender* to *sex*. It refers to socially constructed and culturally determined role that men and women play in their daily lives. Feminist consider gender as the socio-cultural manifestation of sexual difference between male and female. Gender involves power structure and economic relationships and encompasses the social differentiation and cultural distinctions between women and men.

Individuals born in biological categories of male or female get into the social categories of men and women as they possess certain defined attributes as masculinity in males and feminity in females.

According to a famous sociologist, A. Masefield, 'Gender is a notion offering a set of frameworks and within that framework the social and ideological construction and representation of differences between sexes can be understood'.

Basically the gender involves power structure and economic relationships and it is used for analysing the role, responsibilities, status, constraints, needs of men and women in various fields. It also specifies social division and cultural differences between women and men. Gender distinction also plays an important role in shaping various practices and organizations in every society.

DIFFERENCES BETWEEN GENDER AND SEX

The term *gender* is not a substitute for the term *sex*. *Sex* refers to physical differences in the bodies of male and female but not all the differences are biological in origin. Gender is a structural feature of the society and a much broader term indicative of social, cultural and psychological differences between the two. While the biological differences remain the same over time and space, the socioculturally constructed differences vary from one place to the other and also over a period of time, making the term *gender* much more meaningful for sociologists.

REVIEW QUESTIONS

1. What is meant by social mobility? Explain about various types of social mobility.

2. Write short notes on the following:

   a. Stratification and gender

   b. Stratification and caste

CHAPTER

29

Race as a Biological Concept: Criteria of Racial Classification

LEARNING OBJECTIVES

After reading this chapter the learner should be able to

- Understand the basis of racial classification.
- Have knowledge about the determinants of race.

Race is a reality and a part of our daily existence. Without a proper understanding of the meaning of the term and unmindful of the real implications we are affected by it in everyday life as we come across people of various colours and other physical attributes. In the common understanding race refers to a category of people who share certain inherited physical characteristics, like colour of the skin, facial features, stature and other physical attributes. With advancements in science, particularly in the field of genetics, the study of races has become a more important and interesting area for anthropologists, sociologists, biologists and medical scientists.

The emergence of new scientific discipline of genetics has brought about a drastic change in the approach of scholars to the concept of race, which originated long before genetics arrived. It has now become possible to trace the geographical ancestry of a person through genetic analysis. The history of migration of a person's ancestors can be traced through genetic analysis and thus one can now ascertain with a fair degree of accuracy how the populations moved from one geographical area to the other.

The meaning of the term has also undergone a radical change over the years and the debate has been going on whether race is more of a biological concept or a social construct. Most people think of race in biological terms and for almost three centuries, but the approach has changed in recent years and differences not only of skin colour and physical features but also of language, nationality and religion are being taken into consideration. There is a major difference between the biological and sociological views of race. The difference in physical features led to the development of such racial categories, anthropologists, sociologists and many biologists raised questions regarding the value of such categorization.

Historically, the white dominant groups in the United States used the colour line to justify and perpetuate their hegemony over the black population and that led to the initial biological understanding of race on basis of the colour of the skin. The meaning of the term has undergone changes over the years but colour of the skin is still embedded in the minds as a primary indicator of race. The dominant group in society imposed the boundaries of group membership by defining race in terms of biology. The black population was downgraded and made biologically inferior to white population.

The concept of race has historically classified human species into a small number of groups on the basis of biological characteristics attributes inherited from generation to generation. This historical concept of race was rejected by some important thinkers, who found it lacking in both the logical coherence and the very existence of races. Others defended the concept of race but with changes in the foundations of racial identity.

The main problem with the concept has been that no boundaries of discrete races could be determined and it is believed that a great variety of human races exist in this world. Humans have been categorized into four races by some sociologists and these are white or Caucasian, black or African, yellow or Asian and red or Native American, whereas biological or phenotypic variation within racial groups has not been considered. Other thinkers classified humans into many more racial categories, maintaining that the *indigenous* natives of Europe could be distinguished into discrete Nordic, Alpine and Mediterranean races.

Race is, thus, one of the most intricate concepts in sociology and in the following section race as a biological concept is discussed in detail.

Definition of Race

A simple widely accepted definition is that 'race is a group that shares a certain common physical characteristics and a geographical origin'.

In the words of A.W. Green 'A race is a large botanical human grouping with a number of distinctive inherited features which may vary within a range', while A.L. Kroeber described 'a race as a valid biological concept, a group united by heredity, a breed or genetic strain or subspecies'.

According to Sutherland and Woodword, a race is 'a broad association of persons of similar biological heritage, who are united in sentiment by common cultural traditions and who in time of conflict seek to claim rights to a better social position of the basis of an inherited quality'.

J. Biesanz and M. Biesanz have given a very simple definition that 'A race is a large group of people distinguished by inherited physical differences'.

Ian Robertson states that the term race refers to the genetically transmitted physical characteristics of different groups.

The wide variations in the definitions of race prompted The United Nations Educational, Scientific and Cultural Organization (UNESCO) to convene a conference of sociologists, anthropologists and psychologists to have a single concept of race. It concluded that

1. Races can be differentiated on the basis of physical characteristics but not on the basis of cultural characteristics.
2. The differences found to exist in the physical characteristics of men is due to both hereditary and environment.
3. Human races can be classified solely on the basis of physical traits.
4. Pure races cannot be found anywhere in the world and the process of mixing of races originated long back and the belief that it is deleterious from biological viewpoint is incorrect. The claims of purity by some races are not true.
5. Every race has equal capacity for the development of mind and culture.
6. It is possible that degree of racial difference may vary from one nation to the other.

7. There is evidence to support the fact that race has no significant effect in the social and cultural differences between human groups.

Thus, race is a group of intermarrying people who are born of common ancestors and have similar physical attributes and share a we-feeling. Their physical characteristics achieve permanency due to inbreeding and the races can be distinguished from each other on the basis of these characteristics. Apart from geographic isolation, a race also evolves due to mutation, migration, selection and adaptation.

Determination of Race

A race is determined on the basis of physical characteristics and is broadly classified into two categories:

1. Indefinite physical traits
2. Definite physical traits

INDEFINITE PHYSICAL TRAITS

These traits are not amenable to any measurement like colour of the skin. These traits can only be described.

French racial theorist Joseph Arthur de Gobineau is the first to propound the theory that there were only three races categorized on the basis of the skin of the people as white, yellow and black but since it is difficult to make out the subtle variations as colour of skin changes due to climate, the anthropologists do not rely much on it. Further, every colour has many intermediate distinctions such as blood red, white skin of Kashmiri people and white skin of superior castes of Northern India.

Following distinctions are made on basis of the colour of the skin.

1. Leucoderm (white) as Caucasina
2. Xanthoderm (yellow) as Mongolian
3. Melanoderm (black) as Negro

Texture and Colour of Hair: There are three types of distinguishing textures and colours of hair.

1. *Leiotrichy (soft and straight hair):* Mongols and Chinese
2. *Cymotrichy (smooth and curly hair):* Natives of India, Western Europe, Australia and North-East Africa
3. *Ulotrichy (thick and curly hair):* The Negroes

Structure and Colour of Eyes: There are three colours of eyes: white, gray and yellow. The structure of the orifice of the eyes is usually horizontal but in some places like North America and Southern Europe it is diagonal.

Definite Physical Traits: These are measurable traits like stature, shape of the nose and structure of the head.

Stature: It is one of the features on the basis of which people from different races are distinguished as various races have different height. Tall stature (170 cm and above), average stature (165 cm and above) and short stature (160 cm and below) as classified by Topinard on the basis of height.

Structure of the Head: The structure of the head can be determined by the ratio of its length to its breadth. The cephalic index or cranial index is the ratio of the maximum width of the head divided by its maximum length multiplied by 100. Heads can be classified into three categories on the basis of cephalic index as follows:

1. Dolicocephalic (cephalic index 75)
2. Mesocephalic (cephalic index 75 to 80)
3. Brachycephalic (cephalic index 80)

The structure of head is not given much importance now in determination of race as it has been established by Boas that changes in environment affect the structure of head. In India brachycephalic, mesocephalic and dolicocephalic people are found in Bengal, Bihar and Uttar Pradesh, respectively.

Structure of Nose: The nose structure has been classified into three categories on the basis of nasal index. The nasal index is calculated by taking the length of nose as 100 and calculating the percentage of its width. The three categories are as follows:

1. Leptorrhine (thin, nasal index 70 per cent)
2. Mesorrhine (medium, nasal index 60 per cent)
3. Platyrrhine (nasal index above 85 per cent)

Blood Group. It is one of the racial traits which remains unaffected by changes in the environment. There are four types of blood groups A, B, AB and O found in every race, though their proportion may differ.

There is no pure race anywhere due to intermixing of various races over the years across the world.

Human Races

There are two important classification of human races as categorized by Hoebel and Kroebar.

Hoebel divided human races into the following three classes:

1. Caucasoid: Nordic, Alpine and Mediterranean
2. Mongoloid: Mongolian, Malenisian and American Indian
3. Negroid: Negro, Malanesians, Pygmy Black and Bushman

Kroebar categorized human races into the following four classes:

1. Caucasoid: Nordic, Alpine and Mediterranean
2. Mongoloid: Mongolian, Malenisian and American Indian
3. Negroid: Negro, Malanesians, Pygmy Black and Bushman
4. Australoid: Australia

Brief characteristics of important human races are as follows:

1. Caucasoid

The Caucasian race is characterized by light skin colour varying from white to dark wheatish and straight to wavy hair with colour from flaxen to brownish to dark ebony. They are of medium built, have prominent eyes, pronounced nose with good shape and sharp features.

There are various subraces of Caucasoids categorized mainly on the bases of geographic location and language. These include Indo-European populations called Aryans, Arabs, Hebrew-speaking people called Semitic, Berber–Cushitic–Egyptian native races named Hamitic, and others are Nordic, Mediterranean, Dinaric, Alpine, Arabid, East Baltic, Turanid, Iranid and Armenoid.

The two important races in this class are as follows:

Nordic: They are distinguished by high forehead, leptorrhine nose, thin lips, blue eyes, yellow hairs, white or red colour of the skin, average height is 170 cm. They are mostly found in Scandinavian, Baltic and British Island.

Alpine: The main features are broad and small forehead, small eyebrows, medium nasal index, medium cephalic index, maximum thin lips, deep grey eyes, light white skin and height 163 cm. The race is found in Central Asia.

Mediterranean: They are characterized by long head, cephalic l index less than 75, small eye-brows, medium lips, leptorrinie nose, light grey eyes, curly hairs and grey skin. They are found in Spain, Portugal, Italy and France.

2. Mongoloid

Mongoloids are distinguished by yellowish or light wheaties skin, extremely straight and black hair, less hair growth on the bodies, small, almond-shaped eyes and slight built. The facial features are usually small but clear. They are found in the far Orients, Northeastern India and certain American countries.

This group includes the following races:

1. **Asian Mongol:** They are found in China, Japan and north-eastern India.
2. **Micronesian:** They are found in the eastern islands of Malenesia.

3. Negroid

Their physical characteristics are dark skin due to dense pigmentation, coarse black and woolly hair, wide noses and foreheads, often thick lips, large built and broad skeletal structure. The Negroid race is subdivided into subraces such as Aborigines, Melanesians, Negritos, Papuans and Dravidians. They are found in Africa.

1. **Negro:** These are found in equatorial regions like Africa and Southern India.
2. **Far Eastern Pygmy:** These are found in the South Pacific islands. Their characteristics are similar to those of Negroes.
3. **Bushman and Hottentots:** These are found in Kala-hari desert of Africa. Their average height is less than 150 cm.

4. Australoid

As the name indicates, Austrloid are found in Australia. They have racial characteristics as high head, low forehead, big and broad nose, medium lips, grey eyes, wavy hair and an average height of about 165 cm. Anthropologists contest the distinctiveness of this race genetically and physiologically, very close to the Negroid race. So natives of the Andaman and Nicobar Islands in the Indian Ocean have racial similarities with Australian aborigines. Many anthropologists and genetic biologists feel that these people should be categorized as subraces of the Negroid race. Thus, the Australoid race is a classification based on geographical location and regional culture rather than genetic and biological traits.

Classification of Indian Races

Indian population presents a mosaic of major races of the world. India has been the melting pot of races and often described as a museum of races. There have been conflicting races and also the process of assimilation and synthesis, building the civilization.

According to Herbert Risley, who attempted first classification of Indian races, there are seven racial types in Indian population.

1. **The Turk-Iranian:** These types are mostly found in the Frontier Province and Baluchistan. They are very tall with fair complexion, dark eyes and narrow nose.
2. **Indo-Aryan:** Found in Punjab, Rajasthan and Kashmir, these people are distinguished by long heads, fair complexion and prominent noses. They are tall and have dark eyes.
3. **Scytho-Dravidian:** It is a mixed racial type of Scythians and Dravidians. Their racial ancestry is traced to Saurashtra, Coorg and hilly tracts of Madhya Pradesh. They are marked by broad head, fine nose, low-medium height, scanty body hair and fair complexion. The upper strata

people are said to be predominantly Scythian and the lower strata people are dominated by Dravidian elements.

4. **Aryo-Dravidian:** A product of intermarriages between the Indo-Aryans and the Dravidians, the racial type have long head with the complexion varying from light brown to black. They are found in Uttar Pradesh, Rajasthan and Bihar.
5. **Mongol-Dravidians:** Predominantly a mixture of Mongolians and Dravidians, the racial type has some element of Indo-Aryan race. The people are generally black with round head and medium nose and height. They are found in Bengal and Orissa. Bengali Brahmins and Kayasthas form the largest percentage.
6. **The Mongoloid:** This racial type are found in Himalayan and sub-Himalayan regions, including Ladakh, Nepal, Assam, Sikkim, Arunachal Pradesh, the Hill states of Northeast India and Burma. They are characterized by short stature, yellow complexion, medium broad nose, flat face and oblique eyes with an epicanthic fold. Their representatives are the Kinnets of Lahul-Spiti and Kullu, the Lepchas and Bhutias of Sikkim, and the Tharus of the Tarai region of Uttar Pradesh and Uttarakhand.
7. **The Dravidian:** They have dark complexion, dark eyes, short stature, long head and broad nose. The racial type is found in Southern India, particularly in Southern Madhya Pradesh, Chotnagpur, Madras and Hyderabad. The Santhals of Chotnagpur represent this type.

Classification of A.C. Haddon

A.C. Haddon contested the classification of races advanced by Herbert Risley and pointed out that the country had various pre-Dravidian jungle tribes. He came out with his own classification of races in India in which the oldest existing stratum is represented by pre-Dravidian jungle tribes. According to him the Indian population comprises:

1. Jungle tribes or Pre-Dravidian
2. Long-headed Dravidians
3. Long-headed and fair complexioned Indo-Aryans
4. Broad headed Indo-Alpines
5. Mongolians

Classification of J.H. Hutton

According to J.H. Hutton the earliest occupants of India were probably the Negrito race but they left with no trace in India. Next came the Proto-Austroloid and then the Mediterranean race speaking an agglutinative tongue from which the present Austro-Asiatic languages are derived.

Hutton also maintains that the broad-headed elements in the Indian population can be traced back to the Armenodi branch of the Alpine race. The Indo-Aryan race came to India in 1500 BC, whereas the Mongolian characteristics came from the East and moved towards the South.

There are various races found in Indian population as Negrito, Proto-Austroloid, Mediterranean, East Mediterranean Armenoid branch of Alpine, Indo-Aryans and Mongoloid.

Classification of B.S. Guha

Dr B.S. Guha has divided the population of India into the following races:

1. **Negrito:** According to Guha, Negrito element is found in the blood of Andaman Islanders, although the presence of Negrito race in India is a controversial issue. He pointed out that Negrito element is found in the blood of some South Indian tribes like the Kadar and blood of Nagas. Although there is controversy, it maybe concluded that the Negrito race existed in the past in India.

2. **Proto-Austroloid:** It is a pre-Dravidian race which dominates the tribal population of central India. Many tribes such as the Santhals, the Mundas, the Juangas, the Soaras and the Kondhs belong to this race.
3. **Mongoloid:** Most of the people in Northeastern India have features of Mongloid race. According to Dr Guha, the race is of two types:
   - **a.** The Palaeo-Mongoloid. They are of two types: long headed and the broad headed. Long-headed Palaeo-Mongoloid race is the Angami Nagas, whereas brood headed Palaeo-Mongoloid race is people in the Himalayan foot hills from Kashmir to Assam.
   - **b.** The Tibeto-Mongoloid. The people of Sikkim and Bhutan belong to the Tibeto-Mongoloid branch of Mongoloid race.
4. **The Mediterranean:** It is the dominant race in India and it is divided into three types.
   - **a.** The Palaeo-Mediterranean. Brahmins of South India from Tamilnadu and Madras represent this racial type.
   - **b.** The Mediterranean. People of this race are believed to be the builders of the Indus valley civilization.
   - **c.** Oriental. It is very much similar to the Mediterranean type.
5. **Western Brachycephals:** It is of three types:
   - **a.** The Alpendoid. People of this race are found in Sourashtra, Gujarat and also Bengal.
   - **b.** The Dinaric. People of Bengal, Orissa and Coorg belong to the race Dinaric.
   - **c.** The Armenia. The Parsees in India are the representatives of Armenian race.
6. **Nordic Race:** People of this race came to India from the North and Southeast Asia and spread all over Northern India. In North India, it is mainly found in a mixed form with the Mediterranean race.

The Negrito, the Proto-Austroloid and the Mongoloid mainly comprise tribal population, while the Mediterranean, the Western Brachycephals and the Nordic races constitute the general population of India.

REVIEW QUESTIONS

1. What are the various determinants of race?
2. Write short notes on the following:
   - **a.** Classification of race by B.S. Guha
   - **b.** Classification of race by J.H. Hutton

CHAPTER

30

Effect of Caste, Class and Race on Health and Health Practices

LEARNING OBJECTIVES

After reading this chapter the learner should be able to

- Find out the effect of caste on health.
- Know various social factors influencing health.

Caste, class and race continue to be dominant influences in the Indian society, perpetuating the socioeconomic inequalities, which have been the bane of the country. The negative impact of caste and these inequalities are all too visible in various spheres, particularly the health status of the section at the receiving end of these social constructs, which have been responsible for the propagation of unjust and unequal societal structures.

Some upper castes and classes and certain races are very dominant and exploit placed lower in the social ladder and this has often led to violence in society. The inequalities engendered in caste, class and race not only lead to socioeconomic disparities but also have implications on the health and well-being of the exploited lot. Caste is similar to race, which is also a social concept without genetic basis. Various health indicators bring out that people of lower castes and class have problems in accessing health care. The comparatively lower coverage under vaccination, antenatal care and institutional deliveries and higher percentage of underweight children and anaemia among adults in case of lower classes and castes provide an indication of the negative impact on the health.

The scheduled castes (SCs) and other backward classes (OBCs) are socioeconomically weaker sections and they account for a majority of people living below poverty line. Scheduled tribes (STs) are basically the races that have suffered due to discrimination and exploitation. While some barriers have been broken in urban settings, caste, class and race-related inequalities continue to persist in rural India. The efforts to enforce the secular, socialistic and democratic principles enshrined in the constitution that guarantee equality in all respects are making a slow progress. The focus of remedial measures has been on reservation in educational institutions and employment and the impact of these inherent inequalities on health has not attracted due attention.

A large percentage of SCs live in rural areas and they are mostly landless agricultural labourers, while some of them live in urban slums under pathetic conditions. The STs, or adivasis, also suffer economic and social deprivation much like the SCs. Most of them live in the remote hill areas of hills or deep forests. They comprise around 8 per cent of India's population. The major forms of inequalities influencing health and health practices are the poor availability, accessibility and affordability of health care services and this has been largely responsible for the persistently widening differentials in health outcomes.

CAUSES

Poor socioeconomic status: Sociodemographic factors and societal forces like discrimination and poverty create circumstances that negatively influence health status. Persons of lower socioeconomic status face greater social and community demands, while having fewer resources in terms of money, access to medical care, social support system and coping mechanisms. The health status of individuals varies with socioeconomic status because of these resources.

Lack of knowledge: Use of contraceptives is lower among the SCs and the STs compared to forward castes mainly due to lack of awareness. The SCs, STs and other sections of poor people have limited health literacy and they do not have much knowledge about the causes of disease and their effects. They are unable to understand the relationship between lifestyle factors such as diet, hygiene and exercise and health outcomes. People with limited health literacy often may not know when and how to seek health care.

Accessibility to health: SCs, STs and poor class people face problem in getting access to health care services. Even utilization of maternal health care services and immunization coverage is not much among these people. This is evident from lower levels of antenatal care, institutional deliveries and immunization coverage among the lower castes. Consequently, underweight and anaemic children and anaemia in adults is common among the lower castes. Neonatal, infant, child and under-five statistics show a higher mortality among the SCs and the STs.

Migration: Poverty makes SCs, STs and poor to migrate to different parts of the country in search of work. They are denied many benefits offered to the economically weaker section because of their migrant status. Their ration cards may not be valid in other states. Migrants are often thought to be the carriers of many communicable diseases and their services are not hired by many industries leading to unemployment and poverty. Their children are unable to go to schools and lack of education implies a continuation of the cycle of poverty. Their welfare is neglected by politicians and political parties as most of them are not registered as voters in the state to which they have migrated.

Communal violence: The poor and the lower castes are the victims of communal violence. Especially lower castes (particularly dalits) face lot of social discrimination and most of the time are made targets of communal violence also. Dalits are subjected to assault, rape and murder by the *upper* castes. It is commonly seen that these crimes are not properly investigated due to which the culprits escape punishment.

Health and human rights: There is a strong link between health and human rights. The violations of human rights can have serious health consequences. Discrimination against SCs and STs in terms of rights to health, education and housing renders these underprivileged sections vulnerable to various diseases and health-related problems.

Social determinants of health: Determinants of health are social and economic rather than medical. The poor health of people from the lower castes is a consequence of their social exclusion and unequal distribution of power, income, material and public health services. Caste has strong relationship with socioeconomic status of individuals in India. Though lot of schemes are there for the upliftment of low-caste people but they still have limited access to clean water, sanitation, adequate nutrition, proper housing, education, health care and employment. Poor social policies and unfair economic arrangement are some of the factors responsible for it.

Social interventions should form the core of all health and prevention programmes that require population interventions instead of individual.

Barriers to scaling up interventions: The major barrier to mainstreaming health care is discrimination on the basis of caste. The systematic discrimination against lower castes is based on various sociocultural, traditional and religious issues that need to be tackled. Failure to recognize this relationship and the refusal to tackle these issues result in poorer health standards in the SCs and the STs. Poverty and social exclusion have tremendous effect on the social determinants of health. Individuals at higher risk for diseases have a higher probability of being denied health care services.

Continuing the current affirmative action in education and employment is crucial. The Right to Education Act, the National Rural Employment Guarantee Act, the Food Security Act, the National Rural Health Mission, the Mid-Day Meal scheme and Sarva Shiksha Abhiyan, all steps taken by Government of India for the welfare of SCs and STs are in the right direction. There is need to increase resource allocation for the social determinants of health. Social and political inclusion of the poor and lower castes in policy and decision-making are required. The provision of fair and continuous employment and effective coverage under the public distribution system are necessary for improving their health status.

REVIEW QUESTIONS

1. Describe the impact of socioeconomic status of an individual on his health.
2. What are the various issues that need to be tackled to make health care services equally available for all?

UNIT - 8

TYPES OF COMMUNITIES IN INDIA

CHAPTER

31

Community

LEARNING OBJECTIVES

After reading this chapter the learner should be able to

- Gain knowledge about features of community.
- Draw a comparison between community and society.

Human beings have been from time immemorial living in groups. However, community life evolved after people started living in settlements in specific territorial area sharing similar environment.

A community is a rather small unit whose members are bound together by the sense of belonging, created by daily interaction on a personal basis involving a whole range of human activities. Its size is limited by the ability of the people to intimately interact with each other. Thus, it is a much smaller group compared to a society.

A community is essentially a collection of people living in a specified geographical area, sharing close relationships and having a strong sense of belonging. The members have intimate interaction and shared common values, beliefs and culture. The daily activities of a community take place within the geographical area, which is self-contained.

Well-known sociologist Karl Mannheim refers to 'community' as a group of closely bound people living together and sharing a whole set of interests. Talcott Parsons, on the other hand, defined community as a collective unit the members of which share a common territorial area as their base of operation for daily activities.

Similarly, another sociologist Kingsley Davis defined it as the smallest territorial group that can embrace all aspects of social life.

COMPARISON BETWEEN SOCIETY AND COMMUNITY

While a community is a small group of people bound by intimate relationships, a society is a wider entity and can comprise many communities. Thus, a society is much wider entity encompassing the whole web of relationships, organized or unorganized, but there cannot be more than one society in a community.

A community is rooted to a particular geographical area and its existence can be located. A society is pervasive and not confined to a particular territory.

A strong community sentiment is the hallmark of a community but such a feeling is not essential in a society.

In a community, people live together to pursue common interests and common objectives, whereas in a society diverse interests prevail and common interests and common objectives are not necessary.

TYPES OF COMMUNITY ORGANIZATION

Human communities can be classified on the basis of different criteria for various purposes but the most commonly used classification is based on size and density of population.

The first community is the neighbourhood, followed by village, town, city, country, region and the world.

Neighbourhood

It is a loosely bound community consisting of many family groups living in the neighbourhood. It is the first community a child comes into contact.

In rural neighbourhood, the inhabitants know each other well even if they are not living in close proximity. However, in urban neighbourhood, the people may not have close interaction even if they live close by and at times they may not even know each other. Women and children love to live in neighbourhood much more than men.

Village Community

Villages came into existence after the migratory groups acquired skills in agriculture to lead a settled life. Thus, village is the oldest permanent human community. The primitive villages were very small in size consisting of a few families and thus the members were related by kinship. Land was the main resource and it was tilled jointly.

Thereafter, a feudal system emerged and the land no longer remained under collective ownership and it came under the control of some village chieftain.

The modern villages have come a long way and urbanization has made great impact on the lifestyle. The bond of kinship, which fostered a strong feeling of community living, is no longer there due to increased size and high mobility of population.

Agricultural operations have been modernized and mechanized and that has made a huge socio-economic impact on village life. However, the inhabitants continue to share rural and urban categories, though a new category of slum, where mostly the migrant population lives, has emerged in recent years.

Rural Community

Traditionally the rural communities comprise the farmers who are engaged in the production of food grains, fibres and other required raw materials. Farming has been a way of life with the rural communities in India. They adhered to traditional values and the members shared intimate relationships.

The people live in large families and agriculture remains the main economic activity. The vocation of farming is passed on from one generation to the next. The process of change is relatively slow as the rural areas do not have access to modern education and advanced technology.

Rural inhabitants live in a natural environment and work with familiar people with whom they mostly share a close relationship. They are very hospitable and treat guests as family members.

Characteristics of Rural Community

India is predominantly a rural country with over 70 per cent of population residing in villages. The rural community comprises the people living in villages whose main occupation is agriculture. Villages are by and large peaceful and people lead a simple life, bereft of modern amenities.

Occupation: Agriculture is the main occupation of village community, though cottage industry also plays an important part in the rural economy as it provides livelihood to the landless people.

Density of population: With vast open land used for agricultural activities, the density of population is very low. The houses are usually big in villages and the number of houses is also limited.

Joint families: The traditional joint family system is very much intact in the rural community and it plays an important part in controlling the social behaviour. The father usually heads and manages the affairs of the joint family. He commands respect and exercises control over the members to maintain discipline.

Immobility: Population is by and large stable in rural areas. People hardly migrate from villages as their main occupation is agriculture.

Education: Literacy in rural areas is low. Villages lack facilities for higher education. The birth rate is high and the community views it as a positive feature as more hands are required to work in fields.

Environment: People in rural areas live very close to the nature and live a very simple life. The villages still enjoy a pollution-free environment.

Caste system: The roots of the traditional caste system are very strong in the rural communities and segregation on the basis of castes continues to prevail in some form. Social status is largely determined by caste and discrimination on the basis of caste still prevalent in interior areas.

Family system: The traditional joint family system is prevalent in rural areas and the inhabitants follow the old customs, beliefs and values. Most of the families in rural community are large in size. There is still a lot of respect given to elderly people. The head of the family has full control over the family members.

Marriage system: Marriages are usually arranged by the elders of the family. People get married at an early age because of low literacy.

Living standards: The living standards are improving with the changing economy of villages. Better road connectivity, telecommunication facility and other means of communication have made an impact on rural life.

Panchayati Raj Institutions

Panchayati Raj

Villages in India are having a local self-government under the panchayati raj system. A three-tier democratic structure comprising of gram panchayat at village level, panchayat samiti at block level and zilla parishad at district level has been provided. The representatives are elected and to ensure adequate representation seats have been reserved for scheduled castes, scheduled tribes and women.

Village Panchayat

The gram panchayat is accountable for all its actions to the gram sabha, the general body consisting of all adult villagers residing in the panchayat area. The number of members in a panchayat varies from 5 to 13 depending on the population of the villages. The president of the panchayat, also called Pradhan or Sarpanch, and members are elected by the voters. There is also provision for co-option of women and Scheduled Castes and Scheduled Tribes, if they do not get adequate representation through the normal electoral process.

The village panchayat is required to hold regular mandatory meetings of the general house of the gram sabha. It has to present the annual budget, accounts and administrative report before the gram sabha. It is also required get the village development plan and tax proposals approved by the gram sabha. The sarpanch is the key functionary who supervises and coordinates all the activities of panchayat. He is assisted by panchayat secretary in carrying out various administrative functions.

The panchayat carries out various development activities in its jurisdiction and also involved in implementation of various policies and programmes of the government. Its functions include construction and maintenance of roads, village paths, wells, funeral grounds, sanitation, and public libraries, reading rooms, community centre and other such amenities. The panchayat is also required to maintain a record of births and deaths. It also adjudicates minor disputes among residents.

Panchayat Samiti

It is the second tier, an intermediary unit between gram panchayat and zila parishad, and its prime function is execution of community development in the block, subunit of the district. It takes care of larger works functions which the village panchayat cannot perform but are of interests to the residents.

The president and vice president of the panchayat samite are elected by members of the panchayat samiti and all the panchas of the gram panchayat falling within the area. The pradhan convenes and presides over the panchayat samiti meetings.

The prime function of the panchayat samiti is to coordinate the activities of the various panchayats within its jurisdiction. The panchayat samiti oversees the functioning of the panchayats and regulates their budgets. It has a right to suggest measures for improving the functioning of the panchayats. The samiti has a role in preparing and implementing plans for the development of agriculture, animal husbandry, fisheries, small-scale and cottage industries, rural health and other related sectors.

The chairperson of the samiti who is also a member of zila parishad by virtue of his position ensures that the decisions and resolutions of the panchayat samiti and its standing committees are implemented. He has authority to have full administrative control over the vikas adhikari or block development officer (BDO) and his staff. He is the ex-officio chairperson of the standing committees of the samiti also.

Zila Parishad

It is the apex body of the three-tier structure and also called district panchayat or district development council. Its jurisdiction covers all gram panchayats, block samitis under the district. All the directly elected candidates, panchayat samiti heads, MPs and MLAs of the district are its members. They elect the chairperson and vice-chairperson of zila parishads, chairperson and vice chairperson have administrative control over the chief executive officer and all other officers and subordinate staff of the zila parishad.

Powers, functions and duties of zila parishads include implementation of projects and programmes to increase agriculture productivity, expand and maintain irrigation network, promote cultivation of fruits and vegetables, develop agriculture markets, conserve soil, facilitate fodder production and construct and maintain rural roads. Besides, it is also involved in implementation of poverty alleviation and immunization programmes, health education activities, rural housing projects and other activities for socio-economic uplift of the people.

A zila parishad is empowered to supervise and coordinate the functions of the panchayat samitis, examine and approve their budget and issue directives to them to ensure efficient performance of duties. It co-ordinates and consolidates development plans of panchayat samitis and advise the state government on all matters relating to development activities and maintenance of services. It has a number of standing committees namely, general committee, finance audit and planning committee, social justice committee, education and health committee, agriculture and industry committee to take care of various functions.

URBAN COMMUNITY

The country has witnessed rapid urbanization over the past century, particularly after independence, though a vast majority of people still lives in villages. There has been large-scale migration of people from rural to urban areas and the proportion of a population living in towns and cities if increasing by the day.

The process of urbanization got impetus due to industrialization and increase in trade and commercial activities. The word 'urban' is derived from the Latin word *urbanus*, which literally means pertaining to a city. The process and its implications have attracted the attention of sociologist and as a result a new field of 'urban sociology' has emerged.

Urban sociology is the study of people living in groups and social relationship in urban environment. Demographer Thompson Warren has defined it as a process whereby population tends to agglomerate in clusters. The movement of people from rural areas is also accompanied by a shift from agriculture to other economic activities like trade, manufacturing, business, service and other avocations. Large-scale migration of people also leads to change in attitudes, beliefs, values and the overall behaviour patterns in the urban community.

The main reason for migration is the availability of facilities like education, health care system and basic civic amenities, besides employment opportunities. The urban clusters are classified into towns, cities and metros on the basis of population criteria.

Characteristics of Urban Community

Heterogeneous Population

With people moving in from different places, the urban community is a heterogeneous and constitutes a rather diverse sociocultural mix. The urban hubs are more densely populated than the rural areas. The eating habits, costumes, living conditions, religious beliefs and customs and cultural traditions vary greatly.

Family: Individual is more important than family and nuclear families are in vogue in urban areas. Family unit is not all that stable and the number of joint families is far less. The community is not as closely knit entity as the rural community and there is predominance of secondary relations.

Boys and girls have much freedom to choose their life partners and there is a surfeit of love marriages and intercaste marriages but at the same time the number of divorces is also higher.

Mobility: The urban community is mobile and open. The people are more class-conscious, progressive and amenable to changes. The status is not ascribed by heredity or birth but achieved by merit and hardwork, affording ample scope for social mobility.

Occupations: With numerous occupations, there is widespread division of labour and specialization opportunities. The major occupations are in the industrial, business, administrative and service sectors.

Economic disparity: There is huge economic disparity in towns and cities, which are inhabited by very rich and very poor people. Palatial houses and slums exist side by side. Financial standing, property, income and other assets are the symbols of status in the community steeped in materialism.

Environment: People live in heavily built-up areas far away from nature. They have to put up with industrial and vehicular pollution and contaminated water.

Class system: People are not known by their caste but by their class based on the economic status. Most of the people in urban areas fall in the middle class. The urbanites do not care for their neighbours and have very little contact. They hardly know each other and there is abject lack of personal involvement in the affairs of others.

Social control: There is no social control in urban community and individual behaviour is regulated by formal agencies such as police, jails and courts of law.

Rational attitude: The urban community has a rational approach and people tend to reason and argue. Their relationship with others is governed by self-interest and on consideration of personal gain or loss.

Emergence of Slums

Slums come up due to large-scale migration of people from villages and small towns to big cities in search of jobs and a better life. As most of the migrants are poor and in no position to afford good housing and civic amenities in the city, they are forced live on the outskirts. The urban poor also have no choice and they illegally build shelters on any available piece of land.

Disturbing situation created by prolonged wars, insurgency and terrorism and natural calamities like earthquakes, floods and tsunamis often cause uprooting of people who settle in vicinity of towns and cities, giving rise to slums.

Slum areas are in fact urban hubs without the basic amenities like proper housing, clean drinking water, power and sanitary services. There are other problems like congestion, crime, drug menace, prostitution and communicable diseases.

As per official estimates, India's slum population will touch 104 million by 2017, around 9 per cent of the total projected national population of 1.28 billion that year. These slums will mostly come up in small towns and semi-rural areas, owing to accelerated shift from rural to urban areas across the country.

Main Features of Slums

Location: Slums generally come up in the outskirts of towns and cities and they lack the basic amenities.

Poverty: Slum dwellers are mostly poor as they are forced to live on the outskirts as they cannot afford the expensive housing within main township and cities.

Overcrowding: Slum areas are overcrowded and most of the families live in a single-room accommodation, some of which do not even have kitchens and toilets. There is no privacy in the family as all the members live in the same room.

Poor environmental hygiene: Slum areas have poor sanitation as there are no toilets and most of the people go for open defecation. The lack of proper drainage system adds to the problem.

Social problems: Drug trafficking, prostitution and other criminal activities are widely prevalent in slum areas. There is high incidence of deviant behaviour among slum dwellers.

Communicable diseases: Lack of drinking water, poor nutrition, overcrowding and insanitary conditions make people in slum areas vulnerable to communicable diseases. The diseases commonly prevalent include diarrhoea, hepatitis, acquired immunodeficiency syndrome (AIDS), parasitic infestation and andanaemia.

Domestic violence: Addiction to drugs, alcohol and other narcotic substances lead to problems like domestic violence, particularly against women and children. It is a major concern among slum dwellers.

Slums are marked by dilapidated housing structures, often made from scrap materials, overcrowding and congestion and lack of public utilities. These areas are neglected and looked down upon as inferior.

TOWN

The towns are essentially semiurban dwellings and an intermediate between rural and urban communities. Social behaviour is more close to that of rural community than cities. A town is quite large for all inhabitants to be well acquainted but not large enough to prevent predominance of informal relationships.

Towns are places with population of 5,000 and more, subject to the conditions that the density of population is not less than 400 sq.km and at least 75 per cent of the adult male population is engaged in nonagricultural activities.

Cities

Towns with population of 100,000 and above are classified as cities.

Mega Cities

The word *mega* indicates very large habitations and the concept of 'mega city' is a recent phenomenon. It is defined as a metropolitan city with high growth and population of 10 million and more.

They have peculiar management problems due to their large size like proper waste disposal, ensuring adequate water supply and easing traffic congestion.

REVIEW QUESTIONS

1. What are the characteristics of a community?
2. Make a comparison between community and society.

CHAPTER

32

Community Development Project and Planning

LEARNING OBJECTIVES

After reading this chapter the learner should be able to

- Get acquainted with various community development projects.
- Know about the features of Panchayati Raj.

The process of community development (CD) primarily concerns the issues pertaining to the disadvantaged and aims at addressing these issues by involving all members of the society. It is about participation of the people in the process of social change to enhance their power, skills, knowledge and experience.

The objective of a CD initiative is to facilitate and enable individuals and communities to undertake initiatives of their own to combat social, economic, political and environmental problems. It is a process whereby members of the community come together to collectively generate solutions to their common problems and undertake initiatives that will benefit all.

Sociologists have found it difficult to come out with a precise and universal definition of CD, and they have defined it differently. However, the basic definition given by the United Nation in 1948 provides a good idea of the concept.

It states that 'Community Development is a process designed to create conditions of economic and social progress for the whole community with its active participation and fullest possible reliance upon the community's initiative'.

In Chris Maser's words definition of CD is 'the capacity of people to work collectively in addressing their common interests'. According to Christenson 'Community development is a group of people in a community reaching a decision to initiate a social action process to change their economic, social, cultural and environmental situation'.

Kenyon described it as 'Community economic development is about identifying and harnessing local community resources and opportunities and stimulating sustainable economic and employment activity'. According to A.R. Desai 'Community development plan tries to begin the process of transformation in the economic and social life of villages'.

Essential Features of a Community Development Initiative

Flexible and focused: A CD initiative has to be flexible and aim at addressing the existing concern of the community.

Community spirit: It must ensure active involvement of the members and help develop the spirit of community life.

Inclusive: While the will of the majority must prevail, the voices of all concerned should be heard and considered. The barriers of caste, creed, religion, age race and political ideology should not come in the way of participation and all community members should be associated and afforded equal opportunity.

Self-determination: The community members should discuss issues, take advice from experts and arrive at their own decisions and implement them.

Community awareness of issues: There should be awareness in the community about issues and concerns and that a problem existed. Members are more likely to come forward to work together if community accepts that it is 'their' problem.

Capacity building: The existing capacity of the members and the community has to be recognized for creating opportunities for them to build on and enhance the capacity. The focus should be on taking advantage of informal networks and social support systems to avoid duplication of existing structures and functions.

Local leadership: Committed local leadership, formal and informal, is essential for championing the cause of community and effective implementation of development initiatives.

Aims and Objectives of Community Development Projects

Aims and objectives of community development projects are listed hereunder:

1. Integrated development of the rural community to bring transformation in social, cultural, economic and other aspects of village life.
2. Realization of full potential of material and human resources and focus should be on encouraging and training local leadership.
3. Elimination of unemployment, poverty and gender bias from the rural community and provide economic and other assistance to the weaker sections to reduce the economic disparities.
4. Increase farm productivity by encouraging farmers to adopt latest scientific know-how and modern technology.
5. The development effort should aim at making the villages self-reliant in basic needs like food, clothing and shelter.

Community Development Programme

Concept of CD in India was initiated before independence and considerable attention was given to uplift rural community. Mahatma Gandhi advocated communal harmony, economic equity, social equality, deaddiction from alcohol and narcotics, promotion of village industries, sanitation, health care, education and empowerment of women, with the aim of generating gainful employment in rural areas.

After independence CD assumed high priority and a pilot CD project was launched through the Etawah Project in 1948. Later, the Government of India launched 55 CD projects in 1952, each covering about 300 villages or a population of 30,000. The major emphasis was on improving agricultural production. The National Extension Service Project was initiated with similar aim to cover larger areas, including the dry regions. These CD blocks are normal administrative units for allocating budget, planning and development.

There were 1114 blocks covering 1,63,000 villages by the end of the First Five Year Plan (1952–1957). The CD programme covered the entire country by the 1960s. The programme aimed at uplift of the rural poor, covering agriculture, animal husbandry, roads, health, education, housing, employment, social and cultural activities. Efforts were also made to improve literacy, health, sanitation, housing, transport and communication. A block development officer (BDO) was appointed at each block or the revenue tehsil, with a team of subject specialists and village-level workers (VLW) to implement the multidimensional programme. Each VLW covered 5 to 10 villages having a population of 5000–6000 to implement various development programmes. The VLWs persuade the farmers to take part in various development schemes.

The BDO has various staff under him, as extension officers for different departments as each department like agriculture, animal husbandry, panchayat, cooperation, rural industries, rural engineering, social education and women and child welfare is headed by an extension officer. Each block has a medical officer with supporting staff for medical care. Advisory committees were established from block level to state level to ensure people's participation.

There was no significant achievement and poverty kept on increasing till mid-1970s. The Land Reforms Act of 1956 did remove vestiges of the feudal-colonial rule but it did not help the poor and landless to gain control over the land, particularly in North India. Even the core programme of agricultural development failed to raise the food production. India was compelled to import food grains in the 1970s. Even improvement in the agricultural productivity and improvement in the literacy and infrastructural development were not sustainable.

Panchayati Raj Institutions

Government appointed the Balvantrai Mehta Committee in 1957, for suggesting the measures to remove obstacles in implementing the programme, which recommended the formation of a three-tier system of rural local government, to be called *Panchayati Raj* to decentralize the process of decision-making and encourage people's participation and place the bureaucracy under the local people's control. These were Gram Panchayat, Panchayat Samiti and Zilla Parishad.

Central government introduced independent administrative hierarchies to carry out special programmes, under the fourth- and fifth year plan. All these special programmes were financed directly by central government. Some of these programmes are Small Farmers' Development Agency (SFDA), Intensive Agricultural Areas Programme (IAAP), Drought Prone Area and Hill Area Development Programmes, Intensive Agricultural District Programme (IADP), Tribal Development Agency (TDA), Marginal, Small Farmers and Agricultural Labourers Development Agency (MFAL) and few areas have development agencies such as Command Area Development.

Integrated Rural Development Programme

The Integrated Rural Development Programme (IRDP) was introduced in 1979, focusing on the weaker sections, living in poverty. The aim was to involve people's initiatives to build up their economy with dignity, whereas the earlier programmes emphasized on the delivery systems which suppressed self-reliance. Several other schemes as Development of Women and Children in Rural Areas (DWCRA), National Rural Health mission (NRHM), Training of Rural Youth for Self-employment (TRYSEM), National Rural Employment Programme (NREP) and Jawahar Rojgar Yojana (JRY) were also floated with the similar objectives.

Decentralized Planning for Rural Development (1987)

The Planning Commission issued guidelines to all the state governments to consider the block as the unit for planning. The District Planning and Development Council or District Planning Board which had wider representation of the society was given the task of planning at the district level. To implement the development programmes more effectively, plans should be prepared in consultation with the Gram Panchayats, as it can address the problems of rural people directly and facilitate development at the grassroots level.

Emphasis on People's Participation

The Panchayati Raj has contributed a lot to the development of the nation by creating awareness among the public and people's participation. Apart from that it has also helped in filling up the gap between the bureaucracy and the public, the District Planning Committee has been strengthened with members from various government and non government organizations, considering the status of the Gram Panchayats which was too weak to facilitate village level microplanning for development.

Role of Non Government Organizations

In this task of integrated rural development, voluntary agencies can play an important role. Agencies having deep roots in rural areas can serve the community more, as the volunteers and staff are very dedicated, their relationship with the community is excellent, and they have innovative approaches to solve the problems. So, involvement of these organizations can result in greater success.

Indian Ministry of Agriculture formed an organization called 'Freedom from Hunger Campaign' with assistance from international donor agencies. Voluntary organizations involved in rural development were also supported. Later on this organization was reorganized and renamed as 'People's Action for Development-India' (PAD-I). Ultimately PAD-I was merged with Council for Advancement of Rural Technology in 1986 which was renamed as Council for Advancement of People's Action and Rural Technology (CAPART). CAPART has contributed a lot to the rural development by giving financial support to different voluntary organization involved in rural development.

People's Initiatives for Progress

Cooperatives have been established by farmers in several states for processing sugarcane, oil-seeds, milk, fruits and vegetables. These organizations have not only provided economic stability but also checked exploitation by intermediary traders, with professional management and use of modern technology. Such organizations are being encouraged throughout the country.

Involvement of NGO's have been encouraged to prepare the microlevel plan and implement the project directly under a nationwide programme for water resource development. Awareness is being created about the conservation of water and energy resources making a significant impact on the supply of drinking water.

REVIEW QUESTIONS

1. Write in detail about various rural development projects.
2. Write short notes on the following:
   a. IRDP
   b. Voluntary organizations

CHAPTER

33

Changes in Rural Life

LEARNING OBJECTIVES

After reading this chapter the learner should be able to

- Understand the type of changes occurring in the rural life.
- Know the causes of changes in rural life.

India is predominantly a rural country with more than two-thirds of its population living in villages. The country cannot progress without the development of villages. Lot of emphasis has been laid on the rural development in our various 5-year plans. The rural life of India is less susceptible to change as compared to urban life, but it is undergoing a change.

It is truly said that India lives in villages and to know the real India, one must visit the villages. Lifestyle in a village is very simple, very colourful and characterized by natural surroundings and clean and green environment. The lush green farms, flowing rivers, chirping birds and pollution-free environment keep people physically and mentally healthy. Rural people believe in green lifestyle consuming fewer resources and producing less harmful waste. Most of the rural areas have got basic amenities like electricity and water supply. Rapid means of transportation and communication along with advancement in technology have made an impact on villages. They are in touch with the world through satellite-based television networks, Internet, mobile phones and other gadgets. The changes in rural life are visible in every sphere, particularly on social, economic and political fronts.

SOCIOECONOMIC TRANSFORMATION

Scientific methods for cultivation have been adopted by farmers on a large scale and it has improved agricultural productivity. The country has become self-reliant in food production and transformed the village economy and brought prosperity to farmers. The big and rich farmers have mechanized farm operations and installed tube wells for irrigation. They are no longer dependent on weather for crop and do not usually suffer losses. However, poor farmers are still dependent on the weather god and incur losses if it does not rain at the right time. The government has come up with system of minimum support price for agriculture produce to ensure remunerative returns to farmers and farmers have also formed cooperative societies for procuring seeds, fertilizers and other farm inputs and for marketing the produce.

POLITICAL CHANGES

The political scenario of the Indian villages has probably seen the most significant changes. There was no political awareness among rural people earlier and they blindly followed the dictates of the erstwhile kings. The situation has changed radically now and they have become politically aware and actively participate in the political process. Apart from exercising their right to franchise in the Lok Sabha and Assembly elections, they also elect members for Panchayati Raj institutions, the local governance system. It is a decentralized form of government where each village is responsible for its own affairs, also termed *village self-government*. The reservation of seats for women in the Panchayati Raj institutions has tremendously increased their involvement in politics and governance at the grassroots. It has been a major step toward empowerment of women who are now actively engaged in planning and implementation of development works in villages.

The political system and also the political discourse is changing as many women are joining politics and mainstream political parties are getting involved in elections at the Panchayat level. Initially, party-based elections were not known in the villages and caste and community were the key factors in deciding the outcome of the poll.

The term *Panchayati Raj* is the foundation of India's political system. It has three levels, so called the *three-tier system*; Gram Panchayat (village level), Panchayat Samiti (block level) and Zila Parishad (district level). The Panchayats receive funds from three main sources: grants on the recommendation of the Central Finance Commission, the State Finance Commission and under the centrally sponsored schemes.

CASTE SYSTEM

The caste system continues to exist in the rural areas but is getting diluted as more and more villagers are migrating to urban areas and intermingling with their co-workers from different castes. They no more rigidly adhere to the caste system and their outlook is becoming liberal in this regard. Apart from urbanization, the government schemes to raise the status of lower castes have also made an impact in diluting the caste system in villages.

LITERACY

Every Indian village has a school and children do not have to walk long distances for education. The implementation of the Right to Education Act (RTE) has drastically brought down the school dropout rate and most of the children are now going to schools. Consequently, literacy rate is improving in rural areas and girls are also coming forward for higher education. The scope of getting proper education in rural areas has increased in recent times and the various facilities and incentives like mid-day meal, free uniform and books being provided under the RTE are helping in moving forward to achieve the goal of universal elementary education.

LIFESTYLE

People in villages are also living in luxury. The thatched-roof or *kachcha* houses are being replaced by modern brick and concrete structures. The villagers are acquiring expensive items like cars, air conditioners, television with cable connections and washing machines and other gadgets for household chores.

They are using mobile phones and taking advantage of the various services provided through IT (information technology)-based platforms. The improved telecom connectivity is proving a boon for rural people. The gap between rural and urban areas is narrowing down with each passing day.

MEANS OF TRANSPORTATION

With improved road connectivity, the villages have seen drastic changes in transport system. People in rural areas used to walk long distances and were depended on bullock carts, horse carts and boats for transport until recently. But now, with the implementation of the schemes like Pradhan Mantri Gramin Sadak Yojna, villages are well connected with roads and the rural people have, at their disposal, almost all the modern means of transport. Villages are well connected to the cities by link roads and some also have access to rail services.

FAMILY SYSTEM

Joint family system is the unique characteristic of the Indian villages but things are changing now and nuclear families are replacing joint families. With land holdings becoming smaller and smaller, agriculture is becoming unviable and as a result youth is forced to migrate to urban areas for jobs. The implementation of family welfare programmes has also made people go for a small family.

STATUS OF WOMEN

Education is changing the status of the rural women as they are now having access to schools and other educational institutions in villages. A large number of women are contesting Panchayat polls as 33 per cent seats (in some seats even 50%) have been reserved for them. The democratic exercise at the village level is helping in developing leadership among normally shy rural women and they are coming to forefront in various fields.

TRANSFORMATION OF RURAL CULTURE

It's not only the movement of rural people to urban areas that is happening but the rural culture is also undergoing transformation and people in the villages are fast adopting the material culture prevalent in urban areas.

OCCUPATION

The scope for getting into different occupations has increased for the Indian villagers. Many have changed their occupation from agriculture to industry and have moved to the rural areas for getting into alternate occupation or jobs.

REVIEW QUESTIONS

1. What are the different changes happening in the rural life and what are the causes of these changes?
2. Write short notes on the following:
   a. Status of rural women
   b. Changes in family system in rural areas in India

CHAPTER

34

Urbanization

LEARNING OBJECTIVES

After reading this chapter the learner should be able to

- Understand the process of urbanization.
- know about the causes and impact of slum development.

As the countries evolve from agrarian to industrial societies, the people in villages start migrating to cities or towns. The transformation of traditional rural economies to industrial economies also leads to progressive concentration of population in urban areas. This process of urbanization is the natural outcome of socioeconomic development and industrialization. Kingsley Davis has explained urbanization as process of switch from spread out pattern of human settlements to one of concentration in urban centres.

The process of urbanization is relatively a recent phenomenon and started with industrial revolution in Europe. History makes it evident that the process of urbanization is inevitable and universal. The developed countries have already reached a high level of urbanization and some of them are in the final stage of the process and experiencing. The developing countries are undergoing rapid urbanization.

India has witnessed rapid urbanization over the past century, particularly after Independence, but the process has been slower by international standards and a vast majority of people still lives in villages. According to the United Nations data, the urban population in India increased to 31 per cent in 2011, which was much less compared to around 87 per cent in Brazil, 50 per cent in China and Indonesia, 61 per cent in South Africa and 78 per cent in Mexico. India's urban population rose from 17 per cent in 1950 to 31 per cent in 2011, over a period of 60 years. In comparison China's urban population quadrupled from 12 per cent to 49 per cent. As per projections India's urban population will increase to 600 million, 40 per cent of the national population, by 2031.

The process of urbanization got impetus due to industrialization and increase in trade and commercial activities. The word *urban* is derived from the Latin word *urbanus*, which literally means pertaining to a city. The process and its implications have attracted the attention of sociologist and as a result a new field of 'urban sociology' has emerged.

The movement of people from rural areas is also accompanied with shift from agriculture to other economic activities like trade, manufacturing, business, service and other avocation. The main reason for migration is the availability of facilities like education, health care system and basic civic amenities, besides employment opportunities. The urban clusters are classified into towns, cities and metros on the basis of population criteria. Large-scale migration of people also leads to change in attitudes, beliefs, values and the overall behaviour patterns.

CAUSES OF URBANIZATION

The main reason for urbanization is the lack of facilities in the rural areas which compel the people to shift to cities and towns where all modern amenities are available.

Education facilities: Town and cities have much better educational facilities compared to villages and many people migrate to cities for the education of children. Cities have lot of public schools and convents in private sector with modern infrastructure. The youth have to stay in urban areas for higher education. The government has opened school in every village where education is free education but the people prefer to send their children to private schools.

Employment opportunities: There are hardly any job available in the rural areas as the main occupation in the villages is agriculture. The government has been encouraging cottage industry but educated youth prefer white-collared jobs and settle in cities and towns. All the industries, government offices, markets are there in the cities only and as such ample employment opportunities are available in the urban areas.

Life style: Markets, mega stores, multiplexes, gardens and entertainment parks are in big cities and towns. People who want to enjoy a fashionable and trendy lifestyle shift to urban areas.

Transport facilities: Cities have excellent road, rail and air connectivity, while villages only have roads which are in poor conditions. Very few villages in India have rail tracks.

Health care facilities: All the tertiary health care facilities are concentrated in towns and cities which also have big private hospitals with state-of-the-art facilities.

Industrialization: India had the industrial revolution but all the industries are established in the urban areas. It is because of the availability of means of transportation to get raw material and transport the finished material to the market, most of the industries are located in cities. Industrialization is the major cause of movement of masses from rural to urban areas.

Nuclear families: Disintegration of a joint family system is the major outcome of urbanization. Cities and towns have small houses or flats to accommodate small families.

IMPACT OF URBANIZATION

Positive Impact

The positive impacts of the urbanization are as follows:

Education: There are a large number of educational institutions in the cities both in government and private sector which offer a wide range of professional courses. Those who migrate from villages to urban areas have access to better education and they have ample opportunities to pursue higher education. Thus, urbanization enhances the prospects of people from villages going for higher education.

Women's life: Most of the women in urban areas are working and as such they enjoy financial independence. They not only enjoy a better status but also raise the living standards of the entire family.

Health care facilities: Cities have adequate health care facilities. Most of the secondary care and tertiary care hospital are located in urban areas.

Improved standard of living: The availability of basic civic amenities and efficient modes of transportation along with modern education and health care infrastructure ensure that an average person enjoys a descent standard of living.

Employment opportunities: Urbanization has been an outcome of industrialization, which creates a large number of jobs in the cities. Apart from industry, cities have educational institutions, government offices, corporate sectors and business centres providing ample of employment opportunities to people.

Class over caste: In cities and towns, the people are more class-conscious, progressive and amenable to changes. The status of individuals is not ascribed by heredity or birth but achieved by merit and hard work, affording ample scope for social mobility. People lose the caste labels due to strong class identity. Most of the people in cities belong to the middle class, some to high middle class and a few to rich class. A social class consists of people of similar socioeconomic status who regard themselves as equals. Each class has a set of values, attitudes, beliefs and norms of behaviour which differ from those of the other classes. A class of people share common economic resources which influences the type of lifestyle they are able to lead.

Social religious taboos disappear: Urban people do not follow the social and religious norms which are prevalent in villages. They are open to modernization and most of the women also dress up in women covering their head with scarf or covering their face by veil, shaking hand with persons of opposite sex, wearing only Indian dresses or many religious ceremonies are not very common in cities.

Negative Impact

The cities have grown so rapidly that the problems started to outweigh the benefits of industrialization and modernization. Unregulated urbanization has several adverse impacts which degrade the quality of life. The most common urban problem is the ever-increasing population, which is the major cause of congestion, housing problems, environmental pollution and growing unemployment.

As the basic infrastructure and civic amenities have failed to keep pace there is increasing competition for facilities as a result of which the civic infrastructure comes under heavy strain, giving rise to problems like shortage of water, housing, insanitation, traffic congestion and environmental degradation.

Overcrowding: There is crowd everywhere in the cities and it becomes difficult to get access to the public facilities. Bus stations and railway stations are teeming with people and one has to wait in queues to purchase ticket for public transport. Buses and trains are overcrowded and people are seen travelling on the roof tops.

Shortage of housing: Poor people who come to cities and town in search of better employment opportunities cannot afford to buy a house hire a small accommodation for which they have to pay a hefty rent.The extremely poor people are forced to live slums without the basic civic amenities in unhygienic conditions.

Slum development: This is the biggest negative impact of urbanization. Migrants find it difficult to afford houses in the cities so reside in the peripheries of the cities in slum areas. These slum areas are not habitable even as they lack sanitation, potable water, electricity and privacy.

Impersonal relationship: People in villages have good interpersonal relationships as most of them are known to each other, whereas in cities relationships are very impersonal. People hardly bother even about their neighbours.

Deforestation: Urbanization has been taking a heavy toll of forests and it is considered to be one of the major contributing factors to global warming. Trees not only absorb greenhouse gases and carbon emissions but also bring rain and help in preventing floods. Deforestation leads to floods, rain scarcity and air pollution, and it not only affects human beings but also the wild life.

Shortage of water and electricity: Over population results in severe shortage of water and electricity in cities. There is no city or town in India having continuous water supply and most of them face power cuts during peak summer.

Unemployment and underemployment: The level of unemployment is high as the number of job seekers is far more as compared to availability of jobs. Not only that, it also forces well-qualified people to take up small jobs. This leads to psychological problems like job burnout.

Social effects: Urbanization also brings a change in attitudes, beliefs, values and behaviour patterns of the migrants. They feel stressed as they are not used to the hectic city life. Crime in cities is high and offences like thefts, murder, juvenile delinquency and rapes are very common.

Financial insecurity exists among lot of people as they find it difficult to save money and earn on daily basis. The fear of losing job makes survival difficult as there is no job security in the private sector.

Drug addiction and alcoholism are very common because of the various reasons as stressful life, unemployment, broken families and lack of parental attention.

Many people feel lost in the city and lead a life of anonymity. Interaction among people is impersonal and there is no family support also.

Beggars are seen seeking alms near traffic lights and markets. Beggars live on railway stations, bus stands and rain shelters. They live in very unhygienic conditions.

Growth of Slums

The pressure on land grows, the cost of housing and infrastructure also increases and the civic authorities find it difficult to meet the growing service requirement. Scarcity of land leads to spill over human habitations in the form of slums in the peripheries of cities and towns. The spread of habitations leads to deforestation and problems like congestion and insanitation due to lack of adequate civic amenities.

Slum areas are basically part of urban areas lacking most of the facilities like proper housing, environmental hygiene, clean water and electricity. A slum is defined as congested settlement with a cluster of substandard houses built lawfully or unlawfully, mostly of temporary nature, crowded together and usually with inadequate sanitation and lack of drinking water facilities and having unhygienic conditions. These areas are full of problems like overcrowding, crime, prostitution, drug dependence and communicable diseases.

Land is scarce and expensive in towns and cities, and existing urban land policies and the urban poor are left with no choice but to make or take shelter illegally on any available piece of land. This is the main reason for growth of slums as a large number of people, who migrate who cities and towns in search of greener pastures, are poor and cannot afford good housing and amenities in the main city. They start living in the outskirts of the cities where hardly any civic amenities are available.

Besides urbanization, natural disasters like earthquakes, floods, wars and other such events, which cause large-scale dislocation of human habitations, may also lead to growth of slums. People who get uprooted mostly settle in nearby cities in search of livelihood.

Slums have been a major problem in India mainly because of the rapidly increasing population. The magnitude of the problem of slums is alarming. The figures relating to urban population living in slums are not accurately available. However, it is commonly accepted that nearly 20 percent of the total urban population in India lives in slums. The task force on housing and slum development appointed by the Planning Commission of India estimated that nearly 23 percent or over 3 crore persons as the urban slum dwellers. The proportion of the slum dwellers increase with the size of the urban population. Cities with a population less than one lakh have around 17.5 percent slum dwellers, cities with population ranging between one lakh and 10 lakh have 21.5 percent slum dwellers and the big cities having a population more than 10 lakh have 35.5 percent slum dwellers. The four metropolitan cities have around 50 percent of the total population living in slums.

MAIN CHARACTERISTICS OF SLUMS

Location: Slums are located in the outskirts of the cities. The poor migrants who do not have the capacity to buy even a small house and find it beyond their means to rent a house live in slums.

Poor housing and overcrowding: Dilapidated and poor houses in slums are made of poor design and scrap materials like bamboo, straw, low quality wood and tin and plastic sheets. These are often raised on unauthorized land. They are overcrowded and population density in slums ranges from 700 to 4210 per acre and a minimum of 4 to a maximum of 10 people share a room, which is highly congested and unhealthy. Most of the families have single room accommodation. They mostly use wood, cow dung, charcoal, or kerosene for cooking, often with no ventilation leads to respiratory diseases.

Lack of education: Most of the slum areas do not have educational institutions and children are deprived of education. Instead of going to school these children fetch water, take care of younger siblings and sick household members. They also go out to work and play important role in supplementing the finances of the family to make both ends meet. Burdened with these responsibilities, they mostly leave school. Those who do go to school are overage and very irregular. School dropout rate is very high among slum children.

Malnutrition: Most of the children in slums are underweight and anaemic. Being poor the slum dwellers cannot afford to buy enough food and this is the main cause of malnourishment. Since the slums are mostly illegal, their children cannot avail benefits offered under several of welfare schemes. Maximum women are anaemic and their children are also underweight and malnourished.

Health hazards: The poor living conditions in slums affect the health of people mentally and physically. Water-borne diseases like blood dysentery, diarrhoea, malaria, typhoid, jaundice are common. There is no solid waste collection system and children play on heaps of accumulated garbage where they also collect scrap. Garbage with biomedical waste poses a special threat to the health of the slum residents.

Poor environmental hygiene: Slum areas have poor sanitation. There are no toilets and most of the people go for open defecation. There is no drainage system, and garbage is not disposed of properly. As a result both household waste and human excreta finds its way to water bodies or gets accumulated in low-lying areas.

Social problems: Wide resource difference between 'haves' and 'have-nots' living close by weakens the urban poor communities. The economic disparity provides the 'breeding ground for various social problems such as crime, drug abuse and alcoholism'.

Lack of information: It becomes difficult for these people to get access to health care facilities because of lack of awareness. Lack of information about family planning services, immunization of children and antenatal mothers, management of diarrheal diseases among children add to the high mortality and morbidity in slums.

Violence: Prevalence of violence within the families and among the families in slum dwellers is quite high. Reasons are alcoholism, drug dependence and lack of privacy in these areas.

Mitigation: Steps are needed to mitigate the negative impact of urbanization which is a big challenge facing the world today. The only way out is to improve the urban infrastructure and also create opportunities in the rural areas to prevent large-scale migration of people to cities and towns.

REVIEW QUESTIONS

1. What do you mean by industrialization? Write down the causes of industrialization.
2. Write in detail about the characteristics of slum.

UNIT - 9

SOCIAL CHANGE

CHAPTER

35

Social Change

LEARNING OBJECTIVES

After reading this chapter the learner should be able to

- Know the causes of social change.
- Get acquainted with different types of social changes.

A society is a dynamic entity and an ever-changing phenomenon. Social change happens all the time and there is no room for stagnation, which only leads to decay. The society does give an impression of permanence, but it is constantly undergoing the process of growth, decay, renewal and also adjusting to the changing conditions. No change is permanent, it is subject to change. This is true for every sphere of activity. As the process continues unabated the society gets modified over a period time which is reflected in the form of transformation of culture and social institutions.

Social structure and ways of human interaction change; institutional functions and structures undergo reshaping as technologies expand; ideologies and values acquire new components. The change is usually slow and observable only over a period of time but it could be dramatic at times. The social changes caused due to technological advances are rapid, though some societies are slow to adapt to the change. For instance, the advent of computers and, more recently, cell phones, have completely changed the way the world interacts and made a huge impact on societies across the world.

Not every social change is important, some changes matter more than others. Mostly a social change is not planned it occurs unintentionally, it is rarely intentional. Although industrial societies like the United States do promote several types of social changes. For example, many societies dreamed of the day when cell phones would be a common thing, but few could have imagined all the consequences that one device would have.

Changes in hairstyles and clothing patterns are not significant in the 'big picture'. Other changes, such as the invention of the automobile, computer and cell phone have changed the world and the ways of human interaction. Social change is often controversial and a recent example has been the amendment to the Information Technology Act to regulate the social media. It has been opposed on the grounds that it would severely undermine the right freedom of expression.

MEANING AND DEFINITION OF SOCIAL CHANGE

The word *change* denotes a difference in anything observed over some period of time and social change implies variations in human societies that occur in the modes of living of individuals and social relations. It would mean observable differences in any social phenomena over any period of time. Social change refers to any significant alteration over time in behaviour patterns and cultural values' norms and institutions.

Society is a web of social relationships; these ralationships are influenced by social change. Social relationships are social processes, social patterns and social interactions. Thus, the term *social change* is used to describe variations of any aspect of social processes, social patterns, social interaction or social organization. A social change is 'significant' if it leads to profound social consequences.

Social change is discernible when one finds that lot of people are engaged in such activities which differ from those which their immediate forefathers were engaged in some time before.

Human beings constitute the society and whenever modifications in human behaviour are realized one can say that social change is occurring. Men are human beings so social change means human change. Sociologist Davis says that to change society is to change man.

Social system is on the change mode all the time as per theorists of social change. The composition of the population keeps on changing throughout the life cycle and so is the occupation, roles and responsibilities of individual and groups. Members of society even undergo physiological changes, because of the modified attitudes and expectations and the continuing interactions among members. Social changes also involve new knowledge which is being constantly gained and transferred.

Definition of Social Change

The society is ever-changing but what is of interest to sociologist is change of 'what kind' and to 'what degree' has to be considered as social change.

Sociologists have come out with different definitions to conceptualize social change. Jones states that the term social change is used to describe any modifications, alterations or variations in any aspect of social processes, social patterns, social interaction or social organization.

Kingsley Davis explains, 'social change as any alternations that occur in social organization—the change may be structural or functional'.

In the words of Maclver and Page, social change 'refers to a process responsive to many types of changes; changes in the attitudes and beliefs of men , changes in man-made conditions of life; and the changes that may go beyond the human control to the biological and the physical nature of things'.

Morris Ginsberg defines, 'social change as a change in social structure, the size and the composition, of the society, or the change in the balance of its parts or the type of its organization'.

According to B. Kuppuswamy social change is a process in which a significant alternation in the structure and functioning is discernible in a social system.

Merrill and Eldredge explain social change as a change when a large number of persons get engaged in activities that differ from the activities their immediate forefathers were engaged in some time before.

Anderson and Parker said that social change involves structural or functional alternations in societal forms or processes.

According to M.D. Jenson, social change is a modification in ways of doing things and thinking of people.

H.T. Mazumdar says that social change is a new fashion or mode, either modifying or replacing the old, in the life of people.

According to Gillin, social changes are variations from the accepted modes of life, due to various reasons as alternation in cultural equipment, geographical conditions composition of the population or ideologies. These alterations are brought about by diffusion of cultures, or inventions within the group.

If one analyses all these definitions, one comes to the conclusion that the two types of changes should be treated as two facts of the same social phenomenon. These two types of changes are changes in the structure of society and changes in the values and social norms. Values and social norms bind the people together and help in maintaining social order. These two types of changes are dependent on each other and, thus, should not, be treated separately, changes in one type automatically induces changes in the other. A change in the attitude of the people may bring about changes in the social structure as obvious from the following example.

Towards the end of the 19th century, there was a tendency to have small families in the countries of Western Europe. But it was brought about mainly by voluntary restriction of births, which means the attitude of the people.

This indicates that a change in the attitude of the people is basically responsible for change in the social structure. Similarily, a change in the social structure may bring about attitudinal change among the members of the society. Industrialization and changes in the rural society are not simply a changes in the structure of society but also in the attitude of the people. For example, industrialization has caused destruction in the domestic system of production. Another important change was that it made more and more women to step out of their homes for working in the factories and offices. Employment gave women financial independence and that changed their outlook. The spirit of independence has become a personal trait of women and has brought a drastic change in their attitude. This shows that the two types of changes are inter-related and these should not be treated separately and should be studied together.

Characteristics of Social Change

The phenomenon of social change is a complex process and difficult to understand in its entirety. It is essential to analyse the nature of social change to understand it well. The society is a 'web of social relationships' and hence social change obviously means a change in the system of social relationships which are understood in terms of social processes and social interactions and social organizations. A change can be called social change only if it has significant influence on the entire or considerable segment of population.

Social change is universal: Change is the universal law of nature and it keeps on happening constantly at all times in all the societies. No society remains completely static; it is constantly undergoing change, no matter how traditional and conservative it is. Just as a man's life cannot remain static, a society irrespective of place and time cannot be still or stagnant. Demography changes, technology expands, material development takes place and institutional structures and their functions get reshaped. The pace of change varies from one society to the other.

Social change occurs as an essential law: Social change is also natural and an unavoidable law of nature. Our needs keep on changing to satisfy our desire for change and to satisfy these needs, social change becomes a necessity.

Social change is continuous: Society is an ever-changing phenomenon. It grows and decays, there it finds renewal, accommodates itself to various changing conditions. Society is subject to continuous change which cannot be stopped. Human society has been in a state of flux since primitive age when man lived in caves to the present modern era.

Social change involves no-value judgement: Social change does not attach any value judgement. It is neither moral nor immoral. It is ethically neutral. A correct view on what is empirically true is not the same as correct view on what ought to be.

Social change is bound by time factors: Social change is temporal, because society exists only as time-sequences. The factors which cause social change do not remain uniform with the changes in time. For example, the caste system which was a pillar of stability in traditional Indian society is now undergoing considerable changes in the modern India.

Pace of social change is uneven and unequal: The rate, tempo, speed and extent of change is not uniform. It differs from society to society. In some societies it occurs so slowly that it may not be noticed by those who live in them. In the modern, industrial urban society the pace of change is much faster than the traditional, agricultural and rural society.

Social Change may be small or large in scale. Small scale change refers to changes within groups and organizations rather than societies, culture or civilization. According W.E. Moore, small-scale changes pertain to changes in the characteristics of social structures that do not have any immediate and major consequences for the generalized structure of the society as such.

Social change cannot be predicted: Social change is a certainty but it is very much difficult to predict its exact forms. What the society will be in thousand years from now, no one can tell. Similarly, no one can predict what shall be our ideas, attitudes and value in future.

Social change shows chain-reaction sequences: Change in one sphere of our life may bring about a series of changes in other aspects of life. We can say that society is a dynamic system of interrelated parts. For example, educated young women find the traditional type of family and marriage is not to their liking. They desire separate homes. The stability of marriages can no longer be taken for granted.

Social change takes place due to multinumber of factors: One or two factors cannot bring about social change. Multiple factors combine together and become the 'cause' of the change. Sociologist M. Ginsberg says that 'A cause is an assemblage of factors which, in interaction with each other, undergo a change'. Thus, social change is the consequence of a number of factors involved not a single specific factor.

Social changes are chiefly those of modifications or of replacement: Social changes are modifications or replacements of material objects, attitudes or social relationships. For example, the form of our breakfast food has changed, though we eat the same basic materials such as meats, eggs corn but their form has been changed. The old authoritarian family has become the small equalitarian family. Our attitudes towards women's status and rights, religion, coeducation stands modified today.

Short-term and long-term change: The conceptualization of the magnitude of change is another attribute of change in terms of the time span. It may be classified as 'small-scale' from a short-term perspective but may eventually have large-scale consequences over a period of time, for instance, the decreasing crude death rate in India since 1960.

Social change may be peaceful or violent: Usually the attribute *peaceful* has been associated with 'gradual' and 'violent' with 'rapid'. The term *violence* means a threat or use of physical force in attaining a given change. Though rapid change may 'violently' affect the emotions, values and expectations of those involved. 'Peaceful' or gradual changes take place by consent, acceptance or acquisition.

Social change may be planned or unplanned: Social change may occur in the natural course or it is brought about by man intentionally. Unplanned or unintentional change refers to change resulting from wars or natural calamities, such as famines and floods, earthquakes and volcanic eruptions. Intentional or planned social change occurs when these changes are conditioned by human beings through technology. Many community developmental plans, programmes and projects have been formulated by man to determine and control the direction of social change.

Social change may be endogenous or exogenous: Endogenous social changes are those changes which happen due to the factors that are generated within the society. Conflict, communication gap, regionalism, etc., are certain factors responsible for endogenous change.

Exogenous changes occur due to sources from other societies which are external to the system such as earthquake, wars, famine or by certain new factors. Diffusion of cultural traits beyond the limits of single society occurs because of technological transfer and brain drain, political and cultural imperialism.

To conclude, social change is a continuous process, though changes vary in magnitude from small-scale to large-scale changes in terms of, time span, direction, rate of change and amount of violence involved. These dimensions should not be considered as attributes, but as changes along a continuum from one extreme to another: from revolutionary to evolutionary.

REVIEW QUESTIONS

1. What do you mean by social change and what are the various types of social changes?
2. Explain the causes of social change.

CHAPTER

36

Social Evolution, Development and Progress

LEARNING OBJECTIVES

After reading this chapter the learner should be able to
- Have knowledge about the process of social evolution.
- Understand the concept of social evolution with social progress.

The terms *change, evolution, development* and *progress* are related and often used for the same social process or confused as a concept and as such need to understand in the right perspective.

SOCIAL EVOLUTION

The concept of evolution was known to the generation preceding the publication of Darwin's *Origin of Species* but the notion of social evolution is borrowed from biological sciences to sociology. Many social theorists from Herbert Spencer to Sumner applied this concept of *organic evolution* in various ways to the explanation of social change.

The term *evolution* is derived from the Latin word *evolvere*, which means to 'develop' or 'to unfold'. It indicates changes from 'within' and not from 'without'. The word *growth* connotes a direction of change but only of quantitative character. Evolution involves change not merely in size but also in structure.

According to MacIver and Page, 'Evolution involves something more intrinsic, a change not only in size but in structure also'. In the views of Ogburn and Nimkoff, 'Evolution is merely a change in a given direction'.

Ginsberg explains evolution as 'a process of change, which results in the production of something new but revealing an orderly continuity in transition'. Evolution takes place when the series of changes occurring over a period of time appear to be not a mere succession of changes but a 'continuous process', marked by a clear running 'thread of identity'.

In evolution the change must occur within the changing unity and not by forces acting upon it from without.

Characteristics of Social Evolution

Herbert Spencer defines the process of social evolution as a 'change from a state of "incoherent homogeneity" to a state of "coherent heterogeneity".' Evolution is a gradual growth from a simple to complex existence.

Herbert Spencer has laid down four important principles of evolution:

1. Social evolution is the human aspect of the law of change of cosmic evolution.
2. It takes place in the same way, progressing through definite and inevitable stages at all places.
3. Social evolution is gradual.
4. Social evolution is progressive.

Some other features of social evolution are discussed below.

Evolution is a process of differentiation and integration. It was the German sociologist Von Baer who developed the concept of evolution as a process of differentiation and integration. It was later pursued by Spencer and many other sociologists.

In social evolution, new and ever newer circumstances and problems keep appearing and to cope with them, new associations and institutions are evolved. For instance, a small rural habitation is managed by a panchayat, but as it grows into a town, a municipal committee carries out the responsibility, and further transformation into a big city paves for a municipal corporation. In a big city, the management is handled different wings to look after roads, water supply, sanitation, octroi, forests and so on. In this way differentiation increases with the evolution of the town.

However, this differentiation cannot place take without integration. The double processes of differentiation and integration help to increase the efficiency of the society. Social evolution does not always proceed by differentiation as has been observed in the case of modern languages derived from Sanskrit like Bengali, Gujarati, Telugu and Tamil. They cannot be compared in their structure with the richness and diversity of their origin and the process is towards simplification and not towards differentiation. Similarly, in the development of religion too, the transition from fusion to differentiation is not easy to see.

SOCIAL CHANGE AND SOCIAL EVOLUTION

Social change is an ever-present phenomenon everywhere. Many sociologists from Herbert Spencer to Sumner applied this concept of evolution to interpret and explain the process of social change. However, many modern theorists, particularly Americans, have discarded the idea that social change takes place by evolutionary stages.

Evolution is described as a series of interrelated changes in a system in which hidden characters of a thing are revealed to show not merely what happens to a thing but also what happens within it. One cannot speak of evolution when an object or system is changed by forces acting upon it from without. Evolution is a process involving a changing adaptation of the object to its environment, followed by a further manifestation of its own nature. It has to occur from within the changing unity.

PROGRESS

Etymologically, the word progress means *moving forward*. However, it will not be meaningful, unless the direction towards which progress has been made is known. Thus, progress is not a mere change but change in a particular direction. Progress means moving forward in the direction of achievement of some aim. For example, worsening state of agriculture is certainly a change, but it will not be called progress.

Sociologists and thinkers have defined progress in different ways. The important definitions are as follows:

MacIver explains that "Progress is not merely direction, but direction towards some final goal, some destination determined ideally not simply by the objective consideration at work".

According to Lumely, "Progress is a change, but it is a change in a desired or approved direction, not in any direction."

In the words of Ginsberg, progress is "A development or evolution in a direction which satisfies rational criterion of value".

Ogburn defines progress as a movement towards an objective thought to be desirable by the general group for the visible future.

Progress means an advance towards some ideally desirable end. A particular social change may seem to be progressive to one person but it may seem retrogressive to another because they have different values. Thus, the concept of social progress is subjective and largely depends on existing social values, though it has reference to an objective condition.

Criteria of Progress

Social values play a vital role in determining progress and whether a change will be considered as progress or not mainly depends upon the social values which vary with time and place. As the criteria of progress also change with the change of social values, it is difficult to lay down a universally acceptable criteria. However, based on some broad principles the following parameters can be tentatively suggested.

Health and longevity: The average longevity of life, an important indicator of healthy living, is one index of progress but it does not necessarily follow from it that a longer life must be full of joy, bliss, peace and prosperity.

Wealth: Some thinkers consider wealth or economic progress as a criterion of progress.

Moral conduct: Many thinkers maintain that moral conduct is the criterion of progress.

There are many aspects to life and progress has to be viewed in totality. As such, it is not possible to devise any one criterion to determine progress, which is an integrated development process, encompassing all mental, physical and spiritual aspects, including the above criteria.

Nature of Progress

Progress is determined by social values and as such it does not have precisely the same meaning at all times and places. Change is one of its essential attributes without which no progress can take place. The concept of progress presupposes the presence of change.

In Progress the Desired End Is Achieved: Broadly speaking, progress means an advance towards some ideally desirable end. Every change does not imply progress, only the changes that lead to human happiness mean progress.

Progress does not come about through inactivity; efforts have to be made and when these efforts are successful progress happens. It is not uniform and varies from society to society, place to place and from time to time. That which is today considered as the symbol or progress may tomorrow be considered and treated as a sign of regress.

As social values change with time and place, the criteria of progress vary from place to place.

SOCIAL CHANGE AND SOCIAL PROGRESS

Change is integral to both evolution and progress. However, the term *change* is wholly neutral, indicating variation in a phenomena over a period of time. The use of term *progress* becomes essential when specific elements like direction, desirability and value judgement are added to change. Progress is a change in particular direction. It represents forward movement towards some desired goal and or in short change for the better and not for the worse.

Social change is a generic term describing a fundamental process and there is no value judgement attached to it. Some changes are beneficial to humankind and some are harmful. But the concept of social progress implies value judgement.

SOCIAL EVOLUTION AND SOCIAL PROGRESS

The nineteenth-century sociologists right from Auguste Comte to Herbert Spencer termed social evolution as social progress. However, modern sociologists maintain that evolution does not mean progress as a more evolved society does not necessarily be more progressive.

Social evolution has to be distinguished from social progress, which is only one of the many possibilities of social evolution. For example, caste system in India is an outcome of social evolution but it does not signify progress.

Evolution is merely change in a given direction and it is not evaluated as good or bad. On the contrary, progress only means change for the better and not otherwise. Evolution is a scientific concept and an objective phenomena, whereas progress is an ethical concept.

Evolution is a scientific concept and thus the concepts of social change, social evolution and social progress have many common reference points but they have different intellectual frameworks.

PROGRESS VERSUS DEVELOPMENT

The words *progress* and *development* are often used interchangeably and for many people both the words mean the same thing and present the same goal. However, they are similar but not exactly alike and have a few differences.

Progress is defined as 'a movement towards a goal'. Development also indicates movement and growth but is more focused on the expansion of all aspects and in all directions. Progress is a part of development, which is the 'big picture' referring to progress of every concerned area. Development refers to a permanent change, while change and growth in progress is short-lived and only a step to the next level.

The economic side of progress and development are also different. Progress is an ongoing process of upward growth, development is the aftermath and the effect of progress.

REVIEW QUESTIONS

1. How do you relate social evolution and social change?
2. What do you mean by social progress and criteria of social progress?

CHAPTER

37

Factors of Social Change

LEARNING OBJECTIVES

After reading this chapter the learner should be able to

- Understand the various factors responsible for social change.
- Know the causes of resistance of social change.

There cannot be a proper understanding of social change without studying and analysing the factors responsible for the change. Morris Ginsberg has made a systematic analysis of the factors that have been invoked by different writers to explain social change.

Social change is caused and influenced by several factors, including war, flood, earthquake, population, education, environment, culture, technology and other man-made factors.

DEMOGRAPHIC FACTORS

The demographic factor is most important and plays a decisive role in causing social change. The population of every society is always changing in terms of size, numbers, composition, density and the local distribution.

The changes in population have far-reaching implications for the society. The population of most countries in Western Europe declined during the nineteenth century but at the same time, the death rate of these countries also declined. This has been an unprecedented phenomenon in the history. Population changes have occurred through the history due to various reasons such as migration, invasion, war, change in food supply and changing mores. Rapid decline in birth rate and death over the past seven decades has led to a great social transformation.

Events like war, diseases, natural calamities and environmental changes can create an imbalance in the ratio of males and females in population, which directly affect social changes. Many males and females will remain unmarried as a result and this changes the social structure. It also leads to moral deterioration and sexual permissiveness. India is also facing the problem of declining female sex ratio currently.

POLITICAL FACTORS

Society has its customs and social norms but it is also governed by rules and regulations framed by the government that comprises leaders from different sections of people. The political leaders are products of society and any change they effect in the instruments of the state, contributes social change. Political events like partitions of India in 1947 have brought about several social changes in the respective societies.

BIOLOGICAL FACTORS

Biological factors have some indirect influence on social change. The biological principles of natural selection and struggle for survival are constantly producing alterations in society. The qualitative aspect of the population related to heredity is based upon powerful and great men and such biological factor plays a part in social change to an extent.

ECONOMIC FACTORS

As the condition of an individual affects the society, the economy of an individual also influences it. The stratification of people into various class moulds as per their educational qualification and earning influences social changes. It leads to changes in their lifestyle, way of interaction, culture, routine life, languages and other aspects. The best example is the emergence of English in middle-class society in India. Developments on the economic front bring social change in society. The green revolution boosted the rural economy and large amount of money earned by Indians from abroad certainly brought a lot of social change in behaviour, relations, lifestyle, spending patterns, intuitions and the outlook of the world.

INDUSTRIAL FACTORS

Industrialization, particularly establishment of industrial townships, urbanization and trade unionism are responsible for wide ranging social changes in the lives of people concerned. The factors like liberalization, privatization and globalization after industrialization across the world influence the economy of the country, which leads to change in per capita income and, in turn, social changes.

TECHNOLOGICAL FACTORS

The technological factors have immense influence in social change. Invention of electricity, steam-and petrol-driven mechanism for production, the means of transport and communication and various mechanism appliances in everyday life have made a huge change in the society. This advancement affects even institutions like family and marriage.

In the age of technology, no one can live without using mobiles, phones, computers, electricity, radio, television and other appliances that have virtually become necessities of life. These inventions and discoveries have completely changed our style of living, modes of thinking, social relations and even morals. The intellect, creativity and the aspiration of human beings lead to such scientific developments that bring about social changes.

Every technological advance provides new opportunities and establishes new conditions of life. The social effects of technology are far-reaching and often modify the customs and social institutions.

According to W.F. Ogburn, 'technology changes society by changing mostly the material environment to which we, in turn, adapt. The adjustment that members make to cope with these changes, at times, alters the established traditions and social institutions'.

Technological changes have influenced attitudes, beliefs and traditions and demolished old prejudices, dispelled superstitions, weakened casteism and given rise to the class-based society. They have brought new vocations and trades and made possible the vertical mobility. People can now take up occupations with higher status than they could have ever thought of in the pretechnological days.

CULTURAL FACTORS

Technology and material inventions may influence social change but direction and degree of this depends upon the cultural situation as a whole. Culture is a major cause of social change as it is always in flux. Changes in technology can transform culture and changes in culture can change technology. Culture is the internal life forces of society and changes and variations in culture invariably lead to changes in social relationships. Technology alone cannot bring sweeping changes in society unless backed by favourable cultural support. It may be noted that culture not only influences our relationship and values but also influences the direction and character of technological change. The atomic energy can be used for making weapons of mass destruction and also for producing necessities of life. Like fire, technology can be used for both constructive and destructive purposes.

ENVIRONMENTAL FACTORS

Floods, earthquake, excessive rain, drought and other natural calamities directly affect social relationships. Such events have a huge impact on economy, which, in turn, has far-reaching implications for the society. At times, natural disasters cause large-scale migration of people with severe impact on social relationships. Thus, environment as a factor bring out social change.

The increasing environmental concerns like climate change are also affecting society. Many influential environmental groups have become active politically and they are raising related issues like need for energy conservation, controlling air and water pollution. The society is becoming aware about environmental hazards and need to protect wildlife and conserve natural resources. The attitude of people is also changing.

PSYCHOLOGICAL FACTORS

Human beings by hate status quo and monotony and nature love change. This innate psychological quality is the major cause of social change. Man is always keen to discover new things in every sphere of his life and is always eager to explore new areas and for novel experiences. In this process, traditions and customs of every human society are perpetually undergoing change. Change is the law of life; when change do not occur at the appropriate time, major upheavals like revolutions and wars cause change in a violent way.

MODELS OF SOCIAL CHANGE

Sociologists mostly rely on three basic theories of social change: evolutionary, functionalist and conflict theories.

Evolutionary Theory

Taking a cue from Charles Darwin's biological evolution theory, nineteenth century sociologists came out with evolutionary theory of social change. The social evolutionists maintained that the society moves in specific directions and moves progressively to higher and higher levels. The obvious conclusion was that their own cultural attitudes and behaviours were more advanced than those of earlier societies.

Father of sociology, Auguste Comte, and other eminent social thinkers like Emile Durkheim and Herbert Spencer, all subscribed to social evolution theory. They saw human society progressing in one direction and moving from simple to complex social structures. In essence, they all proposed unilinear evolutionary theories as per which all societies pass through the same sequence of stages of evolution to reach the same destination.

Some contemporary social evolutionists like Gerhard Lenski modified it maintaining that *social change* is a multilinear process rather than unilinear. According to multilinear evolutionary theory, change can take place in several ways and does not inevitably lead in the same direction. The proponents of multilinear theory observe that human society has evolved along differing lines and not in one direction.

Functionalist Theory

Functional theory focuses on what maintains society rather than what changes it. It looks at each part of society in terms of how it contributes to the stability of the whole society. Talcott Parsons, a leading functionalist, saw society in its natural state as being stable and balanced. It moves towards a state of homeostasis in natural course. In his views, 'social problems, such as union strikes, represent temporary rifts in the social order'. It is a part of the stabilization process to achieve equilibrium changes in one aspect of society require adjustments in other aspects. In absence of such adjustments, equilibrium is disturbed. While Parsons' equilibrium theory incorporates the evolutionary concept of continuing progress, its main thrust and theme is stability and balance.

Critics argue that functionalist theory does not encourage people to change their social environment. Functionalists view active social change as undesirable as various parts of society contribute in some way to keep its form and shape.

Conflict Theory

Conflict theory lays emphasis on the negative and ever-changing nature of the society and role of the powerful in forcing social order on the weak and poor. The architect of conflict theory, Karl Marx, saw as fragmented groups that compete for political power, social status and economic resources. The wealthy and powerful ensure the status quo to perpetuate social practices and institutions favourable to them and change plays a vital role in remedying social inequalities and injustices.

Karl Marx did not agree with the evolutionary argument that each successive stage in development of society was an improvement over the previous stage. He maintained that the rich always exploit the poor and weak as a class of people and that social change is proactive; it does not rely on people remaining passive in response to exploitation. He believed that conflict was desirable and needed to initiate social change and rid the society of inequalities.

The theory was criticized on the grounds that social upheaval does not inevitably lead to positive or expected outcomes.

According to George Simmel, conflict is a permanent feature of society and not just a temporary passing event. There is also a positive fallout as it is the process that binds people together by interaction. Conflict encourages people of similar interests to unite together to achieve their objectives. Continuous conflict, thus keeps the society dynamic and ever-changing in this way.

RESISTANCE TO SOCIAL CHANGE

While change is the law of nature, some people resist social change. Economic factors have a major role in resistance to change put up by individuals or groups. For instance, technological breakthroughs are resisted by those whose financial or other vested interests are protected in maintaining the status quo. In India, introduction of computers was vehemently opposed by trade unions and various political parties on the grounds that it will lead to massive job loss and further aggravate the problem of unemployment.

Conflict theorists complain that capitalistic systems encourage owners to protect their assets at the expense of workers. They resist all efforts of the government to regulate and enforce safety standards and implement measures for the welfare of workers.

Cultural factors also play a central role in resistance to social change. Nonmaterial culture does not immediately respond to changes in material culture, leading to culture lag. For example, certain religious groups, such as the Roman Catholic Church still advocate large families and term *contraceptive methods* that limit family size as immoral. Currently, movements for gay rights are being strongly resisted by the society in many countries.

REVIEW QUESTIONS

1. Explain different models of social change.
2. What are the various factors that cause and resist social change?

CHAPTER

38

Theories of Social Change

LEARNING OBJECTIVES

After reading this chapter the learner should be able to

- Have knowledge about various theories of social change.
- Get acquainted with the role of nurse as a social agent.

LINEAR, CYLINDRICAL AND MAXIAM FUNCTIONAL

Social change cannot be attributed to any single cause but it occurs during the course of evolution. Some changes are progressive, while others are retrogressive. Different sociologists had different views about the social changes and they have put forth various theories to understand the reasons behind these changes.

Evolutionary Theories

Evolutionary theories are based on the assumption that changes in the societies are gradual from simple beginnings to complex forms. Early sociologists like Auguste Comte believed that human societies evolve in a linear way—that is in one line of development. According to Comte, social change basically meant progress for betterment. These changes are seen as positive and beneficial. To sociologists the evolutionary process implied that societies would necessarily reach new and higher levels of civilization. According to L.H. Morgan there are three basic stages in the process: savagery, barbarism and civilization. Auguste Comte's three stages in the development of human society are the theological, the metaphysical and the positive which represent the basic stages of social change. Charles Darwin's theory of Organic Evolution had great influence on evolutionary theories of social change.

Sociologists who believed in this theory considered that complex and advanced societies must have evolved from very simple and primitive societies. Herbert Spencer, a British sociologist, carried the idea that society is also an organism and believed in Darwin's principle of the survival of the fittest to human societies. Though he stated that every society has been gradually progressing towards a better state and believed in evolution of the industrial society from military society. According to him western races, classes or societies have survived and evolved because of their adaptation to face the conditions of life. The opinion of social Darwinism got widespread popularity in the late nineteenth century and survived throughout the twentieth century. Emile Durkheim says a society's increasing moral density is the cause of societal evolution.

Functionalist or Dynamic Theories

This theory helps us to understand certain social relationships. Sociologists shifted their attention from social dynamics to social stability. As per the functionalist theory different parts of the social systems are like various systems of the human body fitting perfectly and functioning in harmony. Herbert Spencer brought out theories parallel to Darwin's theories. As per Darwin's theory, biological species adapt the changing environmental conditions to survive. But as per the functionalist theory, if one part of the system changes it will influence all the systems. If family system changes with changes in social environment all other social institutes like political, religious and educational get affected, leading to realignment. Functionalist theory explains how changes occur in the society and various social institutions are interrelated and change with each other. As such any society experiencing rapid changes is prone to misalignment if its different institutions do not adapt these changes.

Changes in society are not always disruptive but may alter the state of equilibrium and resulting in a new equilibrium. Social changes may come from within the society to resolve the conflicts and make adjustments. Other sources of changes come from outside the society coming in contact with other societies. Another sociologist Parsons Talcott is of the view that there are two processes involved in social changes. In simple societies one institution performs multiple functions as institutions are undifferentiated. But the society gets complex with process of differentiation and different institutes take over the functions of an institution. Family as an institution performs different functions as reproductive, educational, economical, social and recreational, and many more. But in advanced societies many of these functions of family are performed by other social institutions like schools, crèches and health care centres. Thus, every society has the ability to absorb disruptive forces while maintaining overall stability.

Another sociologist, Durkheim is of the opinion that societies change in the direction of greater differentiation and interdependence. The progress is from relatively undifferentiated social structure with little division of labour and kind of mechanical solidarity to a more differentiated social structure with proper division of labour giving rise to more cohesive organic solidarity.

Linear

Many sociologists consider that social changes are cumulative, developmental, nonrepetitive and permanent. Each society moves to a higher state of civilization as it progresses in a linear fashion and in the direction of improvement though the pace of this advancement may be fast or slow. As per linear hypothesis, each aspect of the society changes constantly in a particular direction. Linear theories of social evolution are based on the assumption that each society must pass through a fixed and limited numbers of stages in a given sequence. This theory is influenced by Charles Darwin's theory which says that the linear model is an economic model which assumes that there are two main causes of social change: (1) innovations in the technology of economic production and (2) urbanization.

Auguste Comte believed that there are three stages and each field of knowledge passes through each of these three stages of growth. These stages are as follows:

Theological stage or religious stage: The primitive man was hunting and gathering and believed that everything is done by supernatural power. God has control over everything.

Metaphysical stage: Reasoning helped human being to find out some order behind the natural world.

Positive or scientific stage: Scientific way of thinking is thought to be positive stage.

Historical development of human societies caused by innovations in the technology of economic production.

Lensiki divided levels of societies into the following five stages:

Hunting and gathering: In almost all hunting and gathering societies, the males hunt large game animals such as deer, elk, moose or whatever else is available in the climate in which they live; and females and children gather plant vegetation and berries.

Pastoral: They are semi-sedentary, and their livelihood is dependent upon the domestication of animals. Basically, they are animal-herders living off the resources readily available from their animals. They also do small-scale trading and selling with other groups.

Horticultural: Horticultural societies engage in small-scale farming and the use of simple hand tools.

Agricultural: These societies use improved technology like fertilizer and irrigation systems for large-scale farming.

Industrial: The production of goods using advanced sources of energy to drive large machinery is the main focus of this society. There is now a centralized workplace, economic interdependence, formal education and complex social systems such as economic, political and government.

Cyclical Theory

Cyclical theory varies from linear theory as some sociologists feel societies change according to cycles of rise, decline and fall just as individual persons are born, mature, grow old and die. Cyclical theory was developed by Oswald Spengler and Arnold J. Toynbee. According to this theory, each society after passing through all these stages of life cycle returns to the original or approximately the same stage.

Civilizations come and go, repeating a recurrent cycle of birth, growth, breakdown and decay, but those who can cope with a changing environment survive and those who cannot die.

P.A. Sorokin, a sociologist is of the opinion that culture oscillates like the pendulum of a clock between two points the 'sensate' and the 'ideational'.

A sensate culture is the one that appeals to the senses and sensual desires, while the ideational culture gives expressions to art, literature, religion and ethics which do not appeal to the senses but to the mind or the spirit.

Like a clock pendulum culture swings and it keeps on swinging through the middle pole from sensate pole towards the ideational pole. The middle of the swinging pendulum is a mixed form of sensate and ideational cultures—a stable mixture of faith, reason and senses as the source of truth.

According to Vilfredo Pareto, societies pass through the periods of political vigour and decline which repeat themselves in a cyclical fashion.

Maxiam Theory

Karl Marx's theory which is also called economic theory of social change emphasizes role of economic factors in the process of social change. This is probably the most widely accepted theory of all the theories of social change. According to Marx, social change takes place because of certain forces. He believes that human society has been fundamentally divided between classes, the rich and the poor, or capitalist and labourer, since its emergence from primitive state, as clashes have been there in the pursuit of class interests. Class interests lead to clash which is the determinant of social and historical process. Class interests develop by occupancy of particular social positions of individuals. A huge crowd of workers unknown to each other gather in the wake of their common interest: maintenance of their wages. Thus, the common interest brings them together against employer even though they have hostile attitude against each other. Not all the exploited classes get a chance to fight against their exploiters. The revolts of the slaves of German peasantry failed because they did not represent a mode of production which could affect the future of production. As per Maxiam theory there are two main aspects of social change, production force and production system. Whenever there is some change in the technology of production because of new inventions or new working skills, production system also gets changed. This relation of production refers to social organization of production: who owns the productive forces and how these forces are controlled.

ROLE OF NURSE: CHANGE AGENT

The change agent needs to understand fully the individual and community. Basically, the change agent is the one who has the knowledge and uses it for the process of change. Nurses can become visible and efficient agents for planned and managed change and avid activists, both in health care and society at large. Nurses act both as change agents and as supporters. Change is possible if there is flexibility and ability for adaptation. Nurses are not only the agents for change but they are also the supporters of social change and they also advocate who assist people to adapt to the myriad of changes that affect their lives.

A nurse plays an important role in changing the mindset of people about existing superstitions which are obstacles in safe health practices.

Having the knowledge of social problems nurses suggest preventive remedial approach to handle the situations related to these problems in efficient manner. Nurses are expected to 'be aware of broader health concerns such as environmental pollution, violation of human rights, world hunger, homelessness, violence and other related issues. Keeping in mind the needs of the coming generation, nurses are encouraged to work individually as citizens to their maximum capability and collectively for policies and procedures to bring about social change'.

A nurse provides educational opportunities to the individuals in the community by propagating health awareness and holding interactive sessions to understand their ideas, emotions and sentiments. A nurse helps in finding the new ways to improve the health care through nursing research.

She maintains liaison between the patient and members of health team. Nursing care involves social justice, involving issues like who should receive its benefits, and who should shoulder the responsibility of providing and paying for it. Nurses are resourceful and try to find out what is available to their patients and use it for their welfare.

REVIEW QUESTIONS

1. Write in detail about dynamic theories of social change.
2. Write in support of 'nurse as an agent for change'.

UNIT - 10

SOCIAL ORGANIZATION AND SOCIAL SYSTEM

CHAPTER

39

Social Organization and Disorganization

LEARNING OBJECTIVES

After reading this chapter the learner should be able to

- Get familiar with process of social organization and disorganization.

A society is never static as the social process continues. It is in a state of a dynamic equilibrium and the groups are held together by the system of social controls and cultural ethos. Changing cultural aspects and the ongoing social process throw up various issues and problems that are an integral part of the society.

However, failure to make necessary adjustments to the changing conditions leads to the lack of functional integration between groups, conflicting social attitudes and personal maladjustment. As a result, the social equilibrium is disturbed and various social problems start arising.

SOCIAL ORGANIZATION

Existence of social order is a prerequisite for smooth functioning of human society but it cannot be taken for granted due to the ongoing process of change that necessitates adjustment of its different parts of the society. There is a social order and the society is well organized when its various parts are properly adjusted.

An organized social unit of people is structured and managed to meet the needs and to pursue collective goals. Social organization is the system of cultural institutions by which the parts of society are inter-related and enable it to function purposefully as a whole. The web of social relationships involving persons and groups remain organized due to a stabilized network of rules, norms habits and institutions.

SOCIAL PROBLEMS

Every society has its share of problems and the Indian society is no exception. Apart from the issues emanating from its history and cultural diversity, which are a cause of social tensions among groups belonging to various caste, community and religion, new problems like corruption, poverty, unemployment, drug abuse, naxalism, terrorism and other issues have cropped up.

The rapid increase in population after independence and the changing demographic profile has also given rise to many problems, while some issues are a legacy of the colonial past of the country. The slackening of social controls, increasing economic disparities and other changes has a disturbing effect on harmonious relationship between various groups and individuals. The undermining of social solidarity and collapse of equilibrium of forces triggers the breakdown of the established social order. The web of relationships that binds the society gets weakened and the process of social disorganization sets in.

Social problems and social disorganization are closely related. When social problems become intractable and start coming in the way of smooth functioning of the society, the process of social disorganization begins.

SOCIAL DISORGANIZATION

The best way to understand the social disorganization is to view it in contrast to social organization. In a well-organized society, there is an orderly relationship of different parts. There is equilibrium of forces and functional balance among various elements of the social structure with harmonious adjustments of institutions.

When the social equilibrium is disturbed owing to the lack of adjustment and parts of social structure are not functioning properly and efficiently, society is thrown out of gear. French sociologist, Emile Durkheim, defined *social disorganization* as 'a state of disequilibrium and a lack of social solidarity or consensus among the members of a society'. Two other sociologists, W.I. Thomas (Polish) and Florien Znaniecki (American), conceptualized *social disorganization* as 'a decrease of the influence of existing rules of behaviour upon individual members of the groups'. There are many such definitions given by sociologists but the important point is that it is prevalent in every society to varying extent.

Social disorganization is a consequence of functional disequilibrium within customs, institutions, groups, communities and societies.

Causes of Social Disorganization

Social disorganization is a result of disruption of existing order caused due to modernization of human societies. Every change on the political, economic and cultural front has implications for the society. There is a constant conflict as the old traditions, customs, habits, norms and institutions refuse to make for the new. Apart from important events like industrial revolution, wars, natural disasters and population explosion, cultural degeneration, erosion of social values, declining social control and other nonmaterial factors are responsible for social disorganization.

Industrialization

Industrialization creates conditions conducive to social disorganization as it affects relationships and family structure and leads to urbanization, migration of people, crime, technological advancements, exploitations and class conflicts. It also raises issues like unemployment, crime, immorality and other evils associated with urbanization.

Extreme Division of Labour

The division of labour within limits increases productivity but when it is excessive, it undermines the social solidarity and leads to social disorganization. Extreme division of labour also leads to economic crises, class struggles, industrial unrest and demoralizes individuals, the family and the community.

Violation of Social Norms

Social values and norms help to strengthen and stabilize the social order and sustain the society. However, with social change, new values emerge and some of the old values decline; however, this leads to a conflict as the people are not in a position to reject the old and accept the new readily. The violation of social norms has a disorganizing effect on social institutions. If the violations of norms are not checked, the existence of social institutions is endangered and cause disorganization.

Cultural Lag

A major cause of disorganization is the different components of culture that do not undergo change at a uniform rate. Some parts, particularly material objects like costumes, architecture, ornaments and modes of transportation, change very quickly, while ideas, beliefs, philosophies, habits, traditions and other nonmaterial elements of culture undergo a gradual transformation. The unequal rates of change of different elements of culture lead to a state of disequilibrium. W.E. Ogburn refers it to this imbalance in the pace of change in various material and nonmaterial elements of culture as cultural lag that sets in the process of disorganization.

The advancements in science and technology are leading to new inventions causing rapid material changes and the consequent social changes cause disorganization. The modern technology has not only made life comfortable but also created problems like unemployment, crime and poverty.

Natural Disasters

Catastrophic events like floods, earthquakes and volcanic eruptions and other calamities also have long-term implications for the society and often cause disorganization. Unlike past, the society is better equipped to control the impact of natural disasters but in the past they had far-reaching consequences. An epidemic can also have a disorganizing effect on the society.

War and Communal Clashes

Societies face serious problems in the aftermath of wars and communal clashes and other type of mass violence. The communal divide that led to the partition of the country provides a glaring example of social disorganization.

REVIEW QUESTIONS

1. Explain the causes of social disorganization in detail.
2. What is meant by social organization?

CHAPTER

40

Democratic and Authoritarian Modes of Participation

LEARNING OBJECTIVES

After reading this chapter the learner should be able to

- Know about the democratic and authoritarian political system.
- Get familiar with characteristics of democracy.

Participation is an essential ingredient of any process of social organization. A social system comprises various subsystems, political, economic, religious, educational and cultural but the state is the most powerful political organization as it regulates the social relationship of individuals and exercises the overall institutional control over the society. The organization of any state depends on the form of political system.

All political systems encouraged participation of the people, though the extent may vary depending on the form of system. Involvement of the people in the matters of state reinforces the legitimacy of political authority and, thus, has a stabilizing influence on the system. The members of the society participate in the political system; they develop various ways to varying degrees.

There are two main types of systems: democratic and authoritarian.

DEMOCRATIC SYSTEM

There are many forms of participation and democratic set-up encourages maximum involvement and participation in the governmental processes. The word democracy is derived from two Greek words: *demos* meaning *people,* and *kratia* meaning *power*. Thus, democracy (demos-kratia) refers to the power to the people who themselves decide the kind of institutions and the laws that will govern them. In simple terms, democracy is defined as political power exercised either directly or indirectly through people's participation.

It is considered a liberal form of political system in which people enjoy a number of basic civil and political rights. Democratic systems have set of institutions that allow people to choose the makers of public policy through competitive elections. There is a clear distinction between state and society, and limits are imposed on the power of the state through constitutional provisions. There are a number of institutions to keep an eye on the functioning of state and ensure that it does not transgress its powers. Abraham Lincoln described democracy as a 'government of the people, by the people and for the people'.

Political and social thinkers have given different definition of democracy. In the words of Gettell democracy is 'a form of government in which the mass of the population possesses the right to share in the exercise of sovereign power'.

Maclver asserts that 'democracy is, not a way of governing whether by majority or otherwise but primarily a way of determining who shall govern and broadly, to what ends'.

According to noted Indian historian Sardar Panikkar 'democracy is not merely a form of government; it is a complex of social, economic and political factors, affecting the relationship of the state of the individual, guaranteeing essential freedoms, personal liberty, and freedom of expression of organization and of governing activities'.

Characteristics of Democracy

It is characterized by an independent judiciary, legal system, election system and media over which the government has no control.

Free and fair elections are held regularly to elect the government in which political parties compete.

The military is under the civilian control.

It works on the principle of majority rule and decisions are taken by the majority and minority submits to facilitate their implementation.

A functioning democratic system ensures the basic rights like the right to franchise, the right to form political parties and freedom of speech, religion and equal opportunity.

Liberal democracies guard against concentrating of power and the functioning is decentralized to regional and local levels to ensure that government is accessible and responsive to the people right down to grassroots.

There is dominance of persuasive and compromising methods, there is no coercion and the approach is marked by nonviolence and nonsuppression.

Types of Democracy

There are two types of democracy: direct and indirect.

Direct democracy: In this form of government, the people directly participate in the affairs of the state. All the adult citizens have the right to participate in the meetings of the assembly or governing bodies where laws are passed, development policies, budget proposals approved and other important decision taken. This type of system is suitable only for the states with a small population to make direct participation of all the citizens possible. This is the reason that it exists only in a few cantons of Switzerland.

Indirect democracy: Indirect democracy exists in almost all the modern states as their large size and population make direct participation of all the citizens in the affairs of the state impossible. In the indirect form of government, people elect their representatives for a specified period to manage the affairs of the state. In case they fail to deliver as per the expectation of the people, they can be changed through the electoral process. People do not directly take part in the affairs of the state.

Merits and Demerits of Democracy

The merits of democracy are as follows:

1. It is a more responsive accountable form of government.
2. It improves the quality of decision-making.
3. It provides a method to deal with differences and conflicts.
4. It enhances the dignity of the citizens and protects their interests.
5. It allows us to correct our own mistakes.
6. It has an independent judiciary and separation of powers.
7. Regular elections give power to the people to change the government.

Demerits

1. Frequent change of leaders makes the government unstable.
2. Delay in implementation of plans as they are to be consulted by many people.
3. Bad decisions taken by the leaders.
4. Leads to corruption as it is based on electoral competition.
5. Democracy is all about power play and there is little room for morality.
6. Illiterate and politically naive leaders may take wrong decisions.
7. Decision-making is slow due to lack of consensus and long time taken in consultations.

DEMOCRACY IN INDIA

There is indirect democracy in India and the country has opted for the parliamentary form of government. Its parliamentary model is largely based on the British system, though several different features have been borrowed from various countries. The chief executive or the head of government is the Prime Minister, who can remain in office till he commands the confidence of the Lok Sabha; enjoys the support of majority of members. There may be a single party or a coalition of parties in power.

In contrast, in presidential democracies, the head of government is the President, who is directly elected by the people and cannot be removed from office except in extreme circumstances through the process of impeachment. As such, presidential democracies provide more stable governments. In a parliamentary system government can be changed before completion of tenure through mid-term elections or political realignments. Such mid-way changes create uncertainty and hinder implementation of policies and programmes.

AUTHORITARIANISM

It is a political regime where one ruler or a small group of individuals exercise the real power over the state without being constitutionally responsible or accountable to the public. Authoritarian governments may have a system of holding elections but the citizens do not have any voice in the affairs of the state. The leaders do not give any freedom to the people who have no choice but to abide by their wishes. Authoritarian regimes may be headed by kings, military leaders, a small group of aristocrats, dictators and even presidents or prime ministers. The leader's title does not automatically indicate a particular type of government.

Autos mean *self* in Greek. So we have *autocracy*, or (autos-kratia) meaning *power to the self*. Authoritarian regimes impose restrictions on individual freedom and with power vested an individual it also termed as *dictatorship*. There is no ideology or political philosophy and the government is run on the whims of those in power.

Another nondemocratic form is totalitarian regime, a highly centralized system which is driven by a strong ideology that seeks to radically transform the state, society and the economy and the feature that distinguishes it from an authoritarian regime.

Authoritarian leaders are autocratic and take decisions without any consultations or inputs from the rest of the group.

Types of Authoritarian Regime

Monarchical rule: It is based on the claim that one person alone is fit to rule a country with no clear regime or roles to constrain that person's rule. Often, this person depends on supporters within the state who derive direct benefits by carrying out the will of the ruler.

Military rule: State undergoing political turbulence and high level of public unrest and violence frequently come under military rule. In such uncertain and unstable situations, the military sees itself as the only organized and cohesive force that could ensure stability. Military leadership often stage coups to throw out the political regimes taking advantage of instability.

One-party rule: In such regimes, a single political party establishes its monopoly by either imposing a ban on other parties or keeping them out from power by using some other tactics. The party actually consists of only a small minority of the population and such regimes can be classified as oligarchies. Members of the party usually enjoy privileges that are denied to the public at large. Such regimes thrive as a large number of people or groups benefit and they are termed as *communism* and *fascism*.

Theocracy: It is a form of government in which clergy have official recognition as the civil ruler. The faith of the people and its leaders are the foundation for these kinds of political regimes guided by the doctrine of a particular religion or religious group.

PARTICIPATION IN AN AUTHORITARIAN REGIME

Political participation is generally restricted in authoritarian regimes; the following forms of participation are often allowed to some citizens or practiced by others in order to gain control of government:

Political Parties in Authoritarian and Democratic Systems

A political party is essentially a social group of like-minded people. These members work together with the sole aim of winning elections and form the government. Political parties compete against one another to grab the political power and try their level best to put their philosophies and policies into effect.

Party organization is the formal structure and leadership of a particular political party. The parties have organizational units at the national, state and local levels. At each level they have executive committees, governing bodies and other formal structures to carry out political activity and organizational functions. Members are enrolled at the grassroots and various organizational bodies come from local to the national level.

Each political party is headed by the national party committee. Though this committee functions as the head of the party, but it cannot force other party organizations to do what it wants.

Sometimes, different party organizations have differences with one another about how to achieve their goals.

The goal of a political party is to secure political power alone or in alliance with other political parties. A political party always works to expand its support base thus it has to be open so that more and more potential members come forward to join the party.

Main Functions of a Political Party

Contesting elections: In democratic regimes, elections to form a government are a regular feature and political parties are the contenders for power. They contest elections by fielding candidates who are selected on various ways and considerations.

Parties come out with different policies, programmes and promises and the voters choose from them. The policies and programmes are framed to muster maximum support of the people.

Parties form governments: The parties contest elections to form government and they train leaders for the purpose. The trained leaders become ministers and run the government as per the policies and programmes of the party.

Enacting laws: On coming to power the parties enact laws for the country. The laws are debated among the members and passed in the legislature. Party leaders issue the directions to its members who follow them, irrespective of their personal opinions.

Role of opposition: Parties that lose in elections play the role of opposition and they continuously evaluate the performance of the government and criticize the ruling party for its failures or wrong policies.

Shaping public opinion: The political parties carry out public campaigns to highlight issues and create public opinion. Their large network of workers enables parties to create public pressure on various issues. At times, big movements are launched for the resolution of urgent problems faced by people.

Link between people and government: The political parties function as a link between people and the government. A common citizen finds it easier to access the government agencies through a local party leader than an officer. Parties have to be responsive to people's needs and demands to gain the confidence of people.

REVIEW QUESTIONS

1. Write short notes on the following:
   a. Functions of a political party in a democracy
   b. Authoritarian regime
2. Write in detail about democratic political system in India.

CHAPTER

41

Voluntary Associations, Inter-Relationship of Institutions

LEARNING OBJECTIVES

After reading this chapter the learner should be able to

- Have knowledge about the voluntary associations in India.
- Get familiar with the role of voluntary associations in India.

Government functions for the welfare of its public but it is a limited agency and there is a lot of work that cannot be performed by the government only as India is a huge country with large population. So there are lot of voluntary associations working for the welfare, integrity and solidarity of the nation.

Voluntary, the word is derived from the Latin word *voluntas*, which means freedom. So, voluntary association means freedom for association. Persons can form an association for promoting a cause they are interested in. Voluntary organizations are also called nongovernmental organizations (NGOs) in which its workers get paid or not paid but governed by its own members and there is no external control.

CHARACTERISTICS OF A VOLUNTARY ASSOCIATION

It has an administrative structure, a management and an executive committee.
It is registered under the Societies Registration Act 1880 and Indian Trusts act 1882.
Every voluntary association has certain aims and objectives and strive to achieve them.

It is governed by its own members without any external control. So these organizations preserve democracy and contribute to the welfare of the society.

The source of money for voluntary associations is grant-in-aid from government, partly from beneficiaries of the programme or the contributions from its members.

FUNCTIONS OF VOLUNTARY ASSOCIATIONS

Voluntary associations are indispensible and work for the welfare of society in addition to bringing the persons together to work for some noble cause.

1. Man is a social animal, so people enjoy working in groups. They form groups and associations for their own benefit and for the welfare of others. Voluntary associations are formed for promotion of health, recreational and cultural activities.
2. Voluntary or nongovernment associations act as buffer between the individuals and the state preventing the government from developing autocratic attitude.
3. Voluntary associations encourage people to exercise their fundamental rights through them.
4. Voluntary associations strengthen the feeling of national solidarity and promote participative kind of democracy.
5. Government may not have adequate financial resources and manpower to meet all the needs of its citizens. So these voluntary associations share the responsibility of state to fulfil the needs of its citizens.
6. Voluntary associations, with their limited resources, may perform some functions in a better way as compared to the government organizations because of dedication and devotion of its members.
7. Voluntary associations not only share the responsibilities of the government but also venture in new areas for the welfare of the society fight against the social evils and give attention to the unattended and unmet needs of people.
8. They act as a force in linking together people who are not politically motivated and work rising above the party politics by concentrating on nonpolitical issues and contribute to national integration.
9. Voluntary associations also make the people aware about the policies and programmes of the government for the welfare of its public and encourage their participation through constructive criticism.
10. Voluntary associations help the underprivileged persons such as the aged, differently abled, scheduled castes and tribes, destitute women and children to live dignified life.

Some of the voluntary associations working in the field of health care are as the following:

Voluntary Health Association of India (VHAI): It was formed in 1970 as a nonprofit registered society. Presently, it is a federation of 27 state voluntary health associations and linking 4500 health institutions.

Indian Red Cross Society: Established in 1920 having 400 branches all over India. Various functions of Red Cross Society are prevention of diseases, promotion of health and rehabilitation.

Hindu Kusht Nivaran Sangh: It was established in 1950 and it mainly works for people having leprosy.

Indian Council for Child Welfare: It was established for the welfare of children to help them develop physically, mentally, socially and spiritually in a normal manner.

Tuberculosis Association of India: This association came into existence in 1932 for controlling tuberculosis. The objectives of the association are to raise funds for training manpower and providing free treatment for tuberculosis.

Bharat Sewak Samaj: It is a nonpolitical and nonprofit organization established in 1952. The aim of the organization is to make people healthy through their own actions and efforts.

Central Social Welfare Board: It is an autonomous organization under the ministry of education set-up in 1953.

Association of Voluntary Agencies for Rural Development (AVARD): Promoted in 1958, it is a well-known, nonpolitical, nonprofit national association having over 700 autonomous voluntary agencies throughout India involved in rural development work. It was set-up by a group of freedom fighters who had renounced power politics to direct people's action to rebuild India during the post-independence period.

Voluntary Association for People Service (VAPS): It is also a nonprofit voluntary organization established in April 1999 by like-minded professionals with social work and health care professionals to render services to the needy and downtrodden in the society.

Voluntary Action Network of India (VANI): As a platform, this organization promotes voluntarism and creates space for voluntary action by workers. As a network, it attempts to take up common sectoral issues for the public interests and make attempts for building a truly national agenda of voluntary actions in the country. It also facilitates linkages of various efforts and initiatives of the different voluntary organizations in the country for a multiplier effect, to create and sustain the process of change in an organized manner. As an apex body of voluntary organizations, VANI makes all efforts for fostering value-based voluntary actions and their long-term sustainability.

VANI Has a Three-Tier Structure

1. **General body:** It is the supreme body of all members of VANI (networks/federations, organizations and individuals).
2. **Working committee:** It makes decisions on behalf of its members and has 21 elected members from the General Body, which also has two office bearers, the Chairperson and Treasurer. This Working Committee has four subcommittees namely: programme, networking committee, membership committee, finance committee and management committee.
3. **Secretariat:** It is headed by a chief executive officer who is appointed by the Working Committee, and is an ex-officio member of the Working Committee. The Secretariat has programme units, each led by programme officers/managers with their respective professional and support staff. The CEO liaises between the Secretariat and the Working Committee for planning, implementation and monitoring of the organization's activities.

REVIEW QUESTIONS

1. What are the functions of voluntary associations in India?
2. Write short notes on the following:
   a. VANI
   b. VAPS

UNIT - 11

SOCIAL CONTROL

CHAPTER

42

Social Control

LEARNING OBJECTIVES

After reading this chapter the learner should be able to

- Get acquainted with kind of social control and its need in the society.
- Know about various means of social control.

Peace, harmony and order are prerequisites for the existence of any human society. All societies have norms and values governing the conduct of individuals. A society without any norms and values is virtually inconceivable. It is essential that all the members abide by the norms and their self-interests are subjugated to the larger concerns of the society as a whole. Otherwise, it will be very difficult to maintain the social organization. Thus, every society has a mechanism in place for ensuring conformity to the generally accepted norms of behaviour and for dealing with deviance. The methods deployed to make the members conform to the norms constitute the social control mechanism and it is a pervasive feature of society.

MEANING OF SOCIAL CONTROL

In simple terms, social control refers to the various means used by a society to bring its members back in line with cultural norms and the accepted pattern of behaviour. In sociology, it means the social processes by which the behaviour of individuals or groups is regulated. The mechanisms for social control vary from one society to the other. Social control mechanisms are generally of two types: formal and informal. Formal social control refers to repressive or coercive forms of control methods, including direct physical constraint components, deployed through institutions like the police and the military. Informal social control is the softer ideological form designed to shape and reinforce ideas, values, attitudes and other cultural elements of society that are designed to ensure conformity to accepted patterns of behaviour.

Thus, social control implies a system through which a society exercises controls over the behaviour and activities of individual members deploying formal and informal methods. American sociologist E.A. Ross was the first to bring out the concept of social control in his famous book *Social Control*, published in 1901. According to him the individual has deep-rooted sentiments that enables him to connect and cooperate with fellow members and collectively work for the welfare of the society. The self-seeking impulses of the individual are so strong that these sentiments are by themselves not enough to overcome the selfish tendencies. Society has to make use of its mechanisms to ensure order and discipline. Ross has stressed upon the roles of public opinion, law, belief, suggestion, religion, ideals, ceremony, etc. in establishing social control.

DEFINITION OF SOCIAL CONTROL

Sociologists have given their own definitions of social control but they all refer to the mechanism by which society influences the behaviour of individual member. In the words of E.A. Ross, social control refers to the 'system of devices whereby society brings its members into conformity with the accepted standards of behaviour'.

Manheim termed it as 'the sum of those methods by which a society tries to influence human behaviour to maintain a given order'. Fairchild defined it as 'the sum total of the processes whereby society, or any subgroup within society, secures conformity to expectation on the part of its constituent units, individuals and groups'.

It is a collective term used to refer to 'those processes planned or unplanned, by which individuals are taught, persuaded or compelled to conform to the usages and life-values of groups' as per J.S. Roucek. Social control refers to 'the patterns of pressure which a society exerts to maintain order and established rules', in the words of Ogburn and Nimkoff.

NATURE OF SOCIAL CONTROL

These definitions bring out that social control denotes some kind of influence that may be exercised by the society or the community by means of public opinion, coercion, religion, morality, ideology and leadership in other ways. The influence is exerted at various levels. It may indicate the entire society's influence over all the innumerable smaller groups, subgroups and individuals. It may denote the influence of a dominant group over several smaller groups. It may signify the group's dominance over the individual members.

The influence is exercised for promoting the welfare of all the individuals or of the group as a whole. Social control aims to serve the general interests of all and to curb the dangerous selfish interests of individuals.

MEANS OF SOCIAL CONTROL

The society or community exercises two types of control over the members: formal and informal.

Informal Means of Social Control

In primary groups, the relationships are close, direct and intimate. Social control is exercised mainly through informal mechanisms such as customs, traditions, folkways, mores and religion. Informal means of social control include institutions like education, family, marriage and religion associated with socialization.

Folkways

Folkways refer to the ways of the people. They are the norms to which individuals conform because it is expected of them and customary to do so. Conformity to folkways is not enforced by law or any other agency of the society. For instance, there is no law that compels people to take bath, to brush teeth and give respect to elders, yet they do it without thinking over. It is the informal acceptance of established practices in each group or society. These are the folkways that are imbibed by individuals from society.

Folkways are manifested in matters of dress, food habits, observance of rituals, forms of worship and methods of greeting. For instance, food habits in North and South India are different and these habits often persist even when the person has moved to a different location away from his earlier surroundings.

Folkways are not as compulsive and obligatory as laws or morals. Those who violate folkways are not punished by formal means. But the violators are subjected to slander and social ridicule. One can ignore a few of the folkways but no one can neglect or violate all of them. They constitute an important part of the social structure.

They contribute to the order and stability of social relations. Human infants learn them through their elders through socialization. They learn different folkways at different stages relevant to their class, caste, ethnic, religious, occupational, marital and other statuses. They are followed by people because they are binding and become a matter of habit.

Mores

'Mores' or 'morals' represent another category of norms of conduct distinct from the customary practice of folkways. When folkways act as regulators of behaviour then they become 'mores'. They are considered to be essential for group welfare as they influence the value system of a society and are in the form of social regulations, which aim to maintain social order. The positive mores prescribe behaviour patterns while the negative mores or taboos prescribe or prohibit behaviour patterns.

Mores seek to regulate the relationship between individuals in defined situations, between wife and husband, parents and children, student and teacher and others. They instruct people to love their country, to look after their wives and children, to tell the truth, to be helpful to others. They also insist on people not to become unpatriotic, not to show disrespect to the god, not to steal or cheat. They may also refer to general social relationships in terms of honesty, truthfulness, hard work and discipline. Mores contribute to the solidarity and harmony of the group. They help the individuals to identify themselves with the group.

Mores represent the living character of the group and are always considered as 'right' by the people who share them. They are more compulsive in nature as they are morally right and their violation morally wrong. Every group has its own mores for each gender, for all ages, for all classes, for all families and so on.

Since mores are consciously designed with a view to preserving them, violations of these often entail penalties. Mores provide the strongest and most mechanisms of informal social control.

Customs

Customs are common practices of people established over a period of time, which come about spontaneously but gradually. These practices not only help to regulate social life, but also bind the people together. In primitive societies, customs were powerful means of social control, however, ever-growing forces of rationality and diversity in modern times have considerably diluted and weakened their role and reduced their effectiveness.

Religion

Religion exercises a powerful influence on its followers. Emile Durkheim defines religion as an integrated system of beliefs and practices related to sacred things. Religion unites and binds together those who have common beliefs and practices into one single moral community.

Formal Means of Social Control

The formal social control is exercised through institutions such as the state, law, education and those empowered by law. They deploy coercive measures in the case of deviance to ensure compliance.

LAW

The folkways, mores and customs were sufficient in controlling the individual behaviour in primitive societies. The groups followed similar occupations and individuals shared a direct, personal and intimate relation among themselves. The compliance was almost universal and unquestioned. However, the situation is different in the modern society where the people have moved away from traditional ways and they are not much under the influence of mores and customs. Relationships have become formal with vast diversity, individualism, division of labour and differentiation in terms of work, ethics and lifestyle. Accelerated movement of people, particularly from rural areas to cities and towns, for a better and dignified life has changed the worldview of social groups. Thus, the informal mechanism of social control is not only ineffective but also inadequate and formal means are required to control diverse population groups.

Law is the most powerful formal means of social control in the modern society and it is used in societies with a political setup, which is a government. The term *law* has been defined in various ways. J.S. Roucek opines that 'Laws are a form of social rule emanating from political agencies'. Roscoe Pound says that 'law is an authoritative canon of value laid down by the force of politically organized society'.

The state has grown stronger and more specialized in nature. It is now in a position to effectively regulate individual behaviour by enforcing common laws backed by the legal, administrative and political machinery. Law enforcement agencies have replaced customs and mores as social regulation of individual behaviour in modern society is not very effective.

Law has been defined in two ways: ideal behavioural norms and rules that are promulgated by the state that are binding in nature. The purpose of law is to impose norms of social behaviour. Individuals abide by laws due to fear of punishment by the state. In the process, the essential freedoms of individuals curtailed and hence acts as a deterrent. A vast majority of the people believe that adherence to laws is necessary for the overall well-being, prosperity, social stability and progress. This is termed as the rule-conforming habit.

Laws are mostly derived from moral notions and enacted on the basis of social doctrines, ideals and mores. Thus, compliance of law will be easier in a society having a healthy moral climate. The maintenance of legal order and effectiveness of law depends upon the moral climate of a society. It cannot be enforced solely on the threat of physical sanctions. It very much depends upon a general attitude of respect for law, and for a particular legal order.

For effective administration of law-enforcing agencies, like the police, the court and sometimes the armed forces, and all the infrastructure is required. Increasing complexity of the modern industrial society has necessitated enormous growth of administrative agencies.

Characteristics of Law

1. Law is definite, clear and precise.
2. Law is framed after due deliberation and meticulous planning and enacted by a proper law-making authority. It is a product of conscious thought.

3. Law applies universally, uniformly and equally to all without any exception.
4. Violation of law attracts stringent action in the form of penalties and punishments prescribed by the authority of the state.
5. Laws are always written down and they cannot be appear in a nonliterate society.
6. Laws are framed and modified in accordance with the requirement of society and they are not a result of voluntary consent of persons against whom they are directed.
7. Laws are the general conditions of human activity prescribed by the state for its members.

The sole purpose of law is to protect the individuals and the society and promote social welfare. Law achieves these objectives by curbing the homicidal activities of individuals and persuade individuals to pay attention to the rights of others.

Differences between Laws and Customs

The laws are different from customs in the following ways:

1. Law is coercive in character and compels people to comply with the legally approved pattern of behaviour, whereas customs are respected and practised out of fear because of the obscurantist nature of traditions and social approval associated with them.
2. Laws have a more general and universal nature, while customs are specific to groups and clans.
3. Contravention of law entails punishment by the state, while disregard of customs is frowned upon by the society but it may lead to strong action like ostracism only in extreme cases.
4. Laws are a more recent phenomenon associated with the emergence of the state and the growth of its institutions, while customs have been there in one form or the other at all times and in all societies.

SOCIAL CONTROL BY EDUCATION

Education has been an important means of social control as it helps in inculcating moral values and a sense of discipline, cooperation, tolerance and integration among children and prepares them for social living. Besides academic knowledge, educational institutions, right from school to university, also teach ethics through formal structured courses. Thus, formal education plays the role of a facilitator and can be considered a kind of social control.

Education is a vital means of social control from infancy to adulthood. Through education, the new generation learns about the social norms and the penalties for violating them. Education has contributed to the regulation of conduct in the early socialization of the child. Without proper education, harmony of the individual and society cannot be achieved. Education makes social control quite normal practice by converting it into self-control.

Educational reformers such as Montessori and Froebel have brought about great changes in the education of young children. These reforms reveal the moral notions external to the educational system. But they have been influential in changing moral ideas in society at large.

The educational system varies from one society to the other, depending on changing social mores and social needs. It keeps changing with time. In ancient Indian society, the main focus was on religious scriptures, philosophy and metaphysics. There has been a radical shift after the Industrial Revolution as social development has raised the quest for knowledge in various other creative areas and managerial skills.

STATE

State is the vital and chief instrument of administering social control in the modern societies. Sociologists have defined the state as 'an association designed primarily to maintain order and security, exercising universal jurisdiction within territorial boundaries, by means of law backed by force and recognized as having sovereign authority'.

State functions through the government and the modern nation-states are concerned about improving the equality of life of the citizens and besides facilities for education they also implement a wide range social security measures like education, medical care, old-age pension and unemployment allowance. Such initiatives are implemented with the cooperation of individuals and through collective efforts of civil society and other social institutions. Thus, the state acts as an informal agency of social control.

AGENCIES OF SOCIAL CONTROL

There are three main agencies of social control:

1. Family
2. Neighbourhood
3. Public opinion

Family

Family is the first and the foremost agency of social control. Every child learns from the immediate environment and the first lessons are provided by the family where a child gets the initial exposure to social life. A child learns etiquettes, values and picks up habits and attitudes from the immediate role models like parents, siblings and kin groups. The family socializes the child into the norms, values, traditions and customs of the group and thus plays the principal role in moulding the personality of a child.

The elders have a dominant role in the shaping of the personality of the child.

In villages, an individual acquires status from the family and these manifest in the individual's attitudes, interests, lifestyles and other facets. Marriages are mostly arranged by the elders and seen as an alliance between families rather than two individuals.

In cities, the situation is much different, though family continues to play a predominant role in the shaping of an individual's personality. The emergence of nuclear families due to factors like industrialization, paucity of income and constraints of space have given rise to individualistic tendencies, unlike the collectivism prevailing in the villages. The families tend to focus more and more upon themselves. The process of socialization in the family is complemented by other secondary institutions like the classroom, playground, peer group and the media. The individual derives status only partly from the family and more from personal achievements.

The parents and elders still have the major say in arranging marriages in cities, though the consent of the girl and the boy is also taken. The barriers of caste and religion are gradually being broken and marriages outside caste and religion are on the rise, indicating that individual choice is becoming increasingly important.

Neighbourhood

Neighbourhood in villages comprises people normally belonging to the same kin group or caste. Hence, relationships that exist are intimate and informal. This is not the case in urban environment where relationships with neighbours are more of formal nature with intermittent interactions. The bonding is far weaker than in the rural environment and in big cities the ties of neighbourhood are almost of no consequence and there is hardly any interaction between neighbours.

The village neighbourhood is vibrant and an enthusiastic participant in many daily activities of a family. It serves as a medium of social control by ensuring uniformity and conformity and correcting deviant behaviour. In cities neighbourhood normally does not have a role controlling individual behaviour as closely as the neighbours come into the picture only when individual actions affect community to monitor his behaviour.

Public Opinion

Public opinion is an important agency of social control. It has immense significance, especially, in democratic societies where the needs of the society regarding knowledge of the needs, ideas, beliefs and values is ascertained through public opinion. Behaviour of the people is influenced by ideas, attitudes and desires, which are reflected by public opinion. People get recognition and respectability when they behave according to accepted social expectations. Public opinion helps us to know what type of behaviour is acceptable and what is not.

In simple words, public opinion may be termed as 'the collective opinion of majority of members of a group'. Public opinion is commonly used to describe the aggregate views that individuals hold regarding matters that affect the interests of a particular community. As K. Young has said, 'Public Opinion consists of the opinion held by a public at a certain time'. According to V.V. Akolkar, 'Public opinion simply refers to that mass of ideas which people have to express on a given issue'. Newspapers, radio, television, motion pictures, legislations and pamphlets mould public opinion.

In the current age of Internet, social networking sites like Facebook, Twitter and other Web portals are also playing a major role in moulding public opinion. The reach of the new media, as the Web-based public platform are refereed to, is increasing by the day and most of the marketing companies and even political parties are using Internet to reach people.

In remote villages, which do not have access to television and newspapers, the communities rely on 'gossip' for information and to express their opinion on various subjects. In recent years, the reach of electronic media, particularly radio and television, has increased tremendously and it is becoming an important source of news, information and events in distant places. In cities, the print and visual media play a dominant role in the shaping of public opinion. The media keeps the public informed about events, issues and policies on a daily basis. Many decisions of the people are influenced by information available through the press.

As an agency of social control the media seeks to influence the tastes, ideas, attitudes and preferences of the readers. It affects their ideology also. It enforces morality by exposing the moral lapses of the leaders.

Radio is another agency of public opinion that influences behaviour. It influences our language, customs and institutions. It can dramatize and popularize events and ideas. In the same way, television has also been influencing people's behaviour.

Films or motion pictures exert great influence on public opinion. They have effectively changed the attitudes and behaviour of the people. Movie-goers are relaxed and unaware of the fact that they are being affected by ideas and values. The leading characters are the role models and the people unconsciously accept the attitudes and values implicit in the role. Through films it is possible to improve people's tastes, ideas and attitudes to some extent.

CONTROL BY SANCTIONS

Sanctions are a device used to force or persuade an individual or group to conform to social expectations. Through sanctions are part of the system of 'rewards or punishments' used to establish social control and their basic purpose is to enforce the norms and bring about conformity and maintain continuity and solidarity of a particular group. With the societies becoming more and more heterogeneous and increasing group conflicts on caste, religion and other basis, there is a danger of strong groups disrupting the ongoing society and threatening its existence. Sanctions help control the individuals or groups who are putting the existence of society to risk. They prevent social disorganization and ensure conformity to expected norms of social conduct.

Sanctions are applied in various ways, depending on the groups and situations. They may be positive or negative, ranging from the use of physical force to symbolic means. Negative sanctions may be anything from a censure to the death sentence and the positive sanction can be nod of approval to an honorary degree. Those sanctions that inflict pain or threaten to do so are negative. They include slander, satire, laughing at others, name-calling, threats, commands, censorship and finally overt action. Positive sanctions include verbal methods such as praise, flattery, suggestion, persuasion, some of education, indoctrination, advertising, propaganda, slogans, giving rewards, medals, badges, uniforms and conferment of titles.

Social Control by Fashion

Fashion is an important means of social control as it is style that is widely followed by the individuals. It permits and regulates variety and thereby avoids a dull and deadening uniformity. They help to express individuality without going against norms. Conforming to fashion amounts to imitating the contemporaries and in this way becomes an instrument of social control.

According to Maclver, 'Fashion is the socially approved sequence of variation on customary theme'. Lundberg described fashion as 'folkways that service for only a short time'. Fashion has an element of social sanction and it is not something that the society merely tolerates but something that the society accepts. Sanctions that support conformity to fashion in dress are very powerful as evident from the fact that no woman can go to a dinner party in a night dress.

Fashion in some ways is like custom but there are features which differentiate the two.

1. Customs evolve, whereas fashion is artificial
2. Customs are traditional and enduring; fashion has a short span and changeable
3. Customs signify sociality, fashion stands for individuality
4. Fashion grows where custom breaks
5. Customs are related to important matters, fashion to flimsy ones.

Fashion is group choice and has tempo. It is changeable, all pervading, and may or may not have utility.

Social Control by Customs

Customs are an integral part of every society and they involve sentiment of the community. They are followed voluntarily due to the emotional element and require no agency to enforce and ensure compliance. A custom is 'a rule or norm of action'.

Custom is still a strong force in group ways. Any disregard shown to it invokes social censure. The general custom as a social discipline is at vanishing point due to failure to adjust to the requirements of the fast-changing society. A custom may, with the change of circumstances, fade into nonexistence but it is a force at a given time and reflects the social consensus.

Law cannot be made in disregard of customs and a law maker has to take it into consideration. Custom evolves with time.

Characteristics of Customs

1. Customs are effective means of control as those who break them attract social ridicule and punished.
2. Customs are traditional and evolve over a period of time. They are accepted and established form of behaviour.
3. Folkways, when continued over generations, take the form of customs.
4. Customs are regulatory in nature.
5. Customs may change gradually over a period of time.
6. Customs are the code of accepted behaviour.

Social Control Belief System

Behaviour of individuals and groups has been profoundly influenced by the belief system. Belief in the existence of the unseen power has been with man from the primitive age. It has worked as a means of informal social control. Some of the beliefs hold a significant place in the social system.

It has provided the sanction to the social norms and conditioned the growth of culture. The belief in the theory of incarnation is motivated by the faith in the continuity of life. The belief in the immortality of soul has largely motivated religious thinking and practices. Birth and death came to be viewed as an endless cycle of change from one body to another.

It brought a sea change in the thinking and attitude of man and strengthen his belief in virtue, ethics and goodness. Wrongful actions, he feared, were bound to have bad consequences. The belief in the theory of *karma* has been accepted fundamental in all the Indian religious systems.

Ideology and Religion

Social thinking has always been influenced by ideology, which has played a vital role in political unity of the country.

Religion is a very powerful agency of social control as includes a host of customs, rituals, prohibitions and standard of conduct. The extent to which religion controls the behaviour of men depends upon the degree to which the followers accept its teachings.

REVIEW QUESTIONS

1. What is meant by social control? Why social control is required?
2. Explain about informal means of social control.
3. Which are various agencies for social control?

CHAPTER

43

Social Norms and Values

LEARNING OBJECTIVES

After reading this chapter the learner should be able to

- Get acquainted with the importance of various norms and values.

Norms and values are indispensable pillars on which the survival of a society rests. These are guidelines for culturally appropriate and socially correct behaviour that evolve over a period of time. Each society has its own set of norms and values that dictate the behaviour of the members. Every individual learns the norms during socialization at different stages of life right from childhood to old age.

DEFINITION OF NORMS

Norms are the set of groups-shared standards that regulate social conduct. Based on social values, norms are the social rules that define correct and acceptable behaviour to which the members of a group or society are expected to conform.

According to Broom and Selznick, norms are 'a blueprint for behaviour, setting limits within which individuals may seek alternate ways to achieve their goals'.

In the words of Young and Mack, *norms* refer to the *group-shared expectations,* while H.M. Johnson says 'A norm is an abstract pattern held in the mind that sets certain limits for behaviour'.

Donald Light Jr. and Suzanne refer to norms as 'the rules that guide behaviour in everyday situations and are derived from the value'.

As per Robert Bierstedt, a norm can be treated as a cultural specification that guides the conduct of members in society. He maintains that 'a norm is a rule or standard that governs our conduct in the social situations in which we participate'.

It is clear from these definitions that norms lay down the standard of behaviour that are regulatory in nature. They prescribe the way the people should behave in particular situation. Norms are mostly enforced informally, though some of them are formalized by translating into laws. They not only guide but also control behaviours through tools like social sanctions and laws or policies formally created. Violations of norms may invite social ridicule or even a more severe punishment.

CHARACTERISTICS OF SOCIAL NORMS

1. **Social norms are universal:** Every society has its norms and they provide the basis for social order. Norms are essential for smooth functioning of society.
2. **Norms incorporate value judgement:** Norms are derived from social values and represent a *standardized generalization* of the expected modes of behaviour after evaluation by the group. They incorporate value judgement as whether an action is right or wrong, good or bad, expected or unexpected is judged in terms of value.
3. **Norms are relative:** Norms vary from society to society and at times even within the society. All norms are not equally important and they are not equally strict or carry the same kind of punishment for nonconformity.
4. **Norms are internalized by the individuals:** Individuals internalize the norms of the society and they become a part of personality through the process of socialization. Individuals generally behave in accordance with the social norms.

INSTITUTIONALIZATION OF NORMS

Social norms are society-specific, and norm operative in one social system may not be operative in another. According to Johnson, a social norm is *institutionalized* in a particular social system if a large number of members accept it and take it seriously. It is socially sanctioned, implying that certain members of the system are expected to be guided by the norm in appropriate circumstances.

In a social system, the institutionalized norms apply to members in accordance with their social position and some norms do apply to all regardless of their social position. The acceptance of a norm in a social system is a matter of degree and not everyone is required to know the entire norms operative in the system.

IMPORTANCE OF SOCIAL NORMS

1. **Norms essential for maintaining order:** Man depends on society for his existence and norms regulate relationships and social conduct to make living together in a society possible. Norms are essential for maintaining order in society.
2. **Norms regulate behaviour:** Norms provide the controls to regulate the society; they govern the social conduct of its members in a manner.
3. **Norms make society cohesive:** Society achieves a coherent structure through the norms of people. The collective and co-operative life normative system gives to the society an internal cohesion.
4. **Norms encourage self-control:** Norms help individuals to exercise self-control. The constraints imposed by norms help to regulate the conduct of individuals who exercise discipline over their behaviour by themselves.

SOCIAL VALUES

Values are the criteria on the basis of which people assess their daily lives; decide their priorities and make a choice between alternative courses of action.

G.R. Leslie, R.F. Larson and H.L. Gorman say 'Values are group conceptions of the relative desirability of things'.

In the words of H.M. Johnson, 'Values are general standards that may be regarded as higher order norms'.

Young and Mack have a somewhat different view stating that 'Values are assumption, largely unconscious, of what is right and important'.

According to Michael Haralambos, 'A value is a belief that something is good and worthwhile and worth striving for'.

Peter Worsley also gave a similar definition stating that 'Values are general conceptions of *the good*, ideas about the kind of ends that people should pursue and different activities they engage in throughout their lives'.

In simple words, values are standards of social behaviour derived from social interaction and a measure of goodness or desirability. They are culturally defined goals and involve sentiments and significance.

Values provide the basis for judging and evaluating social interaction, goals, means, ideas, feelings and the expected conduct. Without such standards, it would not be possible to judge individual behaviour or social action. Values aim to integrate expected individual behaviour and social action.

RELATION BETWEEN NORMS AND VALUES

Norms and values have a salient relation. The main difference is that norms are specific, values are not. There may be delusion of norms in certain situation, but values are commanding. Norms are rules for behaving; and they lay down the do's and dont's by particular types of actors in given circumstances. Values are standard of desirability that are more or less independent of specific situations.

The same value may be a point of reference for a many specific norms and a particular norm may involve simultaneous application of several separable values. For instance, the value premise of *equality* may enter into norms for relationships between husband and wife.

Values serve as criteria for establishing what should be regarded as desirable, and thus provide the basis for accepting or rejecting a particular norm.

FUNCTIONS OF VALUES

1. Values provide goals or ends for the members to aim for.
2. Values ensure uniformities in group interaction and help bind the society together. Some sociologists maintain that shared values form the basis for social unity. Sharing of same values with others, the members of society are likely to see others as *people like themselves*. It will create a sense of belonging to a wider social group.
3. Values lend legitimacy to the rules that govern specific activities. Rules are accepted and followed mainly because they embody the values that most people accept. For example, the popular belief among Americans is that the capitalist organization is the best as it allows people to seek success in life.
4. Values bring about some kind of adjustment and facilitate reconciliation among different sets of rules. The people seek the same kinds of ends in different spheres of life and it is possible to modify the rules to help the pursuit of the desired ends.

For example, if members of a society cherish the value of *the principle of equality*, then they will have to amend the rules governing the interpersonal relationship of husband and wife. Societies create rules on the basis of their beliefs about what is *good* and *right*.

REVIEW QUESTIONS

1. What is the importance of values in the society?
2. Explain characteristics of norms in detail.

CHAPTER

44

Role of a Nurse in Social Control

LEARNING OBJECTIVES

After reading this chapter the learner should be able to

- Know the role of a nurse in social control.
- Get familiar with various social issues nurses can handle.

All nursing involves some element of social control, the degree may differ. Social control is for the welfare of the individuals. It is basically influence exerted through public opinion, social suggestion, religion, public policies or other means. Absence of a strong social control mechanism in the society can result in deviant behaviour.

Nurses not only provide clinical care in hospitals, they also work in the community and function as an agent of social control, particularly towards socializing patients into their roles and to promote society's view of health. Knowledge of sociology helps nurses to achieve social control in the community. With the rising costs of health care, the trend is towards community-based care and patient teaching has become a necessary part of the nurse's role. They also promote health by educating people and creating awareness in the society about the need to contain deviant behaviour.

Nurses do have a place in social control, particularly to socialize nurses. The phrase *social control* is usually associated with suppression, while many believe that nurses are the agents of advocacy not the agents of social control. However, nurses do have a place in social control, particularly to rehabilitating the patients into their roles and to promote society's view of health.

Social control is exercised in two modes: internal and external. Internal social control is thorough introspection while external social control is achieved with society placing controls to keep an individual from indulging in crime. Sociologists maintain that deviant behaviour is result of insufficient social control.

Their role as agent of social control is quite apparent when it comes to dealing with patients with mental disorders. The forensic mental health nurses as agent of social control have clear-cut historical and professional antecedents. While providing health care to persons who have mental illness, these nurses also play the role of agents of social control for checking their deviant and antisocial behaviour. It is important for nurses to show faith in the patients despite their past and present behaviour. They need competencies to view a mentally disordered offender as a human being. Psychiatric nurse is especially equipped with competencies to assist the community in the design and implementation of its own prevention program by strengthening the bonds among citizens and parents, health agencies and schools, law enforcement and hospitals.

The nurses have an important role as agents of social control in preventing evils like substance abuse and alcoholism. Nurses are capable of moulding behaviour and making it conducive to good health. They lay emphasis on self-determination and choice in health matters to ensure that substance abuse prevention efforts are incorporated by the community. They make the community aware by providing scientific information on addiction and abuse and to promote and enhance its health using her technical knowledge, interpersonal process, research competencies and teaching skills.

Nurses help patients to explore options for change by supporting self-efficacy of the individual by acknowledging the difficulties in effecting change and adopting a compassionate approach. They help the victims of substance abuse to understand and identify the causes of substance dependence or substance abuse and the need for change. They also assist them to identify options to solve the problem and take decision by considering the outcomes.

Substance abuse is a major health issue, which has far-reaching implications for the patient's family and also the community. The problem of substance abuse not only mars the health and well-being of the patient but also affects the entire family, educating the family about problem and its implications are very important. Nurses have to explain to the family members about the need for care, support and concern towards the patient.

The nurses have to develop trust and correct misconceptions to play an effective role as change agent. This is essential as they have to inform about both the effects of drugs and the appropriate strategies for treatment. Besides adequate assessment and decision-making skills, nurses must have knowledge and competency for facilitating the required change.

Behaving with patients in a consistent manner and cautiously avoiding confronting them is important for nurses to succeed as agents of change. They have to be nonjudgemental in a non-punitive manner to assist patients and their families on following the rules.

Nurses also have an important role to play in reducing the harmful effects of drugs in common use today. They help in developing and implementing drug and alcohol prevention strategies and evolving support systems. Restricting access to addiction-causing substances and imparting knowledge and skills for relapse prevention are part of the strategies to deal with the problem.

Educating the patient has become an essential step on the part of nurses in view of the rising costs of health care and increasing focus towards community-based care. The nurses are using the social control process to cope with patients with mental disorders and victims of substance abuse.

Nurses have a vital role in developing and implementing strategies for prevention of drug abuse and alcoholism, particularly in handling crisis and putting in place a support system. They have a key role in detecting health-related issues and creating awareness about perils of substance misuse and advising people, especially the elderly, about the risks.

As agents of social control, they have to perform the duty of advising people not to use tobacco and other such substances. There are a whole lot of related issues like active smoking and passive smoking about which the nurses have to educate the people, particularly in the rural community. The use of tobacco products is a major health issue the country is grappling with as it is socially permitted with no stigma attached.

Nurses play an important role in treatment and rehabilitation of persons suffering from alcohol dependence and drug abuse or substance abuse. They explore options for dealing with stress and help the patients by providing positive reinforcement in case of ineffective coping.

Nurses are conversant with laws, customs and folkways, thus are in a position to help people to conform to these. They can also judge the people who do not conform to the norms of the society.

REVIEW QUESTIONS

1. Which are the various social issues that nurses can handle?
2. Explain in detail the role of nurse in social problems.

UNIT - 12

SOCIAL PROBLEMS

CHAPTER

45

Social Problems

LEARNING OBJECTIVES

After reading this chapter the learner should be able to

- Have knowledge about various social problems in or country.
- Know the causes of major social problems.

No society is perfect. Every society has its own problems depending on its caste, class, racial and religious structure along with beliefs, customs and cultural traditions. Social change is an ongoing process, and it throws up problems that are peculiar to the society. The Indian society, being the oldest, is far more complex and plagued with a number of intricate problems. With people professing different religious faiths like Hinduism, Islam, Jainism, Sikhism, Christianity and Zoroastrianism, the Indian society is a heterogeneous mix of communities. Most of the problems are also rooted in the diverse religious beliefs and varied sociocultural practices of the people. The history of invasions and prolonged foreign rule also had long-term implications for the Indian society and created many problems.

As the society undergoes change, relationship between members get dissolved and the process of disorganization gives rise to new order due to maladjustment or nonadjustment of different components of social structure. The rapid pace of change results in a cultural lag as the social institutions fail to readily adapt to the growing needs. Social problems arise as the traditional informal controls fail to regulate the behaviour of individuals.

DEFINITION OF SOCIAL PROBLEM

Sociologists have described social problem in different ways. The most common terms it is defined as 'an undesirable condition affecting a significant number of people to correct which something can be done through collective social action'.

Richard C. Fuller and Richard A. Meyers defined social problem as 'a condition seen by a number of people as deviation from some social norm they cherish'. As per Lawrence K. Frank, social problem is defined as 'any difficulty of misbehaviour involving significant number of people which requires to be corrected'. Another sociologist Lundberg views social problem as 'deviant behaviour to such a degree that it exceeds the tolerance limit of the community'.

Green defines it slightly differently as 'a set of conditions termed as morally wrong by the majority or substantial minority within a society'.

There is an element of subjectivity in social problems. While one society may consider a situation as a social problem, another society may be comfortable with it. Furthermore, the outlook and attitude could change within a society itself over a period of time and what is being regarded as a problem today may not be so tomorrow.

CAUSES OF SOCIAL PROBLEMS

Most of the social problems are inter-related and have multiple causes. Events like war, natural calamities like floods and earthquakes, poverty and unemployment cannot be attributed to a single cause. Apart from traditional issues like casteism, communalism and gender discrimination, the major problems like poverty, illiteracy, unemployment, malnutrition and increasing incidence of crime are a consequence of population explosion. These problems cannot be solved in isolation and require an integrated approach. For instance, malnutrition can be eradicated only by removing poverty, which, in turn, cannot be alleviated without solving the problem of unemployment. Further, to solve the problem of unemployment, the issue of illiteracy will have to be tackled.

Poverty

Like rest of the developing world, poverty is a major social problem in India. In simple terms, it is the state of being poor, lacking the financial resources to provide for the basic needs like food, clothing and shelter. Despite implementation of several programmes for the socioeconomic uplift of the poor, poverty is widely prevalent and continues to be a major concern. Worse, the economic disparities between the haves and the have-nots have been extremely wide. The economy has been growing but the gap between the rich and the poor is only widening as the benefits have not been spread across evenly.

The urban areas have developed much faster than the rural areas. Some states like Maharashtra, Gujarat, Tamil Nadu and Karnataka have marched far ahead, while big states like Uttar Pradesh, Bihar, Madhya Pradesh, Rajasthan and others have been left behind. These are the states where poverty is a major concern. There are several causes for the continued prevalence of poverty in the country. The main reasons are as follows.

Rapidly Rising Population

The family welfare programme has brought down the birth rate considerably over the past three decades, but still the population has been rising at an alarming rate. The total population has crossed the 125 crore mark and every year 17 million are being added. Thus, the demand for food, shelter, clothing and other basic amenities is increasing rapidly.

Inflation

The production of food grains and other commodities is unable to keep pace with the ever-increasing demand and as a result the prices are rising. The high cost of living adds to the woes of the poor who are the worst hit. Any increase in their income is neutralized by price rise and they continue to reel under poverty.

Low Productivity in Agriculture

Farm productivity has been low due to small and fragmented land holdings, shortage of capital, continued of use of traditional methods of cultivation, lack of irrigation facilities and other related factors. As over 70 per cent of population is still dependent on agriculture, low productivity is a major cause of poverty in the country.

Low Rate of Economic Development

The economic growth has been slow over the years and as such a huge gap persists between availability and requirements of goods and services. Shortage of capital and lack of entrepreneurship are the main bottlenecks impeding growth and as result the problem of poverty is persisting.

Unemployment

The low rate of economic growth is also leading to unemployment as not enough jobs are being created and the number of jobless persons is increasing by the day. The nonutilization and underutilization of human resources is also contributing to poverty.

Social Factors

Archaic social set-up marked by caste system, traditions and customs, laws of inheritance and other social factors are not conducive to accelerated economic development.

POVERTY ESTIMATES

Poverty has conventionally been estimated with reference to a poverty line derived on the basis of notion of a minimum nutritional requirement of a person expressed in calories. The line of cut-off between poor and nonpoor is determined using the household consumption data available from National Sample Survey Organization (NSSO).

The first exercise to determine the poverty line was started in 1977 by the Planning Commission, which constituted a Task Force on 'Projections of Minimum Needs and Effective Consumption Demand' under the chairmanship of Prof. Y.K. Alagh. Based on 1973–1974 prices, it worked out the poverty line by taking into account the per capita daily calorie requirement as monthly per capita consumption expenditure (MPCE) level of Rs. 49.09 for rural areas and Rs. 56.64 for urban areas at national level. The estimate was based on per capita daily calorie requirement of 2,400 kcal in rural areas and 2,100 kcal in urban areas.

An Expert Group on 'Estimation of Proportion and Number of Poor' constituted subsequently under the chairmanship of Prof. D.T. Lakdawala, former Deputy Chairman of Planning Commission, to devise the methodology for estimation of poverty and, if necessary, redefine the poverty line. It recommended in 1993 that the poverty line approach be anchored in a calorie norm and associated with a fixed consumption basket (as recommended by the Task Force). The Government of India accepted the recommendations with minor modifications in

1997. The poverty estimates from 1973–1974 to 2004–2005 based on the methodology was worked out as follows:

Percentage and Number of Poor based on the methodology recommended by Lakdawala Committee:

Year	**Poverty Ratio (%)**			**Number of Poor (in million)**		
	Rural	Urban	Total	Rural	Urban	Total
1973–1974	56.4	49.0	54.9	261.3	60.0	321.3
1977–1978	53.1	45.2	51.3	264.3	64.6	328.9
1983	45.7	40.8	44.5	252.0	70.9	322.9
1987–1988	39.1	38.2	38.9	231.9	75.2	307.1
1993–1994	37.3	32.4	36.0	244.0	76.3	320.3
2004–2005	28.3	25.7	27.5	220.9	80.8	301.7

Thereafter, in 2005, another Expert Group headed by Prof. Suresh D. Tendulkar was set-up to review the methodology and recommend changes in the existing estimation procedures. In its report submitted in 2009, it made significant departures from the existing estimation procedure recommending a uniform 'poverty line basket' for both rural and urban population. Besides, it incorporated an explicit provision in price indices for private expenditure on health and education along with a price adjustment mechanism.

Percentage of poor based on the methodology recommended by Tendulkar Committee:

Year	**Rural**	**Urban**	**Total**
1993–1994	50.1	31.8	45.3
2004–2005	41.8	25.7	37.2
2009–2010	33.8	20.9	29.8

The poverty line has been fixed at Rs. 27 in rural areas and Rs. 33 in urban areas in 2011–2012 on the basis of the Suresh Tendulkar panel's recommendations. As it was considered unrealistic, a committee headed by Rangarajan was set-up to have a relook at the Tendulkar formula for the estimation of poverty. After a review the committee revised it to Rs. 32 a day in rural areas and Rs. 47 in urban areas. As a result the below poverty line population increased by 35 per cent from the estimate of 270 million based on the Tendulkar formula to 363 million in 2011–2012.

Thus, 29.5 per cent of India's population lives below the poverty line as defined by the Rangarajan committee, as against 21.9 per cent based on Tendulkar formula. The below-poverty line (BPL) population almost doubled to 102.5 million based on Rangarajan's estimates from 53 million based on the Tendulkar formula.

REVIEW QUESTIONS

1. Explain in detail about major social problems in India.
2. What are the various causes of social problems?

CHAPTER

46

Control and Planning: Poverty, Housing, Illiteracy, Food Supplies and Prostitution

LEARNING OBJECTIVES

After reading this chapter the learner should be able to

- Get acquainted with major problems of our country.
- Have knowledge about the steps taken by the government to control the problems.

Poverty is the root cause of almost all of the social problems of our nation, though lot of efforts for poverty alleviation have been made and it is one of the important components of the planning process in India. The employment generation is being given the topmost priority by the government by boosting agriculture, tourism and industry. Rapid growth over the decades has made India the fourth largest economy of the world. However, the growing economy is not benefitting all the people uniformly. The benefits have not percolated down to a large section of the people, particularly the economically weaker lot. Modern economy is technology based and it is not generating much employment. People from rural areas are migrating to towns and cities mainly due to acute poverty and lack of employment avenues in villages. But despite accelerated growth and greater economic opportunities in urban areas, not enough employment is being created.

PLANNING AND PROGRAMMES FOR ERADICATION OF POVERTY

Even poverty is not uniformly spread across the country; some states like Orissa, Bihar and Madhya Pradesh have high levels of poverty compared to states like Maharashtra, Tamil Nadu Punjab, Gujarat and Haryana. The poor sections, which are not able to participate in the process of economic development, need government intervention. The levels of poverty also vary and this has to be appreciated and understood for effective interventions.

Different Levels of Poverty

Poverty can be of two types: relative poverty and absolute poverty.

Relative Poverty

It is a comparison of level of poverty among various nations. Indicators like the per capita income and national income provide an idea of relative poverty. Nations with per capita income of less than US$25 per annum are considered to be poor as per the norms of the United Nations.

Absolute Poverty

It is measured in terms of per capita intake of calories and minimum level of consumption. Below poverty line (BPL) is fixed by the government based on minimum food requirement for survival of a human being. The food value is converted into calories and value of the calories is further converted into money. The total equivalent amount is considered to be the poverty line.

Poverty Alleviation Programmes

Poverty is synonymous with poor quality of life, deprivation of basic needs, poor health, malnutrition and illiteracy. So eradication of poverty has been an integral part of the strategy for economic development. The Government of India has implemented a number of programmes for alleviation of poverty since the 1970s. Realizing that a holistic approach was required, the Integrated Rural Development Programme (IRDP) was launched under which agricultural labourers and small farmers were taught new skills to involve them in some vocations other than cultivating land. These vocations were fishery, animal husbandry and forestry. Beneficiaries were given subsidized credit, training and infrastructure, so that they could find new sources of income. But this scheme was extended to schedule castes and schedule tribes, women and rural artisans in 1980.

The IRDP failed to yield the desired results as it sought to develop unskilled labourers into entrepreneurs. With no experience in managing an enterprise they took up unviable projects that failed. Wage employment programmes such as National Rural Employment Programme (NREP) and Rural Landless Employment Guarantee Programme (RLEGP) were launched for employment generation subsequently. Later on both of these programmes were merged into Jawahar Rozgar Yojana (JRY). Indira Awaz Yojana (IAS) was launched in 1990 to provide shelter to homeless people who were living below the poverty line. The Employment Assurance Scheme (EAS) was also initiated in 1990 to provide employment to unemployed people.

However, the various schemes did not have the desired effect and the government came up with the Swarnjayanti Gram Swarozgar Yojana (SGSY) in 1999. Keeping in view the non-enterprising nature of the poor individuals, SGSY focused on groups to lend money and develop microenterprises by organizing the poor into self-help groups (SHGs) and providing credit, technological assistance, infrastructure and training. Banks are generally satisfied with the credit worthiness of the SHGs. Unlike the IRDP, SGSY focused on mainstreaming the poor to join the economic development of the country.

National Rural Employment Guarantee Act

A major initiative on the employment front was taken in 2005 with the enforcement of the National Rural Employment Guarantee Act (NREGA). The NREGA gives a guarantee of 100 days of wage employment in each financial year to a rural household whose adult members are willing to do manual and unskilled work. Under the scheme a minimum of 50 per cent of the funds are transferred to the village panchayats, which carry out various development activities such as rural connectivity, water harvesting structures, drought proofing, minor irrigation and micro irrigation works.

Food Safety Programme

Starvation and malnutrition have been reported in various parts of the country, even in economically developed states like Maharashtra. The Public Distribution System (PDS), which was originally a universal public distribution system (UPDS), was created for benefiting farmers from their produce, and not as an antipoverty programme. It was meant for price stabilization of food grains by giving support price. Then the central government initiated the PDS programme in June 1997 and called it targeted public distribution system (TPDS). The states were to identify families below poverty line (BPL) and provide them 10 kg of food grains at highly subsidized price and later on this amount was raised to 20 kg. PDS has a great potential to protect the poor from starvation and hunger, but there are problems in its implementation.

Social Security Programmes

National Social Assistance Programme (NSAP) initiated in 1995 had three schemes: National Old Age Pension Scheme (NOAPS), National Widow Pension Scheme and National Disability Pension Scheme.

Urban Poverty Alleviation Programme

Urban Basic Services for the Poor (UBSP) was launched in 1991 and integrated it with other urban poverty alleviation programme. These programmes are Nehru Rozgar Yojana (NRY) and Environmental Improvement of Urban Slums (EIUS) by providing clean water supply, electricity and drainage system and low cost latrines, Swarna Jayanti Shahari Rozgar Yojana (SJSRY). It was also a part of Urban Poverty Alleviation programme having the components: Urban Self-Employment Programme (USEP), Urban Women Self-help Programme (UWSP) Urban Wage Employment Programme (UWEP), Urban Community Development Network (UCDN) and Skill Training for Employment Promotion amongst Urban Poor.

PROBLEM OF HOUSING

Population explosion in India has led to housing problem, which has further been compounded by migration of people from across the border. The pressure of urban population and lack of housing is very much evident from growing slums in cities. The general view of policymakers was that India is basically an agricultural and rural economy and urbanization will lead to the drain of resources from the countryside to feed the cities. But the rate of migration of people from rural to urban is so high that it will aggravate the housing problem.

Steps were initiated to cope with challenge and a Ministry of Works and Housing was constituted along with the National Building Organization and Town and Country Planning Organization. An Industrial Housing Scheme was also initiated under which the centre extended subsidy up to 50 per cent towards the cost of land and construction.

The Industrial Housing Scheme was widened to cover all workers and three other schemes – Rural Housing, Slum Clearance and Sweepers Housing – were introduced. Town and Country Planning Legislations were enacted in many states and necessary organizations were also set-up for preparation of Master Plans for large towns. A scheme was introduced in 1959 to provide loans to states for a period of 10 years for the acquisition and development of land in order to make available building sites in sufficient numbers.

The Fourth Five-Year Plan (1969–1974)

It emphasized on prevention of further growth of population and decongestion of urban population. To fund the housing and urban development programmes Housing and Urban Development Corporation (HUDCPO) was established. A scheme Environmental Improvement of Urban Slums (EIUS) was undertaken by the centre in 1971–1972 to provide services like water supply, sewerage, drainage and street pavements in 11 cities.

A task force was set up for development of small and medium towns and the Urban Land (Ceiling and Regulation) Act was implemented to prevent concentration of land holdings in urban areas and to make available urban land for construction of houses for the middle and low-income groups. The Integrated Development of Small and Medium Towns (IDSMT) was launched under Sixth Five-Year Plan (1980–1985) for towns with population below 1 lakh to provide shelter for the poor along with various other amenities like roads, bridges, bus stands, markets and shopping complex.

The Seventh Five-Year Plan (1985–1990) laid down stress on mobilization of resources for housing and also involved the private sector. For housing finance National Housing Bank was set-up and for commercial production of innovative building materials, Building Material Technology Promotion Council (BMTPC) was set-up.

Global Shelter Strategy (GSS) and National Housing Policy (NHP) was announced in 1988 with the goal to provide shelter to houseless, improve the housing conditions and provide a minimum level of basic services and amenities to all.

There is still a widening gap between demand and supply of infrastructural services hitting the poor. Growth of urban population is aggravating the housing shortage, resulting in proliferation of slums. The Government of India has announced Housing for all by 2022 and initiated a scheme after the name of Sardar Vallabhai Patel. The scheme will concentrate on providing housing to weaker sections and low-income group (LIG) citizens and tax incentives will be given to those who are unable to buy their own houses.

Indira Awaz Yojna (IAY)

It was launched in June 1985 as a subscheme of National Rural Employment Programme (RLEGP) by earmarking a part of the fund for construction of houses for SCs and STs and freed bonded labourers. IAY provides assistance to rural BPL families for constructing houses using their own design and technology. It is the Gram Sabha which recommends the names of the IAY beneficiaries.

ILLITERACY

Illiteracy in India is the root cause of many problems like poverty, unemployment, population explosion, child marriage, child labour and many others. There is a wide gap of prevalence of illiteracy between the urban and rural population of India. Agriculture, being the main occupation of people in villages, can be the cause of illiteracy, whereas people in urban India belong to working class and so are more educated. Lack of proper educational facilities in the rural areas is an additional cause of poor literacy in rural India. Another worrisome fact is that illiteracy rate is much higher in females as compared to males. Literacy rate among Indian males is approximately 82 per cent as compared to 65 per cent among females, so there is wide disparity. There is so much of disparity in literacy. The social system in India is such that females are considered to be doing household chores and men are considered to be the earning for the family. So education for the boys is given importance while the female population, especially in the deep interiors of the country, is kept away from schools.

India has the largest illiterate population of the world, so eradication of illiteracy has been one of the major national concerns of the Government of India. Though the literacy rate has come up to 75 per cent from 125 in 1947, still our literacy rate is much lower as compared to other countries like China having literacy rate of more than 95 per cent. The Government of India has taken significant steps for the eradication of illiteracy among adults. Some of the important programmes discussed hereunder.

Social Education Programme: This programme got initiated during First Five-Year Plan (1951–1956) in which literacy, general education, leadership training and social consciousness was given importance.

Farmer's Functional Literacy Project (FFLP): This project was implemented started in 1967–1968 for farmers' training and functional literacy. Apart from adult education for the farmers the project aimed at sowing of high-yielding varieties of seeds in 144 districts.

Nonformal Education (NFE): The scheme was launched in the beginning of Fifth Five-Year Plan for the age group of 15–25 years for different skill development.

Functional Literacy for Adult Women (FLAW): It was started in Integrated Child Development Scheme (ICDS) project areas in 1975–1976 on an experimental basis. The objective was to give functional skills training to adult women along with literacy to gain better awareness of health, hygiene, child-rearing practices.

National Adult Education Programme (NAEP): With the aim of eradication of illiteracy in India this programme was launched on 2 October 1978, at the macrolevel. The target population was 15–35 years of age and aim was educating 100 million illiterate adults within a time frame of five years.

Rural Functional Literacy Project (RFLP): This programme was launched with the aim of providing education to the poor and also to teach them functional skills. The target was all illiterate persons in the 15–35 age group who are living in the rural areas. The Department of Education, Union Ministry of HRD, set the literacy centres as per the need of the various areas.

Mass Programme of Functional Literacy (MPFL): This programme was initiated in 1986 involving volunteers of National Service Scheme (NSS) and other students in colleges and universities.

National Policy on Education (1986): It included Universalization of Elementary Education and retention of children up to 14 years of age. This policy was revised in 1992 for facilitating nonformal education in the educationally backward states and National Literacy Mission to impart functional literacy to adults in the age group of 15–35 years.

National Literacy Mission (NLM): It was launched on 5 May 1988 as a Technology Mission to impart functional literacy to illiterates in the country. The target age group was 15–35 years being the productive and reproductive period of life. The campaigns were launched for literacy, family welfare, immunization, mother and child health care, conservation of environment, communal harmony and national integration clubbed together. The mission also in NFE programmes and basically to cater to the school dropout children. The major objective of these programmes is to promote literacy among women, scheduled castes and tribes and backward classes.

National Literacy Mission carried out Total Literacy Campaigns (TLC), followed by Post-Literacy Programme (PLP) and then moving on to Continuing Education (CE), which provides a life-long learning and creating a learning society.

Constitution (Eighty Sixth Amendment) Act, 2002: This amendment has inserted a new Article 21-A in the Constitution. According to this Act, all children of the age of 6 to 14 years have the right to free and compulsory education. This article became active as Right of Children to Free and Compulsory Education Act, 2009 (Act No. 35 of 2009) was made operative by the central government.

FOOD SUPPLIES

Public distribution of food grains was retained as a social policy and in fact it was an important component of the policy of growth with justice. Initially it was an urban-based system and was extended to all such rural areas also, which suffered from food shortages. The system started losing its relevance due to abundant food grains availability. This situation even resulted in government abandoning procurement of food grains and losing all controls on the private trading in food grains. The government was forced to restart the procurement of cereals, put control on trading of food grains and re-examine the need for public distribution system (PDS). Consequently, other essential commodities like sugar, cooking coal and kerosene oil were added to the commodity basket of PDS. There was also a rapid increase in the number of ration shops and the quantity of food grains distributed through PDS also increased progressively.

The creation of Food Corporation of India and Agricultural Prices Commission in 1965 further strengthened the PDS. The government started announcing a minimum support price (MSP) for wheat and paddy for procurement. The stocks were utilized for maintaining distribution through the PDS and some quantity of food grains are also kept in stores to maintain buffer stocks, in case of stocks happened to be inadequate for distribution through PDS.

The PDS is supposed to provide rice and wheat and four essential commodities, sugar, edible oil, soft coke and kerosene oil, to the beneficiaries. However, state governments managing the system are exhorted to add other essential commodities like pulses, salt, candles, matchboxes and ordinary clothes. Supply of additional items through PDS is especially relevant in interior areas. Most of the state governments have set up Civil Supplies or Essential Commodities Corporations to buy food grains and additional items directly from the manufacturers but distribution is done through the PDS only.

PDS in India is the largest distribution network of its kind in the world. The aim of the PDS is to make the food grains available to pubic at affordable price. It has been very useful for the management of food economy in the country. This system is run by the central and state governments with the help of Food Corporation of India. To improve access of food grains to people living below poverty line and people in hilly and inaccessible areas, PDS was revamped in 1992. The TPDS was launched in 1997 to focus on poor families. The responsibility for the identification of poor was with state governments to ensure the delivery of food grains to the deserving poor people. Antodaya Anna Yojana was launched for the landless agricultural labourers, marginal farmers and rural artisans such as potters and tanners, slum dwellers and daily wagers. such as porters, rickshaw pullers, cobblers, destitute and households headed by widows or terminally ill persons, disabled persons and all primitive tribal households.

The owners of ration shops are licensed under the PDS (Control) Order, 2001, and they have certain responsibilities under the scheme to ensure sale of commodities as per the entitlement of ration card holders at the retail issue prices fixed by state governments. They are also required to maintain records, display information such as the list of BPL and Antyodaya Anna Yojna

(AAY) beneficiaries, entitlements of essential commodities, timings of shops, opening and closing stocks and the balance stock at the end of the month. The food subsidy is the difference between the costs incurred by the centre on MSP (including additional costs) and the central issue price. The MSP is the price at which the centre buys food grains from farmers and it is usually higher than the market price and is intended to provide incentives for the production. The MSPs for various agricultural commodities are fixed by the central government based on rates recommended by the Commission for Agricultural Costs and Prices (CACP). There are several issues to be considered for the implementation of TPDS, as identification of eligible households, trends in procurement of food grains, storage space for food grains, food subsidy and pilferage of food grains. Studies have shown that TPDS are prone to large number of errors in the identification of beneficiaries. It has been found that many ineligible people are taking undue benefits of the scheme, whereas entitled beneficiaries are not getting food grains. An expert group was set-up in 2009 to advise the Ministry of Rural Development on the methodology for conducting the BPL census.

PROSTITUTION

A prostitute is a person 'who allows her body to be used for lewd purposes in return for payment'. A prostitute provides sexual services for money. It is a problem not only in India but exists throughout the world.

But India is home to Asia's largest red-light area, the infamous Kamathipura in Mumbai, which originated as a massive brothel for British occupiers. National Human Rights Commission of the Government of India conducted a survey and the report reveals that after initiation as devadasis, women migrate either to nearby towns or other far-off cities to practise prostitution though the tradition of dedicating devadasis has been declared illegal by the Government of Karnataka in 1982 and by the Government of Andhra Pradesh in 1988. But this practice is still prevails in north Karnataka, Andhra Pradesh and Maharashtra. Karnataka is known to be 'devadasi belt'. Different routes of trafficking exist at various levels. Most of the women in prostitution are either lured in to it or they have been deserted by their husbands.

Causes of Prostitution

Ill treatment by parents, bad company, family profession, social customs, inability to arrange marriage, lack of sex education, victim of incest and rape, early marriage and desertion, poverty and economic distress are some of the causes of prostitution. But these also some of the psychological causes like desire for physical pleasure, greed and dejection.

The laws related to prostitution in India are Suppression of Immoral Traffic in Women and Girl Act (SITA) and Prevention of Immoral Traffic Act.

Immoral Traffic (Prevention) Act (ITPA)

It is the main statute dealing with sex workers in India. This Act does not criminalize prostitutes but mostly punishes those who facilitate prostitution like brothel operators, those living off earnings and procuring, even where sex work is not coerced.

Any person who keeps or manages, or acts or assists in the management of, a brothel is liable to be punished with rigorous imprisonment for a term of one to three years along with a fine which may extend to Rs 2000. In the event of a second or subsequent conviction, a minimum term of rigorous imprisonment will be enhanced to two years and maximum to five years.

Prostitution is not a social problem alone. It also leads to many health problems like dreaded sexually transmitted diseases like human immunodeficiency virus (HIV), cancer of cervix and behavioral disorders. It is not easy to control the problem of acquired immunodeficiency syndrome (AIDS), the reason being most of the people indulge themselves in unprotected sex with prostitutes. AIDS in India was initially identified amongst sex workers and their clients, and later among the other sections of society. Due to AIDS awareness initiatives, the sex workers are themselves taking steps to control the problem and in some brothels like Sonagachi brothel in Kolkata sex workers are insisting on use of condoms to avoid infection. Social workers and NGOs are trying to acquaint the sex workers with the ill-effects of AIDS and they are insisting on protected sex.

REVIEW QUESTIONS

1. Write short notes on the following:
   a. Public Distribution System
   b. Immoral Traffic Prevention Act
   c. National Literacy Mission
2. Explain in detail about various programmes for eradication of poverty in India.

CHAPTER

47

Vulnerable Groups

LEARNING OBJECTIVES

After reading this chapter the learner should be able to

- Get familiar with various vulnerable groups.
- Know why certain groups are considered to be vulnerable.

Certain groups are disadvantaged as compared to others mainly on account of their lack of access to medical care services and other necessities for a healthy life such as safe and potable drinking water, nutrition, housing, and sanitation. Some groups also face discriminatory treatment and need special attention to avoid potential exploitation. These marginalized sections of population constitute the vulnerable groups.

The vulnerable groups that face discrimination include women, scheduled castes (SC), Scheduled Tribes (ST), children, aged, disabled, poor migrants and in recent times people living with HIV/AIDS and sexual minorities. Some of these vulnerable groups may face multiple barriers due to more than one identity for instance a disabled woman faces double discrimination. She is vulnerable being a woman and also as a disabled person.

Women: They are considered to be vulnerable as they are subjected to discrimination right from their birth (even before birth as evident from increasing incidence of female foeticide) and as they grow up they suffer neglect in terms of nutrition, education and health care and also face sexual abuse. Women face domestic violence, sexual harassment, marital rape and honour killing and it has an impact on their health. The low status of women in society makes them vulnerable but SC and ST women are even more vulnerable.

Aged persons: One of the main concerns of growing population in India is increasing number of elderly people. Elderly people not only suffer from various health problems but they are economically dependent also. As per the survey, 50 per cent of these elderly people suffer from one or the other chronic disease. The common chronic diseases among them are cancer, diabetes, hypertension, heart diseases, indigestion, piles, urinary problems, arthritis and osteoporosis, in addition to other old age problems like dementia, visual impairment, and loss of hearing, senility and neurosis. It has also been found that most of the elderly persons did not receive any medication before death. Among elderly disabled, widows and poor are most disadvantaged. Urbanization in India has caused disintegration of joint families which has further added to the problems of elderly people. They are left alone as their children moved to distant places for employment. Crime against these elderly people living alone is on the rise.

Children: Children face vulnerability because of poverty, sex discrimination and it manifests in many forms like child abuse, child trafficking, child labour and commercial sexual exploitation. High mortality and morbidity are caused due to diarrhoeal diseases, measles, respiratory tract infections and tetanus. All these are preventable causes. Poverty and lack of awareness have direct impact on nutrition intake, access to health care, environment and education of children. Street children and children of sex workers are more vulnerable. Many children are living with HIV/AIDS. Common causes are mother to child transmission, blood transfusion, sexual abuse and syringes used for drug injecting. Rehabilitation opportunities for rescued children are scarce despite the Child Protection Act.

Disabled: Persons with disability face lot of discrimination in terms of education and employment opportunities. People with disabilities are a vulnerable population because, for the most part, they are economically disadvantaged. Many of them do not work and are not provided any social security. Furthermore, some disabled people who work get very meagre amount as salary. Thus, most of them are vulnerable being disabled but poverty further accentuates their vulnerability. Number of disabled persons in India is rising with the increasing population. As per surveys, 2–3 per cent of the total population in India are disabled people. One-third of them are born with disabilities, whereas rest of them have acquired disabilities caused by accidents or diseases. Mental sickness is also another form of disability. Dementia and depression are the prominent types of mental sicknesses. Mentally sick people are subjected to human rights violation. Most of the mental hospital, asylums and special homes lack basic facilities like proper food, clothes, hygiene and medicines. Furthermore, women with mental sicknesses face sexual exploitation and physical violence. Mental retardation is also a form of disability and severe form of mental retardation lead to dependence making them vulnerable to all sorts of social atrocities.

Poor migrants: Migrants within and across the country are vulnerable especially unskilled migrants. They are poor and devoid of adequate nutrition, proper housing, sanitation and medical care. Most affected among them are internally displaced people (IDPs.) Because of religious or ethnic conflicts, construction of projects or dams, wars or natural disasters they get displaced. These IDPs suffer lot of mental sicknesses such as depression and nervous breakdown apart from hypertension, musculoskeletal stress, cardiovascular diseases and skin infections. Female and children among them are even more vulnerable as they are associated migrants. In most of the cases men decide to migrate and women and children are associated migrants. They are economically deprived, lack social support and live under absolute adverse conditions.

HIV/AIDS patients: HIV positive persons are vulnerable to multiple infections. There is so much social stigma associated with the disease. Millions of people across the world are living with HIV positive infection in resource-poor communities which have no access to antiretroviral drugs. Even where the drugs are available, they do not have access to proper medical care for preventing and treating opportunistic infections. As per medical experts, people with acute opportunistic infections should be, with a few exceptions, given HIV treatment right away, especially if the infection is difficult to treat. However, in certain conditions, when there are concerns about drug interactions or possibility of toxicities due to overlapping drug actions, it may be better to delay the beginning of HIV treatment.

Scheduled castes: They were economically weak, politically powerless and dominated by upper caste people. They have been most neglected; marginalized and exploited people.

A major proportion of the lower castes and Dalits are still dependent on others for their livelihood. SCs are in a state of oppression, social disability, helplessness and poverty. They were earlier referred as *untouchables* mainly due to their occupation as cobbler, scavenger or sweeper. Discrimination against them is in the form of physical, psychological, emotional and cultural abuse. Though they constitute one-sixth of the total population of the country, they face discrimination in the form of denial to get access to land, housing, education and employment. The negative attitude of health personals also affects their utilization of health care facilities by them.

Scheduled tribes: They are also socially disadvantaged like SC persons. STs, who were the proud masters of their traditional territory, are being progressively dislocated from their home lands reduced to landless refugees. The process has been going on for centuries but it gained momentum after independence. The policy of economic liberalization has made things worse over the last two decades and large chunks of land have been acquired for various projects. Some government projects in the tribal areas for creating dams and mines are causing submerging of tribal lands, uprooting their settlements. Thus, a large number of STs are forced into agricultural wage labour. Traditional tribal rights in forests which they have been enjoying through their symbiotic relationship with forests are being exploited and making STs dependent on others for their basic requirements and survival. Tribals are specialized in collection of minor forest produce (MFP) which is the main or a substantial source of livelihood for a large percentage of STs. They are being exploited in trading of MFP, both by private traders as well as by corporations set-up by governments.

Incidentally, almost all the mineral resources and other raw materials needed by the industry are located in the tribal areas and forests. The tribals are now opposing the acquisition of their lands, which meant loss of livelihood, displacement from ancestral lands and total disruption of their community-based cooperative living. Instead, they are forced to lead an undignified life by working as labourers for rich outsiders and migrate to distant places into outside society where they are vulnerable to all types of exploitation. The officials dealing with land records connive with the rich and powerful to deprive them of the only mean of survival. The poor tribals often fall prey to moneylenders who also exploit them in the garb of extending help in crisis only to put them in bigger trouble later. The government assistance and efforts for rehabilitation of those uprooted from their homelands has been inadequate.

Sexual minorities: Eunuchs *(hijras)* are *neither male nor female*, these transsexual transvestites are usually castrated and are attributed with certain ritual powers of blessing. Eunuchs might have an accepted place in Indian society, but at the bottom of the social pyramid—making them a highly deprived social minority. Transsexuality as a phenomenon has gained very little visibility or knowledge in our society which contains one of the most visible transgender cultures in the world of the *eunuch* (hijras). Eunuchs in India have virtually no safe place, not even in their families, where they should be protected from prejudice and abuse. Many across the globe do not know whether eunuchs are born the way they are or do they become so later in life. It is believed that many are castrated at some point of time in life and transformed into the identity of an eunuch.

There are over 1 million of such people in India. They live in unhygienic conditions, poverty and internal disharmony. While at one hand they are unaccepted in a society of *normal* beings, they also live in dissonance among themselves only with the hope to survive in a slightly better condition than the other sleeping next to them on the other. The kind of life led by this group, especially in India, is marred with more than just one problem. They live as outcasts in society. Transgender people are very often affected by HIV. Prevalence of HIV among this group ranging from 8 to 68 per cent, and yet they remain severely overlooked in the HIV and AIDS programmes worldwide.

REVIEW QUESTIONS

1. Why are SCs and STs are vulnerable?
2. Write short notes on the following vulnerable groups:
   a. Migrant labour
   b. Children
   c. Sexual minorities

CHAPTER

48

Problems of Women, Children and the Elderly

LEARNING OBJECTIVES

After reading this chapter the learner should be able to

- Gain knowledge about the problems of women, children and old people in India.
- Understand the consequences of the social problems.

The Indian society has come a long way since Independence. It has evolved and undergone reforms but there are still many sociocultural issues, pertaining to the vulnerable sections like women, children and the aged people it has to address. The security of women, children, the elderly people and other vulnerable sections is currently a major concern in the contemporary Indian society.

The Constitution of India guarantees equal rights to all the citizens but still these vulnerable sections are at the receiving end. They are denied their basic rights and women, in particular, face a host of problems and are subjected to discrimination right from the prenatal stage in the form of female foeticide. The aged people are suffering due to lack of care and facing all the problems like western countries owing to breaking down of the joint family system. Children are being denied their right to education and made to work to supplement income of the family.

PROBLEMS OF WOMEN

In India, women are discriminated in various fields like health, education, jobs and other fields and they also live with evil practises like dowry. In fact, the birth of a female child is still considered as a curse in many communities and it has led to emergence of detestable crime of female foeticide. The girls are seen as a liability as they have to leave their parents' home after marriage, while male offsprings are considered by parents as assets to safeguard their old age.

The data of 2011 Census brings out how women are losing out due to undesirable and discriminatory social customs and practices. Out of the total population of 1,210,569,573, males account for 623,121,843 and females just 587,447,730. The female sex ratio comes to

940 per 1000 males, which is slightly better than 933 recorded during 2001 Census, but still far from ideal ratio. This is the highest sex ratio recorded since 1971 Census and slightly lower than 1961.

However, the situation is alarming as the child sex ratio (CSR) has declined from 927 in 2001 to 914 in 2011 and it is the lowest CSR at the all India level since Independence. Many female babies are aborted, abandoned, deliberately neglected and underfed simply because they are girls.

GENDER DISCRIMINATION

Our Constitution guarantees equal rights to both men and women in every field and several laws pertaining to marriage, inheritance of property, education and other spheres to safeguard and promote the interests of females. However, in spite of these provisions, we find a lot of discrimination against women. Women play an important role as a mother and the same makes it unique. However, they have been subjected to discrimination in the Indian society and the impact is now manifesting in the declining female sex ratio in the country. Women are considered major contributors to family and society and they once enjoyed equal status to men. The Ardhanareeshwar, an incarnation of the Lord Shiva, is half male and half female symbolizing equality. Unfortunately, this equality does not translate into reality in practice.

However, a lot of women have gone down and problems like dowry deaths and exploitations of various kinds, incidences of infanticide and early marriage have become a cause of concern. Discrimination in education and emphasis on domestic activities, rather than making career has made women's lives full of problems. They are discriminated from early childhood and remain dependent on parents and husbands throughout their lives. They are assigned diverse responsibilities but treated as relatively weaker and less competent compared to men.

The girl child is usually burdened with responsibilities that are beyond her capacity. This hampers the process of development and growth of the girl child. On maturing as an adult, she is often found to be physically weak and mentally constrained.

Consequently, they are not able to realize their potentials and their contributions are often limited to the family. In many communities, women and girls get less food or poor-quality food compared to men and boys. Adult women have their development problems due to lack of protein input during their childhood.

LOW LITERACY

In a majority of the countries, rates of women literacy are significantly lower than that of men. In 66 countries, the difference between the male and the female literacy rates is higher than 10 percentage points and in 40 countries, it is higher than 20 percentage points in the 6–11 age groups, which corresponds to primary level education.

In India, the overall literacy rate has gone up from 64.83% in 2001 to 74.04% in 2011, a significant increase of 9.21 percentage points. The literacy rate for males is 82.14% and for females is 65.46%. The increase in literacy rate of 11.79 in females is higher than 6.88% in males. It is encouraging to note that out of total 217,700,941 literates added during the decade, females (110,069,001) outnumbered males (107,631,940).

The gap of 21.59 percentage points recorded between male and female literacy rates in 2001 has reduced to 16.68 percentage points in 2011 but it was higher than the target of 10 percentage points set by the Planning Commission by the year 2011–2012. Another remarkable feature was that there was a decline of 31,196,847 among illiterates, and females (17,122,197) contributed more to the decline compared to males (14,074,650).

Traditionally, the Indian society places greater value on sons but instances of daughters excelling in academics are increasing. Still daughters are viewed as an economic burden, particularly in the interior areas.

The government has introduced many schemes to promote education of girls. Reservation of jobs for women and even 6 months maternity leave is provided to them besides many other schemes.

DOWRY SYSTEM

The practice of dowry is one of the worst social practises and it has turned into a major problem with the increasing number of dowry-related deaths of women. The practice was barred with the passing of the Dowry Prohibition Act in 1961 under which giving and accepting dowry were made punishable offences. However, deeply embedded in the culture, the practise continues unabated. The law is being observed more in breach and the incidence of dowry deaths and even the acts of domestic violence against women are on the increase. However, of late some girls stand firm to assert their rights against dowry but effective social, economic, political and administrative measures are needed to end this archaic practice in order to free Indian society from this disease.

ELDERLY PROBLEMS

The world population is ageing. Globally, the percentage of aged has risen from 8 in 1950 to 10 in 2000 and as per projections, it will increase to 21 in 2050. The elderly persons in the country accounted for 5.8% (25.5 million) in 1961, 6.7% (56.6 million) in 1991, 8.1% (96 million) in 2011 and estimated to reach 137 million in 2021. The number of elderly persons (60 years and above) in the country is expected to be tripled in the next few decades. Providing social, economic and psychological support to the ever-increasing number of elderly persons is a huge challenge for the country. Due to the breakdown of the joint family system and emergence of nuclear families as the trend, particularly in the urban areas, the aged persons are facing a lot of neglect. More so, the community support system is not very strong in the country. In Indian culture, highest respect is given to the elders and there is an urgent need to inculcate the cultural values in the young generations. The members of the next generation have to be made aware that when they were young, they were looked after well and now it was their turn to pay back by ensuring that the elderly lived with dignity and self-respect.

PROBLEM OF CHILDREN

Children are the future and no country can progress and prosper without taking good care of them.

A child is the future citizen of the country and it is incumbent on the state and the society to provide a conducive environment for their proper physical, emotional and intellectual development. Only physically fit and mentally and emotionally strong persons can contribute to the development and build a strong country. The country has a large population of children and they have to provide due opportunities for education and overall development of their personality.

A large number of children are kept away from schools because of poverty, while others are withdrawn from schools even before completing their elementary education. Many are forced to work in factories, brick-kilns, restaurants, hotels, shops or take up other menial jobs at a tender age. These children do not have proper physical, mental and emotional growth and harbour hatred and fail to become worthy citizens.

In India, out of the 200 million children in 6–14 years age group, about 11.3 million are labourers. The estimate by some NGOs put the number at 60 million, of which about 2 lakhs work as domestic help and almost an equal number as bonded labourers. These children are highly vulnerable to physical and mental exploitation, and they are often starved, beaten and even sexually abused. The Right to Education Act provides for compulsory education to all children in the age of 6–14 years. Its implementation in letter and spirit will go a long way in improving lots of children.

JUVENILE DELINQUENCY

A crime is termed *juvenile delinquency* when committed by a young person under a certain age. The age of juvenile delinquent is not uniform all over the world. In India, the age for girls is 16 years and 18 years for boys. There are certain behaviours that are not considered criminal in nature if committed by adults but they will be taken note as a crime if committed by youth. For example, a person below the age of 16 years, who is uncontrollable by his parents or guardians by reasons such as disobedient, habitually play truant and trouble maker at school.

Ever since society was organized and codes of conduct were formulated, there have always been individuals including juveniles and adults who have violated the codes. The increase in such behaviour has reached alarming proportions, including unlawful activities that have affected the smooth functioning of the society. The loss of life, property and the pain inflicted is reaching quite serious dimensions.

Family is the first crucial group in the life of a child. Family nurtures a child's social and personal growth. The family environment plays a vital role in shaping the personality of the child. The child is in exclusive contact with the family during the period of dependency and if neglected by the family, the child imbibes negative traits like distrust, hostility or hatred for people. Many times, in broken homes that may have been caused by death, desertion or separation of parents, the negative impact is felt by the children, who tend to find it difficult to conform to social rules. Many studies have pointed to the high incidence of structural breaks in the family backgrounds of delinquent youth. In disharmonious families, children are often pushed from home because of disturbances. They seek outside contacts for resolving feelings of insecurity and frustration. Socialization is the process through which the child becomes aware of the basic values of his society and acquires the attitudes characteristic of it. Each family training influences strongly the inculcation of these values. The child must learn which action is permitted or prohibited.

Poverty in the family has been another popular explanation for delinquency but research has shown that most of those who commit the offence were not driven by hunger rather by the envy and ambition that stimulate petty crimes in the same way that greed urges on the big-time criminals. Conditions of affluence are no sure guarantee against the law violations by youth.

Poverty and unfavourable circumstances also affect the development of children whose options get severely limited. In large families, they have to make do with little living space and inadequate facilities. They are driven to seek their recreations on the streets and other places outside their homes. When there is little money within the family to provide for the minimum basic necessities of food, clothing, education, etc., it imposes extraordinary strains on the family. The parents find themselves quite helpless in such situations and are in no position to fulfil needs of their children.

Slum neighbourhoods also sometimes encourage delinquent behaviour, as pressure to make a decent living is much higher for the people residing there. They also want the same good things that they see others enjoying but at times, it is difficult to get them honestly due to lack of education or opportunity. Many times, crime becomes an accepted way of life, an alternative to the honest work. They are also exposed to the undesirable elements. Crime and delinquency thus become attractive.

There is growing concern these days that the mass media have also become a source of unhealthy influence, particularly on children. Sensational reporting by detailing the modus operandi can affect the readers in dangerous ways. They sometimes indicate that there are methods of evading the law or project unnecessary violence that influence impressionable minds.

REVIEW QUESTIONS

1. What are the causes of juvenile delinquency?
2. Write short notes on the following:
   a. Illiteracy
   b. Dowry system
   c. Gender discrimination

CHAPTER

49

Rights of Women and Children

LEARNING OBJECTIVES

After reading this chapter the learner should be able to

- Have knowledge about various laws to protect the rights of women and children.
- Know how the exploitation of children and women can be prevented.

Children are the future of the country as they constitute a major portion of the Indian population. So the development of the human resource of the nation is only possible by the proper development of children. Thus, taking care of children is even more important than material resources. Children are most vulnerable to exploitation and abuse. Though significant progress has been made in many fields to assure children their basic rights, a lot remains to be done yet. Our nation is committed and determined to give the highest priority to the basic needs of all the children and also to protect their rights. A lot of efforts need to be taken for the health, nutrition and education of children. In addition to it, girls seem to be facing debilitating discrimination at all stages even before their birth. Therefore, specific efforts to improve the life and opportunities of the girl child are of utmost importance. There are several constitutional provisions for children to ensure opportunities and facilities for their development in a healthy manner and among the conditions of freedom and dignity, and that the childhood is protected against exploitation.

JUVENILE JUSTICE ACT, 2000

The Juvenile Justice Board, Child Welfare Committee and state government must abide by the following principles.

Principle of presumption of innocence: Throughout the world, the child is considered to be innocent and the age of criminal responsibility cannot be fixed too low an age level keeping in mind the mental and intellectual maturity.

Principle of dignity and worth: The dignity and worth of the child has to be protected throughout the proceedings.

Principle of right to be heard: Let the child express himself freely in the matters regarding his life and all the decisions related to his welfare.

Principle of best interest: This is to enable a child to survive and reach his full potential by proper physical, emotional, intellectual, social and moral development of a juvenile in conflict with law.

Principle of family responsibility: The basic responsibility of the care and upbringing of the child should be with biological parents. But it can be given to foster parents or adoptive parents in exceptional cases.

Principle of safety: Safety of the child is of utmost importance. So the child should not be subjected to any harm, abuse, neglect, exploitation, or maltreatment while in contact with care and protection system.

Positive measures: Positive measures regarding health, education, livelihood, creativity or games should be taken for the juvenile in conflict with the law.

Principle of nonstigmatizing semantics, decisions and actions: No accusatory words like arrest, remand, accused, charge sheet, trial, warrant, summons, conviction, inmate, delinquent, neglected or custody should be used in the processes relating to the child in conflict with law.

Principle of nonwaiver of rights: Waiving of the fundamental rights of the child in conflict with the law is not permissible.

Principle of equality and nondiscrimination: No discrimination against the child in conflict with the law on the basis of sex, caste, place of birth, disability, religion, status, ethnicity or behaviour of the child or his parents.

Principle of right to privacy and confidentiality: Privacy and confidentiality has to be maintained throughout the proceedings.

Principle of last resort: Institutionalization should be the last resort for the child in conflict with the law, and that too should be for minimum possible period.

Principle of repatriation and restoration: The juvenile in conflict with law should be sent to his family for restoration of his socioeconomic background and culture until and unless this goes against his welfare.

Principle of fresh start: This is for the new beginning of the child who is in conflict with law. Forgetting the past to start afresh by erasing his or her past records.

Juvenile justice board: Each district should have at least one Juvenile Justice Board constituted by state government. This board is headed by the Judicial Magistrate and two social workers and one of these social workers should be a woman. These members will be appointed by the state government on the recommendation of selection committee. All the members and the Magistrate should possess the knowledge of child psychology, child welfare, child rights apart from knowing national and international standards of Juvenile Justice, and the Magistrate will hold the position of Principal Magistrate of the board. Qualification of the members of the board is minimum postgraduation in social work, health, educational psychology, child development or any social science discipline and should be above the age of 35 years. Any person who has been convicted under any law or has indulged in child abuse or child labour stands disqualified to be the member of the boards. Board acts in accordance with Integrated Child Protection Scheme of the central government.

This board is constituted for a period of 3 years and a member can be eligible for two consecutive terms. But the extension of the tenure of any board member is based on recommendation of District Child Protection Unit depending on performance appraisal of the particular member.

Similarly, any board member can resign any time, giving only 1 month prior notice. A new member replaces him from the panel of names with selection committee. Functions of the Juvenile Justice Board are to settle the cases of juveniles in conflict with law, take notice of the crimes committed by juveniles, to ensure proper infrastructure and facilities to maintain minimum standards of justice and treatment to juveniles, liaisoning with the committee regarding cases requiring care or protection, liaisoning with other district boards for speedy justice, and sending regular information to District State Child Protection Unit about juveniles in conflict with law produced before them.

In case juveniles are involved in nonserious cases, the police or child welfare officer from the nearest police station will inform the parents or the guardian about the nature of offence committed by the child. Whereas, if the child is involved in a serious crime, the police or child protection officer can exercise the power of apprehending the juvenile. But the apprehension will also be in the interest of the juvenile. The child involved in such serious crime shall be treated as child in need of care and protection and will be produced before the Board of Juvenile Justice. Even the FIR will be registered only in case of involvement of child in serious crime such as rape, murder or the crime has been committed jointly with adults.

Some voluntary organizations also get recognition as protection agencies from the state government to assist the police or the juvenile welfare officer in preparing the report regarding social background of the child and circumstances of alleged offence. These voluntary organizations should be capable of providing the services of counselling, probation, case work and safe place for the child.

As far as the determination of the age of the child is concerned, the committee decides it on the basis of matriculation or equivalent certificate, date of birth certificate from the school or birth certificate issued by municipal corporation or panchayat. But in case none of these evidences are traceable, Medical Board is constituted to declare the age of the child. If it is not possible for the Medical Board to decide the correct age of the child, then the committee, if necessary, can give the benefit to the child by considering his or her age within the margin of a year on lower side.

If a child between the age of 7 and 12 years does something wrong, that is not considered as an offence under Juvenile Justice Act.

Exploitation of a child by employer: It is the responsibility of the government to build a protective environment for children that safeguards them from exploitation and abuse. Laws that prohibit child labour need to be rigorously enforced. It is the responsibility of the employer to ensure safety of the child in his organization. Child abuse can be physical, psychological or sexual. To protect children from abuse, the Child Abuse Prevention and Treatment Act, 1974 was enacted by Government of India. There are a number of ways children become victims of commercial sexual exploitation, falling prey to persons who exploit children as clients or intermediaries, traffic them for the sex trade within the country or across the borders and use them for live sex shows or pornography, through its International Programme on the Elimination of Child Labour (IPEC). Extensive technical support and advice is provided by the International Labour Organization (ILO) to prevent children from becoming victims of commercial sexual exploitation as well as for rehabilitation of children who have become the victims of exploitation.

Beating or thrashing parents: Parents beating up children is still common, though the incidences of child torture by parents have gone down significantly with the improvement of educational and professional levels of the parents. When kids in primary schools are beaten up and abused by parents, it is usually the result of marital problems and disintegration of the family. The parents take out their frustration on the defenceless kids.

The Child Marriage Restraint Act, 1929: If either party of the marriage is a child, that is called child marriage. A child means if the bride has not completed the age of 18 and bridegroom has not attained the age of 21 years. As per the Act, the person who performs, conducts or directs child marriage is liable to punishment.

Child Labour Act, 1986: This Act prohibits the employment of the children below the age of 14 years and even after this age children are prohibited to work in certain occupations, which are hazardous for the children such as match industry, diamond industry, precious stone industry, glass industry, brass industry, handmade carpet industry, lock making industry, mark pen industry and bidi industry. As the total ban on employment of these children is likely to lead to destitution and making them vagrant and hard-core criminals. So it is the duty of the government to provide education, food, shelter, health care, safety and means of livelihood to all the children so that they can live with dignity and self-respect.

This Act is meant to prohibit the engagement of children in any work below the age of 14 years. As per the right to education, every child should go to school at least till the age of 14. However, even after the child attains the age of 14, the state should ensure that they should not be employed in fireworks factories. There should be separate premises for packing in the matchbox factories where children above the age of 14 are employed. Employers are not allowed to make children work for more than 6 h a day.

There should be facilities for recreation and socialization in the factory or near the factory. One-day meal should be given to the child even if it is possible with the collaboration of state government. Salary should be paid on monthly basis. There should be some welfare fund created by employer's contribution. These children should also be under the insurance cover.

International Labour Organization (ILO): This organization works for eradication of child labour and to safeguard child from industrial exploitation. The major responsibilities of ILO are as follows:

Prohibition of child labour
Safeguarding child labour at work
Tackling the basic problems of child labour
Safeguarding the children of working parents
Assisting the children to adapt to future work

The Young Persons Harmful Publication Act, 1956: Any harmful publication like book, magazine, pamphlet, leaflet or newspaper portraying the commission of offence, acts of violence, incidence of horrible nature or obscenity would corrupt the mind of a young person.

REHABILITATION AND SOCIAL REINTEGRATION

This is done for the children who are in a children's home or special home and is done by (1) Adoption, (2) Foster care, (3) Sponsorship and (4) After care organization.

Adoption: In case of orphan, abandoned and surrendered child, after a trial of restoration of the child to his biological parents the child is given for adoption keeping in view the various guidelines laid down by state government or central government. Usually, there are one or two agencies in each district as specialized adoption agencies. Only those children are available for adoption who have been declared free for adoption by committee.

Central Adoption Resource Agency (CARA): It was set up in 1990 under the union of Ministry of Social Justice and Empowerment and made an autonomous body under the Society Registration Act in 1999. It has framed detailed guidelines for adoption of child within country and also in abroad.

The Prohibition of Child Marriage Act, 2006: It replaced the Child Marriage Restraint Act (1929) with more stringent provisions of declaring a child marriage void at the option of the contracting party, payment of maintenance to minor girl till her remarriage and custody and maintenance of children born out of child marriage.

Under the Act, a male who has not completed 21 years of age and a female who has not completed 18 years of age will be deemed as *Child*.

Immoral Traffic (Prevention) Act: If the age of the girl is below 14 years (minor), punishment can be of 14 years. If girl is a child, punishment may be life imprisonment.

Right to education: It is the fundamental duty of the parents or guardian to provide opportunities for education to his child or ward between the age of 6 and 14 years. Even the early childhood care and education for children until the age of 6 is the responsibility of the state. Anganwadis are there for preschool children. State needs to ensure full physical, mental and social development. Basic needs of all the children should be fulfilled and adequate services to children should be provided before and after birth and throughout the period of growth as per National Health Policy (1974). It is the right of the child to enjoy a healthy and joyful childhood.

Foster care: It may be used for time being for those infants who are to be given for adoption. During foster care, child may be put in another family where child's own parents may visit him regularly. State government may make rules for scheme of foster care programme for children.

Sponsorship: Sponsorship programme may provide support to children's homes to improve the quality of life of the resident children. It can be individual sponsorship or group sponsorship or community sponsorship.

After care organization: State government must provide guidelines for setting up aftercare organization under the Juvenile Justice (Care and Protection of Children) Act 2000. Children require aftercare organization when they leave juvenile homes or children's home to enable them to live a useful life by earning their livelihood honestly.

The Commission for Protection of Child Rights Act, 2005: The central government constitutes the commission for Protection of Child Rights consisting of a chairperson and six members. A chairperson should be an eminent person who is involved in work for promoting welfare of children. Members of the commission should also be the person of eminence from the field of education, child health, child development, child psychology, or person dealing with laws relating to children or elimination of child labour or Juvenile Justice or a person has been involved in the care of children with disabilities or marginalized children. The appointment of the chairperson or the members is for a period of 3 years. However, a member or a chairperson can't hold the office for more than two terms.

The functions of the commission are examination of the measures taken for the safeguards of children, submitting reports to the central government on annual basis, making inquiry into violation of child rights, periodical review of existing policies and programmes for child rights, finding out the factors inhibiting the child rights and spreading the child rights awareness among people.

The Infant Milk Substitutes, Feeding Bottles and Infant Food Act, 1992 (Regulation of Production, Supply and Distribution): This Act came into existence to promote breastfeeding. As per the Act, there should be no advertisement to promote and mislead people that there is substitution for breast milk. So no infant food, feeding bottles and infant milk substitutes shall be advertised and even no expectant mothers should be contacted to promote these products. These products must have warning labels that these products should be used on the advice of health care workers and breast milk is the best milk for the baby. These products should carry clear instructions for use, all the ingredients it contains, and manufacturing and expiry dates, etc. Apart from that, foods for infants and breast milk substitute products should not carry photos of babies or mothers, images or designs for the marketing promotion, words like maternalised or humanized should not be used.

This Act state that no person shall donate or distribute infant food, feeding bottles and infant milk substitutes or any material regarding the same, except the health system.

WELFARE OF WOMEN

Status of women in India is much lower than their counterparts, though as per the Indian constitution women should enjoy equal status with men. States are empowered to take measures of positive discrimination in the favour of women. There are lot of Acts of parliament to safeguard the rights of women. Even reservation for women in the local bodies of panchayats, municipalities, state legislative assemblies and parliament are also ensured for participation in decision making. India has also been the part of various international conventions and human rights organizations committed to secure equal rights of women. The most important among them is the Convention on Elimination of all Forms of Discrimination Against Women (CEDAW) in 1993. There are various Acts to protect the rights of women in India. The aims of these Acts are to make women get access to education, health and productive resources, particularly those women belonging to weaker sections like Scheduled Castes, Scheduled Tribes, Other backward Classes and minorities specifically from rural areas and in the informal and unorganized sector.

The Protection of Women from Domestic Violence Act, 2005: Domestic violence against women though quite prevalent, is a human right issue. Convention on elimination of all forms of Discrimination Against Women (CEDAW) was held by the United Nations Committee in 1989. It recommended that women should be protected from any type of violence, specifically violence happening within the family. Domestic violence is actual abuse which is physical, sexual, verbal emotional or economic deprivation.

As per the law, any woman, a wife or sister or widow or mother or single woman even if living with abuser is entitled to legal protection. The Bill enables any female in a relationship or wife to lodge a complaint against partner, husband or any relative of the husband. But it does not give right to the female relative of husband or the male partner to lodge a complaint against the wife or female partner.

Protection of Women against Sexual Harassment at Workplace Act, 2007: No woman employee at a work place shall be subjected to sexual harassment as this amounts to the gender discrimination and is violation of fundamental right. The cause of sexual harassment is male dominance over women and to make them feel that they are inferior to men. Every working woman is prone to sexual harassment irrespective of her age and profession. Every human being has right to live with dignity. Sexual harassment include any unwelcome sexually determined behaviour, physical contact or making sexual advances, sexually coloured remarks, showing pornography, request for sexual favours, any conduct of sexual nature whether verbal, textual, physical, graphic or electronic.

The Hindu Widows' Remarriage Act, 1856: Basically, this Act came into existence to remove all the obstacles to the marriage of Hindu widows. Hindu widows were subject to extreme hardships for many years like living a miserable life and were outcaste. The second marriage of widow was considered invalid and the offspring of such widow from second marriage were held to be illegitimate. There was practice of sati, a social practice, which required a widow to immolate herself on the funeral pyre of her husband which was ultimately banned in 1826 due a joint effort by social and religious reformers.

The Hindu women's right to property: The Hindu women's Right to property in 1937 was amended to Women and Hindu Succession Act 2005, bringing a drastic change in the Act. A daughter has a right of succession in the joint Hindu family property, no matter whether she is married or unmarried. The share of property she gets is the same as to a son. A Hindu widow also in lieu of her maintenance is given full ownership in the estate of her husband. But in certain tribal areas where polyandry is still in practice, the women are denied the right to property, also in case of unmarried women.

The Medical Termination of Pregnancy Act, 1971 (MTP Act): Termination of pregnancy can be carried out by Registered Medical Practitioner in accordance with the provision of this Act. As per MTP Act, pregnancy can be terminated by a Registered Medical Practitioner if the pregnancy does not exceed 12 weeks of duration.

If the pregnancy period exceeds 12 weeks but does not exceed 20 weeks, the opinion of not less than two Registered Medical Practitioners is as follows:

1. Continuation of pregnancy will pose a risk to pregnant woman (physical or mental)
2. If pregnancy is continued and the baby to be born is likely to suffer from physical or mental abnormalities or will be seriously handicapped
3. If the pregnancy was caused by rape and continuation of pregnancy will affect the mental health of the woman
4. If pregnancy has happened because of failure of family planning method
5. No pregnancy will be terminated without the consent of pregnant woman except mentally ill woman.

The place for conducting MTP should be approved by government or a district-level committee.

The Preconception and Prenatal Diagnostic Techniques (Prohibition of Sex Selection) Act, 1994: This Act is basically to prohibit prenatal diagnostic techniques for determination of sex of the foetus to stop female foeticide. The Act came into existence to prohibit the misuse of prenatal determination of sex of foetus, prohibit advertisement of prenatal diagnostic techniques for sex detection, regulate the use of prenatal diagnostic techniques for the purpose of detecting genetic abnormalities, permitting the use of prenatal diagnostic techniques for certain conditions by registered institutions only, punishing the persons violating the provisions of the proposed legislation.

National Commission for Women Act, 1990: The unequal status of women in all the spheres of life led to the introduction of National Commission for Women Bill in Lok Sabha in 1990. The commission is constituted by central government and consists of chairperson and five members nominated by central government. Chairperson should be committed to the cause of women and members nominated should be persons of ability, integrity, having experience in law, management of an industry committed to increasing the employment potential of women, economic development, health education or social welfare. But at least one member should be Scheduled Caste and one member should be Scheduled Tribe, respectively. One Member Secretary nominated by central government should be from the field of management and an officer who has been the member of civil service of the union. The various functions of this commission are as follows:

- To investigate all the matters relating to legal safeguards for women.
- Presenting the reports to central government annually regarding working of the safeguards.
- To review the existing laws and suggests amendments if necessary.
- Looking into complaints involving deprivation of rights of women to provide them legal support.

- To monitor all the implementation of all the laws meant to protect the rights of women to achieve equality in each sphere of life so that they can equally participate in the development of the nation.

The Maternity Benefit Act, 1961: As per this Act, every woman is entitled to the payment of maternity benefits at least for 12 weeks. Till 6 weeks after delivery, miscarriage or medical termination of pregnancy, a woman would not work in any establishment. Similarly, pregnant women cannot be hired for arduous work or any work requiring long hours of standing even if request is made by the woman herself before 6 weeks of expected date of delivery.

A total of 6 weeks leave with wages is given to a woman after MTP, or miscarriage. Whereas 2 weeks leave with wages is given to a woman after Tubectomy operation.

As per this Act, a woman is entitled for maternity benefit at the rate of average daily wages for maternity leave. But to avail this benefit she should have worked for 1 year in the establishment.

Nursing breaks: Every woman returning to duty after delivery is allowed two breaks for nursing her baby in addition to interval for rest.

The Factories Act, 1948 (Provisions Relating to Women)—Latrines and Urinals: Separate latrines for women should be there in the factories and number of latrines should be in proportion to number of workers. These should be cleaned at least once a week.

Creches: Any factory having substantial number of female workers should have a creche. If there are more than 30 women working in a factory, a room should be there to keep their children below the age of 6 years. Facilities should be there for washing and changing clothes of children in addition to the facilities for the mother to feed them.

Law also provides for the following:

- Prohibition on taking work from women from 10 pm to 5 am in any establishment.
- No woman should be employed in mines, beedi and cigar factories.

Dowry Prohibition Act, 1961: Though legislation cannot solve this deep rooted social evil but it is essential to have laws to curb the menace, so that action can be taken against those who are found guilty. Any person demanding dowry from the parents or relatives of the bride or bridegroom shall be imprisoned for 6 months to 2 years if proven guilty.

The Immoral Traffic (Prevention) Act, 1956: There is punishment of rigorous imprisonment from 1 to 3 years for running a brothel. Even if someone is proven to be guilty of living on the earning of prostitution shall be imprisoned for 2 years or fined or both. In case this earning relates to the prostitution of a child, then imprisonment shall be for 2–10 years.

Hindu Adoption and Maintenance Act, 1956: Any Hindu woman having sound mind and capacity to adopt a child has right to adopt a son or a daughter. But if she has a husband, then consent of the husband for adoption is necessary until and unless husband is not of sound mind or has renounced the world.

As per this Act, a Hindu wife is entitled to be maintained by her husband for her life time and she has every right to live separately from her husband if she being neglected or has been treated with cruelty by her husband. In case husband is having virulent leprosy or having another wife or living with a concubine or ceased to be a Hindu by converting to another religion, wife can live separately and get maintenance from her husband. The amount of maintenance is decided by court keeping in view the position and status of the parties, reasonable demand of the claimant, value of claimant's property and income, and the number of persons entitled to maintenance.

A widowed daughter-in-law is also entitled for maintenance from her father-in-law, if she is unable to maintain herself.

REVIEW QUESTIONS

1. What do you mean by domestic violence and how can it be prevented?
2. Write short notes on the following:
   a. Child Labour Act
   b. Immoral Traffic Prevention Act
   c. National Commission for Women

CHAPTER

50

Substance Abuse and Alcoholism

LEARNING OBJECTIVES

After reading this chapter the learner should be able to

- Have knowledge about the different causes of drug abuse.
- Get familiar with various types of drugs leading to drug abuse.

One of the many problems that the human society faces in today's fast-evolving world is substance abuse, more commonly referred to as drug abuse. Substance abuse may have been in prevalence long before we even coined a term for it; there were times when no one cared to understand the deeper aspects of the problem. The modern world, with its vast array of substances susceptible to abuse on offer, has become a breeding ground for addicts of all proportions and categories. The *ease of availability* and the choices on offer create further complications wherein the society not only has to deal with addiction and abuse but also with the ever-increasing numbers of people dependent on such substances.

Drug abuse is a complex phenomenon, as people think it only requires *will power* to give up the drugs, which is not the fact. Drugs create an impact on the brain fostering the compulsive drug abuse. So giving up drug does not require only *will power* because drug abuse has different social, cultural, biological, geographical, historical and economic aspects. Some of the causes of drug abuse among youth are, accessibility of drugs, disintegration of the old joint family system, absence of parental love and care, specially where both parents are working, decline of old religious and moral values, etc. Drug dependence is on the rise as many people take drugs to escape hard realities of life.

The constant abuse comes with a price and takes a heavy toll on the physical and mental health of an individual. It eventually gives rise to all kinds of problems leaving no aspect of one's life untouched, be it social or personal. Addiction ultimately hampers a person's ability to function naturally in the world. Apart from all of this, there are the usual scenarios that include family, professional, behavioral and psychological problems that the addict may have to face in day-to-day life.

Substance abuse also gives rise to widespread crime. The roots of the multibillion-dollar drug industry which uses crime as a means to facilitate the production and movement of drugs across the globe can be traced almost directly to the addicts and abusers. In other words, if there are no consumers, there is no market and if there is no market, there is no industry. The drug industry would virtually collapse if there were no consumers of drugs. The mafias are in a constant battle for gaining control over the illegal drug trade. Coupled with this, the crime addicts and abusers commit in order to get access to the substance. These include everything from thefts, robberies, physical assaults and heinous crimes like murder in some cases. Years of substance abuse and the fear of withdrawal symptoms may make an addict so determined that it becomes an absolute necessity to obtain what is desired and may sometimes force a person to commit heinous crimes.

The substances prone to abuse and sometimes leading to addiction are available in various forms. There are legally accessible options like alcohol and tobacco; on the other hand you have a multitude of illegal substances on offer. Chronic heavy consumption of alcohol leads to alcoholism, the person experiences an irresistible urge to drink more and more alcohol and end up as an addict.

Substance abuse is a serious problem and the curse of drug trafficking and drug addiction has spread across the whole world. Substance abuse in the young generation in India has assumed alarming proportions and the number of drug addicts is increasing day by day.

Declining social and cultural values, increasing economic stress, and dismantling of the support system are pushing more and more youth into substance use. According to a UN report, there are one million heroin addicts and the unofficial number is much higher at five million. Intravenous drug use in combination with other sedatives and painkillers has made the process of recovery complicated.

ALCOHOLISM

It is classified as a chronic and progressive disease. An alcohol addict requires help to get rid of the addiction, yet it is consumed and socially accepted in almost all countries across the world. Alcohol abuse is the root cause of many problems in our country, ranging from domestic violence to road mishaps and crimes committed each year by people under the influence of alcohol.

Alcoholism or alcohol dependence is like any other addiction. The alcoholic, a person suffering from alcoholism, is addicted to alcoholic beverages. Alcoholism is a chronic disease and if left untreated it leads to multiple health disorders affecting all the vital organs of the body, in some cases it proves fatal. Alcoholism has severe ill effects on the health of a person, gradually but surely it starts to affect all the aspects of their life and ultimately it controls their life with alcohol consumption becoming the sole purpose of their existence. The unfavourable circumstances that an alcoholic faces on a daily basis are overlooked. The physical dependence of an addict on alcohol is so strong that nothing that would deter him or her from consuming it.

Alcoholism gives rise to a host of problems but being legal and socially accepted it is not easy to contain. Liquor is available at government licensed shops and can be easily obtained. Addiction to alcohol is the main factor responsible for increasing domestic violence across our country. Aggressive behaviour after consumption of liquor invariably leads to domestic violence. Besides, drunken driving is responsible for a large number of road accidents and it is a serious hazard for the road users. Several studies have found a linkage between violence and alcohol and it is not possible to reduce crime without stamping out alcoholism in the society.

It is very difficult to create awareness and convince people that alcoholism is a serious problem as consumption of liquor is socially permitted. Once a person becomes physically dependent on alcohol, it becomes even more difficult to treat him or her.

SUBSTANCE ABUSE

The World Health Organization (WHO) has defined substance abuse as 'persistent or sporadic drug use inconsistent with or unrelated to acceptable medical practice'. A drug is a substance when taken by a living being alters one or more of its functions. Drug abuse or substance abuse is self-administration of drug for nonmedical reasons. In case of substance abuse, a person needs alcohol or another substance (drug) to function normally. Abruptly stopping the substance leads to withdrawal symptoms. No clear line indicates when substance use becomes a problem that is severe enough to need treatment.

Cannabis, heroin and Indian-produced pharmaceutical drugs are the most frequently abused drugs in India. However, cannabis products, often called charas, bhang or ganja, are the most abused as they have attained religious sanctity because of its association with some Hindu deities. Several pharmaceutical products containing narcotic drugs are also increasingly being abused. The intravenous injections of analgesics like dextropropoxyphene are also being abused as it is damn cheap compared to heroin. Even codeine-based cough syrups are being abused.

The products derived from opium are the most addictive. While some are derived from opium itself like morphine, codeine and heroine, some derivatives formulated synthetically do not contain opium. There are also semisynthetics which are partially synthetic and partial derivatives of opium. Vicodin and Demerol are both derived from Morphine. Certain semisynthetic drugs also contain a combination of Morphine and synthetic material. Synthetic drugs are actually created in laboratories and although they may have similar effects as opium. Synthetic and intravenous drug use has led to HIV/AIDS adding a new dimension.

Synthetic drugs amphetamines and cocaine–amphetamines are structurally similar to Adrenaline, which is used to treat narcolepsy, obesity, depression and other such disorders. They act upon central nervous system and produce heightened awareness, self-confidence and energy along with mood elevation.

Extracted from the leaves of coca plant, cocaine is a central nervous system stimulant and produces excitement and hallucinations. It has powerful negative effects on the heart, brain and emotions. Its long-term use can have life threatening consequences and even occasional users run the risk of sudden death. Powdered cocaine dissolves in water and users can snort or inject it, while crack cocaine can be smoked.

Barbiturates

It is the class of drugs known as sedative-hypnotics, which generally describes their sleep-inducing and anxiety-decreasing effects. Addiction to these sedatives is the worst as it leads to physical and psychic dependence. Barbiturates are a group of drugs considered extremely dangerous as even a slight overdose can cause death.

Symptoms and Behaviours of Drug Use

The person who is addicted to drugs exhibits discernible symptoms like confusion, violent behaviour and continuing with the use drugs even when health, work or family are being harmed. They are unable to give up drugs and turn hostile when confronted about drug dependence. Their performance declines and they need regular dose of drug use to function. They are not bothered about their physical appearance and indulge in secretive behaviour to hide drug use.

TOBACCO AND TOBACCO PRODUCTS

Tobacco is no less of a menace and it is legal and easily available. It is consumed in heavy quantities in different forms, some can be smoked and others are suitable for eating, but all of them lead to an addiction. It is addictive because of the presence of a chemical called nicotine. Smoking not only harms the addict but also those around him who become passive smokers and vulnerable to all the health risk associated with smoking.

There is a strong need to effectively address the problem of substance addiction which is not only destroying the addicts but also taking a heavy toll on the society. It is being seen as more of a medical and psychological condition that cannot be ignored and requires medical intervention. It is very difficult for addicts who pick up the bad habit at an early age to quit and lead a normal life again.

Medical help is essential to treat addiction as it changes the way body and mind function. Basic interaction chemistry between the body and the mind is altered due to drug dependence. The body becomes accustomed to the presences of the drug. If the body stops getting its regular supply, it goes into withdrawal. This cycle of abuse and the subsequent appearance of withdrawal symptoms when the drug leaves the body compels an addict to look out for the desired substances. The addict ultimately becomes a slave of his circumstances and the only way out is undergoing de-addiction. The need is to create awareness that drug addiction is a curable problem.

REVIEW QUESTIONS

1. What are the signs and symptoms of drug abuse?
2. What are the consequences of drug abuse?
3. Write short notes on the following:
   a. Alcoholism
   b. Tobacco and tobacco products

CHAPTER

51

HIV and AIDS

LEARNING OBJECTIVES

After reading this chapter the learner should be able to

- Know about the extent of the AIDS problem.
- Have knowledge about the National AIDS control programme.

Acquired immuno deficiency syndrome (AIDS) is a group of symptoms caused by a virus called human immunodeficiency virus (HIV). Initially, symptoms are mild and like influenza followed by a latent stage which is almost asymptomatic varying from 3–20 years and the later stage is called AIDS.

As the name indicates, the virus affects the immune system of the person in such a way that he gets prone to all sorts of opportunistic infections like tuberculosis, meningitis, pneumocystis pneumonia, gastrointestinal infections and skin infections, thus affecting nearly every organ. Person with AIDS may get a type of cancer called Kaposi's sarcoma. Usually, these bacterial, viral, fungal and parasitic infections are normally controlled by the immune system. The major signs of AIDS are weight loss, chronic diarrhoea, prolonged fever, persistent cough, sore throat, and itching and inflamed skin.

Transmission: Routes of transmission are unprotected sexual intercourse, through blood transfusion, hypodermic needles and from mother to baby during pregnancy, delivery or breastfeeding. The HIV is found in blood and semen in abundance, though virus has also been found in breast milk, saliva, urine and vaginal secretions but in very low concentration. There are lot of wrong notions about the disease as staying with a person with AIDS or eating with him or touching him may transmit disease.

Treatment: There is no cure for the disease; however, antiretroviral treatment can lower down the progression of the disease apart from reducing the risk of death and complications of the disease. Though the antiretroviral treatment is very expensive and has lot of side effects, it is effective to control the signs and symptoms of AIDS. Without treatment the person with HIV infection may survive at the most for 9–11 years. So it can be said prevention is the only cure for AIDS.

MAGNITUDE OF THE PROBLEM

Origin of AIDS is thought to be from West Central Asia during early 20th century. However, AIDS was first discovered by Centre for Disease Control, (CDC) USA in 1981. There are more than 35 million people in the world suffering from AIDS and more than 36 million have died of AIDS.

The influence of AIDS on society is beyond our imagination. As AIDS has social stigma, it is a source of discrimination. It is difficult to survive for a person who is diagnosed to be HIV positive as he or she faces so much public humiliation.

National AIDS Control Programme (NACP): AIDS being a new disease, very little is known about its epidemiology, but it is believed that the first case of AIDS was detected in 1986 in India. So National AIDS Programme was initiated by the Ministry of Health and Family Welfare in 1987 with the help of World Bank, to coordinate the national response to HIV/AIDS. The programme's main aim was screening of the *sexually promiscuous population,* and blood donors, creating awareness about HIV/AIDS and carrying out some educational programmes. A medium-term plan for AIDS control was developed in 1989 with the support of the World Health Organization, Swedish International Development Agency (SIDA) and the United States Agency for International Development (USAID). Various components of this programme are constitution of National AIDS Control Organization (NACO), Surveillance to find out the magnitude of the problem, Information Education and Communication (IEC), safe blood supply for people in need, HIV testing labs and treatment of AIDS.

National AIDS Control Organization (NACO): It was constituted for implementing this programme. State AIDS control cells were established. NGOs were also involved in the National AIDS Control Programme, to identify high risk groups as commercial sex workers, gays, drug addicts using injectable drugs, people staying away from their families like truckers and migrants. HIV testing labs for screening were set up. Blood banks with screening facilities for AIDS were established for the supply of safe blood to people in need. Free antiretroviral treatment is given in selected hospitals. HIV test kits and ELISA machines were given to blood banks throughout the country. National AIDS Control Programme was the first effort in India to develop a national public health programme to prevent and control HIV/AIDS. The main aim of the programme was to prevent HIV transmission, decrease the morbidity and mortality associated with HIV infection, and most importantly to minimize the socioeconomic impact of HIV infection.

State AIDS Prevention and Control Society (SACS): An autonomous and decentralized society run by each state of India. State AIDS Prevention and Control Society have a governing body, its highest policy-making structure, headed either by the health minister or the chief secretary of the state. It approves new policy initiatives, annual plan and budget and the administrative and financial powers are vested in the executive committee to ensure better financial and operational efficiency.

The mandate of SACS is to provide medical and public health services, communication and social sector services along with looking after administration, planning, coordination, monitoring and evaluation, finance and procurement. State AIDS cells were set up in 32 states and union territories for implementation of the National AIDS Control Programme.

District AIDS Prevention and Control Unit (DAPCU): It is a district-level decentralized monitoring unit of National AIDS Control Organization in India. They have been established in 1989, comprising high priority districts across the country as a step towards decentralization of the coordination and management of Government of India's National AIDS Control

Programme, by working in close coordination with the district administration to take up district-specific initiatives by leveraging local resources.

Education campaigns (information, education and communication) were launched to create public awareness of HIV/AIDS using various media against AIDS, safe blood supply, condom promotion, a system to monitor the prevalence of HIV, treatment of sexually transmitted diseases and AIDS-related conditions. It is taboo talking about sex in our society, so information regarding safe sex and use of condoms was transmitted to public. Condoms were known to be effective in preventing the transmission of HIV and other STDs. National AIDS Control Programme initiated to popularize the use of condoms, improve the quality of condoms and increase their availability. Condom vending machines were set at various public places like bus terminus and railway stations. NGOs were also involved to promote and distribute condoms through social marketing.

Blood banks: National blood policy was made and guidelines were issued to blood banks regarding screening of blood (for HIV and other infections) its storage and distribution. Existing blood bank were modernized. It was mandatory to obtain license to run a blood bank.

Surveillance: An appropriate surveillance system was instituted to monitor trends in HIV prevalence. Blood samples collected from the sentinel sites. Initially, 180 sites were set up to monitor HIV prevalence. These clinics were also meant for antenatal care and for the treatment of sexually transmitted diseases. Integrated Biological and Behavioural Surveillance (IBBS) is being implemented to strengthen surveillance among high risk groups like sex workers, homosexuals, persons having other sexually transmitted diseases, family members of HIV positive persons and migrant population to generate evidence on prevalence of HIV/AIDS and risk behaviours. Keeping in view the low-concentration nature of AIDS epidemics in India, IBBS supports planning and prioritization of programme efforts at district, state and national levels.

HIV testing labs and counselling centres: People with untreated sexually transmitted diseases (STDs) are much more at risk of HIV infection. Controlling STDs is an important strategy for HIV prevention. In the first phase, 504 existing STD clinics, which have requisite equipment, and laboratory facilities were to be upgraded. Besides, training was to be provided to doctors so that they could provide symptomatic treatment of STDs if laboratory facilities were unavailable.

Finally, it was decided to have a multispectral approach in NACP. So the collaboration of various government departments, the private sector, the corporate sector, different national and international organizations were involved in controlling HIV/AIDS. Later on, Voluntary Counselling and Testing Centres (VCTCs) were introduced in NACP. Apart from counselling and testing, VCTCs also provided referral services for treatment and care. For the prevention of transmission of HIV from mother to child (programme for prevention of mother-to-child transmission) services are given and antiretroviral drugs are given to people with AIDS and all these services were linked to the VCTCs. Ultimately, PPTCT centres and VCTCs were combined to form Integrated Counselling and Testing Centres (ICTCs).

TREATMENT

HIV positive persons can survive for long and lead a healthy life with appropriate treatment. There are more than 20 antiretroviral drugs available as research and development in HIV/AIDS drugs has made lot of progress in the field.

Antiretroviral treatment (ART): The aim of antiretroviral treatment is to keep the amount of HIV in the body at a low level. If only one drug was taken, HIV would quickly become resistant to it and the drug would stop working. This stops weakening of the immune system and allows it to recover from any damage that HIV might have caused already. HIV treatment requires much commitment as drugs have to be taken at exact times daily. Some patients may experience serious side effects or may not respond to certain drugs. Family support can help patients to adhere to treatment schedule and address any problems relating to their treatment regimen.

Highly Active Antiretroviral Therapy (HAART): Taking two or more antiretroviral drugs at a time is called combination therapy. Taking a combination of three or more anti-HIV/AIDS drugs is called highly active antiretroviral therapy (HAART). The choice of drugs to take depends on many factors, as availability of drugs, price of drugs, the number of tablets to be taken, the side effects of the drugs, requirements of the laboratory monitoring and whether there are combination blister packs or fixed dose combinations available.

Now, National AIDS Control Programme aims to accelerate the process of reversal of epidemic of HIV/AIDS though there is shortage of drugs and testing kits. The next phase of NACP will make available the third line drugs for HIV/AIDS. As one third of the world's HIV/AIDS patients are in India.

REVIEW QUESTIONS

1. What is the magnitude of the AIDS problem in India?
2. Write short notes on the following:
   a. ART
   b. HIV counselling centres

CHAPTER

52

Social Welfare Programmes in India

LEARNING OBJECTIVES

After reading this chapter the learner should be able to

- Get familiar with various schemes for the welfare of women.
- Have knowledge about child welfare schemes.

India is a welfare state and the uplift of the weaker sections of the country has been a prime concern of the government. The Constitution of India has certain special provisions for the welfare and uplift of scheduled castes, scheduled tribes and other weaker sections, ensuring them their rightful place in the community.

Despite resource crunch and various other difficulties, the social welfare movement has made much headway in the country. The Planning Commission (restructured as Niti Aayog) was set up soon after independence with the objective of preparing plans for the 'most effective and balanced utilization of the country's resource'. The first five-year plan formulated by it was implemented from 1951 to 1956 in which Rs 1.60 crore were allocated for social welfare. So far, 11 five-year plans have been implemented and the 12th plan (2012–2017) is under implementation.

Though the term social welfare means the well-being of each individual in the society, the basic objective is to provide basic facilities like food, water, shelter and clean environment, especially to the weaker and deprived sections. Besides fulfilling the basic needs of the people, the social welfare aims at providing accessibility to health care facilities, equal opportunities to work and social justice.

Besides Planning Commission, an independent ministry of social welfare has been set up along with a department of social welfare in the Government of India. Similar set-up has been provided in all the states for effective implementation of social welfare programmes in the country.

SOCIAL JUSTICE AND EMPOWERMENT

As the social welfare programme gained momentum, its scope was also widened and diversified. The focus was shifted to empowerment and rights of underprivileged for which an array of new administrative structures were created. The Union Ministry of Welfare was bifurcated into the Department of Women and Child Development and the Department of Welfare in the year 1985–1986. At the same time, the divisions looking after the development of scheduled castes and scheduled tribes and the Minorities and Backward Classes Welfare Division were moved to the Ministry of Welfare to implement the new initiative and programmes on an enhanced scale.

The ministry was renamed as Ministry of Social Justice and Empowerment in May 1998. The Tribal Development Division was moved out to create as a separate Ministry of Tribal Affairs in October 1999 and the Minorities Division along with Wakf Unit was taken away to carve out another ministry in January 2007. Adopting a proactive with regard to the disability sector, the Government of India established seven National Institutes (NIs), dealing with various types on disabilities and as many composite regional centres (CRCs) to provide rehabilitation services and training to rehabilitation professionals. A National Handicapped Finance and Development Corporation (NHFDC) was also set up to extend soft loans to people with disabilities (PwDs) for taking up self-employment ventures.

Several other statutory commissions, boards and corporations have also been set up to provide assistance to the weaker sections and ensure their speedy socioeconomic uplift. These include the Central Social Welfare Board (CSWB), National Commission for Scheduled Castes, National Commission for Backward Classes, National Commission for Safai Karamcharis, National Backward Classes Finance and Development Corporation (NBCFDC), National Scheduled Castes Finance and Development Corporation (NSCFDC), National Institute of Social Defence (NISD) and National Handicapped Finance and Development Corporation (NHFDC).

The CSWB was set up in August 1953, with the objective of mainstreaming the neglected, weak, handicapped and backward sections of the society. It has initiated several programmes for the welfare of the most backward, marginalized and deprived sections of the society. Similar boards were set up in various states for implementation and monitoring various schemes of the CSWB. Over the years, the Board has expanded its activities and emerged as a pioneering national level organization in the field of development and empowerment of women in the country and also moved in policy approach from welfare to development to empowerment. The board also serves as an interface between the government and the voluntary sector in the social sector and today there are nearly 25,000 voluntary organizations actively working for the welfare of the neglected women and children of the country.

PROGRAMMES AND SCHEMES

Besides launching various schemes to provide incentives and assistance to the deprived sections, several drives were also launched to educate and make the masses aware about various socioeconomic issues and programmes started by the government for their benefit. Special focus was on poor rural women and the awareness generation programme for rural and poor women was specifically implemented for the purpose. A lot of efforts are made to bring awareness among rural women through programmes implemented through mahila mandals and adolescent girls groups. Apart from the awareness about nutrition, income-generating schemes, hygiene and family planning, women are also made aware about their rights.

Condensed courses of education for women: Illiterate women are given short course of basic education.

Vocational training for women: Industrial training institutes are also running vocational programmes for women as tailoring, embroidery, painting, making soft toys, etc.

Socioeconomic programme: Employment for destitute women, disabled women and loans to women for setting up business and industry.

Agro-based units: Preparing the plants in nursery for sale, floriculture, rose plantation, growing mushrooms, bee keeping, etc., are some agro-based units run by rural folks. They are given loans for these units and also get seeds and other material at subsidized rate from the government.

Food processing units: Food processing units such as pickles, jams, packaged food, dairy products, etc. are set up with the help of government. People are also given prior training.

Family counselling centres: There are centres for child counselling, marriage counselling and pre-marital counselling and career counselling for youth in the major cities of the country.

Women welfare: The Constitution of India guarantees gender equality and also empowers the state to adopt measures of positive discrimination in favour of women through policies and legislative measures.

National Commission for Women: It was established in 1990. It was formed as the apex national level organization of India with the mandate of protecting and promoting the interests of women. The commission has the following functions:

- It reviews the legal and constitutional safeguards for women.
- It recommends the remedial legislative measures.
- It facilitates the redressal of grievances.
- It advices government on all policy matters affecting women.

The social empowerment of women aims at ensuring girls' equal access to education on a par with boys. Special measures are being taken to end discrimination, universalize education, eradicate illiteracy and create a gender-sensitive educational system. Concerted efforts are being made to increase enrolment and retention rates of girls schools and improve the quality of education to impart vocational training to women. Emphasis is on reducing the gender gap in education at secondary and higher levels and develop a gender-sensitive curriculum at all levels to address sex stereotyping as a cause of discrimination against women.

Several initiatives have been implemented for improving the lot of women and these include employment/income generating schemes.

Support to Training and Employment Programme for Women (STEP): Under the scheme, training is provided to women to attain the following:

- Enhance learning capacity of women groups through employment-cum-income generation programmes.
- Develop managerial, entrepreneurial and marketing skills in them so that both backward and forward linkages can be established.
- Assist women in asset formation in income generation.
- Create legal awareness and educate about gender sensitization and health, education.

Allocation for these schemes for the 12th 5-year plan is Rs. 200 crore and under the scheme, 90% of the project cost is given by the Government of India and 10% is to be borne by the implementing agency.

Working women hostels scheme: It was aimed to make life easier for the working women living in urban areas away from home by providing hostel facility along with day-care centres. Working women have been facing problems in finding suitable and safe accommodation in towns and cities. The Government of India came out with the scheme appreciating the concerns raised by voluntary organizations regarding safety of working women.

Mahila mandals: Mahila Mandal is a community-based rural women organization created at village level. Generally, it has more than 20 members. It has an elected executive body of Pradhan, UP Pradhan, secretary and treasurer. Mahila mandal is playing a pivotal role in implementation of many schemes for empowerment of women. It continues to be the hub around which the integrated programmes have been designed. Women have played a crucial role in strengthening these groups and accelerating the pace of development. In the process, many women have been empowered and, with this new found strength, they are not only helping themselves, but also those around them. The forum of mahila mandals has developed among the ability to think together, be together and act together. The Mahila Mandals hold monthly meetings to analyse their problems and find solutions within their means.

Child welfare: Integrated Child Development Scheme (ICDS) is the basic social welfare scheme to address the issue of malnutrition and health problems in children aged up to 6 years and their mothers. The aim was to target the children, pregnant and lactating mothers and adolescent girls. The objective of the scheme was also to bring the girl child on a par with the male child, immunization, supplementary nutrition, health check-up, referral services, preschool nonformal education and nutrition and health information. Objectives of ICDS are as follows:

- To improve the health and nutritional status of poor Indian children aged up to 6 years
- To create a base for proper mental, physical and social development of children in India
- To bring down instances of mortality, malnutrition and school dropouts among children
- To coordinate activities of policy formulation and ensure their effective enforcement through various departments concerned with the implementation schemes related to child development in the country
- To educate mothers of young children about health and nutrition to enhance child-rearing capabilities
- To ensure nutritional food to pregnant women and the mothers of young children

Day-care centres and creches: The need for child care services has been stressed in various national policies pertaining to education of children and empowerment of women. Besides, the National Plan of Action for Children, 2005, also recommended that all sections of the society should be allowed to avail the services of creches. The National Common Minimum Programme also lays emphasis on expansion of child care and development services.

As per norms, a creche centre must have a minimum space of 6–8 sq. ft. per child to ensure enough space to play, rest and learn without any hindrance. Essential material for playing, learning and teaching has to be provided to meet the needs of preschool children. These centres must be linked with the local primary health centres and also have a tie-up with the nearby anganwadi centres. Such linkages are essential for effective immunization, administration of polio drops and basic health monitoring. Nominal user charges of Rs 20 per child per month for children from below poverty line (BPL) families and Rs 60 per child per month from others were also allowed to ensure of participation of the community.

Mid-Day Meal scheme: It was launched in 1995, National Programme of Nutritional Support to Primary Education, popular as the Mid-Day Meal scheme (MDM), aimed at reducing the school dropout rates, besides improving nutritional levels among children. The main objectives of the scheme (revised in 2006) are to improve the nutritional status of children from Class I to V and encourage children from disadvantaged backgrounds to attend school regularly. In October 2007, children in the upper primary section from Class VI to VIII were also covered under the scheme. Cooked mid-day meal with a minimum of 300 calories is provided to children up to Class V and meals containing 700 calories is provided to children of Classes VI–VIII. The central government supplies free food grains (wheat/rice) at 100 g per child per school day to states and cooking cost is also provided under the scheme.

National Institute of Cooperation and Child Development: It was set up in 1966, the National Institute of Public Cooperation and Child Development (NIPCCD) is devoted to promotion of voluntary action research, training and documentation. The institute functions under the aegis of the Ministry of Women and Child Development and has established four Regional Centres at Guwahati (1978), Bangalore (1980), Lucknow (1982) and Indore (2001).

Welfare of old people: Maintenance and Welfare of Parents and Senior Citizens Act, 2007 aims to ensure more effective provision for maintenance and welfare of parents and senior citizens. The Act makes it obligatory for children and heirs to look after the senior citizens and parents or give monthly allowance to them. This Act also provides simple, speedy and inexpensive mechanism for the protection of life and property of the older persons.

Protection of Women from Domestic Violence Act, 2005: In Indian society, domestic violence is often downplayed and internalized as *natural*. The Protection of Women from Domestic Violence Act 2005 (PWDVA) addresses these unspoken issues by providing a legal recourse to women (wives and live-in partners) facing domestic violence of all types, physical, mental, sexual, emotional or economical. The Act provides an appointment of Protection Officers and Service Providers and Medical Officers. An offender is liable to a fine of Rs 20,000/- and a jail sentence up to 1 year. Aggrieved women may file an FIR with the police or a DIR (Domestic Incidence Report) under the PWDV Act. Immediate monetary relief is to be provided to the victim by the government. Further, noncompliance of the order of the court is a criminal offence under the Act and the victim can complain to the magistrate or the police or the appointed Protection Officer and the abuser can be arrested.

Age-Care India: It is a premier voluntary organization for the welfare of the elderly people. It raises various issues concerning the aged population and also undertakes various activities for their welfare like free medical camp.

National Policy on Older Persons: The Union Ministry of Social Justice and Empowerment has formulated a policy, which stipulates that state governments, will take affirmative action to provide facilities, concessions and relief to senior citizens to improve the quality of their life. The state also have to ensure that the existing public services are elder-friendly. It covers many areas like financial security, health care, shelter, welfare, protection of life and property.

Other benefits for old people are railway travelling concession, preference in hospital care, separate counters for paying bills and purchasing tickets and some bus seats reserved for senior citizens.

Welfare of disabled: The Constitution of India mandates an inclusive society for all, including person with disabilities. The government has taken several initiatives in this direction including enforcement of the persons with disabilities (PwD) Act.

Scheme for stipends to physically handicapped students: Financial assistance and other facilities are provided to disabled students from class I to postgraduate level. Disability covers blindness, low-vision, leprosy-cured, hearing impairment, locomotor disability and mental retardation.

Samarthya scheme: The scheme aims to empower the persons with disabilities by facilitating their physical, social, economic and psychological rehabilitation. Aids and appliances such as tricycles, hearing aid, callipers are also provided to the disabled persons.

Indira Gandhi National Disability Pension Scheme: Indira Gandhi National Disability Pension Scheme was introduced in Bihar in 2009–2010 for which funds are provided by the Government of India. Under this scheme, pension is provided to the persons with disabilities in the age group of 18–79 years belonging to the BPL families.

Mukhya Mantri Nihshaktjan Shiksha Rin (Loan) Yojana: The scheme offers loans to students with disabilities for pursuing higher education. The only condition is that the degree, diploma or any other equivalent course should be duly recognized by government and concerned bodies like the Universities Grants Commission and All India Council for Technical Education.

Mukhya Mantri Nihshaktjan Swarojgar Yojana: Loans are advanced for self-employment ventures to persons with disabilities at very low interest rates to persons with disabilities wishing to be entrepreneurs. A wide range of ventures from small-scale industries and manufacturing to agriculture could be set up.

Assistance to disabled persons for purchase/fitting of aids and appliances (ADIP Scheme): The scheme is very useful for disabled persons as it enables them to procure durable and sophisticated standard aids and appliances that facilitates their physical, social and psychological rehabilitation by minimizing the effects of disabilities. It helps them in leading an active life and enhances their economic potential.

Scholarship for disabled students: Under the scheme, financial support in the form of scholarships and grants is provided to students with disabilities for pursuing education. The scholarships are available at all levels, from Class I to postgraduate studies, and for all kind of courses: general, vocational and technical courses.

National Institute for Empowerment of Persons with Multiple Disabilities (NIEPMD): This institute was established in the year 2005 at Chennai to serve as a national resource centre for empowerment of persons with multiple disabilities.

National Institute for the Visually Impaired: It is a premier institute in the field of visual disability set up by Government of India to promote rights and dignity of persons with visual impairments. The institute produces specially trained manpower for providing quality education, vocational training and rehabilitation services to the visually impaired persons. It also undertakes research and developmental activities to help formulate inclusive policies, programmes and practices for disabled persons. The institute is largest producer of braille literature and devices, including talking books, which are distributed across the country.

National Institute for Mentally Handicapped: It was set up in 1984 in Secunderabad (AP) and is an autonomous body that provides various services to persons with mental retardation. It has three regional centres located at New Delhi, Kolkata and Mumbai. The institute is engaged in building capacities to empower persons with mental retardation so that they could live a better life and become independent to the extent possible.

Rehabilitation Council of India (RCI): The council is mandated to regulate and monitor services given to persons with disability. It is also responsible for standardizing the syllabi and maintaining the Central Rehabilitation Register. All the qualified professionals and personnel working in the field of rehabilitation and special education are registered by it. The Act also empowers the council to take punitive action against unqualified persons in case they are found delivering services to persons with disability.

District Rehabilitation Centres: The District Disability Rehabilitation Centre (DDRC) scheme was implemented from 1999 to 2000 to provide comprehensive services to the persons with disabilities through creation of the infrastructure and capacity building. These centres also create awareness regarding, rehabilitation and training of grass-roots-level functionaries.

DDRC have a group of rehabilitations professionals for providing services like identification of persons with disabilities, early detection and intervention.

Welfare of drug addicts: Management of drug addict has traditionally been the responsibility of the family in the country but there has been an increasing demand on the state to provide facilities for their treatment. Psychiatry departments in many hospitals have been offering facilities for indoor treatment to hard-core addicts. It is widely considered as a psycho-socio-medical problem, and thus has to be tackled in the entirety of the life situations of addicts.

Apart from state-run treatment deaddiction centres, many voluntary organizations are also providing such facilities. The deaddiction centres run by nongovernmental organizations; employ various systems of medicines, including naturopathy and Yoga.

Various welfare programmes for addicts: Public awareness and prevention education, stringent legislation, Narcotic Drugs and Psychotropic Substances (NDPS) Act, 1985 and the Prevention of Illicit Traffic in Narcotic Drugs and Psychotropic Substances Act, 1988 and Enforcement agencies.

Welfare of underprivileged section of the society: Scheduled caste, scheduled tribes and other backward classes have been suppressed, exploited, humiliated and virtually enslaved for centuries. These people have been discriminated in almost all the spheres of life as education, housing, food, water, employment and even religious places. They were treated as untouchables. Though there are downtrodden among all the sections of the community but major chunk is from scheduled caste, scheduled tribes and other backward classes.

Constitutional safeguards: Indian constitution includes safeguards for the underprivileged, keeping in view their educational and economic interests.

National Commission for Scheduled Castes and Scheduled Tribes: Commission for scheduled castes and scheduled tribes was set up in 1978 to investigate and monitor all matters relating to the safeguards provided for the two categories under the Constitution and various other laws. It is also mandated to look into specific complaints with respect to the deprivation of rights of the scheduled castes and to advise on the planning process for their socioeconomic development.

Centrally sponsored schemes: Post-matric scholarships, prematric scholarship, book banks for scheduled caste's and scheduled tribe's students studying in medical and engineering colleges. Girls hostel schemes for scheduled caste's girls, coaching and allied scheme for scheduled castes and scheduled tribes, aid to voluntary organizations engaged in the welfare of scheduled castes and scheduled tribes.

Protection of Civil Rights Act, 1955: The Untouchability (Offence) Act, 1955 has been renamed as the Protection of Civil Rights, 1955. As per this act, a person will be prosecuted if he or she prevents scheduled caste community from entering places like a public temple, using a well, water room, hotel, inn, if a barber disagrees to cut the hair of a member belonging to scheduled caste or a laundryman refuses to wash his clothes will be punished, if anybody preventing scheduled caste member from occupying a seat along with other people without any discrimination at the place of religious service or prayer at a public place in the village will be prosecuted.

Twenty Point Programme: The prime objective of the programme is alleviation of poverty, removal of gender inequality, justice to scheduled caste and scheduled tribes. There are other components like provision of potable drinking water, health care for all, food security and housing for all, environment protection, and social security.

Tribal development and welfare: A separate ministry was carved out of the Ministry of Social Justice and Empowerment to look after tribal affairs in October 1999. It is responsible for everything concerning tribal welfare from policy, planning, project formulation, monitoring, research, and training to promotion and development of voluntary efforts on tribal welfare.

Tribal Cooperative Marketing Federation (TRIFED): The apex cooperative institution was set up to serve the interest of the tribal community and facilitate marketing of tribal products. The federation also works for their socioeconomic development by bringing in professionalism in managing the affairs of tribal people.

REVIEW QUESTIONS

1. Which are the welfare schemes for disabled persons in India?
2. Write short notes on Mid-Day Meal programme and Age-Care India.

CHAPTER

53

Role of Nurse as a Change Agent

LEARNING OBJECTIVES

After reading this chapter the learner should be able to

- Know about the qualities of a change agent.
- Have knowledge about the role of a nurse as change agent.

Nurses play a vital role in promoting health of people at individual, family and community level. They can also play the role of change agent in health settings at health institutions, family or community. The nurse can play role of change agent in community, research, hospital and health educational institutions.

Change agent means the person who helps or facilitates change in any area related to health. A change agent takes lead and works for a positive outcome. Nurses have to be proactive as change agent and take action rather than waiting for others to take decisions. They have to take informed decision like whether a change is worthwhile or not. The process of change is much like nursing as it involves assessment, planning, decision-making, implementation and evaluation.

To play effective role of change agent, a nurse has to be far-sighted, a facilitator and an ideal person. A nurse communicates, advices, coaches and provides feedback to bring change in any health and educational setting. She has to play the role of a facilitator to bring change and that of an educator to make the people aware of the kind of change needed. She should be a person with ideas to solve problems to effectively play the role of a change agent.

QUALITIES OF A CHANGE AGENT

A change agent has the most important role and requires high level of competency. The outcome of any initiative to effect change depends on the leadership and capabilities of the change agent. Apart from the ability to objectively assess the need for change, the agent must have the power to convince everyone that it was required to create a receptive environment.

A change agent must have leadership qualities and ability to motivate people and ensure their full support and commitment. Interpersonal skills are a must to build a rapport with the people, put across the viewpoint and persuade them. Communication skills and ability to appreciate and understand the opinion of others and remove doubts, if any, are essential. Besides, cultural competence in terms of basic knowledge about the values, beliefs and customs of the people are also required. Any change affecting the traditional values or customs is likely to face resistance and make the task of implementing the change a tough proposition.

The most important task of the change agent is to generate acceptance to facilitate the process of change and this can be best achieved by ensuring involvement of the people. They must not feel that they were the subjects of change. People should be encouraged and afforded an opportunity to become a part of the solution.

Credibility, integrity and reliability of the change agent are immensely important for effectively motivating people and bringing the desired change. Above all, a change agent needs to be passionate about the task for effectively implementing change. The process of change may not lead to the expected results if the change agent lacks commitment in implementation.

NURSES AS CHANGE AGENTS

One of the major roles of the nurses in the health care system is that of a change agent. They can be key agents to spearhead change not only in health care but also other aspects of society. Nurses effect on the transformations of lives of both ill and healthy people through the various functions they perform.

Societal change requires a great deal of flexibility and the ability to adapt and nurses have both these qualities to play the role of change agent. They are involved in influencing change at various levels in the family, institutions and community at large.

Nurses are in a unique position to facilitate new development both as activists and agents of change themselves. They can become visible and efficient agents for planned change by adopting a proactive approach. Being a change agent means that a nurse will help to come out of the usual scenario, identify the need for the change and implement the change.

As a change agent, a nurse has to be a leader, an educator, a communicator and an advocate, besides the usual role of care provider.

Advocacy: Advocacy is an essential process that involves coordinated efforts of people to change the existing practices and ideas. Advocacy is a positive force for change and apart from facilitating the process of change, it gives people a voice. It empowers and educates the people and helps in generating acceptance.

Communicator: Communication skills are very important in the field of nursing. A nurse has to be an accomplished communicator to effectively play the role of a change agent. As communication means giving and receiving information, a communicator has to be a good listener too.

Counsellor: The process of change usually leads to stress and there comes the role of a counsellor. Since stress is a natural outcome of any situation that requires adaptation or change, nurses also serve counsellors helping people to develop mechanism to cope with it. The role encompasses the emotional, intellectual and psychological support to the people.

Leader: As a change agent, a nurse must have leadership quality to be able to influence others and motivate them to achieve the common goal or objective. A nurse must be able to move a step ahead of others and take responsibility. Nurse leaders are role models who inspire others and often challenge the status quo with more innovative methods to effect change.

Educator: Nurses have to play the role of educators to function effectively as change agents. Awareness regarding need to implement change can be created only through education and the nurses have to update their own knowledge and have an integrated long-term perspective to take informed decisions to shape and implement the change.

Nurses play the role of an empowering agent by emphasizing the active role of the recipient of care in improving the health. They empower the individual, family, the community and groups related to the patient's situation and this process helps in improving the health status of communities.

Nurses can successfully usher in social change by making use of evidence-based change concepts like opting for right leadership skill, foresee the response to change and adopt the appropriate implementation strategies. Bringing about social change involves working for changes in organizations and government policies with a view towards reducing or eliminating poverty, social exclusion and other social inequalities.

One cannot expect to effect change by simply asking people to change, it will not work. Nurse leaders have to involve others to co-construct realities and concepts by helping them discover their strengths to put plans in place to deliver.

Action plans for social change can be implemented through many ways by providing information, lobbying, carrying out media campaigns for creating new attitudes and approaches to policies that affect them.

A nurse in the role of a change agent has to be an innovative thinker and active listener, besides leadership qualities. It also involves creativity, accountability and role modelling. Every nurse has the potential to be a change agent; all that is needed is to acquire these soft skills, which are better developed through life experiences, feedback and self-reflection.

REVIEW QUESTIONS

1. Describe the characteristics of a change agent.
2. Explain the role of a nurse as a change agent.

CHAPTER

54

Resources of the Country: Natural, Occupational and Industrial

LEARNING OBJECTIVES

After reading this chapter the learner should be able to

- Get acquainted with the natural resources of India.
- Have knowledge about the occupational resources of our country.

NATURAL RESOURCES

Natural resources are the things that are available in the environment above and under the surface of the earth and can be utilized by human beings. Natural resources are important as they influence the economy of the country. But it is the exploitation of the natural resources that influences economy of the nation rather than the availability of these resources. There are some countries that have rich natural resources but are still underdeveloped. India has 2.42% of the total area of the world, which means it has huge area of land but density of population is very high. So the land is being fragmented as the large holdings of land are reduced to marginal holdings because of population explosion. All the economic activities are performed on land only, such as agriculture, plant growth and setting up industrial units. Even the commercial activities require land.

India is endowed with a rich and vast diversity of natural resources. There are two types of natural materials available for the consumption of human beings, biotic and abiotic.

Biotic

These are organic materials from living things and are renewable except fossil fuels, which are considered to be biotic as they are from decayed organic matter but are not renewable.

Forest: It constitutes 21.02% of the total geographical area of our country; some of it is very dense while some is moderately dense and open forest area. Due to variations in climatic conditions and differences in altitude, different types of forests are present in India. Variety of forest vegetation is large. Forests are the main source of firewoods, furniture wood, bamboos, paper, spices, drugs, herbs, gums, raisin and more. Forests contribute significant amount to nation's economy.

Fish: With its rich marine and inland water resources, India has a long tradition of fishing and aquaculture. Besides the 8129-km-long coastline, the country has vast inland fishery resources in the shape of rivers, reservoirs and lakes. There are more than 400 species of fish in the rivers, many of which are economically important such as shrimps, sardines, mackerels, carangid and croaker. Major fish species available are carp catfish, murrel and weed fish.

Coal: India has the fourth largest reserves of coal in the world. Coal is easy to mine and found in abundance; particularly in the Chota Nagpur Plateau, which is the principal source area for coking coal with a large number of surface and deep-pit spread over a number of states. By far, the most important coal-producing region is along the Damodar River, including the Jharia and Raniganj fields in Bihar, Jharkhand, Chhattisgarh and West Bengal, which account for most of the country's coal output.

Oil: India does not have the amount of crude oil to make it self-sufficient. Rising consumption of oil and comparatively less production makes India dependent on import of oil from other countries. Most oil reserves are located in the western coasts (Mumbai) and in the north-eastern parts of the country. Some of the reserves are located in the offshore Bay of Bengal and in the state of Rajasthan.

Natural gas: India's main source of natural gas is western offshore regions in Mumbai. The other sources are in the state of Assam, Andhra Pradesh and Gujarat. Oil and Natural Gas Commission (ONGC) and Oil India are the leading companies as far as the production volume is concerned apart from some foreign companies involved in joint ventures with private sector.

Abiotic

These materials are nonorganic and obtained from nonliving things. These are not renewable except water and air. Other abiotic materials are nonrenewable. Minerals are of two types, metallic and nonmetallic.

Metallic are copper, iron ore, chromite, gold, bauxite, lead and Zinc, etc.

Copper: It is found in Singhbhum (Bihar), Balaghat (Madhya Pradesh), Jhunjhunu and Alwar (Rajasthan), Khammam (Andhra Pradesh), Chitradurga and Hassan (Karnataka), and Sikkim.

Chromite: It is the only commercial source of chromium. Chromite deposits of economic significance occur in Andhra Pradesh, Bihar, Karnataka, Maharashtra, Manipur, Odisha and Tamil Nadu. About 96% of the total geographical resource is accounted by Cuttack district in Odisha.

Gold: India has very limited gold reserve. Three main gold mine regions are, Kolar gold field in Kolar, Hutti gold field in Raichur in Karnataka and Ramgiri gold field in Anantapur in Andhra Pradesh.

Bauxite: Major deposits of bauxite, main source of metal like aluminium, are mostly concentrated in Odisha and Andhra Pradesh. It is also found in Jharkhand, Gujarat, Jammu and Kashmir, Karnataka, Kerala, Chhattisgarh, Maharashtra, Tamil Nadu and Uttar Pradesh.

Lead and Zinc: Almost 95% of known reserves of lead and zinc are concentrated in Rajasthan and Gujarat. The main deposits are in Meghalaya, West Bengal, Uttar Pradesh, Andhra Pradesh, Tamil Nadu, Odisha and Sikkim, besides Rajasthan and Gujarat.

Iron ore: Iron ore is found in several parts of the country but the major part of the reserves are in Jharkhand, Orissa, Madhya Pradesh, Chhattisgarh, Karnataka and Goa. Jharkhand alone accounts for about 25% of the total reserves. Very high-grade ore is found only in Bailadila sector of Chhattisgarh.

Minor minerals—marble, granite, gravel, clay and sand, nuclear–uranium, thorium, plutonium

Marble: It is found in different colours and textures in many states of India.

Uranium: Tumalapalli mine in Andhra Pradesh is the world's largest uranium mine with more than 170,000 tonnes of uranium.

Thorium: Found in the three eastern coastal states of Andhra Pradesh, Tamil Nadu and Odisha. Probably, India possesses the largest share of world's thorium deposits.

OCCUPATIONAL RESOURCES

Agriculture: It has been the primary occupation of Indian people since ancient time. Initially, farming was dependent on rain so most of the crops were cultivated in monsoon; but now with advancement in irrigation technology, crops are grown throughout the year. There are rich farmers having their own land and hire labour for cultivation. But some people do not have their own land so do contract farming. They take the land on contract to cultivate and take the portion of produce. Thus, lot of people are dependent on agriculture for their earning.

Fishing: India has lot of rivers flowing through it and huge sea along its borders. Hence, fishing is the occupation for many, especially for the people living in the coastal areas. There is lot of consumption of sea food in India so local market is there for the fisherman to sell fish and earn their livelihood. Fresh water fish such as carp, catfish and brackish-water fish are liked by many so sold at good price. Other variety of fishes found in Indian seas are mackerel, sardines, Bombay duck, perch, croaker, carangid, sole, ribbonfish, whitebait, tuna, silver belly, prawn and cuttlefish. Some of the fishes are exported also and bring huge amount of foreign exchange.

Handicrafts: A wide range of handicrafts are made in India and many of the products have made their mark in the international market. Handicraft sector is a major employment-generating sector in rural India and a large number of people earn their livelihoods by making different types of handicrafts like pottery, metal craft, gold and silver jewellery, wood craft, shell craft, cane craft, embroidery, ivory craft, glass craft, paper craft, sholapith craft and weaving.

Health care sector: It is a major source of jobs of various levels from ward attendants to doctors, nurse and other paramedical staff deployed in hospitals. Initially, only government hospitals used to be there in the country apart from private practitioners, but now many multinational companies and corporate sectors are also running private hospitals. Health care sector is now a big industry with a lot of job options.

Teaching jobs: Educational institutes like schools, colleges and universities are the resources for teaching and nonteaching jobs.

INDUSTRIAL REVOLUTION

Industrial revolution changed the economy of India to the extent that it is emerging as the third biggest global economy after the United States and China. India has established number of modern industries like steel plants, chemical industries, textiles, fertilizers, cement, thermal power, atomic power, heavy engineering, electrical and electronic.

Textile industry: It covers a whole range of activities right from production of raw materials like jute, wool, silk and cotton to manufacture of ready-made garments. The industry uses both, man-made or natural, fibres. It has 4% share in GDP and accounts for over 35% of the gross export income.

Food processing industry: The country accounts for just about 1.5% of the global food business, despite being a major food producing nation. Food processing industry provides job opportunities to 1.6 million people and the number is estimated to reach 37 million by 2025.

Chemical industry: The Indian chemical industry produces about 70,000 commercial items ranging from plastic to toiletries and pesticides to beauty products. It is perhaps the oldest domestic sector in the country and the sheer volume of production gives it a sense of pride. In fact, India is the 12th largest producer of chemicals. Some other rapidly growing industries under the sector are petrochemical, agrochemical and pharmaceutical industries.

Cement industry: India is the second largest market of cement after China and the country accounts for about 8% of the total global production. Its total installed capacity of the country is 360 million tonnes (MT) as of financial year ended (2013–2014). The housing sector is the biggest driver of demand of cement and accounts for about 67% of the total consumption.

Steel industry: The nearly four-centuries-old steel industry in the country has been growing steadily over the years. The total steel production capacity touched 101.02 million tonnes (MT) in 2013–2014, when the output was 81.7 MT. India is set to become the world's second largest producer of crude steel with an annual outturn of 112.5 MT in 2016.

Software industry: Software industry registered a phenomenal growth in the last decade of the 20th century and first decade of the 21st century. The country is the world's largest sourcing destination for the information technology (IT) industry, and it has approximately 52% of the US$ 124–130 billion market (2014–2015). The industry employs about 10 million Indians and has not only given a big boost to the economy of the country but also transformed its image in the eyes of the world.

Mining industry: The GDP contribution of the mining industry varies from 2.2 to 2/5%, though it touched 3.4% in 1993–1994. Even mining done on a small scale contributes 6% to the entire cost of mineral production. Indian mining industry provides job opportunities to around 0.7 million individuals.

REVIEW QUESTIONS

1. How industrial revolution has changed the economy of our country?
2. What are the important occupational resources of India?

CHAPTER

55

Social Security in India

LEARNING OBJECTIVES

After reading this chapter the learner should be able to

- Have knowledge about the requirement of the social security in our country.
- Get familiar with various social welfare schemes in India.

The concept of social security is not new; it has been there in all the western countries for ages. However, family system being very strong in India, the need for social security was not felt by the state as most of the families were joint families and elderly people were well looked after. Widows were not allowed to remarry but they had economic support from the family, though these widows used to live a very miserable life. Elderly people held a lot of respect in the family; and being experienced, younger family members used to seek the advice from them. All the male members were involved in the family business and women used to look after the household chores and take care of elderly people. Following the cultural traditions, family members and relatives always discharged a sense of shared responsibility towards one another. Thus, the elderly people, widows, members having special needs and poor health were the joint responsibility of all other members of the family.

The situation has undergone many changes over the past few decades and large sections of the Indian society are facing all the problems and social concerns hitherto experienced in the western world. Rapid urbanization has led to the collapse of the joint family system and most of the families in the urban areas are nuclear. Housing problem is there almost in all the small and big cities and the nuclear families are not able to accommodate elderly people in their small houses. Consequently, elderly people are left alone to fend for themselves. Similarly, widows also don't have any family support despite the Widow' Remarriage Act, which came into existence way back in 1856. Widows and divorcee women still have to face social stigma and there is not much acceptance of remarriage.

Unemployment is another outcome of the population explosion and urbanization. The number of educated jobless people is increasing day by day and even professionally qualified youth are unemployed. It is leading to a lot of frustration among the youth who are under tremendous mental stress and indulging in erratic behaviour. This is a major reason for growing mental health problems and even rising suicide rate in India.

Changing scenario of Indian society has attracted the attention of the government and it has been forced to implement various schemes to provide the social security to people who don't have any financial support. The schemes cover the industrial workers, aged, destitute, widows, unemployed youth, persons with disabilities and other vulnerable lot.

The Employees' State Insurance Act, 1948 (ESI Act): It came into existence for health care and cash benefit payments to employee in the case of sickness. The Act applies to all factories and establishments that are run with power, having 20 or more employees and provides for comprehensive medical care to the employees. It is provided for an integrated need-based social insurance scheme that would protect the interest of workers and provides six benefits such as sickness benefit, maternity benefit, medical benefit, disablement benefit, dependants' benefit and funeral benefit. The cash benefits are given by Government of India through the Employees' State Insurance Corporation (ESIC), whereas medical care is administered by state government.

The Employees' State Insurance Corporation (ESIC): This corporation ensures the appropriate functioning of ESI scheme. It comprises members from state government and central government. Chairman of the corporation is Union Minister of Labour. This is the leading social security organization of our country. ESIC takes measures for the welfare of the insured persons apart from their health and rehabilitation in case of disability and injury.

Contribution for this scheme is partly from the employer and partly from the employee and rates of contributions are prescribed by central government. All the contributions received are put into a fund called *Employees' State Insurance Fund*. Anybody making a false statement to get benefit or payment is authorized under this Act, and shall be punished with imprisonment and fine; and if this offence is committed by the company, the in-charge of the company shall be punished.

The Employees' Provident Funds and Miscellaneous Provisions Act, 1952: The Act applies to all the factories and establishments employing 20 or more employees. The main objective of this Act is to make the future of the employee financially secure after retirement and in case of his death while in job, his dependents get the financial assistance. New establishment are exempted for a period of 3 years. This Act is also not applicable to organizations under central or state government whose employees are entitled to contributory provident fund.

Employees' Provident Fund Organization (EPFO): Government of India implemented this Act through EPFO, which is under the Ministry of Labour. It contributes substantially to the economy of the country. EPFO is the largest provident fund organization in the world as it has largest number of members and financial transactions. There are three schemes operational under this Act: Provident Fund, Family Pension and Deposit-Linked Insurance Funds. An old age and survivorship benefits, a long-term protection and security to the employee and to his family members after his death and advance payments, including advances for treatment of sickness and for possessing house during the period of membership are also some of the functions of EPFO. The contributions made by employer to the fund is 8 and 1/3% of the basic wages, dearness allowances and retaining allowance, the employees' contribution shall be equal to the contribution payable by the employer. Moreover, any employee may desire to contribute more subject to the condition that the employer shall not be under an obligation to pay any contribution over and above his contribution.

Employees' Deposit-Linked Insurance Scheme, 1976: The central government started this scheme with the objective of providing additional social security in the form of life insurance to the family in case of the death of the member of the Provident Fund Scheme. The benefit of the scheme is to encourage the members to save more in their Provident Fund account. As the name of the scheme indicates, the amount of benefit depends on the amount of money in the Provident Fund account of the member. This scheme is mandatory for all the organizations that are covered under the Employees' Provident Fund Scheme. All the members of the Employees' Provident Fund Scheme are covered under the Employees' Deposit-Linked Insurance Scheme. Employee does not have to make any contribution under this scheme, nor the government makes any contribution; only the employer pays an amount of 0.5% of the total wages paid to the members.

Employees' Pension Scheme, 1995: All the members of EPF are beneficiary of this scheme. If the employee works for more than 10 years in an organization before cessation of employment then he will be eligible for the monthly pension. In case the employee has not put in 10 years of service then he shall be entitled to withdrawal benefits. If the worker suffers permanent and total disablement during the service he/she shall be entitled to a pension of minimum Rs 250 per month for the lifetime. Family of the employee is entitled for the pension in case of death of the employee. Contribution is 8.33% from employer and 1.16% from government and the employee does not have to pay anything.

The Employees' Compensation Act, 1923: Employer is supposed to pay compensation to the workman or his family in case of occupational injuries resulting in death or disability, arising out of and in the course of employment, also if a worker contracts any disease, specified in the Act as an occupational disease. Minimum and maximum amount of compensation payable for death and disability are fixed. Certain things like salary of the worker, age of the worker and severity of the injury matter in case of amount of compensation and for disability have been fixed. And this compensation amount is subject to revision from time to time.

Social Security Division: Ministry of Labour and Employment has set up this division to implement various social security schemes.

The Maternity Benefit Act, 1961 (MB Act): The Act means to provide 12-weeks wages during maternity leave. But the employee must have completed 1 year of job in that organization. The employer is supposed to pay the amount in advance on production of proof of pregnancy by the worker and the amount is to be paid within 48 h of production of the proof that she has delivered the baby. An employer cannot dismiss the woman worker if she is absent due to pregnancy or delivery. A woman can avail 1-month leave with salary if she is having any illness related to pregnancy, delivery, premature birth or miscarriage.

The Payment of Gratuity Act, 1972 (PG Act): The is an Act introduced under Social Security scheme, which provides 15-days wages for each year of service to employees who have worked for 5 years or more in an organization under industrial law. An employee is entitled for gratuity on his retirement or on the termination of his employment or resignation after completion of continuous service of 5 years. The amount of gratuity is at the rate of 15-days wages per year and the wages will be based on the rate of wages last drawn by the employee concerned.

The National Social Assistance Programme (NSAP): The programme came into existence on 15th August, 1995. The basic aim of this programme is to provide social assistance to the poor in addition to the social assistance being given by states.

Indira Gandhi National Old Age Pension Scheme (IGNOAPS): Central government formed this scheme and instructed the state government to give old age pension to helpless elderly people who don't have any other financial sources. Amount of pension varies from state to state. Punjab was the first state to implement Old Age Pension Scheme.

Indira Gandhi National Disability Pension Scheme (IGNDPS): It was launched by Ministry of Social Welfare in the year 2000. The scheme benefits the person with 80% disability and family is in the BPL list.

National Family Benefit Scheme (NFBS): The scheme was introduced by Department of Social Welfare, Government of India. Basically, this scheme is meant to help families living below the poverty line. Amount of Rs 10,000 is given to the family in case the primary breadwinner of the family dies due to natural cause or accident. The family benefit is given to the surviving member of the bereaved family who is proven to be the head of the family. Application is submitted to Deputy Commissioner of the district and directed to the Directorate of Social Welfare of the state. Documents required are family income certificate, death certificate of the person who died and two photographs of the applicant.

Widow pension: All those widows who don't have any financial support are entitled for Widow Pensions, though the amount varies from state to state in the country.

Mahatma Gandhi National Rural Employment Guarantee Act (MNERGA): It is aimed at creating employment in villages and enhancing the livelihood security by providing at least 100-days employment to the family members of the rural people who are unskilled and do manual work. If no work is given to the applicant then unemployment compensation is given to him or her. MGNREGA also helps to create durable assets (such as roads, canals, ponds, wells). According to this act, the person should get the employment within 5 km of his residence and minimum wages fixed by the Government. MNERGA is an Indian labour law and social security measure that aims to guarantee the *right to work*. It is the largest and most ambitious social security and public works programme in the world. MNERGA not only provides economic security and create rural assets, but it also helps in protecting the environment, empowering rural women and helps in reducing rural–urban migration.

National Rural Employment Programme (NREP): It was introduced in 1980. The programme was expected to generate additional gainful employment in the rural areas, create durable community assets and improve nutritional status and living standards of the poor.

Food for Work Programme (NFFWP): It was initiated in 2004, which provided food grains to complement wages.

Jawahar Rozgar Yojna (JRY): Government of India initiated this scheme on 1st April, 1989 to converge employment generation, infrastructure development and food security in rural areas. The government integrated National Rural Employment Programme (NREP) and Rural Landless Employment Guarantee Programme (RLEGP) into this new scheme JRY.

On 1st April, 1999, it was revamped and renamed to Jawahar Gram SamridhiYojana (JGSY) with a similar objective. It was reinforced with the local self-government at the village level called the *Village Panchayats* as the sole implementing authority.

Employment Assurance Scheme (EAS): This scheme was started on 2nd October, 1993 with the objective of providing employment during the lean agricultural season. Later, EAS was merged with Sampoorna Grameen Rozgar Yojana (SGRY) in 2001.

A new scheme SGRY was initiated on 25th September, 2001 for employment generation, infrastructure development and food security in rural areas and EAS and JGSY both were merged into this scheme. This scheme was ultimately merged with Mahatma Gandhi NREGA in 2006.

Sampoorna Grameen Rojgar Yojana: The primary objective of the scheme is to provide skilled and local employment and thereby improve skills levels in all rural and urban areas. The scheme is meant for all the unemployed educated youth from rural and urban areas land looking for employment and willing to do manual and skilled work in and around his locality. Beneficiary gets fixed basic payment of wages and incentives based on performance.

National Rural Livelihoods Programme—Aajeevika: It was launched by the Ministry of Rural Development, Government of India in June 2011. Aajeevika's objective is to cover 7 crore rural poor households, across 600 districts, 6000 blocks, 2.5 lakh Gram Panchayats and 6 lakh villages in the country through self-managed Self Help Groups (SHGs).

Prime Minister's Employment Generation Programme (PMEGP): The scheme was announced on 15th August, 2008. This is Credit-Linked Scheme of Government of India by merging erstwhile REGP and PMRY scheme. KVIC is the Nodal Agency at national level. The primary objective is to generate continuous and sustainable employment opportunities in rural and urban areas of the country.

Unemployment allowance: Some states plan to pay different amount of unemployment allowance to unemployed youth. As Haryana government pays Rs 300 per month to all the registered 10+2 passed in science stream and Rs 700 per month to each registered unemployed graduate. Uttar Pradesh government recently launched a scheme to pay Rs 1000 per month to unemployed youth between 25 and 40 years of age. The amount is credited to the bank account directly.

SCHEMES FOR SENIOR CITIZENS

Ministry of Social Justice and Empowerment, which is responsible for the welfare of the senior citizens, has announced the National Policy on older persons. This National Policy covers almost all the aspects of the welfare of elderly persons (a person aged 60 or above). Grant is given for construction of old age homes and care of elderly people apart from various schemes for the welfare of senior citizens. The Ministry of Social Justice and Empowerment is also implementing various schemes for the benefit of senior citizens. For example, an Integrated Programme for Elderly Persons—under this programme there is provision of Assistance to Voluntary Organizations for the welfare programmes of the aged. Financial assistance up to 90% of the project cost is provided to NGOs for constructing and maintaining old age homes, day care centres, mobile medicare units and many such services provided to elderly people.

Scheme of assistance to Panchayati Raj Institutions/voluntary organizations/self-help groups for construction of old age homes: One time construction grant is given to Nongovernmental Organisations (NGOs) under this scheme for old age homes on the recommendation of the state governments.

Ministry of Finance and Income tax also gives rebate up to an income of Rs 1.85 lakh p.a. to the senior citizens. They are also given higher rates of interest on saving schemes of senior citizens—Senior Citizens Savings Schemes and banks have been introduced by the Government of India.

Ministry of Social Justice and Empowerment: It has announced National Policy for senior citizen in which 90% of financial assistance for old age homes is given to NGOs.

Ministry of Road Transport and Highways: Reservation of seats for senior citizens in buses and railways and concession of fair in buses and trains and planes.

Ministry of Health and Family Welfare: Separate queues for senior citizens or some hospitals run special OPDs for senior citizens.

Department of Telecommunications: Complaints of senior citizens are given priority.

Ministry of Railways: Concession of 30% in fare, wheel chairs for them, separate counters for senior citizens.

Annapurna Scheme: Government of India launched this scheme in 2000 through Ministry of Rural Development. Basically, this scheme was initiated for the food security of the senior citizens who are not covered under the targeted Public Distribution System (PDS) and who are not financially independent. A total of 10 kg of food grains per month are given under the scheme, free of cost, to all such person who are not getting old age pension. It is the duty of the Gram Panchayat to identify such persons who are eligible for this scheme and give the list of such persons to the government.

Antyodaya Scheme: The BPL families with elderly persons are provided food grains at the rate of 35 kg per family per month at the rate of Rs 3/- per kg for rice and Rs 2/- per kg for wheat. Priority is given to persons aged 60 or above from the BPL category.

REVIEW QUESTIONS

1. Write short notes on the following:
   a. MNREGA
   b. JRY
   c. Annapurna scheme
2. What do you mean by social security and why is it required?

CHAPTER

56

Budgeting for Family

LEARNING OBJECTIVES

After reading this chapter the learner should be able to

- Get familiar with the process of family budgeting.
- Have knowledge about the benefits of budgeting.

Budgeting is the most effective basic tool for managing your money. It virtually allows you to see from where your money comes and how it is being spent. It is very useful exercise for the situations where the income is limited as it helps in controlling the extravagancy. More importantly, it ensures that the financial resources are wisely spent. People mostly end up spending money on things that are hardly of any use and repent later. This can be avoided by proper budgeting that clearly shows how one should allocate money for different things within one's financial limitations.

Family budgeting is required to ensure that the basic needs of the family are met. It becomes absolutely essential when the income is fixed and prices are spiralling all the time. Before undertaking the exercise, it is advisable to have an account of the monthly expenditure to have an idea of how much money is being spent and on what items. Once the average monthly expenditure being incurred is known, a plan could be drawn up on the basis of the monthly income.

Family budgeting is just like preparing budget for a company. Budgeting is a tool that helps to ensure that the company's financial resources are used prudently and efficiently. The budgeting process is a guide to ensure that resources are allocated for most profitable and efficient activities to achieve financial and business goals of the company. The objective of family budget is to ensure that basic needs are met and some part of the income is saved for emergencies and financial security during old age.

Unlike company budgets, which are made for a financial year, family budgets are made on a monthly basis. Family budgeting means drawing up a plan for spending the money available as per the family income. Lack of proper household budgeting could lead to many financial problems and wasteful and irrational spending. Family budgeting is not a difficult task and all one needs to do is to decide the amount of money to be spent on specified items such as food, telephone and electricity bills, tuition fee of children, recreation and clothing's and money to be saved. Of course, the entire exercise depends on the monthly income available for spending.

BENEFITS OF HOUSEHOLD BUDGET

A household budget helps in curtailing expenditure on nonessential items and prioritizing the needs of the family and allocating the required amount to a particular need.

Provides control over money: Budget helps us in exercising control over finances as it presents an accurate picture of the financial health of the family. One knows how much money one can spend or save for any exigency.

Inculcates prudent spending habits: Efforts to stay within the budget will develop prudent spending habits, which can be maintained over time. Working within the budget will shift actual expenses from unnecessary categories to the most essential household categories.

Budget blue print: Budget reveals where every penny is currently being spent. The actual expenditures reveal whether the budget has been followed. The budget is a living document and the changes occurring in life from time to time should be taken into account.

Misuse of money can be detected: A detailed budget, when compared against the actual monthly expenditures, reveals the misuse of money. If money is not spent as planned, then corrective action can be taken for the future use by identifying source of waste.

Reduces financial stress: Household budgeting prevents financial stress as proper planning ensures that there is no dearth of money. All the committed expenses and priorities are taken care of while preparing the budget.

Budget changes family's mindset: Budgeting involves all the family members and they not only provide inputs but also try their level best to stick to it. Budget changes the mindset of the family members and instead of spending recklessly, money is well utilized to achieve goals and fulfil the needs of the family. Involving the family members in the budgeting exercise makes them realise the value of money.

Creates financial space: Managing within the budget will help create financial space as excess money becomes available for other purposes.

Encourages savings and financial discipline: Budgeting encourages frugal habits and saving becomes a priority. As every expense is closely monitored and compared to the budget, the focus is on maintaining financial discipline. Adherence to budget plan brings financial health of the family in line.

Keeps focus on financial goals: Budgeting prevents unnecessary spending on items and services that do not contribute to attaining family's financial goals. It allows scope to set aside money for emergency and unexpected events such as sickness or wedding of a relative.

PREPARING FAMILY BUDGET

While preparing budget, besides family income, their needs and the locality where the family lives, and size of the family has also to be taken into consideration. A practical budget can be prepared only if the income of family is enough to meet the basic needs and priorities, as listed below.

1. **Food**: As balanced diet is essential for the family members to stay healthy to enjoy, adequate money must be allocated for food items. In case there is a baby in the family, a special diet is needed for the mother and the baby has to be taken care of by providing additional money. A pregnant woman or a family member suffering from a chronic disease such as diabetes or cancer will also require similar consideration.

2. **Housing:** Living in its own is a boon for a family as little money is to be set aside for carrying out routine repair and maintenance. If the family lives in a rented accommodation then a large amount of money is required to be set aside for paying rent every month.
3. **Clothing:** Clothing needs of a family is varied as every member has different requirement. The amount of budget to be allocated for clothing depends on the family status.
4. **Education:** It is an important head as providing good education is essential to secure the future of the family members. Money has to be allocated for tuition fees, books and other school expenditure on monthly basis, if there are schoolgoing children in the family. More money is also required if any of the member is pursuing professional degree.
5. **Household operations:** Most of the middle-class families these days engage helpers, and provisions for their salaries have to be a part of the monthly budget.
6. **Utilities:** Bills for various services like water supply, electricity, sewerage and telephone, which are paid monthly, should be included in the budget.
7. **Health care:** Adequate money should be kept aside for meeting the health care expenses of the family. If a member having special condition like pregnancy or breastfeeding, additional money should be provided to meet the requirements.
8. **Recreation:** Recreation is an integral part of family life and provision has to be there in the budget for organizing family get-togethers, picnics, movies or going out for vacations and other social activities.
9. **Savings:** It is very important for every family to save money on regular basis to meet emergency situations. It can grow in the form of investment for a financially secure future.

PER CAPITA INCOME

Per capita income is often used as a measure for average income. It is also used as a parameter to compare the wealth and relative prosperity of nations. Expressed in commonly used international currency, such as the US dollar, per capita income is often used to measure a country's standard of living. *Capita* is a Latin word, which means *head*, and per capita literally means *by the head*. Per capita income is the ratio of the gross domestic product (GDP) and the total population of a country. It is easily calculated from readily available GDP and population estimates to generate useful statistics for comparison of wealth development status of countries. Per capita income is a measurement of economic output per person of a country. Countries with high population will tend to have low per capita income as compared to those with low population.

Initially called as gross national product (GNP), GDP is considered as the best way to measure the economy of a country. It is the value of all the goods and services at market prices produced by all the people and companies that are in the country, typically during one fiscal year. The comparison of the GDP for two successive years provides the growth rate, the most important indicator of economic health. It provides an indication of how fast or how slow the economy of a country is growing. When the economy is expanding, the GDP growth rate is positive and a growing economy means flourishing businesses, more jobs and good personal income. If there is a slowdown, the businesses will put investments on hold and defer hiring new employees, till the economy shows signs of revival.

If the GDP growth rate actually turns negative, then it means that the country's economy is heading towards or is already slipped into a recession. This happens when the economy actually contracts and GDP is less than the quarter or year before. The consumers have less money to spend on purchases and it further slows down the economy.

GROSS NATIONAL INCOME (GNI)

Another frequently used measurement is GNI per capita, which is calculated by converting gross national income to U.S. dollars using the World Bank Atlas method and dividing it by the mid-year population. The GNI is defined as the total income earned by a nation's residents by various means such as agriculture, industry or business. No matter where these people are working or where the business is located. This income includes income from abroad also.

IMPACT OF PER CAPITA INCOME ON HEALTH AND ILLNESS

The income of family has a bearing on the wellbeing of members as socioeconomic status is a fundamental cause of health. In a situation where many people do not have adequate money to fulfil basic needs like food; adults and children often suffer the short and long-term effects of a poor diet. Besides nourishing food, maintenance of good health also requires clean water, good sanitation, adequate nutrition, and adequate housing and warmth. All these conditions are correlated with income. There is threshold income requirement to afford these necessities and once safe water is available, a higher income will not make it safer. However, income that is lower than the threshold requirement will have an adverse impact on health.

For instance, infant mortality rate (IMR), the most sensitive indicator of the health status of a country, is associated with poverty, lack of sanitation, malnutrition, poor-quality housing and overcrowding. Other important factor is lack of medical care, including care before, during and after childbirth, which also depends on economic status.

It has been observed that the higher the income, the lower the mortality. Adequate income and technical knowledge have allowed the community to change the conditions that lead to high infant mortality.

Like IMR, there is a strong correlation between measures of health indicators like life expectancy and the level of economic development. Budget allocations of each state include the allocation to health sector programmes. The state governments, central government also allocate budget to centrally sponsored programmes and various national programmes. The amount of budget allocated to the health-related programmes depends on the GDP.

Our nation spends very little on health because of poor per capita income. This adversely affects the health of its people. India is ranked 184 among 191 countries in terms of public expenditure on health, and ranked 164 among 191 countries as far as per capita expenditure is concerned, but it is spending just about \$29 on health. This is around a third of Sri Lanka's, less than 30% of China's and 14% of Thailand's spending.

India's spending on health as a percent of GDP has stagnated in the past two decades and it plunged to 1.3% in 2014–2015. It was drastically disproportionate to its 21% contribution to the global burden of disease. The health budget has witnessed a 29% decline over the past year from Rs 29,165 crore in 2013–2014 to Rs 20,431.4 crore in 2014–2015.

India's per capita income is projected to be Rs 88,533 in the year 2014–2015 as compared to Rs 64,316 in 2011–2012. It has registered a growth of 37% over the 4-year period. The per capita income was Rs 71,593 in 2012–2013 and Rs 80,388 in 2013–2014.

The national income in 2014–2015 stood at Rs 11,217,079 crore as compared to Rs 10,056,523 crore in 2013–2014. It was Rs 8,841,733 crore in 2012–2013 and Rs 7,846,531 crore in 2011–2012.

REVIEW QUESTIONS

1. What are the advantages of family budgeting?
2. What are the most important factors to be considered while preparing family budget?

APPENDIX

Multiple-Choice Questions

1. Sociological perspective is primarily related to an attempt to
   a. Transform the social order
   b. Improve the social order
   c. Understand the social order through behaviour and relationships
   d. Regulate the social order
2. Who is commonly known as the father of sociology?
   a. Durkheim
   b. Comte
   c. Spencer
   d. Cooley
3. _____________ has described *society* as a web of social relationships.
   a. Mead
   b. Ogburn
   c. Leacock
   d. MacIver
4. The book *Primitive Culture* has been authored by
   a. Majumdar
   b. Lundberg
   c. Tylor
   d. Malinowski
5. Who presented the classification of groups into in-group and out-group?
   a. Sumner
   b. Cooley
   c. Homans
   d. Tonnies
6. _____________ is the achieved status
   a. Sex
   b. Age
   c. Marital
   d. Caste
7. _____________ is not a characteristic of primary group?
   a. Intimacy
   b. Closeness
   c. Familiarity
   d. Impersonality
8. Which among the following is an informal method of social control?
   a. Education
   b. Coercion
   c. Law
   d. Customs
9. Studies of social interaction, groups belong to _____________ sociology.
   a. Micro
   b. Macro
   c. Applied
   d. Urban
10. Which among the following is an example of a community?
    a. Family
    b. Marriage
    c. Refugee Camp
    d. Village
11. Weber conceived of sociology as a comprehensive science of social
    a. Groups
    b. Action
    c. Interaction
    d. Institutions
12. The term *primary group* coined by
    a. Comte
    b. Ginsberg
    c. Gisbert
    d. Cooley

13. Who among the following was a macro sociologist?
    a. Simmel
    b. Goffman
    c. Durkheim
    d. Weber
14. Group characterized by impersonal relationships and self-interests is
    a. In-group
    b. Gesellschaft
    c. Secondary
    d. Both B and C
15. Contradictory demands of the same role is termed as
    a. Competition
    b. Role-play
    c. Role conflict
    d. Role strain
16. A role is the ____________ aspect of status.
    a. Counter
    b. Dynamic
    c. Static
    d. Latent
17. ____________ help meet the basic needs of society.
    a. Associations
    b. Social groups
    c. Social institutions
    d. Interactions
18. 'Contact and communication are the two main conditions of social interaction.' Who said so?
    a. Horton and Hunt
    b. Park and Burgess
    c. Ogburn and Nimkoff
    d. MacIver and Page
19. ____________ is the vehicle of culture.
    a. Technology
    b. Language
    c. Society
    d. Man
20. Who said, 'Culture is the man-made part of environment.'?
    a. E.B. Tylor
    b. M.J. Herskovits
    c. R. Brown
    d. K. Davis
21. *The Presentation of Self in Everyday Life* (1959) was written by
    a. Garfinkel
    b. Goffman
    c. Gillin and Gillin
    d. Giddings
22. The term *sociology* was coined in the year
    a. 1798
    b. 1829
    c. 1818
    d. 1839
23. The term *sociology* is derived from the ____________ words *socius* and *logos*, respectively.
    a. Latin, Greek
    b. Greek, Latin
    c. Hebrew, Latin
    d. Hebrew, Greek
24. According to ____________ theory, 'people are motivated by self-interest in the interactions with other people'.
    a. Conflict
    b. Structural
    c. Interaction
    d. Exchange
25. The idea of 'cultural lag' was thrown up by
    a. MacIver
    b. Malinowski
    c. Ogburn
    d. Risley
26. ____________ is a socially defined position in a group or society.
    a. Role
    b. Interaction
    c. Deviance
    d. Status
27. The smallest group possible.
    a. Dyad
    b. Family
    c. Peer group
    d. Primary group
28. The term *reference group* was introduced by
    a. MacIver
    b. H.M. Johnson
    c. Horton and Hunt
    d. Muzafer Sherif

29. Who propounded the social exchange theory?
   a. G. Homans
   b. G.H. Mead
   c. Goffman
   d. Peter Blau
30. Demography essentially means the study of
   a. Migration of population
   b. Implication of mortality and birth rates for development
   c. The prevention of overpopulation in a society
   d. The levels and trends in population size and its components
31. An interaction not involving social contact
   a. Conflict
   b. Exchange
   c. Cooperation
   d. Competition
32. Groups were classified into small groups and large groups by
   a. Simmel
   b. Park and Burgess
   c. Weber
   d. Sumner
33. ____________ was an American sociologist is widely regarded as the founder of behavioural sociology.
   a. G.C. Homans
   b. B.F. Skinner
   c. H. Blumer
   d. A. Comte
34. ____________ coined the term *sociology*.
   a. Spencer
   b. Durkheim
   c. W. Thomson
   d. A. Comte
35. Human interaction is essentially _________ interaction.
   a. Competitive
   b. Cooperative
   c. Deliberate
   d. Communicative
36. The idea of pursuing scientific study of society was pioneered by
   a. Auguste Comte
   b. Adam Smith
   c. Simmel
   d. John Graunt
37. Sociology sheds light on the ____________ nature of man.
   a. Animal
   b. Rational
   c. Psychological
   d. Social
38. Population pyramid deal with
   a. Net migration of a population
   b. Age and sex structure
   c. Age and marriage structure
   d. Age and literacy spread
39. ____________ defined *culture* as the sum total of knowledge, belief, art morals, law, customs and any other capabilities and habits acquired by man as a member of society.
   a. Tylor
   b. Spencer
   c. Redfield
   d. G.C. Homans
40. The components of material culture are ____________ and objective.
   a. Internal
   b. External
   c. Tangible
   d. Both B and C
41. A definite role and status are assigned to individual by
   a. Institution
   b. Society
   c. Collectivity
   d. Group
42. The most superficial manifestation of culture is represented by
   a. Values
   b. Rituals
   c. Symbols
   d. Norms
43. Blood relationships in the family are guided by
   a. Taboos
   b. Culture
   c. Kinship
   d. Marriage
44. The parts of social structure are ____________ everywhere.
   a. Distinct
   b. Different
   c. Irregular
   d. The same

45. ____________ form the core of a culture.
a. Values
b. Arts
c. Traditions
d. Customs

46. An important feature of social group is ____________ of individuals.
a. Contact
b. Relation
c. Communication
d. Interaction

47. Sociology is the science of interpretative understanding of social
a. Action
b. Interaction
c. Group
d. Institution

48. Who carried out the pioneering work to throw light on the structure of society?
a. Spencer
b. Durkheim
c. Comte
d. Parsons

49. Social structure is of no use useless without
a. Role
b. Order
c. Function
d. Status

50. The foundation of society rests on _______ among human beings.
a. Action
b. Interaction
c. Roles
d. Culture

51. ____________ is the basic ingredient of social relationships.
a. Interaction
b. Awareness
c. Bonding
d. Group

52. Institution is relatively
a. Transitory
b. Temporary
c. Artificial
d. Permanent

53. Name the reciprocal influence that humans exert on each other through interstimulation and response.
a. Social groups
b. Social relation
c. Social interaction
d. Cooperation

54. Human interaction is essentially a ________ interaction.
a. Communicative
b. Cooperative
c. Competitive
d. Deliberate

55. Human beings organize themselves into groups called ____________, to achieve some object or goal.
a. Community
b. Institutions
c. Society
d. None of the above

56. In the view of Talcott Parsons, all the units of social structure are
a. Abstract
b. Tangible
c. Concrete
d. Explicit

57. ____________ denotes the functional significance of the actor for the social system.
a. Role
b. Action
c. Mores
d. Status

58. A ____________ may be defined as plurality of individuals who are in contact with each another.
a. Social structure
b. Village
c. Group
d. Society

59. A social group is a ____________ entity.
a. Static
b. Cooperative
c. Spontaneous
d. Dynamic

60. The criterion for classifying groups put forward by German sociologist Simmel was based on ____________
    a. Nature of contact
    b. Size
    c. Nature of membership
    d. Interaction
61. ____________ is an involuntary group.
    a. Political party
    b. Club
    c. Race
    d. Dyad
62. Groups classified into genetic and congregate groups by
    a. Giddings
    b. Charles A. Ellwood
    c. Sumner
    d. Simmel
63. The ____________ group is the nucleus of all social organization.
    a. Secondary
    b. Formal
    c. Primary
    d. Small
64. The concept of social control was pioneered by
    a. E.A. Ross
    b. Ogburn
    c. Durkheim
    d. G.H. Mead
65. Gemeinschaft is translated into English as
    a. Association
    b. Institution
    c. Corporation
    d. Community
66. The ____________ groups are characterized by sympathetic contact.
    a. Secondary
    b. Primary
    c. Reference
    d. Congregate
67. ____________ refers to the tendency on the part of members to identify themselves with the groups.
    a. We-feeling
    b. Mutual awareness
    c. Group unity
    d. Group norms
68. Culture bound or culture specific traits are known as ____________ culture.
    a. Emic
    b. Etic
    c. Counter
    d. Universal
69. ____________ is a process by which cultural borrowing and lending take place
    a. Assimilation
    b. Diffusion
    c. Enculturation
    d. Acculturation
70. A group to which individuals refer when making judgments.
    a. Voluntary group
    b. Membership group
    c. In-group
    d. Reference group
71. An artificial and highly commercialized culture popularized through mass media.
    a. Universal culture
    b. Urban culture
    c. Mass culture
    d. None of the above
72. ____________ is the most fundamental term in sociology
    a. Caste
    b. Society
    c. Individual
    d. Organization
73. The ____________ revolution is largely considered responsible for the emergence of sociology as a discipline.
    a. Chinese
    b. Russian
    c. French
    d. American
74. According to ____________ sociological imagination is the vivid awareness of the relationship between experience and the wider society.
    a. Mills
    b. Berger
    c. Giddens
    d. Goffman

75. One requires sociological ____________ to see the relationship between their personal experiences and broader social and historical events.
 a. Consciousness
 b. Understanding
 c. Questions
 d. Imagination

76. ____________ authored the book *The Sociological Imagination*.
 a. Comte
 b. Brewer
 c. Elliot
 d. Wright Mills

77. ____________ is an indirect method of social control.
 a. Folkways
 b. Customs
 c. Propaganda
 d. Religion

78. Action oriented to a social norm or norms is
 a. Acceptance
 b. Control
 c. Conformity
 d. Approval

79. ____________ is a loss or fault of a critical part in a complicated mechanism.
 a. Corruption
 b. Rejection
 c. Rebellion
 d. Deviance

80. The book *The Sociological Imagination* was published in year
 a. 1959
 b. 1896
 c. 1904
 d. 1839

81. Emotional warmth and spontaneity are an important feature of ____________ group.
 a. Out-group
 b. Special
 c. Secondary
 d. Primary

82. Who coined the term *cultural lag*?
 a. Ogburn
 b. MacIver
 c. Weber
 d. Comte

83. ____________ culture is communicated mostly to the like-minded.
 a. Material
 b. Explicit
 c. Nonmaterial
 d. Utilitarian

84. The process of spread of cultural traits from one culture area to another is called
 a. Culture diffusion
 b. Assimilation
 c. Cultural evolution
 d. Acculturation

85. The opinion held by people on any important issue concerning larger interests of the society is called
 a. National opinion
 b. Public opinion
 c. Verdict
 d. Personal opinion

86. ____________ is not a characteristic of groups.
 a. Cooperation
 b. Reciprocity
 c. Antagonism
 d. We-feeling

87. Membership is ____________ in secondary groups.
 a. Ascribed
 b. Mandatory
 c. Involuntary
 d. Voluntary

88. Who defined religion as 'unified system of beliefs and practices relative to sacred things'?
 a. Durkheim
 b. Comte
 c. Weber
 d. MacIver

89. The material and nonmaterial components of culture are often referred to as the ________ of culture.
 a. Theme
 b. Combination
 c. Concept
 d. Content

90. The members of a ____________ group lack intimacy.
- **a.** Family
- **b.** Primary group
- **c.** Secondary group
- **d.** Peer group

91. Presence of ____________ is a prerequisite for a group to come into existence.
- **a.** Society
- **b.** Culture
- **c.** Relation
- **d.** Individuals

92. Values and knowledge are examples of ____________ culture.
- **a.** Material
- **b.** External
- **c.** Explicit
- **d.** Nonmaterial

93. The functioning of a secondary group is regulated by ____________ rules.
- **a.** Informal
- **b.** Natural
- **c.** Formal
- **d.** Personal

94. ____________ is an ascribed status.
- **a.** Class
- **b.** Marital status
- **c.** Caste
- **d.** Master status

95. Interaction is impersonal and transient in ____________ groups.
- **a.** Secondary
- **b.** Close
- **c.** Social
- **d.** Primary

96. Uttar Pradesh accounts for the highest ____________ per cent of the country's population as per 2011 census.
- **a.** 12
- **b.** 8.50
- **c.** 16.50
- **d.** 20

97. The number of live births per thousand persons in a year is termed as
- **a.** Death rate
- **b.** Birth rate
- **c.** Growth rate
- **d.** Infant birth rate

98. Working population comprises all persons in the age group of
- **a.** All male population
- **b.** 0–15 years
- **c.** 60 years and more
- **d.** 15–59 years

99. According to 2011 census life expectancy at birth has increased to
- **a.** 58 years
- **b.** 63 years
- **c.** 74 years
- **d.** 67 years

100. The literacy rate has gone up from 64.83 per cent in 2001 to ____________ per cent in 2011.
- **a.** 67.5
- **b.** 69
- **c.** 74.04
- **d.** 83

ANSWERS

1. c, **2.** b, **3.** d, **4.** c, **5.** a, **6.** c, **7.** d, **8.** d, **9.** a, **10.** d, **11.** b, **12.** d, **13.** c, **14.** d, **15.** d, **16.** b, **17.** c, **18.** b, **19.** b, **20.** b, **21.** b, **22.** c, **23.** a, **24.** d, **25.** c, **26.** d, **27.** a, **28.** d, **29.** a, **30.** d, **31.** d, **32.** a, **33.** a, **34.** d, **35.** d, **36.** a, **37.** d, **38.** b, **39.** a, **40.** d, **41.** a, **42.** c, **43.** c, **44.** d, **45.** a, **46.** d, **47.** a, **48.** a, **49.** c, **50.** b, **51.** a, **52.** d, **53.** c, **54.** a, **55.** b **56.** a **57.** a, **58.** c, **59.** d **60.** b, **61.** c, **62.** a, **63.** c, **64.** a, **65.** d, **66.** b, **67.** a, **68.** a, **69.** d, **70.** d, **71.** c, **72.** b, **73.** c, **74.** a, **75.** d, **76.** d, **77.** c, **78.** c, **79.** d, **80.** a, **81.** d, **82.** a, **83.** c, **84.** a, **85.** b, **86.** c, **87.** d, **88.** a, **89.** d, **90.** c, **91.** d, **92.** d, **93.** c, **94.** c, **95.** a, **96.** c, **97.** c, **98.** d, **99.** d, **100.** c.

Index

U

V

W